Boob Jubilee

Other Salvos from *The Baffler:*

Commodify Your Dissent

B
BAFFLER
RAPTUS REGALITER REVIRESCO
PATRICIUS WELCH FECIT AD MMII

BOOB JUBILEE

The Cultural Politics of the New Economy

Edited by
Thomas Frank and David Mulcahey

W. W. Norton & Company

New York • London

Printed in the United States of America
First Edition

Manufacturing by The Haddon Craftsmen, Inc.
Book design by Julia Druskin
Production manager: Anna Oler

Library of Congress Cataloging-in-Publication Data

Boob jubilee : the cultural politics of the new economy / edited by
Thomas Frank and David Mulcahey.— 1st ed.
p. cm.
Includes index.
ISBN 0-393-05777-1 (hardcover) — ISBN 0-393-32430-3 (pbk.)
1. Speculation—United States. 2. Investments—United States. 3. United States—
Economic conditions—1981–2001. I. Frank, Thomas, 1965–
II. Mulcahey, David.
HG6041.B658 2003
306.3'0973'0207—dc21

2003006566

W. W. Norton & Company, Inc., 500 Fifth Avenue, New York, N.Y. 10110
www.wwnorton.com

W. W. Norton & Company Ltd., Castle House, 75/76 Wells Street, London W1T 3QT

1 2 3 4 5 6 7 8 9 0

Contents

Foreword

THOMAS FRANK, DAVID MULCAHEY, and their giftedly irreverent colleagues offer here an assemblage of agnostic essays on our new national religion, the Free Market. The title they've chosen is a natural, evoking memories of H. L. Mencken's catchword, "booboisie." Yet there is something else here.

Mencken, master of the American language, nonpareil literary critic, never really tackled the truly Big Boys. He did have a high old time with poor Bryan and the Creationists during the Monkey Trial. He did a real number on the Babbitts of the day. He walloped small-mindedness wherever it popped up, even though he had a few blemishes himself. But never did he challenge the true religion—called Free Enterprise at the time.

The Bafflers have, in their writing styles, the buoyancy of Mencken; but in substance, they're in the tradition of the old-time muckrakers—those who *did* challenge the power pillars of our society. I've a hunch that Lincoln Steffens, Upton Sinclair, George Seldes, and I. F. Stone would have approved.

I'm especially enthralled by a phrase from the Introduction: "a catastrophic failure of critical intelligence." It might otherwise be called our national Alzheimer's disease. There is no memory of yesterday, let alone what happened sixty-five or so years ago, when the New Deal of FDR, Henry Wallace, Rex Tugwell, Harry Hopkins, and Harold Ickes saw to it that the have-nots and the have-somewhats would get a fighting chance against the have-everythings. It was something called regulation—Federal Governmental Regulation—harnessing corporate greed. And in the process, the corporate greedies' asses were also saved.

After half a century of the Cold War and labor-management ententes, we saw the end of such regulations and we were rewarded with Enron-and-on-and-on thieveries, described by Kenneth Galbraith as "innocent fraud." Millions of the have-somewhats were euchred out of life savings as well as grand illusions. What has happened to the have-nots is grievously self-evident. The Bafflers do a splendiferous job on this one.

As for the obscene myth of the "liberal media," it has never been more widely believed than it is today. Among our bestsellers are the "findings" of the vulgar press, TV, and radio toadies of the Big Boys. There is no need to name them; they are all properly identified in this revelatory book.

Yet, something unexpected, though long overdue, is also happening. There appears to be a slow catching-on by the anonymous many of the con job that has been perpetrated for much too long. At least I hope so. The "wanton boy" of Shakespeare's *Lear*, our appointed chieftain in the White House, didn't know when to quit. A private servant of the Big Boys, he went too far, proclaiming, "I

Am the World," let alone the United States. The whole cockeyed scenario appears to have been conceived by W. C. Fields as much as by Rupert Murdoch. It is all this crazy stuff that is reflected on and exposed by our young muckrakers in high and exuberant fashion. That's why this is a hell of an important book.

—*Studs Terkel*

Overture

1

This Car Climbed Mount Nasdaq

Thomas Frank
Greg Lane
David Mulcahey
Emily Vogt

For a magazine dedicated to debunking the fantasies generated by the American business culture, the final years of the twentieth century overflowed with bounty. What was for others the dawn of a "New Economy," a final leave-taking from the problems of history, was for us a cornucopia of absurdity. It was, without a doubt, the most spectacular outbreak of mass pundit delusion that we are likely to see in our lifetimes.

The almighty Free Market, through the agency of the Internet, its enforcer here on earth, was going to "change everything." It had become the model for nations, for governments, for corporations, and even for individuals. Alone among the peoples of the world, American entrepreneurs knew the way forward. We had figured it out, deduced the truth about life from the pattern of the microchip, from the mind-blowing magnitude of our new billionaires' fortunes. History was moving at Internet speed, rewarding the faithful with limitless lucre and leaving the stubborn behind in their crumbling analog slums. The universe was in the grip of primal powers that mankind could not hope to control; the only choice was to go along for the ecstatic ride. The market was sifting out the hearts of every human enterprise before its judgment seat.

And for a few years the whole world seemed to believe it. Libertarianism in all its flavors—cocksure or surly, learned or selfish—was the universal conviction of the moment. The language of the corporate manager, which had once been a fairly obscure tongue, grew to fill all available space.

We, on the other hand, were the sort of people of whom it was fashionable to say, *They just don't get it.* We were political dinosaurs, supposedly, writing about things like organized labor from a city in the rusting Midwest. Our very medium—a paper magazine, painstakingly composed and arranged, and with no online presence to speak of—was hopelessly, laughably obsolete. Compared to what our college classmates were pulling down at Goldman Sachs or in Silicon Valley, what we were doing was so self-evidently foolish that it did not warrant consideration.

But we kept at it. As the decade's big thinkers generated evermore-ethereal descriptions of what was going on—the weightless economy, the end of scarcity, the angelic nature of fiber optics—The Baffler stayed resolutely on the ground. The pundits told us that a new, frictionless form of toil was supplanting the old, that labor unions and even industry itself were obsolete in a nonexploitative "knowledge economy." We decided to investigate the actual mechanics of work. They told us that inconceivable opportunities awaited the faithful—the entrepreneur, the investor. We pointed out that it was the already-rich who benefited most from the spread of the stock market religion. They insisted that the libertarianism so fashionable in the Nineties was a bold breakthrough, a new politics opening onto a glorious future. We traced its origins to some of the ugliest chapters in recent political history.

The North Star in this glittering galaxy of bad ideas, though, was the infallibility of the market. Freed to do their thing, we were told, market forces would give us prosperity, diversity, democracy, justice, and every last little material thing we had ever coveted.

But what, we asked, had market forces done to our intellectual life? Far from delivering a robust exchange of divergent views, money had simply hired a glee club of one-note yodelers—Gilder, D'Souza, Samuelson, Glassman, Friedman, Cramer, Kudlow—to lead us into a deafening crescendo of folly. If this was what a "marketplace of ideas" looked like, then the experience of the Nineties should be sufficiently disastrous to discredit the free-market superstition for all times.

With the culture of the nation being brought under the control of five or six megacorporations, we argued, the oft-remarked fact that people had access to all manner of pseudosubversive lifestyles did not really mitigate matters. Yes, we had *Dilbert*, and yes, the land overflowed with Xtreme products, but something terrible was happening to the American critical tradition. Where were all the revolutionaries and creative individualists and prude-defiers and boss-shockers the Nineties were supposed to be producing in such great abundance? Swept away like all the rest, it seemed, in the irresistible current of world-historical bullshit. We all had 'tude by the ton, but no dissent to speak of.

We now know that the New Economy was a financial swindle, with Wall Street analysts assuring us that companies like Enron and WorldCom represented the way of the future. But it was also a cultural con game in which professional optimists and foundation-subsidized libertarians sang similarly sweet songs of golden inevitability. Both analysts and pundits seem to have been motivated by other concerns: For the Wall Street gang, it was the business they would rake in from the companies whose shares were praised; for the authors of all those futuristic books, it was the political promise of the thing, the heights of deregulation and privatization and tax-reduction that could be scaled if the public were persuaded of the virtue and irresistibility of free markets. The great management theorists of the Nineties did not dissect the corporation so much as propagandize for it, tell us how fulfilling it was to submit to the discipline of the market. The stock market gurus of the age, with their fond dreams of a nation of small shareholders, openly looked forward to the destruction of the New Deal regulatory state, to a time when "the little people" would identify more with the corporation than the government. The pundits offered up their theory-bong and the nation drifted off on dreams of millionaires next door, liberation management, new rules for new economies, and the virtue of prosperity.

What made it all possible, though, was a catastrophic failure of critical intelligence. Thanks to advertising pressure and conglomerate ownership, business journalism—the institution that bore primary responsibility for warning of the impending disaster—became so deeply committed to business ideology that it often read more like stock-selling than stock-taking. So predictable had the stuff become that by the mid-Nineties, our own Paul Maliszewski was able to trick a business newspaper into printing fake articles that mimicked the genre's characteristic optimism, thuggish politics, and slavish regard for free markets. In the realm of broadcasting, where thirty years of complaints about liberal bias finally brought massive deregulation, what we got was not a lively national debate but more indistinguishable pundits and stock tickers streaming across the bottom of the screen. Finance programs, unswervingly upbeat, turned brokerage personnel into celebrities and newsreaders into statesmen, moguls, and starlets. In politics, the unleashing of the dollar brought similar results. Rather than vigorously contesting the free-market fad, New Democrats worked hard to prevent their colleagues from assuming their traditionally skeptical role. Instead, they made their party safe for corporate patronage, renounced big government, picked on the weak, sealed sweetheart trade deals, and turned somersaults for Wall Street. And in academia, even the most "radical" seemed to have no problem with the triumph of the market ideology, just as long as TV audiences remained free to invent their own subversive interpretations of *Star Trek* or *The X Files*.

Without countervailing cultural forces to limit it, the rhetoric of the booster crowd simply expanded, making ever-more-grandiose claims about ever more aspects of life. It was a boob's jubilee, a chiseler's millennium. The prophets of profit were speaking in tongues in the *Wall Street Journal*, levitating solemnly for the cameras down at the Nasdaq market-site, graciously acknowledging the accolades of the awestruck commentator, snorting greedily at the magnificent golden trough that had been placed before their snouts by God-only-knows what forces. And suckers across the land, meeting in chatrooms and barrooms, discoursed gravely in the mysterious new lingo they had picked up on CNBC.

THESE DAYS, things are slightly different. The superstar pundits are desperately dishing out blame for the Dow's failure to hit 36,000, while ordinary journalists are trying to explain why their lousy reporting wasn't their fault.

The tide has turned, yes, but superficial apologies of the sort now in fashion will not suffice. Financial abuses of the Enron/WorldCom variety are not some random misfortune resolved by a few mea culpas; they are systemic. They are what happens when we let our guard down, when we believe the sanguine tales of the free-market faithful. The New Economy hustle happened precisely because we allowed the American critical tradition to become so feeble. Without its renewal, we can look forward only to endless repetitions of the same game: spectacular booms and crushing busts, wages that go nowhere, shitty health care, unaffordable schools, an ever-wider prison roundup, and a culture in which organs of opinion are prostituted to boosterism of one sort or another.

Against that day we offer the following essays. We understand that reprinting them here may expose us to charges of premature anti-libertarianism, but we believe it's worth the risk.

2

The God That Sucked

THOMAS FRANK

> Despite this, many economists still think that electricity deregulation will work. A product is a product, they say, and competition always works better than state control.
>
> "I believe in that premise as a matter of religious faith," said Philip J. Romero, dean of the business school at the University of Oregon and one of the architects of California's deregulation plan. —New York Times, *February 4, 2001*

TIME WAS, the only place a guy could expound the mumbo jumbo of the free market was in the country club locker room or the pages of *Reader's Digest*. Spout off about it anywhere else and you'd be taken for a Bircher or some new strain of Jehovah's Witness. After all, in the America of 1968, when the great backlash began, the average citizen, whether housewife or hardhat or salaryman, still had an all-too-vivid recollection of the Great Depression—not to mention a fairly clear understanding of what social class was all about. Pushing laissez-faire ideology back then had all the prestige and credibility of hosting a Tupperware party.

But thirty-odd years of culture war have changed all that. Mention "elites" these days and nobody thinks of factory owners or gated-community dwellers. Instead, they assume that what you're mad as hell about is the liberal media, or the pro-criminal judiciary, or the tenured radicals, or the know-it-all bureaucrats.

For the guys down at the country club, all these inverted forms of class war worked spectacularly well. This is not to say that the right-wing culture warriors ever outsmarted the liberal college professors or shut down the Hollywood studios or repealed rock 'n' roll. Shout though they might, they never quite got cultural history to stop. But what they did win was far more important: political power, a free hand to turn back the clock on such unglamorous issues as welfare, taxes, OSHA, even the bankruptcy laws, for chrissake. Assuring their millionaire clients that culture war got the deregulatory job done, they simply averted their eyes as bizarre backlash variants flowered in the burned-over districts of conservatism: posses comitatus, backyard Confederacies mounting mini-secessions, crusades against Darwin.

For most of the duration of the thirty-year backlash, the free-market faiths of the economists and the bosses were kept discreetly in the background. To be sure, market worship was always the established church in the halls of Republican power, but in public the chant was usually *States' Rights*, or *Down with Big Gummint*, or *Watch out for Commies*, or *Speak English Goddammit*. "All Power to the Markets" has never been too persuasive as a rallying cry.

So confidently did the right proceed from triumph to triumph, though, that eventually they forgot this. Inspired by a generous bull market and puffed up by a sense of historical righteousness so cocksure that it might have been lifted from *The God That Failed*—that old book in which ex-Communists disavowed their former convictions—the right evidently decided in the Nineties that the time had come to tell the world about the wonders of the market.

JUST WATCH AS THE CULTURE WARRIORS come out of the closet. Dinesh D'Souza, pedagogical product of the Jesuits, these days can be found swinging the censer for Mammon and thrilling to the mayhem his ruthless "god of the market" visits on the undeserving poor. George Gilder, erstwhile elder of the Christian right, is now the Thirty-Third Degree Poobah in the Temple of Telecosm, where he channels the libertarian commandments of his digital Juggernaut in the language of the angels.

A host of awesome myths attest to the power of this new god. Markets must rule, some right-wing prophets tell us, because of "globalization," because the moral weight of the entire world somehow demands it. Others bear tidings of a "New Economy," a spontaneous recombination of the DNA of social life according to which, again, markets simply must rule. The papers fill with rapturous talk of historical corners turned, of old structures abandoned, of endless booms and weightless work.

The new god makes great demands on us, and its demands must be appeased. None can be shielded from its will. The welfare of AFDC mothers must be entrusted unhesitatingly to its mercies. Workers of every description must learn its discipline, must sacrifice all to achieve flexibility, to create shareholder value. The professional, the intellectual, the manager must each shed their pride and own up to their flawed, lowly natures, must acknowledge their impotence and insensibility before the new god's divine logic. We put our health care system in its invisible hands, and to all appearances it botches the job. Yet the faith of the believers is not shaken. We deregulate the banking industry. Deregulate the broadcasters. Deregulate electricity. Halt antitrust. Make plans to privatize Social Security and to privatize the public schools.

And to those who worry about the cost of all this, the market's disciples speak of mutual funds, of IPOs, of online trading, of early retirement. All we have to do is believe, take our little pile of treasure down to the god's house on Wall Street, and the market rewards us with riches undreamed-of in human history. It gives us a Nasdaq that is the envy of the world and a 401(k) for each of us to call our own.

Then, one fine day, you log in at Ameritrade and find that your tech portfolio is off 90 percent. Your department at work has been right-sized, meaning you spend a lot more time at the office—without getting a raise. You have one kid in college to the tune of $30,000 a year, another with no health insurance because she's working as a temp. Or maybe you lost your job because they can do it cheaper in Alabama or Mexico. Your daughter's got a disease that requires $400 a month in drugs, and your COBRA insurance benefits are due to run out in two months. Or maybe you're the Mexican worker who just got a new *maquiladora* job. You have no electricity, no running water, no school for your children, no health care, and your wage is below subsistence level. And should you make any effort to change these conditions—say, by organizing a union not aligned with the corrupt PRI—you're likely to get blacklisted by local factory managers.

That's when it dawns on you: The market is a god that sucks. Yes, it cashed a few out at the tippy-top, piled up the loot of the world at their feet, delivered shiny Lexuses into the driveways of their ten-bedroom suburban chateaux. But for the rest of us the very principles that make the market the object of D'Souza's worship, of Gilder's awestruck piety, are the forces that conspire to make life shitty in a million ways great and small. The market is the reason our housing is so expensive. It is the reason our public transportation is lousy. It is the reason our cities sprawl idiotically all across the map. It is the reason our word-processing programs stink and our medicine costs more than anyone else's. In order that a fortunate few might enjoy a kind of prosperity unequaled in human history, the rest of us have had to abandon ourselves to a lifetime of casual employment, to unquestioning obedience within an ever-more-arbitrary and despotic corporate regime, to medical care available on a maybe/maybe-not basis, to a housing market interested in catering only to the fortunate. In order for the libertarians of Orange County to enjoy the smug sleep of the true believer, the thirty millions among whom they live must join them in the dark.

. . .

BUT IT IS NOT ENOUGH to count the ways in which the market sucks. This is a deity of spectacular theological agility, supported by a priesthood of millions: journalists, admen, politicians, op-ed writers, think-tankers, cyberspace scrawlers, Sunday morning talk-show libertarians, and, of course, bosses—all united in the conviction that, no matter what, the market can't be held responsible. When things go wrong, only we are to blame. After all, they remind us, every step in the economic process is a matter of choice. We choose Ford over Dodge and Colgate Total over Colgate Ultra-Whitening; we choose to take that temp job at Microsoft, to live in those suburbs, to watch Channel 4 rather than Channel 5. We participate in markets; we build markets; markets, in fact, are us. Markets are a straightforward expression of the popular will. Since markets are the product of our choices, we have essentially authorized whatever the market does to us. This is the world that we have made, let us rejoice and be glad in it.

Virtually any deed can be excused by this logic. The stock market, in recent years a scene of no small amount of deceit, misinformation, and manipulation, can be made to seem quite benign when the high priests roll up their sleeves. In October 1999, a heady time for small investors, Andy Serwer of *Fortune* could be heard telling the inspiring story of an investment "revolution" in which the financial power of "a few thousand white males" in New York was "being seized by Everyman and Everywoman." We the people had great, unquestionable power: Serwer's article was even illustrated with clenched fists. We had built this market, and it was rewarding us accordingly.

But these days Serwer is pondering the problem of "stock market rage" as those same Everyman investors are turned inside out by the destruction of $4 trillion of Nasdaq value. Now that the country is in the sort of situation where brokers and bankers might find themselves in deep political shit, Serwer observes that we have become quite powerless. Investors are "mad as hell," Serwer notes, but "there isn't much [they] can do about it." The explanation for this supposed impotence is, strangely, a moral one: choice. Since those lovable little guys acted of their own free will when they invested in Lucent, PMC Sierra, and Cisco, today there is no claim they can make that deserves a hearing. What has happened is their fault and theirs alone.

The market only fails us, it seems, when we fail it—when our piety is somehow incomplete, when we don't give the market *enough* power, when we balk at entrusting it with our last dime. Electricity deregulation didn't work in California, the true believers chant, because the scheming elitist political class of that state betrayed the people, refusing to give them enough choice, to deregulate all the way.

"FREE TO CHOOSE" is a painfully ironic slogan for the market order. While markets do indeed sometimes provide a great array of consumer choices, the clear intention of much of the chatter about technology, "globalization," and the "New Economy" is, in fact, to deny us any choice at all. Moving from rhetoric to the world of financial politics, the same logic holds true: Markets show a clear preference for the shutting down of intellectual dissent and political choice. Markets romp joyfully when word arrives that the vote-counting has been halted. Markets punish the bond prices of countries where substantial left parties still flourish. Markets reward those lands—like Bill Clinton's USA—where left parties have been triangulated into impotence. So predictably do markets celebrate the suppression of political difference that Thomas Friedman, the highly respected *New York Times* columnist, has actually come up with a term for the trade-off: "the golden straitjacket." Since all alternatives to laissez-faire are now historically discredited, Friedman maintains, all countries must now adopt the same rigidly pro-business stance. When they do, "your economy grows and your politics shrink." The pseudodemocracy of markets replaces the real democracy of democracy; the great multinational corporations nod their approval; and the way is clear for (some) people to get fantastically rich.

Friedman has a point. Consider the case of Singapore, long the inamorata of market heavies and their press agents. As we all know by now, Singapore is an economic miracle, a land arisen from Third World to First in a handful of decades. Singapore is the land with the most economic freedom in the world. Singapore is more comprehensively wired than anywhere else. Singapore is the best place to do business in all the earth. And as proof you need look no further than a postcard of Singapore's glittering downtown, with all the spanking new skyscrapers erupting from the earth in stern testimony to the market's approval.

And what the market loves best about Singapore is what is absent: politics. Singapore's shopping malls—heavenly landscapes of chrome and polished granite, of flashing jumbotrons and free floor shows for the kids—trump those of our own land. But politically the country is a dull monotone. There is little danger that opposition parties will come to power or that crusading journalists will violate the rules of what Singaporeans call "self-censorship."

So what replaces politics? What fills the blank space left when a country has sacrificed dissent on the altar of the market? In Singapore, the answer seems to be management theory. Settling down one Sunday afternoon in that country with a copy of the *Straits Times*, the more or less official newspaper, I turned to the section most American newspapers reserve for book reviews and think pieces and instead found: a profile of the management guru who cowrote the *One to One* series of marketing books; a column about the urgent need to adapt to waves of workplace "change" (you know, like "outsourcing"); an enthusiastic story about the new president of PepsiCo, a native of India who reportedly studies videotapes of

Michael Jordan's greatest basketball moments in order to "catch insights about the value of teamwork"; a profile of the management guru who cowrote *The Individualized Corporation* ("Power to the people is [his] motto"); a profile of one of the paper's writers in which the concept of "the journalist as a brand" is the point of departure; and a review of one of those sweeping, pseudohistorical books so beloved of business readers that start out with the Neanderthals and end up affirming various contemporary management homilies about creativity and entrepreneurship.

Management theory has become so variegated in recent years that, for some, it now constitutes a perfectly viable replacement for old-fashioned intellectual life. There's so much to choose from—so many deep thinkers, so many flashy popularizers, so many schools of thought, so many bold predictions, so many controversies!

For all this vast and sparkling intellectual production, though, we hear surprisingly little about what it's like to be managed. Perhaps the reason for this is that, when viewed from below, all the glittering, dazzling theories of management seem to come down to the same ugly thing. This is the lesson Barbara Ehrenreich learns from the series of low-wage jobs that she works and then describes in bitter detail in *Nickel and Dimed*. Pious chatter about "free agents" and "empowered workers" may illuminate the covers of *Fast Company* and *Business 2.0*, but what strikes one most forcefully about the world of waitresses, maids, and Wal-Mart workers that Ehrenreich enters is the overwhelming power of management, the intimidating array of advantages it holds in its endless war on wages. This is a place where even jobs such as housecleaning have been Taylorized to extract maximum output from workers ("You know, all this was figured out with a stopwatch," Ehrenreich is told by a proud maid-service manager), where omnipresent personality and drug tests screen out those of assertive nature, where even the lowliest of employees are overseen by professional-grade hierarchs who crack the whip without remorse or relent, where workers are cautioned against "stealing time" from their employers by thinking about anything other than their immediate tasks, and where every bit of legal, moral, psychological, and anthropological guile available to advanced civilization is deployed to prevent the problem of pay from ever impeding the upward curve of profitability. This is the real story of life under markets.

But the point where all the "New Economy" glory and promise really start to suck, where all the vaunted choice and empowerment of free markets are revealed as so many creaking stage devices, is when Ehrenreich takes on the shiniest of all the Nineties myths—productivity. In 1999 and 2000, with the country as close to full employment as it had ever been, wages did not increase as much as standard economic theory held they ought. Among the devout this was cause for great rejoicing: Through a titanic national effort we had detached productivity from wages, handing the gains over to owners and shareholders. But this was less a "choice" that Americans consciously made than it was, as Ehrenreich makes undeniably evident, the simple triumph of the nation's managers—always encouraging employees to think of themselves as stakeholders or team members even as they unilaterally dictate every aspect of the work experience.

The social panorama that Ehrenreich describes should stand as an eternal shrine to the god that sucked: slum housing that is affordable only if workers take on two jobs at once; exhausted maids lunching on packages of hot-dog buns; women in their twenties so enfeebled by this regimen that they can no longer lift the vacuum cleaners that the maid service demands they carry about *on their backs;* purse searches, drug tests, personality tests, corporate pep rallies. Were we not so determined to worship the market and its boogie-boarding billionaires, Ehrenreich suggests, we might even view their desperate, spent employees as philanthropists of a sort, giving selflessly of their well-being so that the comfortable might live even more comfortably. "They neglect their own children so that the children of others will be cared for," she writes; "they live in substandard housing so that other homes will be shiny and perfect; they endure privation so that inflation will be low and stock prices high."

THESE ARE THE FRUITS of thirty years of culture war. Hell-bent to get government off our backs, you installed a tyrant infinitely better equipped to suck the joy out of life. Cuckoo to get God back in the schools, you enshrined a god of unappeasable malice. Raging against the snobs, you enthroned a rum bunch of two-fisted boodlers, upper-class twits, and hang-'em-high moralists. Ain't irony grand.

—BAFFLER 14, 2001

SUCCESSITUDES™

Incenting the extreme professional since 1993

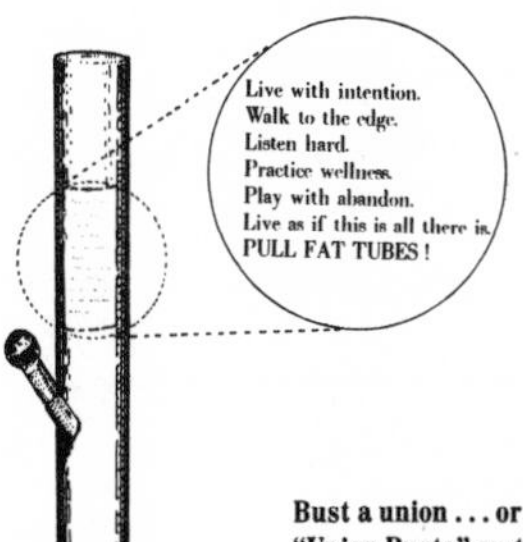

Live with intention.
Walk to the edge.
Listen hard.
Practice wellness.
Play with abandon.
Live as if this is all there is.
PULL FAT TUBES !

The "Pursuit of Wow" bong
Para-sailing at Cabo and snowboarding at Crested Butte may help you to "get to yes," but deep-lung a couple of plumes out of this baby and you'll be at "Fuck yeah!" What executive go-getter wouldn't like to have a hit or two of what Tom Peters has been smoking? 2' plastic Grafix. Red, blue, or green. Brass plaque engraved with inspirational verse of extreme business poet Pringle Pypkin. $129.95.

Bust a union . . . or bust a move with our "Union Busta" motorcycle jacket
Let your restive work force know that you wouldn't think twice about shutting down your box factory and moving it to Arkansas or Mexico. Labor Board approved. Black top-grain leather. $329.95.

Unlock the asshole within . . . with WordBastard™ cassettes
Corporate difference-makers know that the key to extracting peak employee performance is a regime of random and terroristic intimidation. In this nine-tape WordBastard™ set, Dirk Polnschlaeger, the Dean of Executive Intimidation Training, unlocks the secret to life-transforming viciousness. Each day, Dirk will guide you through a series of mental exercises that will teach you the 10 timeless principles of business contumely, the 7 styles of tactical truculence, 6 tips for the up-and-coming martinet, and the 4 qualities of an effective tyrant. The information-packed workbook will hone your skills, and your Personal Bastard Diary will chart your progress. More than a thousand colorful and humiliating commands, imprecations and insults (almost 200 of which refer to the testicles). $89.95.

A Word From Our Chairman
Successitudes™ began with my life-long passion for acquiring stuff — money, cars, fine cigars like this one in my mouth, chicks (of course). I learned long ago that if you want a piece of the action, you gotta strap on a pair of brass ones. Now, some inspirational merchandisers talk a good game about positive mental attitude. They'd have you festoon your office with posters telling you how life is like a golf course and paperweights telling you what T-E-A-M stands for. If that kind of candy-ass uplift makes you feel better about your dead-end middle-management job, fine. But just remember — high-net-worth individuals like myself find chunks of suckers like you in our stools every morning. And that, asshole, is why you should write for our catalog today. P.O. Box 378293, Chicago, IL 60637.

James Hatt

—Baffler 10, 1997

Cyclorama of the Great Debauch

4
Give the Millionaire a Drink

Mike Newirth

THEY COME from all over to the town of East Hampton, this celebrated place at the end of the island. Private jets shoot off hourly from Dallas and LA, the chilled Porsches and Saabs arrive from Montclair and Rye, matron busloads depart the Park Avenue swelter in a huff of opera and facials, and they come packed five to a Camaro from Woodside and Asbury Park. They crowd the same streets gridded by Dutch burghers of centuries past, and with their tanned arms thrown up and their eyes upon their lord they sing of the alchemical wish: *I can buy this.* I can pull things near to me, I levitate as you descend, I will pile the stuff of cash so high as to keep me forever out of my grave. . . .

. . .

NOBODY COULD GUESS why the internationally known supermodel decided to piss in the bar sink at the Apex Grill. Two A.M., the hour most socially permissible for decadent stunts, barroom crowded with angular bodies and faces gone shiny with cosmopolitans and blue martinis, called for again and again with the same stubby wave. The bartender, blurred bulk in white shirt and French apron, watched idly as the tall woman with the charred gold mop of hair crawled up top of the bar, nailed hand rubbing the makeup from her face. As she stepped to the chrome rails and rucked up her dress, silk scraping silk, there were shrieks and the sound of a man slapping himself to vulgar effect, and the bartender remembered an afternoon decades past, lying in bed with his first girlfriend, she sashaying above him in his boxer shorts, giggling, this as piss of drink sprays from the center of that trained and shaped and photographed body, and the bar sink fills like a cistern.

After, a distinguished anesthesiologist, lean, leathery, hair varnished like a helmet, holds up a credit card. "Buy the lovely lady whatever she wants to drink." Cheers, applause, the bartender straightens up and, moving so slowly through time, reaches for the cassis and champagne.

His date, a twenty-year-old with an unblemished, accusing Andover face: "What is your fucking *problem*."

"You need to be more celebratory." His gaze locked to the swaying, flushed model, all the swelled faces in the long mirror, cell phone before him on the bar like a gray fish. "I already *told* you what you're here for."

SLOW LATE AFTERNOON: Stray cats prowl the village dumpsters. All the good people—those drowning in that hearty moral sea of accumulated wealth—are stretched out at the gleaming beach. A famous comic actor known for his films of family entertainment (homespun wisdom interspersed with hilarious belches and pratfalls), and for his witty endorsements of a fine tortilla chip, walks up and down the main street carrying a large bottle of vodka. His fishing vest and floppy hat add a near-tint of gentility. The actor's eyes resemble cathode-ray tubes. When his cell phone rings he shifts the bottle, flips it open, and keeps on walking. He speaks with an air like that trapped for years at the bottom of a western mine.

Three teenage girls stand before the window of a crowded shop. Stylish clothes for women, all and entirely in the color of white. Frocks and gowns and underwear, all the same hue of elegance and emptiness. Beside those white garments, the girls throb in their hiphuggers and tight striped shirts, slurping on pacifiers. Sixteen and already their faces are engraved with a Russian century of bored malaise. "There is nothing I wouldn't do to spite my father," says one.

"If only I wasn't *here*," says another.

Tea is served on the veranda of the American Hotel to a rowdy party of options traders. Oh, they've done all the good drugs, been tapped for entrance at many velvet ropes; they've fucked all the slim blonde women (and then watched, snifters in hand, as all the women melted together in the foamy hot tub on the moonlit deck, every last gawky white boy fantasy fulfilled categorically). But now the intrusion of china cups and pale sandwiches flusters their paid-for vacation hoohrah. Their practiced repose comes apart; up through the mucus of the body's past rise the fumbling second-string ballplayers and zitty homeroom monitors. "This is *bogus*," Troy says.

"Hey. Waitress. Can't you bring us some *port*, or something?" calls out Ken, twisting for assurance his gold-flashing diver's watch.

"The bar will not be open until six, sir," she replies.

"Bitch," says Trevor, knocking a teacup off the rail.

At the Telephone Mama, the choice nightspot of this season, the one the Jersey tourists and Astoria orthodontists are *simply* better off not even knowing about, the line snakes out into the parking lot. Who are these people? Zombie extras from *Night of the Flesh-Eating Corporate Raiders*, the never-made Corman salute to the rapacious 1980s? The men fluff their chest hair through the slits of silk shirts, if they have it; the smooth-skinned blondies, those delicate boys with pursed mouths disparaging, are either blood-leached and serious old money or else homosexual. Reaching the door, three black kids from Valley Stream are turned away: "We have a dress code," says the enormous doorman. Through the door thumps a vintage Funkadelic side; inside the young women twitch like wraiths on the dance floor, white shawls slipping from their shoulders and breasts. Cursing, the blacks drive off into the night.

In the narrow aisles of the town supermarket: A wealthy man in his fifties argues with his girlfriend, half his age. She is wearing a thong bikini, and her tanned skin is like fine fudge or mink: a thing sheiks might buy by the yard. When he sweeps his arm, his IWC chronometer and gold bracelet tick, clanking: his voice is low, savaging. She flips her ashy hair precisely. "I won't go," she says. "Not unless André goes." At the cash register, a townie—belly, navel, nipples distended, jaw shame-slacked, oily hair—hands over a sheaf of food stamps. The proper patrons line up elsewhere, piling up their soda crackers and Pellegrino on the other conveyor, as if something were catching.

That well-known actor loiters in the Rexall, chatting discreetly with the pharmacist. He leaves, buying quantities of cough drops and breath mints. In five years, perforated liver shipping poison to his brain, he'll have taken to passing out candy from his pockets to alarmed children on the streets.

An internationally famous woman, even locally a celebrity of some substance, watches the washed-up wetbrain cross the street from within the armored capsule of her Range Rover. She feels toward him a chundering mix of contempt and fear: He's a has-been, for sure, reduced to kiddie pablum and shilling for snacks, but once he was actually a Hollywood player, the realest kind. She's on top now, the ultimate hostess, a lasery visionary of taste and purchases and decor, with magazines and recipe clubs and catalogs, a carpet-bombing of commerce spread across the hick heartland; but, you know, she doesn't really *do* anything that any Miss Baltimore Homemaker of 1961 could not have improved upon. Behind the flat, flawless heatproof glass of the vehicle, her smile is pulled into place by hydraulics, exposed teeth carved from a single block of titanium. But she's shaking as though from a palsy. Recently, one of the dowagers she courted had whispered to her the cruel, glittering news—"for your own good, dear," the withered bitch had said—that her daughter, that hard-cheeked rider of ponies and deceit, was sleeping with the contractor on her Sag Harbor cottage, with whom, truthfully (and known to none other), she had herself slept not two weeks earlier. Unlikely, but it *could* get around. Ten thousand dollars had gone toward quieting the tale of baby ducks (briefly needed for a photo shoot) murdered beneath the wheels of her vehicle. This perfect hostess, no one guesses at her days of shudder and terror, what she endures to prop up her exemplary life of buying and placing. *Cross me and die*, she thinks, waiting for the light to change.

July glides into August, the frictionless summer everlasting. Everybody is from England or into junk bonds or forcing themselves to vomit or working on a novel or bisexual temporarily. More telephones are stolen out of Range Rovers. Most of the dogs receive grooming. Some of the townies get laid.

It is still 2 a.m. at the Apex Grill. The supermodel lurches in, shaky, bad news. Her miniskirt offers up her sintered ass. Nobody is surprised by this, no one notices. Bound to her shoulders is the soft black leather Prada knapsack that every woman here was required on peril of her soul to purchase for this summer. The Prada bags, shapeless, hang from the backs of the women like elegant hide pupae. But the model has replaced the Prada bag's signature gold-plated zipper ornament with a Tiffany keychain, a miniature infant's bottle in platinum. This particular Prada bag was made in Malaysia, in a factory thrown up in an enormous corrugated shed, hand-stitched by women whose arms bear curing burns and knife scars, women with hair coarse as rope, and some weeks later the model purchased it at the East Hampton Saddlery for $570 because her agent and *Country* magazine had touted it as the summer's prime accessory, and of course, they were right.

"I would like a . . . cosmopolitan," she whispers to the bartender. Her mind has been expertly muted to a soft blue Xanax blur. Beneath it, though, is something real: a throbbing Kodachrome snapshot of the night, five years earlier, when she sucked a photographer, somewhere in the Montauk dunes. Two months later she had a shoot in *Interview*, so it was undoubtedly worth it, she knows, but still. . . . The memory's buzz will outlast her looks and career. The bartender sets a cocktail glass before her and spills out her drink. Her fingers flutter like moths on the hard stem of the glass.

The bartender slips farther down his bar, wiping spills with a white dinner napkin. He pauses before a man and two women sagged with drink and exhaustion, but the man waves him away. "We still have our ménage to look forward to," says the black woman with grayed skin and drooping gold jewelry.

"Yes," the man agrees. "If only for its own sake."

"Oh, you think that's the important thing," says the other woman. She looks close to forty, as do they all.

"What I think," he says, "is it is something we are going to do. Any other definition is just somebody being intentionally morbid and obtuse, *Nancy*."

"Pay up," says the first woman.

"Have another drink," says the man, words leaking out through his puffy face. "Let the impatience build a little."

"Is your head up your ass or what," the bartender says, quietly, to the barback, a pocked, stumbling local boy, who has let the ice tub deplete to meltings. "Fill that up and then go home. Get out of my sight."

He's not really a good person, this bartender.

But this is his life, East Hampton to Aspen and back, selling the best legal drug in America to the rich folk, enabling their little scenes and gaudy reckless purchasing, all that passes for history these days. His secret knowledge tends to weigh him down: that the dollar's what it's all about, and this is just a dance of fancy smoke and notions.

Out in the parking lot, watched only by the stars and the valet, that sly, pretty Andover girl wanders in slow, dazed circles. The anesthesiologist is long gone, back to Scarsdale. Tonight there was a late supper with a stocky, rapacious bond trader, a manic transplant from Kansas for whom all the dollars made and spent were their own nonstop coitus. They went to Apex, where his waved credit card produced champagne. She listened to his mouth saying things like, "Damn shit, I sure do love this Dom." He followed her into the toilet. "Let's ignite ourselves," holding out the vial of cocaine. Then went right up her *skirt*, $30 panties split down the middle, her forearms bruised where he planted her against the hot-air blower. The entrance of three dazed Chanel matrons gave her a chance to run. "*What?*" he said behind her; "bitch," as she slipped coins into the phone. She cries, wondering only what, specifically, she'd expected—the bastard dropped two hundreds on dinner, to say nothing of the drugs and bar tabs, the cost of it all, she knows to what sum the numbers add up—cries nonetheless, and waits for her taxi to come.

—BAFFLER 8, 1996

5
American Heartworm

Ben Metcalf

1.

I PROCEED FROM RAGE: rage at those whose ignorance, either God-given or self-consciously homespun, has excited in them a wrongheaded desire to peddle as the font of all that is virtuous and productive and eternal about our nation that shallow and putrid trough we call the Mississippi River. For generations we have suffered such fools to create unworthy riverside wetland areas and disappointing overlook sites and unventilated paddleboat museums and disturbing amusement parks on the theme of the American frontier; to form historical societies so that we might come to think a great deal more than we should of a rill no deeper in places than a backyard swimming pool and far less apt to hold its water; to lay bicycle paths along the levees so that we might crack open our heads within sight of chemical wastes bound for the Gulf of

Mexico; to clutter the calendar with steamboat festivals and "Big Muddy" days so that we might pay a premium for corn dogs and warm cola, and grow red and sullen under the midwestern sun, and slap our children before a congregation of strangers acquainted with the impulse and approving of the act. Yet as much as I detest those who would pound the pig iron of history into the tinfoil of folklore, and despite the ease with which I could build a case against these people, and ascribe all that is trumped-up and harmful and loathsome about their region to a native failure to work the algebra of decency and taste, my hatred of the Mississippi itself is greater still, and conscience will not let me sight the lesser target.

For what manmade entity has worked more evil upon the land than has this accident of nature? What other waterway has been the seat of more shame, or has inspired us to greater stupidity, or has inflicted more brutal and embarrassing wounds upon our culture? Have not the basest qualities to be found in the people of the middle states been quickened by the river's example, or by its seeming impulse for self-promotion? And have not these lessons been learned so well that the region now has little more to recommend it than the various log-cabin homes of Abraham Lincoln (hundreds of these), a handful of competing grain-based gasoline concerns, and the fat substitute Olestra? But I hardly mean to confine myself to generalities here: My grievances against the river are specific and they are personal, for so thoroughly have the ideals it teaches laid waste to the soul and imagination of my own family, the Metcalfs of southern Illinois, that a high degree of emotional suffering and moral decay has become almost a point of pride among its members as they walk life's dreary dirt road.

2.

The Mississippi's lessons are not "hard" in the familiar sense, wherein some touching bit of wisdom is had for a nominal fee, payable in humility and gratitude; they are hard precisely because, being wholly bad lessons, they exact a cost in wisdom, and because the river's students pay a dear tuition in sanity and health and self-esteem for the privilege of learning that which can only harm them further. Moreover, history records an almost conscious effort by the "old man" to clear his classroom of all those who recognize bunk when they see it and to gather in those who do not, a task accomplished in large part through the importation of white men. The first of these, De Soto, saw the river in 1542 but was of a reasonable bent and did not think the discovery worth bragging about; the river killed him. One hundred and thirty-one years later came Marquette the priest (now a Wisconsin basketball power) and Joliet the salesman (now an Illinois prison), who canoed downstream despite being asked not to by the local Indians and who, along with La Salle et al., set in motion a process by which the hospitable natives of the area became first trinket wholesalers, then Christians manqués, and finally a market to saturate with whiskey and firearms. Once this last goal had been achieved, the Choctaw helped the French annihilate or enslave the Natchez, while the Ojibwa scattered the Sioux, drove off the Winnebago, and ran the Fox, already shot full of holes by the French, into the desolate reaches of northeastern Wisconsin, where the Packers now play. Then arrived the European smallpox in 1782, ably ferried from village to village by the obliging Mississippi, and what few natives the plague left breathing were thereafter loath to crane their necks around the bend for fear of what was coming to get them next.

I imagine that after such a convincing bit of treachery only the stubborn or the foolish would not make some effort to get as far away from the river as they possibly could. One of those who stayed, or was born of those who stayed, was my great-great-great-grandmother "Grutch," most likely a Chickasaw, who married Joshua Metcalf, a widowed southern Illinois farmer, and bore him a son, Frank, to complement the lot his dead wife had left him, and who died herself, along with the first wife's children and those of a neighboring farm couple who had asked her to baby-sit, when at lunchtime one day she poured out tall glasses of milk laced with rat poison. The neighboring parents were never seen again, and it might be assumed that they poisoned the milk and the children much in the same way that an animal chews off its own foot to be free of a trap, the trap in this instance being the river and all that it had cost them.

Young Frank did not fancy milk and drank only half of what was in his glass, enough to stunt and disfigure him but not enough to discontinue the line. In spite of his flaws, and his half-breed hair and features, the boy managed to secure a local farm girl for a mate and to avoid her outraged brothers, who had sworn vengeance not for the insult of the seduction but because a general by the name of Metcalf had once enthusiastically slaughtered their Irish cousins at the behest of the English crown. Frank tilled the soil in southern Illinois as had his father before him, leaving only briefly to make some ranching money in the Indian Territory (later Oklahoma) but returning when the Arkansas, a tentacle of the Mississippi, dried up one summer, as did the sum of his herd and profit.

My great-grandfather, Otto, was just a boy when he watched his father's fortune blow away in the Oklahoma dust, and when he grew into manhood all the obstinacy of his forebears, and all the bitterness and disappointment this trait had sowed over the generations, took full root in him. Otto sought to revisit his father's dream without leaving Illinois, *without leaving the river*, and because he could not afford the acreage required to graze even a moderate herd there, and because this circumstance served only to affirm his small place in the world, he made a habit of reversing the inevitable stampedes with shotgun blasts; all that could not be controlled in this manner he struck out at with his fists.

His firstborn, Max, tolerated these outbursts and the whippings because he believed, incongruously, that his place in the world was not small but large. He rode boxcars and flew crop dusters and caroused and married and in the end could no more escape the river's gravity than had his ancestors. Max's large place in the world had convinced him to people it as best he could, and with thirteen mouths to feed, my father's wide among them, he was forced at last to take work along the river as a conductor on the same north–south freight trains that as a young man he had jumped and that a century earlier had killed off the steamboats, which had killed off the keelboats, which had killed off the flatboats, which had killed off the Indians. After nearly two decades of sitting idle in cabooses, catching sight now and then of the Mississippi and all the while smoking tobacco, trade in which the river had graciously abetted, my grandfather was stricken with cancer and found himself being driven, in what the clownish side of circumstance had arranged to be a De Soto, across the muddy water to a hospital in St. Louis, where, after a devastating operation, he would taste the painkillers that in time would weaken first his will, and then his heart, and then his earthly grip.

3.

In the mid-Seventies an aunt and uncle were part of a Ma Barkeresque gang whose sad tale ended one afternoon with a raid on a warehouse by local authorities and a standoff in which my pregnant, foul-mouthed, shotgun-wielding aunt used up what social credit was still being extended to the family in those days. My own father has said, with some regret in his voice, that he once passed up the opportunity to help rob the Denny's between Charleston and Mattoon, Illinois. He had no moral qualms with the plan but could not find the energy to participate, or to do much else over the next twenty-odd years, once he understood how little a week's take at the only place in the area worth robbing would improve his ability to feed and clothe his children.

What tripped up my aunt and uncle, and I suspect would have undone my father as well, was an irrepressible urge to brag about what had been stolen and to exaggerate its worth well beyond the bounds of good sense. The police might not have troubled themselves with the warehouse, which of course had been left unlocked, had they not been led to believe that they would find there countless stolen Cadillacs, bags full of laundered mob money, and stacks of Fort Knox gold. As it was, and no doubt owing to the truculent stupidity the river had bred into the Metcalfs over the generations, my aunt made her stand over a few broken-down refrigerators and a lone pig.

Most of America's national resources, and the despoliation of same, have their mythic personifications: the northwestern forests have Paul Bunyan, who, like the trees he felled, was immensely tall and who, if we are to believe the American lumber industry, created all that we now see before us; the Great Plains have Pecos Bill, whose bronco rides were apparently so intense that they whipped up the tornadoes that now regularly flatten trailer parks filled with Metcalfs; and I suppose all of America lays claim to John Henry, who represented the railroad, which has always wanted us to regard it as a natural resource. To this list the Mississippi adds an unmedicated schizophrenic named Mike Fink, a flatboat pilot who, to hear him tell it, was "half horse, half alligator" and could eat "you for breakfast, your folks for supper, and all of your cousins for a snack in between," which is to say that the river is personified, and aptly so, by a stunted and belligerent liar.

The damage done to my family by this monster Fink, and by Huck and Tom, those young liars Fink prefigured, is close to immeasurable. When my father speaks of a youthful altercation, he does not say that both parties were injured some, as is the usual way with fights; rather he says, "I hit that motherfucker so hard he actually complimented me on it later—said he was shitting teeth for a week." When I hear the tale of how my great-uncle Walter threatened my grandfather with a knife, I am not told that there was some nod toward calm, or some recognition that Walter was mentally ill and needed to be dealt with accordingly; I hear that "Max had that silly fucker on his knees before he could blink and told him, 'If you ever pull a knife on me again, you sonofabitch, I'll stick it so far up your ass you won't have to cut your meat come suppertime.'"

I do not know exactly what led Walter to draw on Grandpa. By all accounts Walter was a miserable drunk who spent his days whitewashing clapboard houses that eventually would rot because of the flooding and the humidity, and would collapse into sticks if a twister came near, but could not be built of stone or brick because the boy in Mr. Twain's story had painted a *wooden* fence, and so Walter, who might have made a decent and sober bricklayer, was forced instead to cover house after wooden house with the whitest paint he could find, which contained an extraordinary helping of lead, which may or may not have given him the bone cancer that would eventually spread to his skull and torture him there until he died but certainly did not help his sanity or intelligence in the meantime and may have been a factor in both the drinking and the knife pulled on Grandpa. I do not know. What I do know is that Walter might have lived and died beyond humiliation's shadow if the river had not driven him to drink, and Tom Sawyer had not poisoned him with lead, and Mike Fink had not encouraged him to pull a knife on a man three times as fast, ten times as smart, and fully twice his size.

4.

I used to consider it odd that the word most often called upon by those compelled to describe their feelings for a river that had just washed away their crops, or their homes, or their livestock, or their neighbors, was "respect," because to my mind a river worthy of respect put up a fight against the rain, and made some show of absorbing what fell, and did not run its banks at the first sign of darkening clouds and heat lightning. I did not know then that to the river's victims, "respect" is but a theatrical means of invoking the notions "fear" and "helplessness," and that so familiar are these notions to the river-warped mind as to render a more direct reference to them absurd.

Fear in the Midwest bears relation not only to the river's senseless attacks but to the flattened land beyond its banks, which promises the paranoid (and the river has made many of these) that he will be able to see Armageddon coming a long way off but reminds him always that there will be precious little barring its way. My father has said that when lazy old Basil Metcalf, my great-great-great-great-great-grandfather, reached the Mississippi somewhere in the lower half of Illinois, he stopped there simply because it was the first thing he had encountered since leaving the East that could not be walked around or over; he intended to press on, the story goes, but perished before he could manage it. In time, he would see a son taken away by the Union Army and would sit outside his farmhouse and scan the horizon until one morning he spotted what he took to be a visitor far across his fields and by evening held a note informing him that his son was dead, or nearly so, in a measles epidemic on the Kentucky shore. Basil set off to help the boy, or to claim his remains, sure now that fate and the landscape had conspired against him, and promptly vanished. He may have simply kept going, having concluded too late that his course need not have been stayed by such a petty obstacle as the river, but more likely he was murdered in Cairo, a common occurrence in those days and not unheard of in these. At any rate, the river failed to make delivery on either corpse.

The midwestern strain of helplessness is in part a function of the river's exaggerated capacity, for although much is made of the fact that it attains a width of 3,000 feet (generally rounded to "a mile") and a depth of 200 feet (also "a mile"), this holds true only if one attempts to swim across in the vicinity of New Orleans; upstream the soundings are less impressive: From Baton Rouge to St. Paul a shipping channel of just nine feet is maintained. It is well worth asking what chance those feet have against a flow of the sort reported in 1993, when eleven times the volume of Niagara Falls threatened St. Louis, and it is equally well worth asking what chance is afforded even inland trailer homes against a river so ill-equipped to contain the water, or to teach by its example anything more hopeful than that weakness and chaos are the natural law.

The power of this lesson is made clear to me when I learn that a cousin of mine has burned down his high school because a bully told him to do so, or has molested a child for his own reasons, or has run off with his brother's wife (and offered his own in recompense), or has deserted his pregnant girlfriend for a woman old enough to buy him beer, or has somehow managed to electrocute himself, or has tattooed an infant, or has been beaten so badly that her kidney was removed, or has not spoken to her aunt since her aunt married the man who ruined the kidney, or has rolled a car because his father never taught him to slow down on corners (and because the thought never occurred to him privately), or has attempted to run down his wife and her lover in a combine, or has been shotgunned in the chest at close range but is "too ornery to die," or has been arrested for growing marijuana *in the front yard*, or has made no effort to pay the telephone bill and must now communicate solely by CB radio, or has become some sort of humorless Christian, or has been delivered of yet another child so that this jug band of woe might play on.

I can no more doubt that the river has turned and perverted my cousins' lives than that it has done the same to its own course, at will and at random, over the eleven thousand or so years since it was brought into existence by what looks to have been an honest mistake on the part of a glacier. In his book *The Control of Nature,* Mr. McPhee writes that "southern Louisiana exists in its present form because the Mississippi River has jumped here and there within an arc of about two hundred miles wide, like a pianist playing with one hand. . . . Always it is the river's purpose to get to the Gulf by the shortest and steepest gradient." Although I concur with the notion that the river's selfish meanderings have cursed us with southern Louisiana, I prefer the image of a drunken blind man carelessly whipping his cane back and forth in unfamiliar surrounds to that of a tasteful pianist. And I do not think that the river's purpose is "to get to the Gulf" so much as it is to cause the greatest amount of suffering on the way there. Consider the river's capricious disregard for the boundaries between our states: Arkansas has been forced to sue Tennessee on numerous occasions (1918, 1940, 1970) in order to retrieve land and taxpayers carved from its eastern flank by the river and handed over to the Volunteer State. Louisiana has sued Mississippi (1906, 1931, 1966) for like cause, and Mississippi has sued Louisiana, and Arkansas has sued Mississippi, and Missouri has sued Kentucky, and Iowa has sued Illinois, and Minnesota has sued Wisconsin, until the very identities of these states have been eroded, and the wisdom of entrusting their shapes to a slithering and deceitful border impeached.

This epidemic of strife and distrust has spread elsewhere, to other rivers and other states (e.g., *Texas v. Louisiana, Missouri v. Nebraska, Nebraska v. Iowa, Indiana v. Kentucky, Virginia v. Tennessee, Maryland v. West Virginia, Rhode Island v. Massachusetts*), and has so intensified our citizenry's penchant for litigation that judges in many fluvial districts no longer have even the time required to perform a marriage or to entertain a bribe. In those areas directly scarred by the Mississippi, neighbors sue one another with a frequency and a fervor that belie the small gains to be had, having learned at the foot of the river hard lessons in desperation that have left them suckers for the bittersweet lies of the American justice system. I consider it a mere accident that to date, and to the best of my knowledge, no Metcalf has sued another Metcalf, and I do not doubt that this fact will reverse itself soon. Already the midwestern milieu is such that involvement in a petty lawsuit is held to be the height of glamour and achievement and therefore suitable excuse not to hold down a job.

My grandmother once spoke proudly to me of a cousin who had finally "growed up a little." The cause of the improvement was not parenthood, for he was a father many times over, and by numerous women; nor was it some semblance of a career, for he was minimally employed at that time and, as far as I know, since. What impressed my grandmother was that he had found the gumption to sue someone (or to do something that got him sued; I cannot remember which, nor does it particularly matter) and at last stood to make a man of himself. He failed, of course, even on these terms. Petition lost, courtroom fees owed and unpayable, he ceded control to the panic that was his birthright and fled to Missouri, across the river but really no farther from it, where I suppose he became, at least until the next chance to play the river's fool[1] presented, a child again.

5.

There runs through this continent a river worthy at least of the praise heaped upon the paltry Mississippi; that drains 9,715 square miles of Canada without once crossing the border, as well as 523,000 square miles, or fully one-sixth, of these United States; that rises up out of the Continental Divide in Montana and wends

[1] Mr. Russell "Rusty" Weston Jr., late of Valmeyer, Illinois, and a small pied-à-gulch in Montana, who in July 1998 allegedly took it upon himself to gun down a dozen cats and two Capitol Police officers before being shot himself, was so perfect an example of Mississippi victimhood that I wondered at the time of his spree if he did not have some Metcalf blood in him. Here was a man who had seen his town washed away in the 1993 floods and (stubbornly, pointlessly) rebuilt just a stone's throw to the east to await the river's next assault, who was terrified of television sets and satellite dishes (this is common even among midwesterners who own and enjoy them), who believed that the president of the United States had sent a Navy SEAL to kill him (the SEAL is an unusual variation here, but the claim of persecution at the hands of the president certainly is not), and whose acute schizophrenia deviated so slightly from the midwestern norm that his father thought it sufficient to offer the following gloss to the *Miami Herald:* "His mind doesn't work real good." More familiar still, and what finally locates Mr. Weston Jr. on the middle bands of the riverine behavioral spectrum, is his comfort with, and obvious flair for, the lawsuit. In addition to considering a suit against the Secret Service, who had questioned him regarding threats he had made against the president, Mr. Weston Jr. is known to have sued a pickup-truck dealer in Illinois and to have fought his eighty-six-year-old landlady, who he claimed had beaten him with a cane, all the way to the Montana Supreme Court, where, in true Mississippian fashion, he lost.

its way across the American heartland, flowing in places north and elsewhere east and in the balance south, having decided its course a long time ago and having for the most part stuck to it; that at 2,315 miles is without challenge the longest stream around and if allowed by mapmakers to claim its southernmost leg (that is, "the Mississippi River" below St. Louis) would reach 3,495 miles, a length bested only by those great rivers of the tropics, the Nile and the Amazon. I refer, of course, to the Missouri River.

In addition to doing its own job, the Missouri drains nearly three-quarters of the upper Mississippi basin, leaving the rest not to the Mississippi, which is incapable of doing what by rights should come naturally to it, but to the Ohio, the Iowa, the Illinois, the Des Moines, the Wisconsin, the Minnesota, the Meramec, the Kaskaskia, and the St. Croix, fine rivers all. That they, along with the White, the St. Francis, the Salt, and the Rock, should be deemed "tributaries" of the Mississippi I can only regard as fraud of the highest order, considering that the Mississippi, which receives nearly half of its annual flow from the Ohio alone, and a good deal of the remainder from the Missouri, is but where these streams happen to collide and not, as is commonly supposed, the mythic force that draws them together or, more ludicrous still, created them.

The Mississippi is in reality a thin creek issuing from a nondescript pond in Minnesota and would likely trickle away to nothing before it reached St. Louis if on the way it did not loot every proper river in sight. Even availed of the extra water, the Mississippi is so wasteful with the stuff, and so fickle with its bearings, that only the constant attentions of the Army Corps of Engineers enable it to reach the Gulf at all. Unaided, it would pour off into the Louisiana swampland known as Atchafalaya and form a fetid inland sea. Should it therefore surprise us that the Mississippi's pupils have developed a habit for public assistance unrivaled even by that to be found in our decaying coastal cities; that there is scarcely a household in my extended family that does not have at least one potential breadwinner sitting it out on some sort of "disability"; that there are stores in these people's communities where a food stamp is met with less suspicion than a five- or ten-dollar bill?

Some years ago an uncle made a break with family tradition and found work in the oil fields near his house, doing so not because he saw any need to improve himself or his situation but because the job allowed him to tell people he was an "oilman," which he thought had a ring to it. He did not care much for the actual work, though, and began to send his eldest son out in his stead, a practice tolerated by my uncle's employers only because they considered it unlikely that the son could be any lazier than the father. The boy soon opened their minds, and one afternoon he arrived home to tell his father, "We've been fired." My parents visited shortly after the incident and found the entire household in good spirits. My uncle had been angry at first, and he did express concern that his son might never learn how to hold down a job, but he believed that things might work out after all: As he saw it, both he and the boy were now eligible for unemployment. My parents did not disabuse him of the notion.

6.

Having taught the midwesterner to freeload, and to lie, and to steal, and to work violence against his brother, the Mississippi now rings its doleful school bell once more. My father heeds the call as he always has, emptying the family bank account and driving to one of several riverboat casinos tethered off the coasts of Illinois, Iowa, and Missouri, where he plays at blackjack and roulette until he has entirely lost what sum my mother has managed to save up since his last unfortunate visit. He goes not because he believes that the river will make a winner of him, for he surrendered that fantasy long ago, if indeed he ever entertained it at all. He goes because he believes, or needs to believe, that one day the river might look more kindly upon its son than it has in the past, and teach him some lesson not predicated on havoc and despair, and allow him just once to recoup the losses that have imperiled both his marriage and his sanity.

And of course it never will.

Ecce Mississippi. We might well ask how much longer the republic can stand with a worm such as this slithering through its heart.

—Baffler 11, 1998

6
A Partial History of Alarms

Nelson Smith

The history of property and theft is a large subject, more or less the history of humankind. Fully considered, it extends to the bulk of our achievements in government, culture, and commerce, along with the greater share of our technical advances, from the earliest architecture and mightiest engines of war to the humbler topic at hand: electric and electronic security alarms—the various buzzing, shrieking, whooping, clanging, yeeping anti-theft devices so familiar to anyone who lives and sleeps in a modern city.

Though mechanical alarms are fairly recent, the idea is as old as property itself. Undoubtedly, mankind's earliest alarm system consisted of a few strategically tethered dogs. With their jittery, blusterous temperaments and zeal for authority, dogs fully prefigured the basic operating principles of the modern security alarm.

Like mechanical alarms—which do not themselves directly attack, roust, or mangle thieves (though such spectacular accessories are now available)—dogs repel intruders with a kind of sonic illusion. Riled, they emit a warning cry in the lowest tone they can muster—a plangent growl whose deep, resonant pitch implies a larger chest, and thus vocal cords attached to a mightier beast. Likewise, security alarms—not in their pitch, but in their broad, systemic reach—imply the attachment of private property to a larger, more brutal entity: the state.

This ventriloquial strategy first took mechanical form in humble alarms for private homes. Before electricity, such devices were relatively feckless, as in the case of an eighteenth-century apparatus of pull-strings and jingle-bells rigged to emit, in the words of its English inventor, "a plaintive air that inspires such sentiments in the mind of the housebreaker that will doubtless prompt him to take precipitous flight."[1] With electricity, however, plaintiveness became an octave of the alarm's past. According to patent records, the first voltaic "burglar annunciator" was registered in Boston in 1853, making security alarms arguably the earliest form of electrified mass communication. Versions of this novel, window-sprung buzzer were used primarily to protect the homes of affluent city dwellers. Their jurisdiction was domestic, their advantage surprise. Yet with the technology in place, electric security alarms would soon spread beyond this limited purview in a steady, raucous encroachment of private distress on public domain.

COMMERCIAL ALARMS marked the next major epoch of alarm development. By the turn of the last century, on-premise commercial alarms formed part of the emerging urban network of telegraphs, telephones, pneumatic tubes, fire bells, traffic signals,

[1] From *A History of Alarm Security*, by The National Burglar and Fire Alarm Association.

and other conveyers of modern urgency. Proliferating along the new overhead wireways, a growing alarm industry affixed its clamorous wares to banks, furriers, jewelers, and, above all, to department-store windows, where newly fashionable dioramas of mannequins reveling in convenience formed the stroll-by television of the day. Able to reinforce glass without obstructing the view, electric window alarms thus advanced to new heights the technical fusion of display and restriction so essential to the formation of a well-stoked consumer economy. Soon store windows everywhere sported that quaint iconography still visible to any appreciative urban stroller today: badge-shaped decals bearing the Kiwanian-era trademarks of the early alarm manufacturers—a goddess in helmet (Holmes Electric Protection), an eagle volant (Merchant Central), a pony expressman (Wells Fargo Security), a winged griffin (DGA Alarm Systems), a grenadier in a halo of electric bolts (National Guardsman, Inc.)—depictions of the alarms as a constabulary of stern little genies inhabiting the glass.

With this widening protectorate came a fundamental change in the security alarm's mode of operation. While household alarms were designed primarily to consternate burglars and jangle awake the slumbering homeowner, alarms in the commercial setting required third-party intervention. After business hours, that is, the property owner may be nowhere about, and the alarm must act not merely as a warning signal but as an instrument of makeshift recruitment and random public address. In this evolved capacity, then, the security alarm assumes an implicitly civic function. It appeals, like the clarions or church bells of old, to the sense of duty that undergirds all social order, to those nobler instincts of citizenship, reciprocity, and the commonweal by which we band ourselves into stable, productive nations. Naturally, coercion is involved. Amplified with colossal buzzers, pneumatic sirens, and rapid-fire, wall-bolted gongs, the din of a detonated store alarm blaring, ringing, clanging away in the night forcibly conscripts everyone within earshot into the defense of property that isn't theirs and from which they themselves, let us pause to remember, derive neither profit nor reciprocal protection. All the logic of patriotism is there.

Yet while these peace-rending machines spread rapidly through the commercial realm, their placement remained limited to more or less clear physical bounds. Soon, however, alarm technology would take a decidedly metaphysical turn. By the 1940s, the outsized break-ins of world warfare had inspired the development of a new array of infrared and ultrasonic detectors. Incorporating these advances and hewing to the twentieth century's emerging spirit of global surveillance and aerial attack, the simple burglar alarm began to evolve into the more intricate and ethereal "security system." Augmented with electromagnetic sensors, the alarm's trip-circuits could now be beamed through the air rather than puttied or taped to breachable surfaces. This refinement proved especially useful for settings of conditional public access. In banks, museums, and other secular institutions, concealed alarms served to reinforce a sense of gloom-based authority, while half reviving, through a sort of technological animism, the modern public's waning dread of unseen powers.

The hidden security system thus established a new courtliness of interior space. In these hushed, tingly atmospheres of withheld outburst, the visitor feels vaguely incriminated, while any object under the alarm's scan acquires an aura of baleful superlegitimacy. Consider, for example, an encounter with an institutional treasure like the *Mona Lisa,* one of the first artworks accoutered with alarms. You arrive through guarded corridors amid a restrained, pensive crowd. You take your turn and stand beneath the masterpiece, pondering deeply, awaiting its aesthetical effects. As you wait, you notice how old it looks, how remote and small. The longer you stare, the more its value seems manifest not in the dim little rectangle of crackulating paint, but in the assault-proof glass, the surveillance cameras, the softly militarized setting. Peering closer now, as if through freshly criminalized eyes, you imagine the alarm behind the portrait itself, the alarm surely underlying that famous, bemused face like a suppressed scream that twitches delicately at the corners of her mouth: One touch and she shrieks, one bump and her role in the history of art is instantly superseded by her role in the history of property and punishment.

Whether guarding a store window, then, or a priceless work of art, alarms illustrate the appeal to force implicit in the very concept of property. Yet if the interior security system advanced this coercive function to new heights, the alarms themselves remained as stationary and wire-fixtured as the earliest burglar-buzzers. It was only with the development of the transistor in the late fifties and the advent of smaller, wireless parts that alarms assumed a policing power as dispersed and flexible as property itself in a commodity-flooded world. With electronic components and plastic housings, no longer were alarms bound to place. Even the sounds, the twitters and whines, of this new "remote control" technology suggested a boundless penetration of external authority into internal conscience. By the end of the decade these qualities had been brought to ingenious perfection in the anti-shoplifting systems of the Sensormatic and Knogo corporations, whereby even the meagerest store merchandise could be tagged electronically with its own powers of adjudication and self-avenging squeals.

First installed in department stores in the Sixties, such systems have become so common now that it is difficult for us to truly appreciate the horror they must have inspired in their first unwitting victims—that special, revelatory horror reserved for lab animals, infantry, and other prey of new machines. Imagine yourself as an innocent young shopper in that dawn of the electronic age deliberating over some extravagant vendible—say, a costly pair of gloves. On an impulse you slip the gloves under your coat, cough, and glance around: so far, so good. Now with casual aplomb and excruciating restraint you saunter down the aisle, past the distracted clerks and toward the store exit, your heart tugging and panting on its leash, trembling in the anticipation of life's most incomparable triumph: successful theft. The exit is just four, three, two steps away. . . . Then suddenly, a scream! A high-pitched, oscillating whine, as if some dentalish instrument were extracting the pulp of your very conscience. A guard steps forward and seizes you by the arm. And whatever your immediate fate, you will surely experience for years to come the after-twitches of this utter betrayal by the inanimate universe: like the fairy tale in which the broom or bucket—or in this case, the pricey gloves—suddenly springs to life, crying, Thief! Thief! Thief!

AS SUCH HIGH-TECH AMBUSHES proliferated through the Sixties, they seemed at first to herald the push-button totalitarianism grimly prognosticated in those days. Yet just as the path of human logic is so often unpredictable, so the technologies it dreams into existence rarely progress along clear trajectories. While hidden alarm networks continue to enclose more and more of our public space, the idea of a totally ordered, big-brotherly society now stands in our growing collection of antique futurisms. Where we once feared the perfection of social order, we now sense order fragmenting all around us. Suitably enough, then, the most recent phase of alarm development has a clearly discordant, regressive ring to it, as the sporadic howls of car alarms fill our city nights with echoes of the device's distant zoological origins.

Technically speaking, this latest "postmodern" genre of security alarm cannot be considered much of an advance. Yet more forcefully than any of its predecessors, the car alarm intones a central irony in the history of alarm technology. The automobile itself, as we know, represented the mechanical triumph of individual over collective. Enthroned in his roaming, honking intransigence, the motorist becomes a creature against all others. With alarms, this territorial self-acclaim can be sustained even when the motorist has called it a day. The early horn-triggering alarms of the Seventies clearly evinced this surrogate function, emitting an autistically methodical honk like an enraged driver pounding his forehead on the horn. As later car alarms grew more ubiquitous and expressive, filling neighborhoods with their now-familiar idiom of whoooops, dweeeeps, and whirligig wails, they clearly demonstrated a paradox evident in so many areas of human progress: that our achievements tend to expand to the point of their own self-diminishment. Here the very line of technology first designed to protect the sanctity of the home has evolved into that sanctum's most persistent disrupter.

The history of security alarms, then, chronicles yet another case of social failures amplified by mechanical successes. On the purely technical side, the successes will undoubtedly proceed. In the line of detached alarms we already have accessory shriekers for luggage, pets, children, home-incarcerated felons, and habitually wandering victims of senility. In the field of security networks, we can envision future advances linking breakthroughs in digital encoding, bioengineering, and satellite surveillance. Whatever our minds can imagine owning we will surely find noisier ways to secure. Yet it is here that the limitations arise. For we have come far and acquired much since our earliest, dog-guarded days. Indeed, the world is now so thoroughly and irreversibly *owned* that each new generation arrives into a state of increasingly aggravated mutual trespass. And in such a state the laws configuring social relations appear to us more and more like a shrill, misfiring system of coercion into which we are all unwillingly deputized. In the end, we grow inured. For who today actually responds to these mechanical invokers of civic duty? When a car alarm shrieks under our window at night, don't we all simply curse, pack the pillows over our ears, and burrow back to sleep? . . . sleeping until startled awake by yet another alarm: the peep, jingle, or buzz of our bedside alarm clock, that most intimate of all security devices, the alarm by which property itself secures our daily labor, guarding its ever-expanding claims against the trespass of our dreams.

—BAFFLER 10, 1997

7

Bring Us Your Chained and Huddled Masses

Christian Parenti

Massive waves pound the quarter-mile concrete jetty that shelters the bay off Crescent City, California. On either side of the inlet rise small and mangy hills, ravaged by cycles of clear-cut logging. Beneath these slopes is Highway 101 and the gaudy motel-littered strip of a typical California highway town. Miles from nowhere, Crescent City is a working-class burg with middle-class pretensions and aspirations. Normality radiates from its low bungalows, laid out on a bleak and arbitrary grid. Both geography and politics cast a pall over this desolate piece of coast, nestled just below the Oregon border. It's a town only a mayor could love.

Crescent City hasn't had an easy time clinging to normality. With its major industries, timber and fishing, depressed and dying by the mid-Eighties and its economy reeling under the hammer blows of recession, Reaganomics, and globalization, Crescent City was desperate for a new way to finance its version of the American Dream. It found salvation in the arms of the California Department of Corrections (CDC). Today, prison is the number-one industry in Crescent City and surrounding Del Norte County. Thanks to the sprawling $277 million Pelican Bay State Prison—a "super-max" lockdown renowned as a model of sensory deprivation—a new breed of swine grows fat here on human misery and government cash.

As the same forces that ravaged Crescent City wrought havoc on the rest of the state as well, California's predominantly white and suburban electorate began calling for blood in the "war on crime," the "war on drugs," and also in that thinly veiled war on people of color. This is the context in which Crescent City found its new economic function: guarding the POWs at Pelican Bay, the place where the faint trail of California justice dead-ends in a sadistic carnival of violence and petty greed.

Outside attention first focused on the new Pelican Bay prison in 1993, when guards forced a raving, shit-smeared inmate—driven nuts by months of isolation in a small white cell—into a tub of scalding water. The prisoner, already dazed, paranoid, and psychotic, was kept in 148-degree water until his skin began to dissolve. He suffered third-degree burns and loss of pigmentation over much of his body. According to documents cited by a federal judge, one of the attending guards commented thusly on the black man's ravaged flesh: "We're going to have a white boy before this is all through."

Madness among inmates at Pelican Bay is epidemic. More than half of the prisoners are deemed "incorrigible" and are locked away in the prison's Security Housing Unit (SHU), a prison within a prison, where inmates are confined to windowless cells twenty-three hours a day. With no work, no education, no communal activity, and no recreation (save for one hour a day in an eight-by-twelve concrete box open to the sky), many prisoners break down psychologically. According to human rights investigators, psychiatric care for those thus affected often consists of nothing more than watching cartoons from inside a phone booth–size cage. Even this sort of "care" is strictly rationed. As a result, convict insanity quickly spins out of control.

"The psychotic inmates are—unequivocally—the most disturbed people I've ever seen," says Terry Kuppers, a veteran psychiatrist and one of the few independent medical experts to have toured the prison's SHU. "They scream and throw feces all over their cells. In a mental hospital you'd never see anything like that. Patients would be sedated or stabilized with drugs. Their psychosis would be interrupted."

But most folks in Del Norte County aren't consumed with sympathy for Pelican Bay's wards. After all, the prison injects more than $90 million a year into the local economy, feeding almost all other economic activity in the region. Town fathers and local boosters view the imported chattel from LA, Fresno, and Oakland as economic raw material that keeps the town and surrounding county solvent. "Without the prison, we wouldn't exist," says County Assessor Jerry Cochran.

Many suspect that is exactly why the CDC chose Crescent City: Economically weak regions often make gracious hosts for prisons. Hard times, it seems, also have a wonderful way of dulling empathy among the local citizenry. So willing has the town been to accommodate the prison that it sometimes seems like Crescent City has sold its sovereignty to the CDC. Today it is very much a company town, and discipline is its mono-crop.

The county's symbiotic relationship with the prison is most apparent, and appalling, in the local courts. According to research by California Prison Focus (CPF), a human rights group based in San Francisco, even minor disciplinary infractions at Pelican Bay, such as spitting on guards or refusing to return a meal tray, are routinely embellished and prosecuted as felony assault in the local courts. There, the mostly black, Latino, and neo-Nazi prisoners face white jurors, who often are friends or family of prison employees.

"From our investigations it seems that the prison, in conjunction with local judges and prosecutors, is using every excuse it can to keep more people locked up for longer," says CPF's Leslie DiBenedetto-Skopek. "It's job security for the whole region."

In other words, the town benefits directly every time a ten-year sentence can be ratcheted up into a twenty- or thirty-year bid. Making matters worse, the CDC pays fully 35 percent of the Del Norte County District Attorney's budget. Given these facts, it is hardly surprising that the citizen-jurors of Del Norte seem to hand out second and third strikes (i.e., life sentences) like lollipops at a bank. Thanks to the demonic economics of incarceration, those who enter Pelican Bay on small-time charges are often trapped permanently inside.

This is the Faustian bargain upon which Crescent City's version of the American dream—its recent affluence and suburban twee—is being built. For their willingness to destroy human lives, the citizens of this county get to enjoy endless government cheese. It is in the town's interest to keep the prison horrific as well: The more inmates who go mad, the more "three strikes" dollars can be channeled north from Sacramento.

Consider the case of Geza Hayes. At age seventeen, Geza, a white youth from rural Trinity County, got the bright idea of pulling a knife on someone during a brawl. For this Geza received a four-year sentence in the phenomenally brutal Corcoran State Prison. Like most California lockups, Corcoran is Bosnia in a box—a race war managed by local warlords and their outside allies, i.e., prison gangs and allied guards. Organizations such as the Black Guerrilla Family, Nuestra Familia, and the Aryan Brotherhood manage the inside economy; like feudal barons, they wage war and extract money from the masses of inmates in the form of "taxes."

Being white, Geza fell under the jurisdiction of the Aryan Brotherhood (AB). Given the realities of California prisons, Geza had three choices. He could "pay taxes" to the mighty AB, he could join them, or he could become another semi-affiliated foot soldier on "the yard." Whether or not Geza joined the AB is unclear, but as far as authorities are concerned he's an AB soldier. For that he was sent to Corcoran's SHU. And that's where Geza's future went through the meat grinder. To leave the SHU, Geza would have had to rat out other AB soldiers, in a process known as "debriefing." But if he did this and returned to the general population, he most likely would catch a shank in the ribs or worse. So his only real choice was to wait to finish his sentence. But that's easier said than done.

As it turns out, the corrections officers in the Corcoran SHU had an affinity for Roman games. To break the monotony of watching prisoners slowly go mad, the screws would stage fights between members of the rival races on the concrete yards of the SHU. Eventually this practice, exposed by the *Los Angeles Times* and the *San Francisco Chronicle*, led to CDC director James Gomez's "reassignment." But the exposés came too late for many.

Geza, who turned nineteen in the abattoir that is the Corcoran SHU, says he was in nine such gladiator fights there. Even having survived these trials, however, he was eventually ensnared in the extreme violence endemic to the SHU. Due to severe overcrowding, Geza found himself double-celled with an alleged AB "snitch." Quite predictably, Geza did what the masters of the AB expected of him: He attacked his new "cellie" with a homemade garrote.

The videotape of the assault, shot by guards preparing to intervene, looks in through the steel-mesh door of what appears to be an underground cell. Inside one can make out two pale muscular frames: one twitching limply, the other rippling and shaking with rage, bundled like a human explosive behind the neck of the first. It's clear that Geza has snapped. Then the door slides open, the Kevlar-clad screws charge in, and the video stops.

As a result of this incident, Geza, only halfway through his four-year sentence, found himself facing new criminal charges in superior court. He plea-bargained, received an additional four years, and was transferred to the very end of the line—Pelican Bay.

Now classified as "extremely violent," Geza was placed in solitary confinement in the Pelican Bay SHU. But due to overcrowding, administrative error, or some malicious subterfuge, another alleged snitch soon landed in Geza's cell. Not surprisingly, Geza again attacked his cellie. He now faces another attempted murder charge.

"I am afraid I'll never get out," Geza says. The young convict from Trinity is now facing his "third strike." If found guilty, he will remain in prison for the rest of his life. "I spend a lot of time studying Spanish," Geza explains. "I figure I'll be here for awhile."

One other thing: Every year Geza stays inside costs California taxpayers a bit over $25,000, most of which will end up circulated in Del Norte County.

Targeting Attorneys

The CDC's influence doesn't stop at the prison walls. Crescent City criminal-defense attorneys say that they too are targeted by prison officials, who use behind-the-scenes leverage to prevent effective legal defenses of inmates. "Hell, all I know is that in 1995 I won four out of five of my Pelican Bay cases and they were almost all third strikes—hard cases," booms criminal-defense attorney Mario de Solenni, a self-proclaimed "conservative redneck pain-in-the-ass." "Then, in 1996 the judge gave me only one case." According to de Solenni—who owns and drives a large collection of military vehicles—successfully defending prisoners is a no-no in these parts, a taboo that sends authorities far and wide in the search for guaranteed loser lawyers.

"It's bad for the county's economy when the defense wins," agrees another attorney. Numerous Crescent City defense lawyers tell similar stories of beating the prosecution too many times and then finding themselves with no defense appointments. If they want to continue practicing criminal law they often end up leaving town.

Jon Levy, who holds a correspondence law degree, used to make his living defending Pelican Bay inmates charged with committing crimes inside prison. "I don't do defense anymore," says the nervous, balding Levy as he walks his small dog along the rubble-strewn beach. After winning a few cases Levy was cut off; the judges stopped assigning him work. "I can't make a living here. Even if I switched to civil cases, all my potential clients work for the prison." Levy is, quite literally, a victim of a company-town blacklist. And he's not alone.

Tom Easton, a genteel civil rights attorney with the slightly euphoric air of someone who's just survived a major auto wreck, lives with his Russian wife in a modest house overlooking the sea on the north side of town. Copies of *The National Review* and *American Spectator* cover his coffee table, but right-wing reading habits haven't endeared him to the CDC compradors. "The prison and the DA are trying to destroy my career," says Easton with a vacant smile. Until recently Easton faced several felony charges, including soliciting perjury from a prisoner, arising from his defense of Pelican Bay inmates. He says the charges were nothing more than retaliation for providing an effective defense in criminal cases and handling civil rights suits on behalf of convicts. Eventually all the charges against Easton were dropped, reversed, or ended in hung juries. "But the DA could still try to have me disbarred," says Easton. In the meantime, he has been banned from communicating with the seven Pelican Bay prisoners he represents.

Easton's sin was that he strayed from his permitted role as provider of the mandatory feeble defense, and he even dared to file a few civil suits on behalf of maimed and tortured prisoners. "I am convinced they're going after Easton because he helped prisoners," says Paul Gallegos, a defense attorney who, like others representing Pelican Bay convicts, has been harassed by the DA.

Carceral Keynesianism

What's going on in Crescent City isn't just free-floating meanness. The town's culture of civic sadism appears to be the deliberate result of state policy. Economic troubles began here in the Sixties, when the salmon and timber industries, long the lifeblood of the region, began to sputter. Then in 1964 a massive tsunami rolled in and crushed Crescent City's quaint downtown. Only nine people died, but the place never fully recovered. After the waters receded the local planners carried on as best they could, and bulldozed the old town center's twisted rubble across Highway 101 and into the sea—where it still forms a contorted barrier of sidewalk slabs, tiled bathroom walls, and buckled asphalt. In place of the old redwood Victorians, a cheap and shabby imitation of Southern California was erected: minimalls, covered open-air walkways, empty parking spaces, dingy boxlike motels.

By the early Eighties, Crescent City's economy—part of the Golden State only in name—was hemorrhaging badly. All but a handful of the area's sawmills had been shut down, commercial salmon fishing finally died, and businesses collapsed by the hundreds. The small businessmen and real estate boosters who ran the place made a series of clumsy attempts to "reposition" the regional economy. Like other towns, Crescent City latched on to the idea of becoming a tourist destination. And as so often happens, the strategy failed, in part because of the region's isolation and its unfortunate, newly built environment. The tourism strategy ultimately produced a hulking botch of a "convention center" and a few motels now used only by long-haul truckers.

By 1989 unemployment reached 20 percent and population was declining. Crescent City and Del Norte County had sunk into a seemingly terminal economic torpor. Enter the California Department of Corrections, the knight in khaki armor, searching for a site to build a new mega-dungeon. Like any battered and anemic damsel in distress, the local boosters saw their chance: The region would move from exporting fish and trees to importing brown people and renegade white trash. From now on, the town's fate would be tied to the weighty task of justice, its civic culture remade to reflect that somber mission. Facing little opposition, the CDC moved in, commandeered some unincorporated land outside of town, and set about building the state's most feared lockup.

For the most part, the Faustian bargain has paid off. Del Norte County is, in its own distorted way, booming. Pelican Bay provides 1,500 jobs, an annual payroll of $50 million, and a budget of more than $90 million. Indirectly, the concrete beast at the edge of town has created work in everything from construction to domestic-violence counseling to drug-dealing. The contract for hauling away the prison's garbage alone is worth $130,000 a year—big money in the state's poorest county. With the employment boom came almost 6,000 new residents. By the end of the Nineties, the average rate of housing starts had doubled, as had the value of local real estate.

Similar scenarios have been replicated scores of times in recent years. From Bowling Green, Missouri, to Green Haven, New York, economically battered small towns are putting out for new prisons. And they end up paying for economic safety in ways they never imagined. They are beset not only by overloaded sewer systems but also overburdened social-services agencies, as whacked-out wives, children, and corrections officers stumble in, reeling from work-related stress, abuse, and addiction. According to the National Criminal Justice Commission, 5 percent of the growth in the rural population between 1980 and 1990 is accounted for by prisoners captured in the inner city and transported out to the new carceral Arcadia.

The Keynesian stimulus awarded to prison towns does not, of course, explain the whole criminal-justice crackdown. Ultimately, the Big Round-Up is a way of managing the renewed inequality of American capitalism, which itself is the result of the intensified quest for corporate profits. It's also the byproduct of politicians' endless search for compelling issues that don't address the realities of class power and exploitation. Crime mobilizes voters in a very safe way. And building prisons isn't a bad way to dole out the federal pork that—editorial hosannas about American entrepreneurialism notwithstanding—has always been the driving economic force in American capitalism.

The damage from Crescent City's latest tsunami—rule by the CDC—isn't limited to the shattered lives of inmates, whistleblowers, and lawyers. Though prison is often sold as a "clean industry," it does bring with it what economists call "externalities" and "diseconomies." In manufacturing, the externalities are things like pollution. But in the prison business, they are madness and violence. In 1997, an inmate was released directly from the Pelican Bay SHU to the local bus station. He was found two days later, halfway to his hometown, splattered in blood, having raped a woman and put a hammer through her head.

So while capitalism restructures—driving down wages, breaking unions, decimating cities in the name of austerity and profits—a new niche market arises. The business of disciplining the surplus populations of the postindustrial landscape becomes a way of reincorporating the enraged remnants of Middle America. Small cities from Bedford Falls to Peoria must become the Vichy regimes of fortress capitalism; they must either "reinsert" themselves on the winners' terms or wither and die. Today, Middletown's "comparative advantages" are the fury that receding prosperity has engendered and a cruelty sufficient to process the social wreckage of capital's great march forward. The diseconomies of economic restructuring are recycled into politically useful raw material: Dislocation brings rage, and rage contains the dislocation, each movement in the process lubricated with a stupefying political silence.

—Baffler 12, 1999

8
Death Travels West

MIKE NEWIRTH

THESE ARE GROTESQUE TIMES. When the visuals of daily life are punctuated by shaky images of screaming children; of the bloody bodies of Rogers Park Hassidim and of Pittsburgh's Indian grocers; of corpses posed in broken prayer circles and parking lots and libraries, it may help to remember that the lately stricken Ronald Wilson Reagan was a gun-owning man.

Recall him now, ramrod tall against the die-cut Hollywood West, and forget for a moment the chalk outlines among which the rest of us live.

Reagan was a believer, a Life Member of the National Rifle Association back when such designations meant something. For while it's impossible to imagine the permanent gun culture without it, today's NRA is so bereft and so hungry for that good direct-mail cash that it has evolved all sorts of convertible-bed and Ginsu methods: shooting out thick info packs, desperate "threats to your rights!" mailings, and preapproved "membership" cards. And lost among these appeals, among the NRA's "Get tough on crime! Enforce existing laws!" party line, are the origins of the current epidemic of violence. As recently as the early Nineties, the NRA was able to convince many that violent career criminals, pampered by soft-hearted liberal judges, justified unregulated arms for self-defense. But the population of shooters among whom we live now—Harris and Klebold, Barton, Baumhammers, Smith—are essentially the NRA's own creation: Noncriminals steeped in the muck of mainstream revenge culture, they are the vicious product of thirty years of right-wing resentment. This shift from economic criminality to a cultural wellspring of rage can be tracked, as with many elements of the contemporary rightist backlash, to the late Sixties.

If Sixgun Reagan seems anachronistic now—a frail, addled senior beside the steroid-pumped, Glock-toting race killer—one must travel much farther, to an age visible now only in ghostly tracings, to find how the NRA was formed. In *Under Fire* (Holt, 1993), Osha Davidson portrays the organization as a reflection of innocent American ingenuity underpinned by darker paranoias. Following post–Civil War riots in which the National Guard performed badly, the NRA was set up to improve public rifle skills. For several years, the tournaments held at the NRA's state-funded Long Island range attracted both international competitors and social swells. Following the abrupt withdrawal of state support, the organization collapsed in 1880, only to be revived in 1901, again through state monies, amid a bout of enthusiasm for "military preparedness" inspired by the Boer War. In 1903, the NRA urged Congress to create the National Board for the Promotion of Rifle Practice, then secured a nice dispensation in which military rifles were made available at cost (later, gratis) to NRA members.

Membership swelled after World War II, and the organization's public priorities shifted to the "shooting sports," a telling euphemism for hunting. It was during this era that the NRA achieved its Shrineresque mainstream prosperity, a normalness best exemplified by the hard optimism of the steel-on-granite slogan emblazoned on its headquarters in Washington, D.C.: FIREARMS SAFETY EDUCATION, MARKSMANSHIP TRAINING, SHOOTING FOR RECREATION. But some decades knock out all the props, and in 1968, when NRA Executive Vice President Franklin Orth, testifying *in favor* of that year's Gun Control Act, said in reference to the banning of mail-order sales that

> We do not think any sane American, who calls himself an American, can object to placing in this bill the instrument which killed the president

he marked both the terminus of the NRA's mutability and the death of the pro-gun moderation he espoused.

Over the next several years, an internal schism grew between older members, often war veterans, who hewed to the NRA's more traditional, more benign missions, and an alienated coterie of younger members who found a leader in the person of Harlon Carter—a bulky Texan in the Hestonian mode, a former head of the U.S. Border Patrol, a onetime commissioner of the Immigration and Naturalization Service, and an NRA member since age sixteen. Rallying a reactionary circle (including dozens of NRA employees fired in 1976), Carter seized control of the organization at its 1977 annual meeting. Known ever since as the "Cincinnati Revolt," the uprising retains the hot-spark resonance of Chicago '68 and the Boston busing riots: one of those moments at the thin edge of the wedge where a thousand angry Joe Doakses, fed up with the liberal bullshit, cracked skulls and took names. In Cincinnati, Carter's clever band of Babbitts set the template for the NRA's ever-after unwavering stance on gun control of any kind, adding in that same year to the organization's charter an assertion of "the right of the individual of good repute to keep and bear arms as a common law and constitutional right." Yet, as Osha Davidson reports, Carter also possessed a darker qualification for his zeal, one he uncharacteristically obfuscated. In 1931, at age seventeen, he had been convicted of murdering a Mexican teen in a sort-of trespassing incident. The conviction was overturned on appeal; it seems the jury had been inadequately informed about self-defense. Carter later attempted to evade the tale, claiming it involved one Harl*a*n Carter; documents then surfaced, including his original NRA card, confirming that Carter changed the spelling of his name two years after the shooting. Conceal the consequences of violence under comforting myths of home, hearth, defense: Carter's dubious self-justification would become the NRA's ideological stock-in-trade.

None of this is to imply that the NRA hadn't objected to gun-control laws in its various previous incarnations. On the contrary, it organized an intensive letter-writing campaign to ensure that the 1934 National Firearms Act contained no handgun regulations, and focused instead upon "gangster" weapons like fully automatic guns and sawed-off shotguns. (Given that handgun market saturation was basically achieved in the Sixties, the NRA here scuttled perhaps the only opportunity for viable gun controls in the United States.) Generally speaking, however, before 1977 such actions were grassroots-based and semiorganized, tangential to the NRA's larger priorities. Only under Carter's leadership did a militant stance against any and all gun restrictions become the NRA's sole priority, such artful initiatives as the "Eddie Eagle" gun-safety-for-kids program notwithstanding.

The NRA's shift was of a piece with the general culture of sourness that exploded in the Seventies. And guns quickly took their place in the topsy-turvy class war of the backlash. Witness the post–*Easy Rider*/ *Walking Tall* tendencies of backlash cinema, in which primal images of bodily violation and vengeance became ubiquitous features of populist morality. The genre found its apex in the "crime in the streets" films of the Seventies and Eighties, including *Ms. 45, Assault on Precinct 13, Vigilante, The Star Chamber*, and all the other bastard offspring of *Death Wish* and *Dirty Harry*: gory fantasies in which Bronson, Eastwood, and lesser lights like Joe Don Baker raised to archetype the figures of the rogue cop and the armed civilian, taking God's side as they greased sundry punks and humiliated liberals along the way. Unfortunately, backlash culture also left many grossly miseducated in firearms reality. To sample: Wallboard does not stop rounds, even when convenient, and if you fire your overpowered handgun an inch from your boy-buddy's nose (as in the kill-happy opener of 1994's *True Lies*), you will set his face on fire.

THE TEMPLATES REMAIN, weirdly unchanged after twenty-five years. Decades after Hunter S. Thompson and his biker pals first stared down an enraged burgher's .357 Magnum, the quasi-libertarian firearms culture continues to speak in terms of a perverse class defiance that has now come to dominate even our coolest lowbrow and pseudo-lowbrow entertainments: From mall-rat hero Eminem to porno rockers Nashville Pussy, and from white-trash almanac *Hustler* to white-trash hipster Jim Goad, we can all, vicariously and up to our credit limits, put our hands on the Glock. Moreover, liberals' antigun hysteria serves only to stoke the NRA's increasingly isolationist bent. Here, as in other precincts of the culture wars, denunciation just makes the persecution fantasies of the extreme right more credible. This is why the NRA benefits so immensely from antigun statements in the mainstream media: Using its direct-mail connections, it is able to portray the organization, and every last God-fearing gun owner along with it, as rope-a-doped by the big combo of effeminate cultural elites and spineless politicians. Ultimately, every pious exposé of the gun culture's old-boy seaminess, in venues like the *New York Times*, merely rains fresh checks upon the NRA's bought-and-paid-for men such as Tom DeLay—who nimbly attributed the Columbine school massacre to the absence of the Ten Commandments only months after taking sage cover beneath his desk while his security guard took the hollowpoint of Capitol shooter Russell Weston. This is why "Today's NRA," despite the insensate pronouncements of Executive Vice President Wayne LaPierre, continues to hold such valuable cultural real estate, the ombudsman by default for all American firearms owners.

More important than the cultural camouflage of gun rights are the precarious economics of the gun industry. NRA members may prefer to use the bland language of hobbies and collecting to describe gun ownership rather than the red tones of mercenaries, armorers, and obsessives, but they are no more or less a market demographic than is the underworld of crotchety libertarians, right-wing paranoids, conspiracists, separatists, and drug-war foot soldiers whose consumerism ultimately underpins the "legitimate" firearms market. And heading off any simple, disinterested economic analysis of the firearms boondoggle is the NRA's greatest semantic bull's-eye. Turn away from the organization's endless Red-scare bombast for a moment in order to follow the money, however, and a curious narrative begins to emerge.

The shooting industry is the real power behind the American gun battle. Although the major surviving firms are owned overseas (Smith & Wesson, Glock, Beretta, H&K), precariously solvent (Colt), or threatened by novel lawsuits, there is nonetheless a great deal of money in the distribution, sale, and resale of firearms. An unjustly overlooked book by journalist Tom Diaz, *Making a Killing: The Business of Guns in America* (New Press, 1999), seizes on this unorthodox approach in considering our over-armed populace. Diaz sidesteps the ideological foam of the gun debate, examining both the semantics of firearm fetishism and the way market forces (firearm manufacturing is an almost completely unregulated industry) have elevated what he terms the "spiral of lethality" over other concerns. He describes the curious legal patchwork that both exempts firearms exclusively from any consumer safety standards and that reduces to nothing Bureau of Alcohol, Tobacco, and Firearms (ATF) oversight of firearms distribution. Diaz has a keen eye for the free-market absurdities of the industry, which suffers from cyclical downturns and saturated markets, due variously to the decline of hunting and the ironic fact that a well-made gun never "dies." More important, he explores how the increasingly dangerous hardware of recent years has dovetailed with certain rightist cultural tropes. Thus fears of rampant criminality in the Sixties fed price wars among makers of snubnose .38 "Saturday night specials," incidentally flooding the market with the ubiquitous concealable revolvers. Similarly, manufacturers harnessed Reagan-era survivalist paranoia to stoke sales of military-style semiautomatic rifles; and after the 1989 Stockton, California, schoolyard massacre, gun distributors and the gun press pumped up fears of impending controls to spawn an overspeculated market for "grandfathered" weapons and cosmetically altered guns, including huge numbers of Chinese and Eastern bloc AK-47 clones. More disturbing to Diaz is the emergence of "pocket rockets," high-capacity shortened pistols that manufacturers have promoted in recent years without heed for the dangers posed by the proliferation of powerful concealable handguns (and of high-tech hollowpoint bullets, nicknamed "flying scalpels" and valued for their "knockdown"). The elusive corporate histories that Diaz digs up are equally chilling. Consider, for example, California's "Ring of Fire" companies, a family-owned group of small manufacturers that has flooded the market with low-grade pistols retailing for under $150; or Georgia's Sylvia & Wayne Daniel Enterprises, which marketed crude, easily converted knockoffs of the once-obscure MAC-10 to both Miami gangs and the white-sheet market. Such "ugly guns" bob like feces in the market, disdained by nearly all serious shooters for their low quality and inaccuracy, but they are the weapons of choice for spree killers like Giancarlo Ferri and Harris and Klebold. That's how capitalism works, and Diaz makes a case for understanding the gun industry, with its constant upgrading of bodily harm, as the prototype for the reflexive savagery of the market.

Even more unsettling, though, are the ways in which law enforcement feeds the gun industry's escalation of lethality. In the Nineties, as Diaz recounts, police departments nationwide began to fear a perceived "gun gap" between their own long-standard .38 revolvers and the armaments available to the "bad guys." And thanks in part to the fetishization of semiautomatics in *Scarface* and *Miami Vice*, there was some validity to this fear: Recall the 1986 Miami shootout in which two felons, armed with Magnum revolvers, a shotgun, and a .223 semiautomatic rifle, killed two FBI agents and wounded five even after being themselves wounded by 9 mm rounds. This had wide repercussions: Ignoring factors like agent unpreparedness, the FBI publicly denounced the 9 mm as insufficient for earnest firefights and embarked on a sidearm review that, as Diaz documents, ushered into the civilian marketplace numerous new weapons in formerly obscure calibers. Law enforcement's rush to overpowered ammunition had the unintended consequences one might expect from such a mixing of lethality and bureaucracy. Diaz digs up enough obscure stories—like the nest-feathering that Glock provided certain New York officials in order to promote two unnecessary upgrades—to suggest that law-enforcement agencies foster gun technology proliferation even if their rhetoric officially opposes it.

A more insidious effect, perhaps rooted in the fact that many officers are required to range-qualify only twice a year, is the increasing incidence of what police call "spray and pray," in which an officer squeezes off several rounds or the whole clip in response to real or perceived threats. It's strange how quickly multiple-wound police shootings have assumed the cultural weight that 'banger drive-bys had in the Eighties: poled TV lights and grim cops, enraged neighbors tragic in their shabby night-dress, a crystallized moment from a Richard Price novel.

One must finally pin all these darker trends in law enforcement—the upgraded lethality, the reliance on cut corners—upon our contemporary equivalent of Prohibition. What few victories we have achieved in our scorched-earth War on Drugs—and what constitutes a victory in a nation where booze and pills are God-given rights, where "winners" *do* use cocaine and where the chemical apprenticeship of college is every middle class youth's long-sought reward?—are dwarfed by the loss of public safety and the erosion of privacy. It is impossible to separate this war from the gun morass. Manufacturers on every tier benefit—from the "Ring of Fire" .25s that are sized to teenage hands, to companies like Colt that have fitted law-enforcement agencies with devices better suited to Omaha Beach in 1944. Meanwhile police tacticians increasingly elevate doctrines of force over all else: Dozens of our bleak postindustrial towns now field fully armored assault teams carrying the ubiquitous $1200 Heckler & Koch MP5 submachine gun; a generation of young cops has come up with no compunction about using "no knock" warrants whenever possible; a class of administrators has learned how to use asset forfeiture to acquire land and funds that frequently vanish within insular departments; and, of course, we have chosen to imprison millions for ever-lengthier stretches of time. We witness all this, passively, and then must also watch as an *Übermenschen* "tactical" team dithers for hours outside Columbine High, unsure of how to proceed, while inside a martyred teacher dies on a classroom floor. Comfortable with kicking in civilian doors, our cops throw themselves back on procedure when confronted with one-plus sociopaths armed with semiautomatics.

It is true that the April 2000 spectacle of the burly federal agent aiming an MP5 past the head of Elián Gonzalez while his pumped-up peers rampaged through the house, shoving and slamming, bodies fat with the arsenal of democracy, did cause some alarm. But that debacle was the wrapup to a public drama so scripted that Tommy Lee Jones should've been in there somewhere. During most "dynamic entries," of course, neither the set-chewing Mr. Jones nor the balm of television lights attend the forcible discoveries of grow-rooms or the precious, financially stabilizing powder. That the public sees nothing wrong with such "extreme" law enforcement—witness the already wearily accepted police tactic of using pepper spray or tear gas to torment protesters—ensures that the new playbook will become the norm, and that civil life will degrade into something approaching the TV-ready spectacle. Many shall become acquainted with the battering ram's crash, with the tiny apartments filled with immigrants or blacks or working folk, with the glinting MP5s, fine German tools of perfect precision.

Even so, in this age of downsized civil liberties, one feels a perverse empathy for the foot soldiers, the urban cops, and for those who patrol an increasingly tattered, volatile exurbia. Unwilling to face the politicized darkness of their work, the enforcers face instead a combination of weapon-clogged environments, a spreading population of the "controlled"—the poor, immigrants, those with addictions or criminal records—and immediate public approbation, whether earned or otherwise, in the event of a "bad day." If some cops are racists or sadists, experience suggests a stout majority are not. But law enforcement by definition is dictated from above, and to get a glimpse of the future one need only examine the "resurgent" New York, where it's an open NYPD secret that the statistical demands of Giuliani and Safir, as much as macho tac-squad culture, were behind the deaths of Amadou Diallo and Patrick Dorismond. Firepower is routinely chosen over less lethal options, and if Dorismond's shooting occurred during the proverbial struggle, it was still instigated by the weird "pressure point" tactics of "Operation Condor," which evidently presumes that any African-American male under seventy sells marijuana in his spare time.

Which facet of our contemporary gun violence is most intolerable? Is it the racist edge-city rages of Smith and Baumhammers? The cracked-up, nerded-out boy who opts for early revenge at his underfunded hell of a high school in Kentucky or Arkansas or

Washington—states where guns are as common as grain? The Michigan first-grader who gleaned from his ragged home the coding that compelled him to shoot a classmate in the head? The Baltimore or D.C. 'banger who pulls the trigger of his cheap 9 mm for reasons that can barely be understood within their tragic seconds? Or the "tragic miscalculation" of plainclothes officers who empty their high-capacity clips to put down a black man reaching for a wallet? Whichever, it's hard to deny that the national love of guns is wreathed in a bloodthirstiness that somehow negates the caution of millions of responsible gun owners; that it is choked with a quickening rage that, from the penny-ante fascism of spree killers to the "acceptable" casualties of the Drug War, is fast approaching conflagration.

How long will the nation remain lost to this violent dream of itself? We may be haunted by the bland suburban familiarity of those grainy stills from Columbine, but the NRA and its industry backers will continue to ensure that the blood of the poor, unkempt, and tawdry will continue to flow in the streets among the distinctive 9 mm shell casings. They are the grease in the gears of the gun machine.

—BAFFLER 14, 2001

Who Moved My Civility?

The content providers at

The BAFFLER

pioneers in the field of abrasive literarity, have now adapted their dependable neighbor-puzzling mechanisms to a wide range of products that is proving indispensable to industry and commerce. Typical among such developments are those described below—all having as their background years of swiping, grousing, and mocking.

CERTAINTY

THERE is no place for guesswork in modern criticism. The *absolute certainty* with which we at The Baffler address each of the issues of the day is but one of the many factors that make this magazine so valuable, and yet so irritating, to so many. In every hall of learning and house of coffee, both great and small, it has become the world's standard of annoying prose.

Yes, we know all the answers. The same high standards of infallibility and irritation, regardless of length or quality of illustrations, can be found equally in all Baffler literary equipment, whether essay, fiction, prank narrative, found text, or poetry. Stay with us over the remaining years of the American Century as we continue to think up and express the most maddening opinions we know of in the smuggest voice we can find.

Subscribe to THE BAFFLER.
P. O. Box 378293, Chicago, Ill. 60637
www.thebaffler.com

9

I, Faker

Paul Maliszewski

Editor's Note: The hoax articles that Paul Maliszewski managed to publish in a regional business newspaper may have been outrageous in a factual sense, but compared to what passed for genuine, big-league business journalism in the Nineties, his tall tales now seem positively normal. As readers and investors have since discovered, much of mainstream business journalism was little better than a hoax. Business reporters throughout that decade hailed Enron, for example, as a maker of revolution, a harbinger of the future. The substitution of ideology and optimism for observation wasn't just one writer's joke; it was the industry standard, the way the job was done. Whether Americans learned this painful lesson from Maliszewski's exposé or from the Enron fiasco, it is unlikely that we will ever read business journalism the same way again.

I must confess. I must tell what I have done.

I was a staff writer at *The Business Journal of Central New York*, and my job was less than rewarding. When called upon, I cobbled together special sections on annuities, offered tips on executive gift-giving, and wrote brightly about business prospects in Syracuse—whose economy had been stagnant for the previous decade. I was a hack and I knew it. What's more, I had come to see my hackwork as not just flimsy and inconsequential but insidious. One article on a welfare-to-work program was 100 percent free of interviews with any actual workers; the publisher praised it for being balanced. Like Onondaga Lake, located just upwind from where I wrote, my articles not only smelled a little peculiar, they polluted the air around me. They were toxic.

Perhaps I could have endured this job for many more years, but fearing the consequences of my labor, I finally decided that I could no longer look away. I needed somehow to address all the issues the paper consistently ignored. Why, for example, hadn't this journal of business published a single article about the epic, $1.5 billion securities fraud perpetrated by the Syracuse-based Bennett Funding Group—one of the largest Ponzi schemes in history? Why was one of my colleagues writing an editorial about the NAACP, placing at the crux of his analysis the marital history of its current president? While Syracuse burned, the publisher acted as if the civility of the nation depended on the distinction between "who" and "whom"; the managing editor practiced calling himself with a cellular phone he received, compliments of an advertiser, for research purposes; and the other writers debated the merits of "among" vs. "amongst." Disgusted, I wrote a Swiftian letter to my own editor:

> *The Business Journal*, September 1, 1997
> To the Editor:
> Three cheers and then some for Norm Poltenson's "Ladder Without Rungs" editorial in the August 4 issue of *The Business Journal*. Poltenson points out that the United States, with its dynamic, revolutionary economy, is by far the superior of Europe. . . .
>
> However, earlier this week my American reverie was shattered as I read that the ungrateful workers at UPS have gone on strike. The men (and women) in brown are saying the company hired too many part-time workers and that they are required to lift loads that are too heavy and handle too many packages an hour. Please, I thought. First brush aside these sugary, humanist sentiments, and let's get down to facts. UPS carriers are required

to lift packages weighing up to 150 pounds. Sorters are expected to handle 1,600 packages per hour. While I'm not sure I can lift 150 pounds or even count to 1,600 in an hour, the brown people of UPS are, in fact, professional sorters and carriers and naturally suited for this kind of work. It is their job to sort and carry. Moreover, they should cease with their shrill complaints. If the striking brown clowns (workers) should dare seek a more humane corporation, they would do better to seek a good psychotherapist.

To put the complaints of those UPSers in perspective, let's consider the true success of the company. In 1996, UPS made $1 billion in profits. But it hasn't been all up. Since 1990, UPS has paid $4.4 million in penalties for health and safety complaints, for more than 1,300 violations documented by OSHA. Let us assume, conservatively, that those violations and penalty payments were made in equal amounts over the last seven years. Thus, UPS paid about $630,000 for an average of 186 violations a year. I bring this up not to berate UPS, as *The New York Times* did. Rather, I want to suggest that the penalty (a trifle really for a billion-dollar corporation) is in effect one of the wisest investments it could make. Indeed, in order to continue on its path to success and improve its already considerable profit margins, UPS must act aggressively now and take risks. One way to do this is to make its workplace riskier. To wit: would not UPS at least double its profits by raising the number of its OSHA violations to 372 for 1998? Could it not fairly triple or quadruple its profits by budgeting for and investing penalty amounts of $1.2 million or $1.8 million in fiscal years 1999 and 2000?

By considering my simple proposal, corporations like UPS and others will guarantee that the United States remains a vibrant economic dynamo of a country.

What I need to confess is I didn't sign my name to these ravings; I attributed them instead to one "Gary Pike," local firebrand, all-American crank, and fictional creation. Since August 1997, I have written regularly for the newspaper as Pike and others—submitting letters, guest "expert" columns, and bogus reporting—concealing myself behind free e-mail accounts. How many fake writers did I invent? About as many as the months I spent working at *The Business Journal* full-time.

In my spare time I manufactured whole companies. They emerged from my head wildly profitable and fully staffed with ambitious assistants obeying the bidding of sage bosses. If my fictional characters filed tax returns, I probably would have been personally responsible for creating more new jobs in central New York than any nonfictional company.

Just for kicks, I littered my fictions with references, allusions, and bastardized quotations from literature. I quoted Donald Barthelme but made the words pass through the dead lips of Adam Smith. In another counterfeit, I drew names of characters from a *New York Review of Books* essay about Van Gogh forgers and the businessmen who knowingly peddled the knockoffs.

As Paul Maliszewski, I continued to report on quarterly figures and tepidly gauge the effects of proposed regulations. My fake characters, however, were free to engage business issues with everything from unhinged speculation to dimwitted appeals to common sense. I granted my characters as many titles ("a consultant for middle-middle and upper-middle managers in the Los Angeles metropolitan area") as they had tangled points of view and rhetorical tics. I adopted more than a dozen identities, none of them very truthful but all of them, curiously, found worthy of publication. I was Gary Pike, Samuel Collins, T. Michael Bodine, Carl S. Grimm, Grimm's assistant Simone Fletcher, Noah Warren-Mann, Irving T. Fuller, Daniel Martin, and Pavel R. Liberman, and no one—from the publisher, the editor, and my fellow writers to the advertisers whose ads appeared next to my fictions—ever had a clue.

On Tuesdays before an issue of the newspaper went to the printer, Norman Poltenson, *The Business Journal*'s publisher, would give me his latest editorial for proofreading and comment.

The rest of the paper was usually complete but for a yawning white space reserved for him on page four. His byline and a short note about upcoming personal appearances (a minute or so weekly on a local TV news broadcast, at 6:45 A.M.) would already be laid out and, along with the other pages, hanging on either side of a long, narrow hallway for staff inspection. Poltenson's picture, a heavily shaded pencil drawing that I regarded as a very distant and very poor cousin of those copperplate engravings in the *Wall Street Journal*, would look down from the top of the third column, surveying the thirty column inches of nothingness.

Poltenson the man would be upstairs in his office, writing to exact length. He was more familiar with printing than writing and seemed to take a kind of pride in converting the number of unfilled column inches on page four into a frighteningly close approximation of the number of words required, all in his head. Poltenson had come to publish the newspaper not as a writer or an editor, but as the heir of his family's printing business, which he and his brother decided to sell. Starting the newspaper consumed most of Norman's share of the proceeds; buying a competing newspaper (in order to put it out of business) took care of the rest. By the time I began working at *The Business Journal*, the paper reached about 9,000 readers in sixteen counties across central and upstate New York—mostly business owners whose names were culled from a Dun & Bradstreet database and who received their subscriptions gratis. It was the ideal journalistic stepping-stone to not much of anything.

When he finished his latest editorial, Poltenson would come looking for me. "Mr. Maliszewski," he would say, "if you would be so kind as to read this over and offer your comments to me with your usual alacrity, I would appreciate it." For the next half hour, I would grind my teeth and stomp my feet and pound my desk over howlers such as "Any attempt to 'humanize' the corporation should be dismissed as syrupy, corrosive sentiment." Though I'd point out all the holes in his arguments I had the patience to find,

Poltenson only seemed to want a thorough proofreading. He would listen patiently as I expressed my disbelief that, say, mutual funds were society's great equalizer, but then he would thank me and accept only my stylistic suggestions.

Out of this climate were born Gary Pike and Samuel Collins, my two writers of letters to the editor. Both debuted in the same issue, writing in response to a predictable Poltenson editorial on OSHA regulations. All the covert ideological cargo Poltenson slipped by on a raft of ill-gotten statistics, Pike would hail loudly as righteous and true. Collins wrote only on those occasions when I was so angry I couldn't be bothered to invent a satirical perspective.

As the fake letters became more frequent and windy, the white space available to Poltenson dwindled. Finally, one of Pike's letters managed to kick Poltenson off the page altogether. This was not good. Although I enjoyed seeing the editorial page—always home to dozens of statistical fictions—become a venue for my real fiction, it bothered me that my counterfeits allowed Poltenson to skip out on a column or two. Clearly, I had to change tactics. My characters would need to become full-fledged contributors to *The Business Journal,* develop their own subjects, and make forays into expert columns and perhaps even the news section, a kind of promised land for the faker.

As my hackwork piled still higher, I began to think of journalism not as a series of unique assignments or stories but rather as a limited number of ideas and conventions that each story somehow had to affirm. When Poltenson assigned me to write about tort reform legislation proposed by "New Yorkers for Tort Reform," a faux-grassroots effort led by major manufacturers, he suggested I interview a few of the reformers, talk to a trial lawyer, and then write it up with the usual on-the-one-hand-on-the-other-hand equivocation. In the hands of a trained journalist, such back-and-forth disagreements write themselves and can be as long or short as the editorial requirements of the moment. But such a standard telling of the story also includes little or no context or historical perspective, and the reader is left with nothing but a sense of muddled ambivalence. Every story's a toss-up.

But after looking into New Yorkers for Tort Reform, I decided to write about a survey they had commissioned, showing how the study's results came from outrageously worded questions. I had only recently started to work at the paper and unfortunately had not yet mastered the formulas of news writing. Poltenson slugged the story as "analysis," which seemed to me like an apology or a warning label. Analysis, I gathered, was not a staple at *The Business Journal*. Eventually, I learned to stop worrying and love the formulas. I also came to appreciate their efficiency. No matter how contrary and damning the information I unearthed in interviews and research, a few turns of the crank ensured that it all came out looking as indistinguishable as the next story and the next story and the next story.

The Business Journal used all the familiar formulas, each apparently derived from a popular fictional genre: the merger-and-acquisition article (best written using the techniques of a romance novel, with the central metaphor of a wedding); the company under investigation (refer to John Grisham's legal thrillers, casting the company as an innocent yet scrappy underdog); the CEO with an unlikely or nontraditional background (fairy tale); the quarterly report disclosing surprisingly strong/weak earnings (the vignette, tuned to frequencies of sweetness or sadness, as appropriate); bankruptcy (a real tragedy, mournfully rehearsing the standard business verity that a marketing budget is not to be trifled with); the profile of an eccentric (screwball comedy, starring a renegade businessman who walked away from his six-figure salary as a vice president of marketing only to turn to manufacturing decorative mailboxes and—would you believe?—marketing them through mail-order catalogs).

A fictional expert such as Carl S. Grimm, who began writing columns for *The Business Journal* in January 1998, seems like any other dispenser of corporate advice. He follows the rules of the genre. He is casually confident, yet serious. He professes bold, counterintuitive ideas but remains well versed in the deployment of clichés. His background mixes equal parts intrigue and prestige: "A former official with both the State Department and CIA, Grimm frequently speaks at overseas engagements for the U.S. Agency for International Development, Andersen Consulting, and the American Federation of Independent Businesses." He's independent. He's successful. He has a book contract with HarperCollins.

What an amazing life Grimm seems to lead. To crisscross borders and time zones in solitary pursuit of accumulating riches is certainly close to the unacknowledged dreams of many readers of *The Business Journal.* Were they not regrettably bound to this earth and these flabby bodies, to mortgaged homes and long-term leases on Sevilles, they could surely follow in Grimm's footsteps. Failing that, readers can cozy up to his columns, turning to the warm words of an accomplished expert for the moral instruction and diversion traditionally found in genre fiction.

Carl S. Grimm, "Toward a Life of Pure, 100% Liquidity," *The Business Journal*, July 6, 1998

Carl S. Grimm is the author of Living Liquidly: How Being More Like Money Pays Off, *which will be published by HarperCollins in fall 1999. Grimm is a consultant specializing in currency and trade opportunity analysis, foreign risk assessment, industry informational surveys, and market-share projection specification programs. He can be contacted at csg1137@altavista.net.*

I suppose the day was like any other, really. I found myself on the helicopter from LaGuardia to Kennedy, endeavoring to bypass the traffic by flying over the city instead of fighting my way through it. With total lapsed time well shy of 10 minutes, the cloudless skies of postcards, and no symptoms of incipient motion-sickness, I was, I must admit, making quite a success of it.

Along for the ride—in addition to the pilot whose name I forget—was my new friend, whom I'll call Marvin. Poor "Marvin." As Manhattan heaved into sight off to our left, I was commiserating with Marvin, who confided in me how he found himself completely unable to live on $450,000 per year. He had, he claimed, done everything right: educated at a private prep school in Connecticut where the halls are decorated with portraits of past students who became presidents and the classes are attended by young presidents to-be; graduated Harvard with honors and Harvard Law at the very top of his class; been offered a position in more Wall Street firms than he had fingers to count; and been made partner and then senior partner sooner even than his ambitious life-schedule had stipulated. Yet here he was, he said, flat broke and bumming a ride on my helicopter. Strangely, I knew exactly what he meant.

It was later that same day, as the more memorable pieces of my conversation with Marvin bounced and rolled around inside my head like so many shiny coins tossed by well-wishers into a public fountain, that I vowed to achieve a life of pure 100-percent liquidity in order to avoid the fate of "Marvin" and that wretched existence of his. To do so, I had only to make over myself in the image and essential character of money.

WHAT IS THE LIQUID LIFE?

We all know what we mean when we talk of money or capital as liquid wealth; its properties allow it to be applied anywhere for any purpose by anyone who has it. It was Adam Smith, the economist and proto-warrior for free trade, who so presciently wrote, "The practiced accumulation of capital is the topmost taper on the golden candelabrum of existence." Capital, Smith knew, is easily transferable and more widely accepted than a Visa card. The liquid life has in common with money this freedom of movement. The purely liquid among us are always already willing to move—and move quickly. Liquid-lifers find work instead of allowing work to find them. It's a way of traveling light, acting fast, and staying one step ahead.

People of pure liquid move to where it suits them best, they relentlessly seek their level.

Readers may recall my last letter ["Stock Tip: Invest in Welfare," *The Business Journal*, Jan. 19, 1998], which projected handsome profits in the welfare-management industry, what I called the welfare of welfare. When I wrote that letter five months ago, I was living in Philadelphia. Now I'm in Chicago and in between I've probably lived in three or four more places besides. Perhaps "lived" is not the proper word for what I do, because I stay in luxury hotels, the sort of places where the televisions are not chained to the floor, places at which my arrival is eagerly anticipated, my needs met. Really, I light from assignment to assignment, providing billable advice as I go. I move from hotel to hotel, from Hilton to Holiday Dome to Radisson to Adam's Mark to Hilton again.

The liquid life is a state of mind, really. Sure there are modest costs—e.g., the wife, who didn't feel she wanted to accompany me on my quest to obtain the liquid life, though she did try it for a while (one month, not to her liking).

An example should bring the liquid state of mind into sharper focus. Follow the money in this quote from *The Financial Times*: "The return of the capital that fled after Beijing's missile tests in the Taiwan Straits in March last year, a relatively accommodating liquidity policy by the central bank and active buying by government controlled funds have brought doubled share values in little more than a year." First of all, congratulations are in order—way to go, Taiwan. But let's follow the money, shall we?

The money was afraid of political fall-out from Chinese missile tests. Fair enough, money fled. Money went elsewhere. Money canceled lucrative but tentative deals. Money hopped jets with departing business people or rode electronic wires and flew, trailing more zeroes than you or maybe I can imagine through the money-sphere. But then, you can see what happened next. There's a happy ending here. Money returned. Money marched back into Taiwan like conquering soldiers. Money came home to Mom.

"So what's this all mean?" you ask. When I speak of the liquid life, I speak of a life that abides by the rules of money. If you can do better, be better, and achieve more elsewhere, why then, by gosh, be there, go there, now.

Karl Marx had it only partially right. Labor and capital do obey two unique sets of rules. But Marx could not have foreseen the likes of me and the few people like me. He could not have imagined the way we make airports our living rooms, and their long, glassed-in concourses our entryways. That's us on the phone, conducting business on our laps. That's us playing solitaire on color laptop computers, or taking a chance on the video poker machines that lean down over bars. We go where the money goes, to the new lands of opportunity and investment, looking for financial milk and honey.

Here again is Smith, north star to any thinking economist, "Opportunity is the hearty, weathered sailor on the tumultuous seas of loss and gain." We liquid types go how money goes, by air, at cruising altitudes of 12,000 feet or more, and in first class. Be fearless, be quick, be liquid. Who are we? We are the willfully and meaningfully and lucratively transient, living by silence, exile, cunning—and so on. We always shop duty-free.

What's the opposite of the liquid life?

Four words: routine, attachment, sedentary, and home-body, or R.A.S.H. The opposite of the liquid life is a solid one, and solidity is produced by the above four behaviors and worst of all, solidity causes a rash. A real specter is haunting America at the end of the millennium—the specter of solidity. Remember: solidity is the nightmare from which we are trying to awake. But what happened to Marvin? you ask. Marvin did not live the right life. Poor Marvin. He was too heavy and entirely too solid. Regrettably, his occupation—law—drew him back to earth. The law is

> fundamentally concerned with representing the legal considerations of bodies, people or corporations. The law is by definition a material pursuit, uses material means to achieve material remedies. Far better to be like money, I say, and trade in information.
>
> Poor Marvin, he couldn't move like money moves. He didn't even seem to recognize himself in my description of the law. When last I saw him, in Kennedy, he merely looked fed-up and annoyed, no doubt angry with himself. Clearly, he appreciated the wisdom in everything I had so unselfishly shared with him about the liquid life, while both on the helicopter and the ground, during the hour or so after that I walked around after him wherever he went.
>
> Marvin was not and would never be liquid, but he at least was aware of the liquid life. He said to me, "Carl S. Grimm, I wish I never asked you for a ride."

When *The New Republic* writer Stephen Glass was exposed as a journalistic fabulist, I thought I had found a coconspirator. Here, maybe, was someone else who understood the restrictions of journalism and bristled against them. At magazines and newspapers, meanwhile, the hand-wringing and soul-searching went into high gear. Presses all along the eastern seaboard turned out one disingenuous apology after another. *Forgive us, readers. This won't happen again.* Contrite tenders of the journalistic flame suggested that perhaps young writers should be kept from writing articles with unnamed sources, a signature of Glass's style. They're not old enough to use the power tools.

After spending most of a weekend reading Glass's collected works, however, I decided that his writing was not so much satiric as sarcastic. Not a single article tweaked readers' expectations or questioned received opinion. He only made the conventionally wise seem that much wiser. Glass, it appeared, was nothing more than a master of journalism's simple forms, a kind of superfreelancer. Men's magazines, policy magazines—to Glass they were all just outlets. His writing carefully mimicked the style and form of each one, bowing obsequiously to everything its editors valued. The articles hit all the right targets and confirmed all the right stereotypes. Ever think stockbrokers pay too much attention to Alan Greenspan's every utterance? A Glass article confirms what you suspected, inventing an investment company where the traders kneel before a photograph of Chairman Al. Stay up late fretting over the vast right-wing conspiracy to get the president? Glass reports on one so literal it should have been called, "The Right-Wing Conspiracy."

Glass's articles were, as commentator after commentator wrote, too good to be true, but that hardly explains why they were published. Editors didn't judge them to be good articles because they were well written or moving. They ran Glass's writing, I think, because it did everything that good writing in *The New Republic* is expected to do. A Glass article told you that what you assumed was, in fact, true—young Republicans are Visigothic—and it slyly congratulated you on the intelligence of your suspicions. The combination of colorful tales buttressing cherished assumptions was so potent that everyone who came into contact with his stories desperately wanted them to be true, so they printed them.

The best satire makes use of a certain amount of intentional mislabeling. I've often wondered what it would be like to encounter *Gulliver's Travels* without having any prior knowledge about the book or its author. What if it could be published as a guidebook and shelved in the travel section among all the Fodor's and Lonely Planets? Tear off the prefaces by the editors, take away the inevitable essay by Allan Bloom, peel back the thin slices of footnotes, and you'd be left with a book that not only fits the form of the travel guide but also fiendishly parodies it. The book's first two editions tellingly carried Gulliver as its author. Swift was absent from the title page.

I read an excerpt in *Harper's Magazine* from a torture manual used at the School of the Americas and wondered how it might accommodate the language and rhetoric of a manager's how-to. With very few changes—substituting "employee" for "subject," for instance—the piece began to look more and more like an advice column. Now published and with nothing whatsoever to announce it as satire, it lies in wait, looking and reading like just another article. In *The Business Journal* it is oddly at home.

T. Michael Bodine, "Don't Get Caught Being a Weak Manager," *The Business Journal*, November 10, 1997

Bodine is a partner, senior business-to-business consultant and Vice President of Marketing, West Coast Operations with Universal Business Consultants (UBC), a full-service instructional and consultative "academy" for business-owners and managers. UBC offers nine levels of advanced intensive coursework and customized, on-site workshops, publishes the Universal Business Consultant Newsletter (UBCN) for subscribing alumni, and currently has offices in Los Angeles, London, Honolulu, and Hong Kong.

As a long-time consultant and instructor of middle-middle and upper-middle-managers in the Los Angeles metropolitan area, I've seen my fair share of problems. But no manager is ever beyond help. As I gaze back on my years, the number one problem that sticks out in my mind about my business is weak managers. If "weak manager" appeared in the *Webster's Dictionary,* I have a feeling it would be defined as one who rarely or only inconsistently applies adequate force behind his managerial hand. In my advanced courses as well as in my publications I emphasize a set of lessons that are easy to learn and even easier to apply.

First of all, the manager must learn to use coercion effectively. Coercion might sound like a dirty word, but consider its usefulness to managers the world over. Fundamentally, coercion's purpose is to induce psychological regression in an employee by bringing a superior force from outside to bear on his will to resist, resulting in a more effective managerial style. Regression of this sort is basically a controlled loss of autonomy and is marked by the return to an earlier behavioral level. As an employee regresses, his learned personality traits fall away in reverse chronological order. Destructive capacities such as ironic detachment or a regard for one's self are lost. With practice, an employee + coercion will = a worker.

Always remember that an employee's sense of identity depends on continuity in his surroundings, habits, appearance, relations with others, etc. Always remember, too, the four Cs of good managing: Careful Coercion Corrodes Continuity. An example: an employee's desk is an extension of his body, and the manager should look closely at its artifacts for hints at the weakest part of that body. Pictures of children and loved ones might point to the family. Postcards from last summer's vacation point to the importance of leisure. Stuffed animals surely signify a need to be hugged, even loved. Managers, make careful note of these observations.

Disrupting an employee's continuity can always be a productive method of applying managerial pressure. Detention and a deprivation of sensory stimuli are two methods which on the surface sound draconian, but which, on second look, are easily adapted for the workplace. Detention can mean arriving early and staying late. Contrive ways to keep an employee by your side all day, perhaps by making appointments with the employee early in the morning and around 4 P.M., when "quitting time-itis" has been known to set in. Depriving sensory stimuli can be accomplished with embarrassing ease: take away an employee's radio.

I have been suggesting some possible actions for the weak manager. In some cases, perhaps only the threat of action is enough. I always tell the managers in my courses to internalize the difference between threats suggested and threats enacted. Remember a rule I call, "Follow-through is up to you." The threat of coercion usually weakens or destroys resistance more effectively than coercion itself.

Just as an example—the threat to inflict pain can trigger fears far more damaging than the immediate sensation of pain. And sometimes pain causes a sense of hopelessness, nihilism, and despair that is too bleak even to be useful to managers who are experts in these techniques. A reminder: this example has nothing to do with actual conduct in the workplace.

On the subject of coercion, I would be remiss if I didn't mention my experience with hypnosis. I have had some indescribable personal success with the hypnotic arts. Though it's true that answers obtained from an employee under the influence of hypnotism are highly suspect, as they are often based upon the suggestions of the manager and are distorted or fabricated, hypnosis does have its clear benefits and I remain one of its vocal champions.

An employee's strong desire to escape the stress of the situation can create a state of mind called "heightened suggestibility." The manager can then take advantage of this state of mind by creating a situation in which an employee will cooperate because he *believes* he has been hypnotized. This hypnotic situation can be created using a magic room technique.

For example, imagine that an employee is given a hypnotic suggestion that his hand is growing warm. In the magic room, his hand actually does become warm, with the aid of a bi-level, rheostat-controlled diathermy machine previously concealed in the arm of the special office chair. An employee may be given a suggestion that a cigarette will taste bitter and then be given a cigarette prepared to have a slight but noticeably bitter taste.

In view of the litigious nature of U.S. society today, being a business owner and an employer of people has never been more difficult. The bad news is it probably won't get easier. The good news is that there are things you can do, as a manager or business owner, that you probably haven't tried yet.

While there is no drug that can force every employee to divulge all the information he has, in a state of heightened suggestibility and in a duly outfitted magic room, a harmless sugar pill can have extraordinary effects. The manager can tell an employee that the placebo is a truth serum that will make him want to talk and prevent all his lying. Things grow complicated here and can fast become overheated, psychologically speaking, but the end result is that an employee will indeed talk, as it's clearly his only avenue of escape from a depressing situation. He will want to believe that he has been drugged because then nobody can blame him for telling his entire story. A mere sugar pill provides him with the rationalization he needs to cooperate. The manager will keep a number of these sugar pills handy.

I have mentioned some of the more powerful techniques used to create a useful state of regression. Sometimes, however, the manager should consider more subtle means, such as:

- Manipulating time
- Retarding and advancing clocks
- Offering free meals at odd times
- Disrupting sleep schedules with either early morning or late night "emergency" calls
- Unpatterned and aimless questioning sessions
- Vigorous nonsensical questioning
- Ignoring halfhearted attempts to cooperate
- Rewarding noncooperation
- Arbitrary body language

Surely I have suggested that there remains a wide and plentiful universe of options available to the manager who possesses an open mind.

2.

One cubicle away, my managing editor was on the telephone trying to reach a prospective freelance writer who had materialized out of the vast wasteland of New York's north country. "I need a number for Noah Warren-Mann," he told an operator. A query letter had arrived from Noah recently, bearing story ideas aplenty, and my managing editor was apparently eager to speak with the man whose e-mail messages, rich in parentheticals and exclamation points, conveyed a passion for business and an aspiration to join the team. ("That's Warren *hyphen* Mann.") I knew a bit about Noah. ("Could you look under 'Mann' too?") I knew he had no phone, for instance, and that every wild-card search would come up empty. ("You checked Felt Mills *and* Watertown?") I knew this because Noah Warren-Mann was I.

Born and bred in humble Watertown, New York, this up-and-coming young businessman dreamed of the high-tech, gadget-galore life he had read about in *Wired* and *Fast Company,* and he was committed to achieving it in his hometown, a city known, if at all, as the birthplace of the ubiquitous pine tree–shaped air freshener. While Noah had what high school guidance counselors charitably call "potential" and "enthusiasm," his best efforts produced MicroVisions, a one-man computer maintenance company that fit comfortably in the trunk of a small car. True, Watertown barely sustained Noah's most micro of visions and, true, he didn't have a telephone, but the newspaper held him in high regard anyway and published his first article, "Upstate Businesses Recover Slowly from Wicked Ice Storm." Only the ice storm was real.

After paying his dues with such mundane reporting, the stage was set for Noah's star turn. He would profile Teloperators Rex, Inc., a homegrown company with the revolutionary idea of using people to answer telephones. After a number of editorial delays, which had nothing to do with the story's utter lack of veracity, "T.R.I. Brings On-Call Phone Personnel to the North Country" ran in the June 8, 1998, issue of *The Business Journal.* The headline stretched across the top of two inside pages.

The published article delivered exciting glimpses of the habits and musings of TRI's principal, one Irving T. Fuller. In tones of breathless awe, Noah described the owner's lifelong but utterly irrelevant fascination with dinosaurs and, like any good profiler, used detail to offer tinker-toy psychological insights into his entrepreneurial epiphany (a young Irv standing before a *T. Rex*) and resulting character:

> Today, there are large framed prints of a triceratops, an archaeopteryx, and a delta-dromeus on the walls of Fuller's office in Watertown, along with movie posters from *Jurassic Park* and *The Lost World*. On an antique mahogany credenza behind him, pictures of his wife and three children share space with a close-up photo of a stegosaurus skull and an artist's rendering of a brachiosaurus—a slow, gentle-seeming herbivore in muted pastel tones. A cleverly painted plaster cast of a thighbone sits propped up against the back wall of his office, flanking a large picture window on one side, with the U.S. flag on the other. The bone easily stands floor to ceiling, with one panel of the acoustic drop ceiling moved aside so that it continues on up into the wiring and the dark. The replica, he says, was cast in a limited edition from the *Rex* held by the Museum of Natural History, the very skeleton that long ago fired Fuller's imagination.

Naturally, Noah was as eager to explain Fuller's "Darwinian" philosophy of management as he was to tell us about his phone-answering system: "A recent memo to inspire the marketing staff began, 'First, let's cogitate like the advanced primates we supposedly are. Personally, I gave up thinking like a lizard, and you should, too.'" We counted ourselves lucky to sit at the feet of this impressive thinker and merely collect his pearls:

> Evolution is not, as some people believe, about the changes occurring in organisms due to adaptation, natural selection, and other forces that are so minute and gradual as to be not directly observable given their long-term nature. It's really about not missing the next big thing. It's about adapting yourself and mod-

eling yourself and rigorously remaking yourself quickly enough in order to embody the next big thing before it's even big. Evolution is about electing to survive.

"Fuller" was so pleased with Noah's bouquet that he decided to excerpt it on the company's Website. He also created a media kit around the glowing profile and, in the hope of reaching a broader audience, sent it to journalists at local television stations and daily newspapers.

Websites, as we all know, are crucial to reaching that anonymous, broader audience. TRI's site (which a later news article described as "very professional") was in fact designed and placed online in a single night by my brother. We spent no money and settled on a simple aesthetic: Appropriate and cobble together the gaudy dreck of nonfictional corporate Web pages. Like medieval alchemists, we sought to transmute their crap into TRI's gold plating. A pseudo-Celtic symbol, chosen more for its size than any particular meaning, became the perfect corporate logo for a company declaring itself, "Your choice for the new millennium." AT&T's and MCI's Websites coughed up all manner of generic images of telephones and operators. Stock photographs used to gussy up especially thin year-end reports did wonders for TRI's image. An animated Hewlett-Packard banner ad, after a little doctoring, crowed about TRI's Vetracom 2000: "Simply . . . let us answer your telephone." The Website showcased nonnews (Look, new Website!) and the trophies of a year's invented successes (opportunities in Europe and an economic development grant courtesy of Governor Pataki). All very professional, indeed.

I didn't really expect local journalists, once they received the media kit, which included Noah's profile and a sheaf of press releases, to perpetuate the TRI hoax. I figured its days were numbered. Readers in Watertown had, after all, informed *The Business Journal* just days after Noah's article ran that there was no Fuller, no TRI, no Noah, anywhere. What I did expect is that people would look at the Website, the stack of fake press releases, the profile, and realize, without my prompting, that TRI—which clearly doesn't exist—was a lot like other businesses, with their own very professional Websites, press releases, and hagiographic profiles. That this, to put it simply, was a satire.

And, indeed, the reporters who contacted TRI by e-mail were definitely wandering in the country of humor. "Congratulations," a reporter in Syracuse wrote. "It was a fun read." Another, based in Albany, enthused: "Your George E. Pataki press release was dead on. Most of it reads exactly the same way the stuff from the gov's office does. . . . Also, I must tell you, the governor's chief press spokesman is not amused."

Within three days of being mailed, the media kits generated articles in the *Syracuse Post-Standard* and the *Watertown Daily Times*, and WSTM-TV3 ran a story about TRI in both of its evening newscasts. But instead of grasping the satire, as I'd hoped they would, the reporters focused on TRI as a Byzantine flimflam. Setting the tone of the coverage, each article quoted the governor's press secretary, who said, "This falls into the realm of the bizarre"—adding in one account, "It's clearly inappropriate." Eager to lend seriousness to the story, both articles also raised the specter of a government investigation, with the Watertown newspaper suggesting that TRI's media kit provoked widespread panic: "The counterfeit press release had gubernatorial and legislative press aides scrambling to figure out what was going on, and Attorney General Dennis C. Vacco's office is now investigating." State officials did not speculate about TRI's motives, but *The Business Journal*'s managing editor plied local reporters with suggestions of "some kind of elaborate business scam at the heart" of the hoax.

The real scam was the way reporters spun press releases into news. I was pleased to note how the reporters lifted my own strategic phrasings. The Syracuse story—about 40 percent of which was taken word for word from the media kit—concluded with three lengthy quotations from my fake press releases, my Governor Pataki, and my state senator.

AFTER A FEW DAYS and a few articles, the story of TRI expired, the failed yet perplexing swindle of a north country confidence man. Meanwhile, a new misunderstanding was taking shape. It turned out *I* was being investigated. On September 23, 1998, two agents from the state attorney general's office visited me at work (I'd left *The Business Journal* for another job in February) and questioned me for the better part of two hours about TRI and a press release bearing an uncanny resemblance to those issued by Governor Pataki. "Can I call you Paul or should I call you Noah?" asked the senior member of the duo. My impression was that he had thought of this line at least twenty-four hours earlier.

The investigators were very serious men. They told me I was looking at possible charges on multiple counts of criminal forgery and some vaguely defined "computer crimes." They gestured ominously and with noticeable pride to two stuffed accordion folders labeled "Press Release." My bogus publicity circular, just more than a page, had blossomed into their evidence. It looked like the consequence of being misunderstood was being arrested. If I really had awakened in the land of the literally minded, then I wanted to be perfectly clear.

So I explained my project, much as I have in these essays, as a satire. The officers didn't exactly warm to my apologia. The junior investigator was particularly skeptical, repeatedly scolding me. He called my project "selfish," the cause of a costly government investigation, and said that what I'd done was like "the guy who sees a weakness in the security of the bank and so robs the bank to prove it can be done instead of using your gifts and intelligence to fix the problem in a straightforward manner." But I persisted. To their insinuations that I was a forger and even insane, I talked about satire and the use of literary pseudonyms. At last, the skeptic asked, "But doesn't satire require that people recognize it as satire?" I took it less as a follow-up question than a signal that, finally, I was being understood.

Then the investigators asked me to commit myself—on paper. I was to provide a statement about my project—and nothing clever this time. I told them I'd think about what I wanted to say and type something up. "Look, we're not asking you to go off and make some kind of literary creation," the skeptic shot back. "We want you to sit here and write, by hand, what you did and why." And so I explained it all again, filling several pages with short, unmodified declarative sentences. I larded the statement so heavily with keywords such as "literary," "satire," and "fictional project" that even a devotee of *Ally McBeal* could see that underneath their charges of forgery broiled a First Amendment case, with all the attendant media scrutiny and bad publicity that implies.

While I wrote, the officers got down to business with their cell phones. One of them received a call for his partner. Their phones were identical; it seemed they'd accidentally been switched. When I finished writing, the senior officer notarized, signed, and initialed the sheets and had his partner fax them to an attorney. We waited awhile. Then we left my office and went to theirs and waited some more. The attorney, I learned, was to evaluate my written statement, consider the relevant legal statutes, and decide what crimes to have me arrested for. I would be arrested that day, the skeptic assured me. The only question was on what charges.

I found it difficult to eat my lunch. I couldn't imagine keeping my sandwich down. I bit at an apple and polished off my water. We waited some more. Finally, word came back that the attorney did not wish to press charges or make an arrest at this time. At what time would the attorney wish to press charges? I asked. The officers couldn't say. They were going to continue their investigation, they said. I asked when they planned on winding this up. Again, they couldn't say for sure. The senior investigator said: "It may be two weeks or it may be two months. The longer it is, the better off you are."

Before saying goodbye, the skeptic had some final advice for me, which I dutifully pass along to aspiring Swifts out there: "If you want to be a satirist, get a pen and a pad of paper, write something, and then publish it conventionally. If I open the paper one day and see you're on the *New York Times* bestseller list, then I'll know you're a real satirist."

Despairing of ever living up to the officer's standards and becoming a real writer, I hastily looked to tie up loose narrative threads and conclude my fakes project.

IN MID-AUGUST *The Business Journal* had apologized belatedly for the publication of Noah's TRI article, printing "We Apologize," an unsigned notice that was a study in complex obfuscation.

> For twelve years *The Business Journal* has prided itself on providing the Central New York business community with accurate and useful information, information that our readers rely on to keep them informed about businesses and issues in our region.
>
> On June 8, we fell victim to what now appears to be a hoax, in publishing a freelancer's profile of a relatively young company in the Watertown area.

The apology mentioned only a single fake article and not by name—or should I say, *what now appears to be* a fake article. The paper (read: victim) also knew Noah's other article was a fake, and besides that had published sixteen letters to the editor and business columns that were (unbeknownst to its editors) fake as well.

> A subsequent phone call from a well-informed reader in Watertown sparked our initial suspicions about the story, so we immediately began investigating to determine whether the story was

truth or fiction. Despite repeated attempts, we have been unable to make contact with the principals in the firm.

One would, the apology suggested, have to be a well-informed reader in Watertown to spot the fakery, as if advanced knowledge were necessary, including, perhaps, a proficiency with foreign languages and the ability to converse with natives.

> We were continuing our efforts to resolve our questions about the article when we received a mailing from the supposed company on August 3. The mailing included a news release that appeared to be from Governor George Pataki's office and announced that the company had received more than $1 million in state economic development grants. We immediately contacted the state's economic-development arm, Empire State Development Corp., to inform officials about the release. In fact, it was *The Business Journal*'s call that alerted state officials to the apparent escalation of the hoax.

First the victim of a hoax, then the hero of the day? Apparently this was an apology with a happy ending.

> We regret that we originally published an article that appears to be a fabrication. *The Business Journal* prizes its reputation for credibility with our readers and strives always to meet or exceed their expectations.

What appears to be *The Business Journal*'s apology was not the last word on the fakes. Later I saw the newspaper's editorial/opinion page step boldly into the breach, weighing in several times on the "issue" of fakery and journalism scandals, though always neglecting to mention the paper's close acquaintance with both. In his January 15, 1999, call to arms, Poltenson blamed journalism scandals on a loose industry not subject to press scrutiny, overrun with people of "a decidedly left-wing slant," and reporters who are "crusaders, out to change society." Three months later the paper's ersatz media critic could only offer thin, homiletic gruel such as "Don't believe anything you hear and only half of what you see"—sternly concluding, "Let the viewer beware!"

But these implicit responses to the apology were preceded by another. Gary Pike, one of my earliest fictional personae, a man of strong opinions, a conservative's conservative, who had last written in with a bit of impressionistic babble about the future of shopping malls, was first to accept the paper's apology.

"APOLOGY ACCEPTED," *The Business Journal*, September 28, 1998

To the Editor:

I write to congratulate the *Business Journal* for having the editorial guts and wherewithal to stand up and apologize to its readers ("We Apologize," August 17, 1998, p. 3). The fact that you are a) able and b) willing to apologize in a straight-forward and honest manner, admitting that "what now appears to be a hoax" was published in the newspaper, speaks volumes for you and the kind of work you do. I have no idea to what article you refer, but I nevertheless applaud you for having the integrity to tell us the complete story—you were a victim of another's deceit—and come clean about your minor mistake.

In a year in which many mistakes were made in the name of journalism, from Stephen Glass at *The New Republic* to the African-American poet/columnist Patricia Smith and the great Mike Barnicle at the *Boston Globe* to the unnecessary investigation of the corporate practices of the Chiquita Banana Company by a muck-raking trouble-maker at the *Cincinnati Enquirer*, your incident stands out as being minor and your apology magnanimous. I cannot, of course, speak for all your readers, but, as for this reader, apology accepted. . . .

On the same day I read your apology, I later heard President Clinton attempt to apologize to the American people. The two apologies sat down side by side in my mind for the next few days—yours an example of how to do it right and the other a textbook example of extreme disingenuousness and dubious logic. Anyone who tuned in and saw *The Bill Clinton Show* on TV will agree that copping to "a relationship that was inappropriate; in fact, it was wrong" is a far cry from what you say in fewer words and with no misdirection whatsoever. If only our nation's Commander-in-Chief could have taken a hint from your pages and spoken with one-half the percentage of clarity that permeates through your sentences, as in the following: "We regret that we originally published an article that appears to be a fabrication."

In conclusion, what most cheers me is learning that you investigate yourselves. This reader's mind is put at ease knowing that you investigated the article after publishing it and maintained your efforts even as the principals in the firm apparently aimed to foist their apparent deception on unsuspecting victims. Let it escape nobody's attention, therefore, that it was only because of this newspaper's being literally on the ball that state officials were alerted to the hoax's "apparent escalation." I, for one, can rest easily knowing that you are watching the news and watching yourselves watch the news, acting as both guardian of journalism's lighted torch of truth and the watchdog guarding against journalism's occasional mistakes. Once more, my hat is off to you, my head bowed, and pate exposed.

Gary Pike, Syracuse, N.Y.

—BAFFLERS 11 and 13, 1998, 1999

Afterword

Five years later, I have not yet managed to write a bestselling work of satire. In that time, several more writers have published fiction as fact, including: Rodney Rothman, in *The New Yorker*, writing about his do-nothing job at an Internet company; Jay Forman, in *Slate*, writing about fishing for monkeys with fruit as bait; and Michael Finkel, in the *New York Times Magazine*, writing about Youssouf Malé, a young boy forced into a slave's life in Mali. The writers' missteps were as varied as their subjects. Indeed, for all their differences and for all the varieties and degrees of their faking, these cases make clear that journalism is still a game played with a small number of unforgiving formulas, that the formulas don't always accommodate actual stories, that writers sometimes feel they need to fudge to make the stories fit the assignments, and that editors sometimes collude in the process, wittingly or not.

10

Cold Warrior in a Cold Country

CLIVE THOMPSON

CANADA HAS NEVER BEEN a hospitable land for right-wingers. Even so, 1991 was a low point for the country's long-frustrated friends of wealth and established power. Unemployment had soared to almost 11 percent, putting an already well-organized union movement on the offensive. A public-sector strike was raging, with workers campaigning against a wage freeze. Toronto's public-transit employees followed suit, tying the city up in traffic jams. To make matters worse, Ontario had just elected a nakedly left-wing party to run the province—the New Democrats, a tax-and-spend gang headed by one of those fey, bookish elites so loathed by the right.

A bleak spectacle indeed—particularly for Conrad Black, Canada's expatriate media baron. In the Canadian daily business paper the *Financial Post*, he surveyed his home and native land and offered a scathing prognosis. "Only in Canada, especially in Ontario, are the prig stormtroopers of the old, soft, anti-capitalist left still taken seriously when they insolently strive to communize industry, confiscate wealth, and discourage economic growth," he railed. "Only in Ontario in the entire democratic world, is the cant and hypocrisy of union-dominated soak-the-rich, anti-productivity, politics of envy officially approved and po-facedly presented as 'caring and compassion.'" Worse, he moaned, the best and brightest Canadians, "demoralized by the socialist quagmire," were fleeing to the United States.

After a few more desultory stabs at Canada's tweedy left (alternately described as "simpering" and "driveling") Black came to the meat of the matter: What Canada needed, dammit, was a dose of hard-assed American-style values. It needed tax cuts, more tax cuts, and union busting. Black fondly recalled Reagan's legendary beatdown of the air-traffic controllers. It was, he concluded, really quite simple. Canada needed a culture war, a massive backlash of the kind that had propelled his American heroes—and, indeed, the world—into the age of the market.

Only one niggling problem remained: How could the simpering, driveling Canadians be made to see the light?

With a national newspaper, that's how. Before long, Black launched the *National Post*—one of the most aggressive, not to mention expensive, backlash vehicles in Canadian history. From its debut on October 27, 1998, the daily has delivered a virtually nonstop harangue against taxes and organized labor. Many newspapers reflect their owners' viewpoints, of course, but the *National Post* is so thoroughly choked with free-market zealotry that it appears at times to have been written entirely by Black himself, then faxed directly to stunned readers in Moose Jaw or Saskatoon. I'm exaggerating, but only just: Black is, after all, renowned for calling up reporters at some of his most obscure daily papers and dressing them down for false consciousness—as he once did at the *Montreal*

Gazette, bawling out a hack who had dared to criticize his concentrated control of Canada's media.

And so it goes with the *Post*. Day in, day out, the paper adheres religiously to Black's prime directive: Canadians must either pander to the rich, else watch them flee to the risk-and-reward empyrean of the United States or some other tax haven even farther afield. "The yacht clubs in the Caribbean and the slopes of Switzerland are filled with wealthy Canadians who will never pay a penny of taxes here, or anywhere else, again," as one columnist scolded. And it's not just the rich who are fed up! An even more important actor in the make-believe world of Blackian theory is the mad-as-hell middle class, who just aren't going to take it anymore. To read the *National Post* one would believe there is a virtual tsunami of "tax rage" sweeping the country, turning average Canadians into "tax rebels"—refusing to pay up and preparing to hunker down with cans of tuna to await the jackbooted Mounties. "When a nation's citizens are backed against a wall and have little left to lose, they take desperate measures," admonishes *Post* tax columnist Jonathan Chevreau. Black even began using the *Post* to distribute copies of *The Wealthy Boomer*, an antitax magazine whose title—despite its viciously populist, down-with-elites content—is just about the most obnoxious bit of class boasting imaginable. (Okay, calling it *The Contented Yuppie* would have been worse.) Meanwhile, a "special report" in a February 1999 *Post* devoted entirely to the antitax movement offered glowing profiles of marginal tax-rebel groups, musings about Laffer-curve economic theory, and polls categorizing different sectors of the Canadian public as "high rage" or "medium rage."

The really weird thing about Black, though, is that he himself can't really turn on the populist vibe. Quite the contrary; he harbors some very pronounced aristocratic pretensions. For years, Black has lobbied desperately for admittance to—get this—the British House of Lords, bending himself backward in sucking up to the most calcified symbol of class hierarchy in existence. In

2000, Black even went so far as to enlist Tony Blair's aid in an eleventh-hour bid to snag a peerage. Unfortunately, the plan fell afoul of a Canadian government policy prohibiting citizens from accepting honorary titles that "confer any precedence or privilege." When the government told Black he couldn't don an ermine robe in the Sceptr'd Isle, he immediately went apeshit and phoned the Prime Minister to complain. The impudence! The arrogance! The leftism!

Granted, Black has picked his victim well. If you're going to stage a Nixonian freak-out about socialism today, Canada is one of the few places you can still do so without seeming utterly bonkers. It remains an oddly left-wing place in subtle ways and—all the worse for Conrad Black—those ways tend to be the national characteristics most cherished by Canadians themselves. As the Canadian political theorist Gad Horowitz has argued, the country's cultural DNA includes a powerful strand of early British trade unionism, mixed with a lot of pro-union European immigrants. This is not a free-market crowd. The idea of communally pooling money to pay for stuff like health care is the bedrock of the Canadian psyche, not some elitist nostrum imposed from on high by trip-hopping tenured radicals. Canada's would-be backlash warriors are left slightly unsure of whom precisely to attack, which is why the *Post* frequently seems to be flailing at anything. Worse, invocations of the glories of American life are instantly derailed by the fact that Canadians, living right next to the United States, have seen enough hair-raising stuff to realize that *Beverly Hills 90210* and *Friends* don't quite reflect the real state of everyday America, with its medically uninsured middle class and crumbling public-education system. Yeah, sure, it'd be nice if we never had to pay taxes, everyone figures—*but who wants to end up like Detroit?* This quaint xenophobia powers more Canadian politics than you'd imagine, which is why endless surveys and polls have found that, the *Post*'s *jihad* to the contrary, few Canadians are stirred by Black's dream of massive tax cuts.

One study by Ekos Research even shows that antitax sentiment has been *falling* ever since 1977.

This is what has made Conrad Black's great cultural experiment so intriguing to watch: It's almost psychotically divorced from everyday Canadian reality. Ordinarily, even the most deformed backlash politics arise out of some bitter claim of injustice inflicted on the *hoi polloi*, some smoldering sense of being hard done by. Since no such anger really exists in Canada, it leaves the *Post*'s hapless reporters forced to holographically create their own revolt, spinning isolated cases (here, a shopkeeper who decides to stop paying taxes; there, a bug-eyed letter to the editor) into a full-on "rebellion." Meanwhile, the paper's editors feebly protest that what they're doing isn't cravenly serving the ideological (and financial) wishes of their rich-as-Croesus boss; they're "crusading," in old-skool newspaperman style, trying to wake up the country's somnambulant public. At its best, the paper can be a lively, British-style read; anyway, it's always fun to read a paper that actually comes clean about its ideology. But at its worst, the *Post*'s screeds seem simply hallucinatory, directed to the citizens of an alternate universe who lie awake at night, fretting over whether "taxation is legal." Who *are* these people?

Albertans, possibly. Alberta, being soaked in oil and cowboy culture, comes the closest of any region in Canada to producing Texas-style riches, and thus Texas-style right-wing fervor. Black adroitly realized this and appointed a young Albertan, Ken Whyte, as his editor in chief. Under Whyte's guidance, the newspaper has devoted seas of ink to Western concerns, under the assumption that they will metastasize and eventually consume the entire country. This technique can at times work fairly well; even the most po-faced, envious, driveling Toronto intellectual will acknowledge that the West probably has some ideas worth considering about how to run things. Hell, those Albertans are still Canadians, aren't they? Quite, old chap, quite. And many credit the *Post* with single-handedly creating the new right-wing Western protest party, the

Canadian Alliance, by running an endless stream of boosterish stories about its members.

With Western suspicion of taxes has come the Western mania for family values—including ranting denunciations of feminists and other modern-day witches. From day one Whyte has waged a tireless crusade against women's issues. Reporters have argued that pay equity distorts the market (Headline: "Courts in grip of radical feminism"); that boys are subject to rampant discrimination ("It's a bad time to be a boy"); and that battered women are . . . kind of *asking for it,* ain't they? ("Spinning the spousal abuse story"). Indeed, perhaps even more than its antitax crusade, the *Post*'s rabid antifeminism decisively removes the paper from the Canadian political orbit and sends it spinning off somewhere not too far from the moon, or perhaps Pat Robertson.

It is the final irony of Black's project in Canada: For a guy so convinced that free markets will sort everything out, the *Post* has the centrally planned feel of a North Korean government newspaper. And such is Black's mania that he has poured millions into keeping the paper going, even as it geysers red ink. If there's a market for American-style rage in Canada, he hasn't found it.

In fact, he's packing up his tent and leaving. In August 2000, Black announced that he was selling his Canadian newspapers—including 50 percent of the *National Post*—to a Canadian TV mogul named Izzy Asper. Asper is not only considerably more liberal than Black, he's actually a Liberal, having spent a five-year stint as leader of the Liberal Party in Manitoba, a province renowned for left-wing rule. He may have abandoned his homeland to the socialist quagmire, but hopefully there is a happy ending in store for Black himself. Maybe all this will finally clear the way for his admission to the House of Lords, where he can rage and vituperate on behalf of the world's long-suffering rich to a more sympathetic audience.

—Baffler 14, 2001

11
A Sell-Out's Tale

Bryant Urstadt

The Invitation

One day in February I got a message from a woman named Jennifer. As messages go, it was a good one. She worked for Volvo of North America, and she wanted to fly me to Phoenix for a three-day stay in a first-class hotel, all expenses paid.

She had a nice voice. Her message was short. She said: "You are preregistered for the Volvo C70 introduction in Phoenix. Can you call me back to work out the flight details?"

It would have been a cryptic message, but I had already been on one Volvo press trip, and I knew immediately that I had just been offered a cushy free vacation. All Volvo wanted, in return, was for me to mention their car in a national publication. Or, to put it bluntly, all they wanted was my journalistic integrity.

She left a toll-free number so that I could call her to schedule my free vacation without putting a dime on my phone bill. Volvo, as always, had thought of everything. As well they should have done. Like all the major automakers, when Volvo introduces a new car, or even a model change, they fly hundreds of journalists to a carefully scouted exotic location, put them up in royal style, and wait for the glowing reviews. I just had to tell her I would go.

I called Jennifer back.

"Hi. This is Bryant Urstadt. I'm calling about the Volvo trip."

"Yes. Will you be leaving from LaGuardia or Kennedy? Do you have any airline you prefer?"

I preferred any airline anywhere—I had been stuck staring out my New York tenement window for months—but I held my tongue. She was asking because most journalists use these trips to rack up frequent-flyer miles.

"Actually, I just wanted to know a little more about the trip."

"Volvo is introducing journalists to their new C70 line of convertibles. The trip is three days in Phoenix, test-driving the convertibles. If you fly out of Kennedy you can go direct."

"A convertible? That sounds nice. Can I call you back? I'm not sure I've been assigned to write about the C70."

"That's no problem, I'll keep your space open."

I spent a good part of the next day trying to figure out whether to take Volvo up on their offer. Of course I wanted to kick around Phoenix for three days in a convertible. But I had always considered myself a serious person—serious enough to quit my job and write at home, giving up a salary, health care, companionship, and a killer view of downtown Manhattan to fashion my art in solitude, or something like that. Serious writers aren't supposed to suck the corporate teat. They are not supposed to do anything but try to pinch it with a clothespin, or chafe it somehow. The *New York Times*, *Rolling Stone*, and every other "serious" publication forbids their writers to take so much as a free lunch from a corporation.

It's not hard to figure out why publications like these forbid their writers to go on press trips: How seriously would you take my opinion on the Volvo XC All-Wheel-Drive wagon if you knew that last summer I had been flown out to Alaska, served salmon on top of a glacier reached by cable car, and given a fishing rod, shooting lessons, and an all-weather reversible jacket with detachable liner, among other things? If you were feeling principled, you might think it didn't matter what I said about that car, or about anything else.

I resolved the matter with a nice bit of doublethink. I would go to Phoenix and write an article, but not about the wonders of the C70 convertible (although I might have to touch on that), but about how Volvo gets people to write about the wonders of the C70. I would be a spy, you see, and not just another hack fighting for his share of the corporate sow's tasty milk.

Still, I hadn't entirely convinced myself. I may have explained to colleagues that I was headed to Phoenix to expose the phenomenon of the press trip, but I was really dreaming of the sun lighting the prickly arms of the *saguaros* as it dipped behind the sandy mountains of the desert, and wondering if, in the heat of Arizona, the women would be wearing tank tops and cutoff jeans.

Volvo, in the person of their travel agent, Jennifer, seemed delighted to hear from me when I called the next day.

"Mr. Urstadt! I'm glad you called."

In her gracious manner, she beckoned me deeper into the warm and fluffy corporate bosom.

"Would you be going March 24 to 26, or March 31 through April 2?"

"What's the difference?"

"The first wave is lifestyle reporters. The second wave will all be from the automotive papers."

The Alaska trip had been filled with automotive reporters, and I had had my fill of stories about heroically maxing-out some hot car on the test track in Stuttgart, so I chose to join the somewhat anemic-sounding "lifestyle" group.

"Lifestyle" includes all of those publications one reads to fit better into some group, to "live" better in some way. *GQ* would qualify, since it teaches you how to be a better man; *Family Life* would, too, because it teaches you how to be a better parent, and so on through *Modern Bride, Cosmopolitan, Glamour*, et cetera. It's a genre that produces journalists no less annoying than the automotive-geek variety—and even more reliable for Volvo's purposes. Fifteen lifestyle journalists can be dispatched to write about the same subject and generate—working alone in their own offices, spread across the continent, with only a few press releases and their own experience as a guide—fifteen nearly identical articles.

There were to be ten waves of reporters, in groups of about thirty, aimed at a huge span of markets, including South Americans, Japanese, Europeans, and, in their own wave, Brazilians. The American lifestyle writers would be about the fifth wave, after the techno-geeks, before the Japanese.

"Do you have any special requests for your hotel room?"

In my life, I have only ever made one request of a hotel room—that it be as cheap as possible. That wasn't what Jennifer was asking.

"I'd like it to be pretty big, I guess."

She laughed. "I'm sure you'll find it comfortable. Any special pillows or anything?"

"Special pillows?"

"Yes."

"No. I think regular pillows would be fine. Soft, though."

Jennifer called up a few mornings later. She left a message asking me to call her immediately. Naturally, I did. She needed to know my jacket size. Volvo, she explained, wanted to give me a windbreaker with its logo on the breast. I had been needing a windbreaker.

A month or two later, at around 11:30 in the morning, the FedEx man arrived and handed me a package. Inside was an envelope, from "Volvo Travel Headquarters," stamped, "Important Travel Information Enclosed."

I paused to reflect on my temporary grandeur: Important travel information, delivered by courier to my door. It was just how I wanted to live.

The envelope contained a custom Volvo luggage tag, my airline tickets, and a letter from Volvo Travel Headquarters, welcoming me to "sunny Phoenix, Arizona" and explaining that the luggage tag would "expedite handling." Also included was a brochure from the Royal Palms Hotel and Casitas, which appeared to represent the highest achievement in the art of prefab elegance. Finally, there was "The 1998 Volvo C70 Convertible Lifestyle Media Program Event Agenda." This document—its wonderful title hinting at the deadly serious precision that Volvo applied to making sure journalists had "fun"—offered not one but two agendas.

There was Program A, which included a guided tour of Frank Lloyd Wright's Taliesin West, a visit to a vintage airplane restorer, and lunch with survival expert J. D. Holman, and Program B, which included a drive to the red cliffs of Sedona, known by locals as the "cosmic center of the world," followed by a visit to an artist at the Mountain Trails Gallery who specialized in Native American themes. In addition to Native American–"inspired" art, Program B also threatened to expose me to one Lily Dorene Falk, whose "exquisitely crafted creations are worn by celebrities and other high-profile, fashion-conscious clients," so I chose Program A. Both programs seemed a little strange until one considered them in the larger context of Volvo's current image campaign, which aims to reach a "sensitive," educated, semiaffluent consumer. Or, as one of their many press releases put it, the "individualist."

The Journey

Arriving in Phoenix's grandly named Sky Harbor International Airport, I was greeted by a driver holding up a sign with my name on it. His name was Ron, and he was the first man ever to hold up a sign for me. He had scribbled my name with a highlighter, and I could barely read it, but that did nothing to diminish the flattery of the gesture. Ron wore a white short-sleeved shirt, a black tie, and black pants. He shook my hand and we were off, trundling down the endless airport corridors. As I followed him, he began talking about Phoenix the way a tour guide might, giving me details about its founding, and the average yearly temperature and rainfall. He was one of the only Volvo-related people I would meet who didn't treat me as though I was one of the most important people on earth.

After driving me through miles of Jiffy Lubes, RiteAids, and Wal-Marts, Ron delivered me unto the Royal Palms Hotel. Volvo's people had spent months choosing the right hotel, and whatever image it exuded reflected careful decisions on the part of the trip planners. The Royal Palms keeps out the public with a pink adobe wall circling the perimeter of one block in Phoenix. To enter, we passed through an iron gate that looked like it might have been stolen from the set of *Citizen Kane*. The crunchy gravel driveway circled around a verdant flowerbed. Sitting out by the front doors were two teal Volvo C70 convertibles and a sky-blue Volvo convertible dating from 1956.

A blond woman at the registration desk welcomed me with great warmth, gave my key to the bellhop, and explained that Volvo had taken care of the tipping.

"That's what I like to hear," I said, possibly too enthusiastically.

The bellhop was ruddy, chipper, and so happy that I suspected that Volvo must have *really* taken care of the tipping. He picked up my bag, asked me how my flight was and told me how I could get whatever I wanted at a number of locations.

My room was just off the pool. The bellhop placed my bag on a special bag holder at the foot of my bed. He pointed out a pile of fruit in a basket. "That's fresh," he said, "I made sure this morning. I'll bet it'll taste pretty good after hours of traveling."

With a few obsequious nods, telling me to call him if I needed anything, he actually backed out of the room, leaving me alone to admire it.

The room was marvelously appointed in the Southwestern

mode, with a Navajo-style rug on the floor, an ornate hutch holding the TV and minibar, and a heavy wood desk with swirling, Spanish-style legs. The bathroom, too, was elegantly laid out, with its own desk. The toilet paper was folded into an arrow at the first square. And on one side of the sink was a stack of freshly laundered, expertly folded towels.

The desk in the main room was heaped with gifts from Volvo. Beside the bowl of fresh fruit, there was a custom boutique bag, in Volvo blue, emblazoned with a photograph of the C70 in the desert at sunset, under the motto, "Volvo C70 Convertible—Tan Safely." Inside the bag was a tube of sunblock, a tastefully preweathered beige baseball cap, and a new pair of Ray-Ban Wayfarers (approximate retail price $75). Also on the desk was my jacket, a brand-new beige windbreaker with "Volvo" stitched into the breast, and a fancy folder filled with glossy press material about Volvo and the C70, including an expensive-looking magazine called *Open Mind, The Volvo C70 Convertible Magazine*, also available on an enclosed CD-ROM.

The hotel's Palmera Lounge, where the introductory remarks were scheduled for that evening, was less lounge than an open breezeway, and Volvo had taken advantage of its spacious opening by wheeling in a special version of the C70 convertible and surrounding it with conference chairs. Here I got my first introduction to the Volvo corporate employees. They were not hard to spot. Besides looking almost comically Swedish—straw-haired, azure-eyed, and much-reddened by the Southwestern sun—each was wearing black pants topped with a saffron short-sleeved button-down, both embossed with the Volvo C70 logo. There were a few American employees of Volvo mixed in, also in Volvo uniforms. The Americans, I must say, looked a little shaggy compared to the Swedes.

Among the lifestyle editors and journalists there was an air of giddy hilarity. We all must have felt like we had been getting away with something, standing there on the pink adobe stairs that led to the Palmera Lounge in balmy Phoenix. We were all wearing the name tags the Volvo publicity people had left in our hotel rooms. Several of us were from New York, and we made jokes about the grim weather we had left behind. There was Penny, the managing editor of an enormous bride's magazine; Heidi and Andrea, both automobile reporters for a New York tabloid; and other authors or editors from a wide variety of lifestyle periodicals such as *Bikini, Washington CEO, GQ, Good Housekeeping,* and *Flair,* a Canadian fashion magazine.[1]

Ree Hartwell, Volvo's media-relations manager, was also there, and she looked happy to see me, though it was hard to gauge her true feelings, since it was her job to look happy to see me. Ree looked happy to see me because I was officially representing *Family Life,* a publication aimed at parents of kids from three to twelve. The magazine tries to reach readers with higher household incomes—readers that interest Volvo very much. With a circulation of half a million, a nice spread on the Volvo convertible would more than pay for my trip.

We all settled into the conference chairs ranged around the special C70. On each chair lay a sand-colored Volvo pad and a black-and-chrome mechanical pencil/pen with "Volvo" stamped on the lead-dispensing button.

With these gifts we were to record the words of José Diaz de la Vega, the chief designer of the C70's interiors and color trim. Diaz de la Vega's speech was high theater, a campy mélange of catchphrases and carefully designed slogans. He spoke in a way that reminded me of Ricardo Montalban, spreading his hands for emphasis, then bringing them back together in a kind of prayer

[1] Altogether, there were about thirty of us. I've done my best to conceal the identities of the writers by changing their names, trying to balance the importance of naming the publication with a desire to protect the other writers. Like me, they probably went into journalism for decent reasons and got battered along the way by the meagerness of their incomes.

gesture. He frequently laid these same hands on the special C70 in a loving way. (I kept hoping that he might brush its supple, fragrant upholstery with the back of his hand, and purr about its "rich Corinthian leather.")

As for Diaz de la Vega's disquisition—some drivel about the "six senses" Volvo engineers had in mind when designing the C70—I was, after a few minutes, on the verge of tuning out completely. As he mimed his slogans with expertly faked passion, I drifted off into my own thoughts behind that polite, blank face one gives when one is being delivered information one doesn't want. In the chairs around me, however, I noticed my colleagues busily scribbling—some into their new Volvo pads, most into reporter-style notebooks. It occurred to me that Diaz de la Vega's palaver might well show up in C70 reviews (it did), so I started taking notes as well. The Volvo pads, it turned out, were not just a gift, they were a push in what Volvo considered the right direction. They couldn't literally write our reviews for us, but they were willing to dictate.

Diaz de la Vega concluded his talk with a few polished remarks, which had been polished, no doubt, in costly brainstorming sessions with the "creatives." Among these gems were, "Many convertibles have the looks, but few have the brains," "This isn't the Volvo you need, it's the Volvo you want," and his final remark, which we heard and saw over and over again during our stay, "Tan safely."

After the introductory remarks, we were led out to a phalanx of buses, which took us to the Wrigley Mansion on the outskirts of Phoenix. I boarded and sat down next to Heidi, one of the writers for the New York tabloid. She was middle-aged and dressed in a T-shirt with a big black cat on it. I asked her if she went on these trips a lot. She said she did, and that courtesy of various manufacturers, she had been flown all over the United States, to Europe on the Concorde, and once to Japan. The car manufacturers, she related, were currently in a miniwar of extravagance, competing to be the most lavish and the most inviting, and lately the trips, along with the economy, had been getting better and better. It was a pretty good deal, we agreed. She asked me if I would be writing about Volvo. I said I would.

"What's your angle?"

"I think I'm going to be writing about press trips in general."

"An exposé?" she asked, sounding worried.

"Sort of, I guess."

"Don't ruin it for the rest of us," she said, without a trace of humor.

At the Wrigley Mansion, we gathered for a four-course meal in the grand dining room overlooking the ten miles of plain leading to Phoenix. There were a number of writers at my table, and a few Volvo reps. The mood, again, was of the highest joy, as though we were all lottery winners, assembled to be congratulated for our good luck and to be awarded the cash prize.

Over white wine and dessert, a goblet full of fresh berries, and to the soft tinkle of a pianist playing, "You Are So Beautiful," the conversation turned to the press trips themselves. Heidi was at my table, and at some point she mentioned that she had writer friends who, when the press people called up to invite them on a trip, asked first, "What are the gifts?" If her friends didn't like the gifts, they wouldn't go. This launched a whole round of press-trip stories. The writers had been flown all over the world. Mexico had flown them to Mexico, so that they would write good things about Mexico, and so on, through a whole raft of countries, cars, and more general products. They compared gifts and joked about how many frequent-flyer miles they had accumulated. I tried to join in—I had a plush bathrobe from Nickelodeon, and some khaki pants from when The Gap was "introducing" khakis and sent a pair to just about every editor in Manhattan—but I had more to add about my friends than myself. I knew people who had been sent to "check out" the South of France, Scotland, exclusive islands in Florida and the Caribbean. (Anyone sick enough to read the hundreds of magazines that come out each month will pick up on certain mini-trends in travel articles, usually sparked by the enthusiasm of writers who have just flown there on the country's tab.) Writers I had met on the trip to Alaska had been flown to Sweden to test Saabs, given BMWs to drive in Bavaria, and so on.

My best story, though, was about an editor I had worked for in New York. She wrote travel stories and went to several ranches and ski areas—all expenses paid—with her family several times a year. She was scrupulous about kissing their asses. As her assistant, I was constantly sending out clips of her obsequious articles to the ranches she had visited—as thanks and insurance that she would be invited back. I also sent her clips to places she hadn't yet visited, in hopes of an invitation. Her office was literally filled with gifts from companies. They were piled up against every wall, in garish stacks on her desk, under her desk, blocking her door—books, tapes, CDs, software, complicated plastic toys, sports equipment, clothes, and on and on. Many of them were duplicates, for she had been in touch with so many companies for so long that she was frequently on their mailing lists twice, but I never once saw her part with one single gift, no matter how many she had or how irrelevant it was to her life. In contrast to her Scrooge-like personal habits was the witty, fun-loving voice of her articles, which no doubt sent thousands of her several hundred thousand readers flocking to the ranches, ski areas, and product lines of her corporate friends. After a while, I realized that maybe it was a story I shouldn't have been telling, and with so much disdain, to the particular table where I sat, so I decided to be quiet for a bit.

Penny from the wedding magazine was at my table, too. She had also been on Volvo's Alaska trip. A little while after my rant, I asked her how a car review would fit in a magazine aimed at newlyweds. Did they recommend cars for newlyweds?

"I made it into a kind of travel thing," she said. "You know, Alaska for the honeymoon."

"Did you mention Volvo?"

She had. And she would probably be working a similar angle for this trip.

When I got back to my room, my sheets had been folded back, a plush bathrobe had been laid out on my bed, and on my pillow was a foil-wrapped mint, with "Volvo" stamped into the chocolate. I didn't eat it.

The next morning, the journalists of the North American lifestyle wave of the C70 rollout ate breakfast at T. Cook's restaurant, flipping through the complimentary *USA Today*s. As for T. Cook's, I will let the hotel's own material describe it: "A stunning view of Camelback Mountain and a grand wood burning fireplace will take your breath away. The perfect setting for our rustic Mediterranean fare." And at night, the brochure continues, the pianist "plays your favorite 'oldies' and the bartender remembers your 'usual' in an atmosphere that evokes warm memories of recent years past."

I sat with a couple of the younger writers, including Ben, who worked for *Rolling Stone Online*, which strictly bars their employees from hopping press trips. Ben had taken the trip for another magazine. Writing for a publication that forbids trips, and going under the name of another, seemed quite common.

He was a friendly guy, a hip, recently arrived New Yorker. He wore a black T-shirt, jeans, and fat black shoes with lug soles. He had his hair cut short in a spiky do. The trip was cool, he said, but he was just using it to get to LA, so he could visit his girlfriend. He had somehow convinced Volvo to fly him through LA, with Phoenix as a stopover. Not that Volvo had needed much convincing. As far as I could tell, they would bend in just about any direction if the possibility of coverage was at stake.

Afterward, we assembled at the Palmera Meeting Room, just off the Palmera Lounge. There we were given spiral-bound "Road Books" with "Volvo Phoenix 1998" on the cover. Inside were detailed directions to Taliesin West, the Carefree Airpark

Estate, Bartlett Lake, and back to the Royal Palms, accompanied by a foldout road map and important telephone numbers.

Out front were fifteen brand-new convertibles in shimmering metallic gold, each with about ten miles on the odometer and the keys in the ignition. The writers stood around while Volvo's audio test engineer, Andreas Gustafson, showed us journalists how to work both the three-CD magazines and the larger, six-CD changer in the trunk. Andreas and his team had gone so far as to compile special CD mixes of driving music, with uptempo tunes such as Abba's "Dancing Queen" and the single from Madonna's "Ray of Light."

Of course, it was important to choose someone cool to drive with, so I matched up with Ben, because at breakfast he had been brandishing a case of CDs.

Thus briefed, Ben and I pulled out of the Royal Palms and headed south to Taliesin West, onetime headquarters of Frank Lloyd Wright. I drove. I suppose I had some seniority, since I had been on the press trip to Alaska and he had not. This was his first trip. Ben sat in the passenger seat with Volvo's careful directions open on his lap.

We pulled out into the Phoenix traffic.

"Hey," I said. "Could you pass me my Wayfarers?"

"You're going to wear those things?" he said.

"I know, they're stupid, but it's too sunny out. My eyes are sensitive."

He handed me the Wayfarers, stubbornly squinted for about two blocks, and then put his pair on too. Suddenly we were two young guys in a brand-new $45,000 metallic-gold convertible, both wearing Wayfarers.

People stared at us at the stoplights and on the freeways. One guy yelled out the window of his BMW to tell us that we had some cool wheels. We both gave him a big, friendly thumbs-up. As cars pulled alongside and their drivers examined us, I felt like I was riding a thin line between having everyone want to know me and getting the shit beaten out of me by four teenagers in a chopped muscle car.

But it was impossible to be too cynical about the car. We were both delighted to be, for once, the ones on the other side, the ones in the fast car, the car that got the looks.

The C70 drove nicely, although it was, in its essentials, identical to most every other car ever made, in that it was able to stop and start and turn, on demand. At one stoplight, I gunned it.

"Good pickup on this baby," I said.

"Yeah, and the stereo kicks butt," said Ben.

Once I pressed the brakes really hard and screeched to a stop.

"Stops nice," I said.

"Yeah, seems good," said Ben.

Neither of us had any idea what we were talking about, in terms of automobiles, and we admitted to one another that we had no intention of writing about the car, and that we were both simply taking advantage of a free trip.

After a private tour of Taliesin, we were served a box lunch with bubbly water, as we sat in a private courtyard under umbrellas. Afterward, Ben drove and I gave him the directions in our road book, which took us to the Carefree Airpark, a paved strip of desert on the outskirts of town. When we arrived, a World War II P-51 Mustang roared off the runway and tipped its wings at us. We gave him a honk.

I thought for a moment of what I would be doing if, as a journalist, I had done the "right" thing and stayed in New York. I saw myself at my little desk, hunched over my computer, occasionally glancing up at the fire escapes out my window.

Before long, the other Volvo-testers started to show up in their C70s and we gathered by an airplane hangar, where a salty old guy showed us his 1943 Steadman biplane and let us sit in the cockpit.

Then we drove up into the mountains, dutifully following Volvo's entertainment schedule, and met another character hired by Volvo, a fellow by the name of J. D. Holman. He was dressed in period costume dating from about 1880—down to antique pocket watch, handlebar mustache, and ivory-handled pistol—and he gave us a well-rehearsed lecture on the dangers of the desert.

At every event, we were joined by several of Volvo's people, who answered our simple questions—"How many cylinders does it have?"—with grace and enthusiasm. They, too, were tooling around in brand-new C70s and seemed to be having as much fun as we were. Again, they all wore uniforms; they seemed to have had a different one made for each segment of the event. This time, the outfit included black C70-embossed hiking shorts and a T-shirt with a picture of a pair of Wayfarers hanging off the end of the words, "Cruise Brothers."

I asked Andreas, the audio guy, about the T-shirt.

"It's just for fun. Our guys, they like uniforms. They get an idea, they just do it."

In the afternoon, having finally escaped the preplanned activities of Program A, Ben and I took off into the mountains surrounding Phoenix. We happened on a state park and climbed to the top of a hill. There was an abandoned Native American settlement there, six or seven hundred years old. Far below, we could see our C70, looking absurdly luxurious alone in the small parking lot. Mountains and hills stretched out in every direction, reaching up to drifting clouds. The warm feelings for Volvo were overwhelming. Volvo had given us all of this.

That night was the big dinner, at the Royal Palms, in the Estrella Salon by the reflecting pool. Most overnight press trips have their big dinner, where the journalists mix with the corporate officers. In Alaska, we had taken a cable car to the top of a glacial mountain, and there, in a lodge with immense windows overlooking miles of mountains, Seward Bay, and hang gliders suspended against the ten o'clock sunset, we had toasted the Volvo corporate personnel, who had risen to ovations from the journalists and made short, witty speeches about how happy they were to have us there, and how important we were to them.

At the predinner cocktail hour in Phoenix, caterers in black bowties brought around margaritas on trays, and bartenders served up the best of the top shelf. Some of the journalists arrived in jacket and tie. Clearly, they saw this occasion as a real event. While we picked hors d'oeuvres off a long oak table, I tried to do some research, to crack open something big, and to that end, I cornered Jim Borsh, Volvo's director of corporate communications.

A tall, serious man, Borsh had been on the Taliesin tour with me and had not cracked a smile or told one joke, which was unusual for someone in public relations.

As we sipped margaritas and smacked the salt off our lips, he surprised me by saying that Volvo didn't expect to sell many C70s. The car was just part of a vast campaign to change Volvo's image. With its "sensual lines" and "supple skin," as the press release called them, the C70 would sexify the stodgy automaker, making people feel better about buying Volvo sedans and station wagons. The success of the campaign, it was natural to infer, would depend on the articles we journalists would write.

The next day, I packed up my sunglasses, lotion, windbreaker, pen, pad, and preweathered baseball hat and went home. I didn't really want to leave, but I had to. I bumped into Ree Hartwell on the front stoop of the hotel. As I mentioned, she was Volvo's media-relations manager, and in that capacity she was responsible not only for my happiness but also for choosing which journalists to invite on the press trips. As cynical as I was about the quid pro quo implicit in these junkets, I couldn't bring myself to announce it openly, so when she asked me if I had written anything about the Volvos I drove in Alaska, I equivocated.

"I'm not quite sure what I'm going to do with that," I said, sheepishly. Actually, I had never intended to write about it at all. I had told her that when she had invited me, but I still felt a twinge of guilt. Even though it was acknowledged by all parties that there was no pressure, we have all been trained from birth that if someone does something nice for you, you owe them one. "I think I might do something about this trip, though," I added, with more enthusiasm. And then, with the other writers, I stepped into the minivan that took us to the airport. I knew the trip was over when, waiting for my plane, I had to buy my own can of soda.

The Payoff

Based on an examination of some of the articles produced by the writers collaborating in Volvo's marketing plan, I've concluded that the amount it cost to send each journalist to Phoenix and back, in first-class accommodations, was more than paid for by the coverage Volvo received, especially when one considers that a full-page ad in a major magazine can cost up to and sometimes more than $10,000. Volvo, along with other car manufacturers, has clearly concluded the same thing.

Not long after the trip to Alaska, for instance, I came across an article in *Bikini*. The author, in a story touted on the cover, raved about the XC wagon, and his article ran alongside a full-page photograph of him standing in front of the car. You can't buy coverage like that, Volvo knows, but you can barter for it. It reaches exactly the kind of audience Volvo is trying for: younger, "hipper," more style-conscious buyers who might otherwise dismiss the Swedish carmaker as too square.

Another writer, in *The Detroit News*, not only regurgitated the press release's claim that the XC "looks as good at the Ski Haus as it does at the Opera House" but also supplemented it with his own riff, adding that "the wagon did indeed blend in equally well at the Grouse Ridge Shooting Grounds, the banks of the Little Susitna River and the classy Alyeska Prince Hotel."

The Arizona trip bore fruit as well. A search on the Dow Jones network for mentions of "C70 convertible" turned up 440 articles. It would be impossible and, I fear, fatally tedious, to read every one. The hundred or so pages I managed to get through were scarily similar. Clearly, Volvo had gotten its money's worth. I recognized the names of many of the writers. Some mentioned that they had been flown out to Phoenix or Alaska, and some wrote the review without mentioning their trip. Some simply lapped up what Volvo fed them, quoting directly from Diaz de la Vega and the slobbering press material.

New Car Test Drive, a publication available both on and off the Web, pretty much grabbed the first line of Volvo's press release to use as a headline, taking "The winds of change are blowing throughout Volvo" and changing it to "The winds of change are blowing here."

More subtle was the adoption of Volvo-fed words, such as "swoop," which Volvo used in its press release and which at least two writers coopted for their own description of the car. One syndicated author actually sank so low as to use the Volvo catch line, "Tan Safely," as his first sentence. His piece appeared in *The Automotive News* and, through syndication, in such papers as *The Toronto Sun*.

Others busted out a little ersatz erudition, pointing out that the C70 was not Volvo's first attempt at an open car, and mentioning the 1956 P1900, which, of course, had been helpfully parked outside our hotel. *GQ*'s writer, for one, penned a worshipful half-page about the C70, pretty much scooping up the press material and ladling it into his story, talking about the P1900 and adding some filigree about how much he'd like to have had Ursula Andress in the car with him. The excitement the article no doubt generated among *GQ*'s half-million or so affluent readers might well have paid for the whole American lifestyle wave.

Honorable mention for the most obsequious coverage goes to the *Autoweek* writer, who added a nice bit of characterization to Diaz de la Vega's speech, writing, "But what about taste? Diaz de la Vega gets a devilish glint in his eyes: 'A taste of the good life,' he says."

The highest honor in this category, however, must go to the online magazine *Woman Motorist*, whose author took Diaz de la Vega's speech in the Palmera Lounge as the outline for her entire review and ended her piece with the treacly, "Thanks, Volvo, for sensing everything today's driver needs."

—BAFFLER 12, 1999

Afterword

The specu-bubble popped two years after I wrote this piece, and I assumed that lavish press junkets would be one of the first items to be trimmed from the corporate budget. At some point during the darkest days of the downturn, however, I got an e-mail from a colleague, complete with a digital photo of an alpine lake backed by snow-capped mountains. He was in British Columbia, testing station wagons on Volvo's dime, trying to figure out which gifts to keep and which to toss. Meanwhile, I continue to be offered safaris and free vacations in Gstaad. The business of buying supposedly honest opinions seems to be recession-proof.

12

The Eyes of Spiro Are Upon You

The Myth of the Liberal Media

CHRIS LEHMANN

> You fellows got a great ballgame going. As soon as you're through . . . we're going to do a story on all of you.
>
> —*Former Attorney General John Mitchell to Carl Bernstein, 1972*

AMERICANS ENJOY PRECIOUS LITTLE in the way of cultural consensus, in our feverishly fragmented, post-everything new millennium. But we do know one thing: The media are not to be trusted. The press is like a plague of locusts upon the republic: elitist, biased, and forever ideological.

This axiom of public life commands universal assent, from virtually every point along the political spectrum. Its dominant variant comes from the American right and is, by now, wearily familiar. The lords of the press, we are told, use the machinery of mass persuasion to mint a steady stream of agitprop briefs for the liberal order. So widespread has this plaint become that, in a paradox worthy of a Howard Beale, vilifying the elite liberal media has become the fastest path to elite media success. Even though Bill O'Reilly of Fox News, for example, wrote the bestselling political book of the year 2000, commands a market share in the cable talk world rivaled only by Larry King, and signed a six-year contract for $24 million, he still claims that he devotes himself to "things not presented in the elite media." For good measure, O'Reilly also likes to point out that he drives "a 1994 automobile" every day to work. (Forced to concede that the vehicle in question was a Lexus, he protested, "But you know it's a 1994—it's got some dings in it.")

O'Reilly is wrong about many things, but he is right to suppose that his credentials as an opponent of all things elite can be established by referring to his personal bearing and taste preferences. It's not, after all, that O'Reilly or anyone else accuses the "liberal media" of ramming home some identifiable system of thought. That is never the charge. No, the malevolent liberalism that is so frequently found to taint the operations of the press always turns out to be a matter of "bias," of the character and image of the news' deliverers. The very terminology of the indictment is personal and pathological in its overtones: Before the late Sixties, "bias" was largely a clinical term from the social sciences, used to describe the irrational attitudes held by bigots, discriminators, and the generally backward. Bias was an involuntary or irrational impulse, to be brought to light and then duly diagnosed, treated, and cured.

In the view of the right, liberalism was the real bias that infected our culture. And the underlying disorder of which liberalism was a symptom was that most loathsome of social dysfunctions, class snobbery. Liberals were liberal because they were self-important know-it-alls, insulated in their eastern seaboard from the real-world consequences of their bad ideas—and, for that matter, from the real world generally. They adored militant blacks and protesters but wouldn't let them near their fine homes (or their privileged daughters). They wanted to desegregate the schools, as long as they could raise their own kids in lavishly funded, lily-white suburban districts. The only workers they encountered were in Peter, Paul, and Mary's rendition of "Joe Hill."

This key plank of the bias complaint proved to be its greatest political legacy: a readily deployed, readily adaptable rhetoric of pseudo-populism. Although the "media elite" in question—reporters, news readers, editors—weren't owners or plutocrats in the way that traditional populist villains were, the idea that the anchorman's unflappability or the journalist's questioning were merely markers of "snobbery" caught on immediately and has never left us.

Indeed, the basic terms of the bias myth have swollen to engulf the entire nation. In the aftermath of the 2000 contest to elect the nation's new Fundraiser-in-Chief, it dawned simultaneously on nearly every pundit in the land that there were, in fact, "two Americas": one based in the South and West—the mythic homeland of the common man—that turned out in droves for the privileged scion of a Republican political dynasty; and one sequestered along the nation's coasts and in big cities—those dens of cosmopolitanism and foreign influence—that preferred the privileged scion of a Democratic political dynasty. But while the pundit set contemplated this graphic reminder of the villainy of the liberal elite, what may have been the most consequential instance of media distortion in our history went largely unremarked. In the twilight hours of the second Wednesday in November 2000, a producer for Fox News called the state of Florida, and with it the presidency, for the Republican nominee (who also happened to be his cousin) without any empirical basis for doing so, thus setting in motion the irresistible narrative of a state rightfully won by Republicans and then targeted for cunning post facto thievery by power-mad liberal elitists—and (worse!) their retinue of attorneys.

Not even the most significant facts, in other words, are capable of derailing the liberal-bias myth. In view of this samurai-like devotion to the bias critique in all its pointless varieties, it's high time to furnish some historical grounding for the whole gaseous phenomenon. The bias complaint is, after all, a recent offspring of our political scene. Over the course of most of its commercialized, modern career, the press was quite straightforwardly taken to be an instrument of reactionary vanity—owned, operated, and strategically leased by the titans of industry and lovingly molded into whatever image of the country's body politic they happened to prefer. Think of the storied press lords of prewar vintage—the good and great Messrs. Chandler, Hearst, and McCormick, whose papers bestraddled the nation's great metropolises through the first half of the twentieth century—and you have summoned the shades of some of the nation's most bloodthirsty, most unapologetic paleo-cons. And even at the height of the Republican outrage over liberal bias, the nation's newspapers endorsed Richard Nixon over George McGovern by a ratio of 753 to fifty-six.

But that sort of thing has never mattered much in the fury-filled world of the backlash. The emergence of the liberal-bias critique was, indeed, a sort of willed act of secession on the part of the right—the first flourish of what would be a thirty-year cultural counterrevolution. And so powerful did the bias indictment prove to be that during the Seventies (and Eighties, and Nineties, and probably the Oughts too) it got worked up into an all-purpose assault on every leading institution of cultural authority—the university, the judiciary, Hollywood, the literary establishment—all of them now dismissed with the blanket epithet of "the New Class."

From Idiot Box to Ideology Box

In its beginnings, the bias complaint was, as befits the Age of McLuhan, a question of medium, not message. Horrified by the unruly tumult of Sixties antiwar and civil rights protests, conservatives saw a decade's worth of happy Cold War consensus slipping away and concluded that the culprit was . . . *television.*

The argument is almost plausible on paper. A new medium matures into a mass information organ—indeed, the leading source of news, by the time of the Nixon years. It traffics, both for formal reasons of genre and commercial considerations of audience maintenance, in oversimplification and colorful visual sensation. At the same time, dramatic new forms of social discontent sweep across the land—in particular among the country's privileged young, who have spent enormous quantities of time lying about absorbing vast undifferentiated swaths of the cool blue medium's nightly output.

Ergo, *they must be getting their marching orders from the networks!* It was unthinkable, after all, that the civil rights movement had incubated among black church leaders, union representatives, and crusading attorneys ever since the cruelly broken promises of Reconstruction. And certainly no reputable American leader or opinionmaker would have decided on their own to question the principles of Cold War containment then on singularly grim display in Vietnam. Reasoned, historically grounded dissent from consensus Americanism was simply not imaginable.

So all the compass points on the question of the press were demagnetized overnight. Suddenly the stolid array of station managers, big-city press lords, and fledgling TV barons who had done so much to foment uncritical Americanism, shore up civic boosterism, and (last but not least) break the back of organizing drives in their own sunny open shops became, via the sort of polemical alchemy that is only possible in America, "the liberal media."

For all practical purposes, the Magna Carta of the liberal-media critique is Spiro Agnew's fire-breathing November 1969 speech, "The Television News Medium," which he delivered, significantly, in Des Moines, Iowa. Taking as his text a recent TV address on Vietnam strategy by his boss, Richard Nixon, the vice president deplored the "instant analysis and querulous criticism" doled out over the airwaves by "a small band of network commentators and self-appointed analysts, the majority of whom expressed their hostility to what [Nixon] had to say." Warming to his subject, Agnew dubbed the influence wielded by this petulant band of naysayers "a concentration of power over American public opinion unknown in history." "Of the commentators," he continued, his words dripping with populist contempt, "most Americans know little other than that they reflect an urbane and assured presence seemingly well-informed on every important matter." We may not know how they get that way, but "we do know that to a man these commentators live and work in the geographical and intellectual confines of Washington, D.C., or New York City, the latter of which James Reston terms the most unrepresentative community on earth."[1]

As Agnew framed the question, what was important about the media wasn't such tedious, empirical matters as affiliate licensing, cable regulation, and local broadcast fiefdoms; no, it was all about cultural attitudes, about the haughty bearing and perversely "urbane" views of a "small band" of men ensconced at strategic points along the country's eastern seaboard. This proved to be just the sort of symbolism that the American right needed. If the media were minting student radicals out of the suburbs and lavishing black militants with airtime and book contracts, why then the solution was to demonize the media. All of Agnew's most reliable applause lines—"the impudent snobs" and "nattering nabobs of negativity"—were aimed to smear the press as a haughty band of

[1] The invocation of *New York Times* Washington hand James "Scotty" Reston must have given Agnew's audience a moment's pause. Reston was, of course, an avatar of the New York and Washington press establishments, a consummate insider who was once moved to run an article credited, "by Henry Kissinger with James Reston." Reston's political reflexes were far more representative of the Washington–New York axis than any hypothetical "band" of network officials that Agnew darkly summons here. But then Agnew's speech was composed by none other than Pat Buchanan, himself a native of Washington and a former editorial writer for the *St. Louis Post-Dispatch*. Just as Agnew's speech bred a whole right-wing ideology of "bias," so did it mark the de facto launching of Buchanan's own long-running career as the arch insider masquerading as Middle American outsider.

high hats. And they resounded magnificently, much more so than any strategist could have dreamed. After all, the surest path to saturation coverage in the media is to assault the media—as subsequent generations of right-wing media baiters, from Dan Quayle to Newt Gingrich to Dick Armey, have found in the long decades since then.

More important, the Agnew assault also produced a dramatic new topography of American politics, forever muddling the all-important mythos of social class. According to the bias critique, the blue-collar hardhats and the owning class were part of the same persecuted cultural majority, united by their shared marginalization in the press. In the backlash vision, owner and worker stood together in defense of the besieged values of Americanism; whatever differences they had were dwarfed by the colossal arrogance of the real class enemy, the media.

Agnew took pains to assure his listeners on that day in Des Moines that by attacking the dastardly liberal media he was not advocating censorship. Instead, as he put it, he was simply "asking whether a form of censorship already exists when the news that forty million Americans receive each night is determined by a handful of men responsible only to their corporate employers and is filtered through a handful of commentators who admit to their own set of biases."

Of course, the answer to Agnew's question was "no." Not only was the vice president here confusing censorship—the suppression of news—with news judgment, with the *reporting* of news (news that's sometimes unwelcome in official quarters), but he was also assuming, as nearly every critic of liberal bias has ever since, that the media are a simple manufactory of political boilerplate.

But all squares are circled under the master narrative of bias: Broadcasting is censorship; the executive branch of the world's most powerful government is oppressed by a small band of fast-talking New Yorkers. It is all, you see, a matter of ideology. And ideology is an agent capable of producing every imaginable social distortion. Throughout his indictment, Agnew supposes that the stealth bacillus of ideology travels unfiltered through each layer of the bureaucracy hulking behind every network news logo. Of necessity, news copy must bear the fatal imprint of the political proclivities of whatever decisionmaker finally looses it into the broadcast booth.[2]

That this is not an accurate depiction of how network news broadcasts are conceived and redacted is to understate things, well, exponentially. Just consider the world of error squeezed into Agnew's clause, "responsible only to their corporate employers." Those employers were not merely old Cold War propaganda hands such as CBS's William Paley, but more generally—and far more depressingly—earnest gray men of the company, conditioned to regard ideas and opinions of any ideological or, indeed, merely controversial pedigree as nothing short of business-destroying sedition. This is not to say they were engines of right-wing ideology, either—just that they were, and for the most part continue to be, stunningly idea-resistant. As Richard S. Salant, president of CBS News, famously told *TV Guide* in the late Sixties, "Our reporters do not cover stories from *their* point of view. They are presenting them from *nobody's* point of view."

No conspiracy of sinister cosmopolitans is required to explain this state of affairs. Rather, the enterprising media critic only needs to reference the blinding truth that any casual viewer of TV grasps instantly in a good ten minutes of viewing time: All network content is designed to serve as a lubricant for the streamlined transmission of advertising. The last thing advertisers want are audiences absorbing and pondering systematic political analysis—

[2] A subordinate irony of the long-running rightist uproar over liberal media bias is that it has accompanied thirty years of unambiguous electoral triumphs for the right. This suggests, among other things, that if liberals have in fact been running amok in the network sanctums, it would be in the right's political interest just to let them be.

which is why, in the network bazaar of ad buys, the longest advertising dollars go either to the most lurid or the most vacuous fare. Network news broadcasts function primarily as audience placeholders, as gateways to the main programming events in prime time, where the biggest ad buys reign. As such, they strive not to emphasize or screen out facts according to some neo-aristocratic imperative, but just the opposite: to achieve a programming tone of deathly *non*commitment, a sustained, numbing impression of authorial absence.

Revolt of the Burghers

The liberal-bias plaint may be largely imaginary, but the ability of journalists to disrupt or discredit certain initiatives of the executive branch has always been real. For the paranoid Richard Nixon himself, the conflict had a personal edge as well. Long willing to remind any and all listeners of his bitter resentment at being "kicked around" by the American press, he took the first chance he could to declare war. When the general subject of the press came up, Nixon was once able to announce to his cabinet, straightfaced, that "We've got a counter-government here and we've got to fight it." Yet Nixon faced a delicate logistical problem as he took the field. There was little hope of demonizing an institution that was draped in the sacrosanct protections of the First Amendment and that, as a practical matter, was fully capable of conducting its own greatly public counterattacks.

So Nixon took up the fight with the trademark divide-and-conquer strategy of the backlash. His targets were the network execs so reviled by Agnew, and his allies would be the rock-ribbed Republicans who owned most TV and radio franchises. By setting the interests of one against those of the other, Nixon could both silence troublemakers and enrich his supporters. In his first term as president, Nixon set up an "Office of Telecommunications Policy," whose chairman, Clay T. Whitehead, carefully crafted Agnew's outbursts into a series of policy grenades, which he lobbed over the heads of the local franchise owners and into the jittery boardrooms of the "small band" of network executives. Whitehead laid much of the groundwork for the cost-cutting moguls' playground we now call the telecommunications industry. According to the 1971–72 *Alfred I. DuPont–Columbia University Survey of Broadcast Journalism*, Whitehead "called for all the things the broadcasters had been clamoring for over the years and a few they wouldn't have dared mention: the deregulation of radio, the scuttling of the Fairness Doctrine, getting the government out of programming by revising the license-renewal process, and by implication the rewriting of the Communications Act of 1934."

Even though the last of these would not be enacted until the Clinton administration and the Telecommunications Act of 1996, the foundations of today's digitally driven media cartel were being built in those heady early days of the backlash.

All this hectic deregulation and deal-brokering was sold to the public not as a way to build more monopolies and media billionaires, but instead to liberate broadcast journalism from its unmanly thrall to elite liberal groupthink. As Whitehead sternly chided the annual meeting of the press fraternity Sigma Delta Chi in 1972, "The First Amendment's guarantee of a free press was not supposed to create a privileged class of men called journalists, who are immune to criticism by government or restraint by publishers and editors." No, this was a class war in which the interests of the common people were to be protected by corporate management. For, as Whitehead continued, "Who else but management . . . can assure that the audience is being served by journalists devoted to the highest professional standards? Who else but management can or should correct so-called professionals who confuse sensationalism with sense and who dispense elitist gossip in the guise of news analysis?"

It was easy for his audience to grasp the simple point Whitehead was making: The "management" he was invoking was perched atop the hundreds of local TV affiliates that bestride our great nation. These midmarket executives were—and for the most part, still are—the runty, right-wing tails that wag the supposedly all-powerful network dogs; they control the places that register the first, and certainly the most influential, uproars over "controversial" TV fare, be it an unseemly or unpatriotic investigative piece, a perceived slight to believers, or a lesbian kiss.

In his 1973 book, *News From Nowhere*—still by far the most rigorously researched and documented study of the production, distribution, and strategic vetting of network news—Edward Epstein pointed out that the real power in broadcasting is held by the networks' local affiliates. Not only do they possess legal authority over broadcast content, but they are also the building blocks by which networks sell national audiences to national advertisers, generating those corporate goods that are such supposed anathema to liberals—profits and operating revenues. And who, exactly, runs these affiliate operations? As one network vice president confided to Epstein: "Affiliates tend to be owned by people in another business—newspapers, automobile dealers, Coke distributors—and run by salesmen and former announcers. Their politics are Republican, their ideals are pragmatic and their preoccupation with return on invested capital and the safety of their license to broadcast is total."

As a result, any network-produced news feature that strayed too far into unseemly political controversy—most notoriously the 1971 CBS documentary on Vietnam public-relations initiatives, "The Selling of the Pentagon"—would send affiliate owners rising up to denounce it, and (more important) refusing to air it, producing an uncomfortable reminder to already hard-pressed network news divisions of how costly controversy can be. Not to mention how politicized: During a congressional inquiry into that documentary's production, CBS President Frank Stanton actually went to jail for denying Congress access to footage edited out of the broadcast. (Nor was this the most dramatic affiliate-inspired foray into the nation's politics: An ambitious manager of the Raleigh, North Carolina, ABC affiliate named Jesse Helms made liberal bias a central plank of his maiden Senate run in 1972, demanding that network news divisions be dismantled outright and the airtime for national news be relegated entirely to local markets.)

None of this affiliate/network animus was lost on the policy-making arm of the Nixon White House. Indeed, followers of the administration's high-profile war with the media must have been astonished by the number of occasions on which the White House romanced local broadcasters. In June 1972, Nixon hosted thirty local station owners and executives at a White House dinner, assuring his guests that he would stabilize the process of license renewal and suppress a troublesome FTC proposal to force fraudulent advertisers to run "counter-advertisements" confessing their wrongdoing. The following week, 110 local on-air news personalities turned out for a White House briefing and reception. All this activity bore out the shrewd 1971 appraisal of the unnamed observer who said, after the administration called for the repeal of the Fairness Doctrine and the overhaul of the 1934 Communications Act, "If I were the Republican National Committee, I'd set up about fifty dummy committees to handle the broadcaster contributions that are going to be coming in."

Thus, we propose, as a general axiom of the American culture wars: Any time officialdom begins laying into remote and manipulative elites, see if the burghers start to nod their assent.

THE RIGHT'S WAR on the media paid off handsomely. For conservative politicians, it yielded a potent variant of populism they could call their own. For the affiliate owners, prosperity came with the waves of deregulation that followed in the wake of the new populists' electoral victories. The campaign donations rolled in—not just to Nixon but also to his market-happy successors Reagan and Bush; in good time, the broadcasting donor class got everything it paid for. First came children's television, which was transformed under Reagan FCC chair Mark ("Television is just a toaster with pictures") Fowler into a long parade of badly animated advertorial features produced by cheap overseas syndicates. Then came the local news revolution, loosening the FCC's already rudimentary fairness and standards-and-practices regimes and bringing forth the rich ferment of depoliticized ghoulishness and happy talk that is today duplicated with eerie sameness in every major market.

In addition, the cable explosion produced robust new revenue streams for local owners—and eroded network viewership to the point that the Big Three (ABC, CBS, NBC) no longer command the attention of a majority of the country's viewing households, a development that renders the media bias complaint even more objectively idle than it was thirty years ago. The still cheaper and far more ideological medium of talk radio, meanwhile, is experiencing explosive market growth. And with deregulation, cable and radio have been bundled together into enormous audience-delivery systems for advertisers—and for overtly ideological broadcasting moguls of the right such as Rupert Murdoch. (Indeed, the thought of any of today's network or cable presidents landing in the hoosegow for shielding their news operations from hostile government scrutiny, as CBS's Stanton did in 1971, can call forth nothing but a torrent of bitter guffaws.)

As a result of these dramatic market shifts, it is quite impossible to name more than a handful of avowedly liberal commentators on the growing empires of cable and talk radio combined. On the right? Let's see . . . Tony Snow, Brit Hume, Laura Ingraham, Bill O'Reilly, John McLaughlin, Mary Matalin, and Sean Hannity. And that's just cable; talk radio has coughed forth such lovely specimens of temperate debate as Das Limbaugh, Dr. Laura, Gordon Liddy, Larry Elder, Bob Grant, Ollie North, Don Imus, and Neal Boortz. Nor does any of this take into account the obscenely lavish spectrum giveaway known as the Telecommunications Act of

1996, which is sure to launch another wave of low-cost conservative commentary as it, too, efficiently graduates a new class of broadcast burghers into New Economy moguldom—but that is a tangled, grimly instructive policy tale for another occasion.

The Culture Snub

All these quantum rightward realignments of the media market have taken place as the right has steadily insisted, in shriller and shriller tones, that the media are getting worse and worse. In the first flush of the Reagan era, the networks would be reviled as fonts of "secularism" and doyennes of decadence by newly ascendant prophets of the right (many of them, such as Brothers Falwell and Robertson, commanding sprawling regional media empires of their own). Neoconservatives would deride the networks for downplaying the Soviet threat, indulging the sexual and feminist revolutions, and mollycoddling criminals in news broadcasts. And come the Nineties, the right would appropriate the elastic lefty epithet of "political correctness," and the sham war against the liberal media elite would start all over again.

This seems, at first, a paradox: The more the right controls the economic structure of the media, the more freely do its leaders bandy the fiction of their persecution. But such is the twisted logic of culture warfare. Those endlessly debatable matters of attitude, language pitch, and representation, they have found, always trump mundane questions such as ownership and allocation of corporate resources.

Not that conservatives shun the quantitative approach altogether. On the contrary, over the years they have transformed bias-spotting from a matter of spare-time grumbling into a curiously positivist undertaking, a profession for scholars and think tanks. Strictly speaking, this grant-sopping enterprise dates back to the 1971 publication of the frenetic bias classic *The News Twisters*, by former *TV Guide* editor Edith Efron. It was the tireless Efron's conviction that the dread operation of liberal insinuation was performed not by formal content, editorial decision, or even production values. Instead, she sought to document bias much as Secretary of Defense Robert McNamara sought to document victory in Vietnam: by ruthlessly toting up the day's margin of advantage for each opposing side. But whereas McNamara counted body bags, Efron counted individual *words*—words that, in her clumsily conceived "content analysis," bore meanings that threatened to upend the very foundations of the American republic. To encounter one of Efron's copiously annotated bar graphs contrasting the number of words broadcast "for" and "against" some hot-button issue or constituency—"black militants," "the Vietcong," and "violent protesters" on the one hand; the quietly noble "white middle class" on the other—is to behold a peculiar form of right-wing dadaism, an unwittingly arch commentary on the bipolar wasteland that we now accept as political reality.

It's tempting to dismiss Efron's divinations of universal liberal bias as the delusions of a lone crank with a foundation grant. But from her kernel of empirical affront—the timeless plaint that the networks stubbornly *refused to see things like she did*—sprang the mighty oak, and countless swarthy branches, of conservative media demonology. Like the ghost of Tom Joad, this weird epistemology of media persecution has surfaced over the last thirty years everywhere that neoconservatives, New Rightists, Moral Majoritarians, Reaganites, Dittoheads, and Gingrich devotees have sought out a public hearing.

Reed Irvine's Accuracy in Media, founded in 1969, continues to promulgate elaborate conspiracy theories on such pet right-wing hobbyhorses as Vincent Foster's death and the Elián Gonzalez raid. Meanwhile, L. Brent Bozell superintends the Media Research Center (MRC), which carries on over all manner of broadcasting slaps at the good and the faithful, tirelessly tabulating such outrages as the moment when "actress Christine Lahti heralded on HBO how [*sic*] Hillary has 'a huge amount of compassion for people.'"

The MRC also has a book-publishing division, which, alongside a parade of paranoid accounts of Clinton's Rasputin-like hold on the media, issued one of the most inadvertently entertaining diatribes in the history of media criticism: *Out of Focus: Network Television and the American Economy*, by Burton Yale Pines. The book chronicles a grim period in 1992, when Pines and an MRC research associate sat down before a pile of videotaped network and cable broadcasts and took diligent stock of the networks' failure to broadcast flat-out laissez-faire propaganda as news. Like most right-wing media critics, Pines detects a torrent of covert antimarket messages smuggled into network entertainment programming. The affronts are tabulated with ruthless, Efronesque efficiency: "In total, businesspersons accounted for sixty-six of the 154 criminals, or 43 percent" of the law-challenged characters appearing in the sample of TV entertainment Pines so diligently monitored. Among the cruel caricatures: "A classic car dealer fronted for thieves who stole Bonetti's car in the January 31 episode of CBS's *Tequila and Bonetti*"; "Minton, a liquor distributor in the August 8 episode of ABC's *MacGyver*, was a gun supplier and murderer."

Loosed in the harrowing sanctums of the entertainment Moloch, Pines couldn't admit that he'd uncovered nothing more sensational than the age-old device of giving TV villains, you know, day jobs. But things get stranger still when Pines trains his unsparing, bias-mad vision on the nightly news. After reviewing a CNN report on a nationwide high in teen fatalities at fast-food restaurants, for example, Pines starts in with some actuarial caviling: "More teens could have been dying in fast-food restaurants . . . not because the jobs were more dangerous than others, but simply because more teens were working in fast-food restaurants than anywhere else."

You know how it is: Put enough teenagers anywhere, and it's just a matter of time before they start keeling over. But such sentimental oversights are not the heart of the problem, in Pines's view: Again, the media is reproached not so much for its active distortions as for its telltale ideological *silence*. Pines scores the downbeat focus on workplace death for its "failure to tell viewers about the extraordinary role played by fast-food chains in preparing huge numbers of inner-city teenagers for the working world. . . . Rather than being dead-end, low-skilled employment for these teens, fast-food outlets have become apprenticeship launching pads to better jobs."

Even if this sunny claim were demonstrable, it would have little actual bearing on the question of on-the-job safety—unless Pines were to blithely contend that the 139 teen corpses are a small price to pay for procuring access to these "launching pads" of young urban entrepreneurship, "whatever the dangers of the job." (One could make a similar argument on behalf of the illegal drug trade, after adjusting for higher body counts in tandem with higher net revenues.) And it's hard to avoid noting another painfully obvious irony here: Even as the right hysterically fingers the media as the de facto stage manager of the late-Nineties outbreak of school shootings, it can apparently shrug off three-figure body counts when a poorly regulated market regime is the obvious culprit.

But such brutal empirical concerns have never been the real point of compulsive bias-spotting. The goal is to feed, water, and nurture cultural resentment in every venue where it can conceivably take root. And in so doing the sport of bias-cataloguing has produced a fine historical irony all its own. Pawing through great heaps of masscult for the most outlandish of ideological affronts, the commandants of the *Kulturkampf* have overlooked the key consideration that ideology has never mattered less than it does in our own market-addled age. In successive, self-destructive feints of cultural warfare, the American right has found itself exactly where it previously scripted the scheming liberals in its pet passion plays: despising the country's dominant culture, shrilly insisting on the politicization of private life, composing tract after tract teeming with cranky alarmist persecution, setting themselves up as professional know-it-alls. The titles alone betray this sense of pure and utmost exclusion: *The Tempting of America, The Death of Outrage, The Re-Moralization of America, Experiments Against Reality.*

Meanwhile, according to the right's own reckoning, the basic terms by which the old logic of "bias" operated—all-powerful network elites cunningly orchestrating the behavior of the credulous masses—have fatally broken down. By the magic of the market, Americans now enjoy the right to have their intelligence insulted by the cable broadcaster of their choice. And as a New Economy has replaced the old regime that sought to regulate market growth, it has rendered irrelevant the old criteria of balance and fairness even to their onetime enforcers. All of the last five chairmen of the FCC went to work, as either CEOs or attorneys, for brave new Internet startups. A more recent convert, Reed Hundt, the Clinton appointee who left the commission in 1997, has even composed his own New Economy memoir, *You Say You Want a Revolution.* He also possesses a multimillion-dollar stock options fortune, gathered from various fledgling digital enterprises; in 1999, he brokered a deal in which Paul Allen, Microsoft's cofounder, poured $355 million into Allegiance Telecom, one of the many corporate boards that has bid frantically to include Hundt in its ranks. Hundt's predecessor in the Bush administration, Alfred C. Sikes, is now president of Hearst Interactive Media, where he has enjoyed similar portfolio-pleasing experiences. Yesterday's regulators have become tomorrow's populists of the market. The revolt of the burghers is complete. Spiro Agnew, RIP.

—BAFFLER 14, 2001

Afterword

"The Eyes of Spiro Are Upon You" was intended to be a sprightly look back at how the modern American right got its start by taking on the straw demon of "media bias." I had naively thought that the conservative movement, as it tightened its grip on power, had largely outgrown the substance of the bias charge even as its leading lights continued to repurpose its form, finding fresh prey in the "politically correct" university and the vast canvas of "Blue America," which betrayed its cultural birthright by swooning into Al Gore's technocratic arms.

Yet no sooner had BAFFLER 14 lumbered off the production lines than Bernard Goldberg stormed the bestseller lists with his tell-all tract on the subject, *Bias: A CBS Insider Exposes How the Media Distort the News*, which included all the customary plaints about anchorman snobbery and sneaky media social engineering. Soon thereafter, Ann Coulter acceded to Goldberg's number-one bestselling perch with the even more hysterical screed, *Slander: Liberal Lies About the American Right*, a collection of decontextualized whoppers that focus obsessively on the liberal establishment's alleged bible, the *New York Times*. Coulter proudly announced, in tones reminiscent of arch bias hound Edith Efron, that her text was Super-True, since it came bundled with some 780 Lexis-minted footnotes. So not only readers but also many reviewers accepted such bizarre Coulter proclamations as: "The left is itching to silence conservatives once and for all," and "If Americans really knew what [liberals] believed, the public would boil them in oil." (Apparently frustrated with the public's failure to take this not-so-veiled hint, Coulter told an interviewer: "My only regret with Timothy McVeigh was that he didn't go to the *New York Times* building.") The new millennial American right had rediscovered its Spiroid roots, in gloriously unself-conscious fashion.

Authenticity, Inc.

So. You think there's something *subversive* about pleasure. You've read the cultural studies books, you've sat through the lectures, and now you're convinced that when you enjoy yourself, you're not just having fun, you're sticking it to the man.

Well, we at The Baffler disagree. And that's why we've constructed a magazine that goes out of its way to neutralize all those things that give you such joy. Our authors can't just enjoy TV shows—they have to *interrogate* them! When they peruse books and magazines—they *nearly always hate 'em*! And don't even mention the music industry—*grrr*!

That's why we've made The Baffler so extraordinarily difficult to read. Those long, tortuous sentences; those phalanxes of semi-colons and ranks of commas; that positively Prussian layout—all *scientifically designed* to deny you the pleasures you expect from such a literary-looking text

---

Subscribe to THE BAFFLER.
P. O. Box 378293, Chicago, Ill. 60637
www.thebaffler.com

13
Babbitt Rex

Boob and Boho in the Businessman's Republic

THOMAS FRANK

THE CARTESIANS OF THIS WORLD must find it difficult to listen to WYPA, the Chicago AM radio station that fills its broadcast schedule with a torrent of three- and four-minute talks on aspects of success, leadership, and entrepreneurial virtue. Not only does the object of desire shift maddeningly from minute to minute—achievement, goals, "conversation power," the ability to read, big houses, social success for the kiddies—but each of the day's thirty or forty lecturers suggests a different protocol or lifelong regimen for attaining whatever it is, usually something involving numerology or alliteration. There's the "friendly, fair, and flexible" system; there's the fellow who has discovered that the way to go through life is to "match and mirror" other people's gestures, inflections, expressions, and accents. Another exhorts listeners to acquire "the habit of visualization," to run an "instant preplay" of everything we say and do. A fourth instructs us to impose order on our lives by writing a "personal mission statement," just as the Founding Fathers are said to have done with the Constitution, "the standard of excellence for the land." Inspirers pause in midsentence to spell out an acronym for the word they have just uttered, revealing what each letter stands for as though it were the most natural thing in the world, the way Adam or Shakespeare or Webster thought up all of them in the first place. Then there are the zanier exhortations, which understand business endeavor as a transcendental state, a quest for oceanic oneness with the timeless spirit of acquisition: In the summer of 1997, the easy winner in this category was the trippy gospel of "Flow," which counsels all manner of marketing managers and photocopier salesmen on the virtues of "becoming immersed," getting "in-groove," and "learning to enjoy the immediate experience."

Here, it seems, is the last frontier of virgin, unironized kitsch: cheesy soundtracks and tinny voice-overs, transparent hucksterism and pathetic sincerity, all emanating from the low end of the AM—*AM!*—dial. The feeling of bottomless banality is heightened by the peppy patter of the DJs, who introduce each minisermon as though inspiration were just as interchangeable as Top-40 music, with Zig Ziglar in the place of, say, Ace of Base. But however sedulously the various stars of "Personal Achievement Radio" may have embraced current buzzwords, there's an unmistakable echo in their routines of the business patter Sinclair Lewis satirized in his 1922 novel, *Babbitt*. Sometimes the resemblance is so exact that one might well be listening to a radio station whose signals have been bouncing around the solar system since the days of Coolidge. Consider this passage from *Babbitt*, a statement of principle given by one of Zenith's leading advertising men at a meeting of the city's Boosters' Club, but one that could easily (with only a few words changed) enliven the afternoon rotation on WYPA:

> Service finds its broadest opportunity and development only in its broadest and deepest application and the consideration of its per-

> petual action upon reaction. I believe the highest type of Service, like the most progressive tenets of ethics, senses unceasingly and is motived by active adherence and loyalty to that which is the essential principle of Boosterism—Good Citizenship in all its factors and aspects.

From the crude days of Dale Carnegie and One Hundred Percent Pep down to the sophisticated postmodern transcendentalism of Flow, this hollow gospel of affirmation has remained the public mythology of our economic order, relentlessly turning any questions about larger purpose back on the individual, casting any society-wide failings as symptoms of your personal failure to be sufficiently affirmative. While it may be pitiable in its obvious meretriciousness, its sham scholarship, its desperately repeated assurances that the pixies of success will someday promote each of us to "executive" status, it is also the folklore of power, the catechism of our national faith. Like George F. Babbitt, the average WYPA listener is hardly a great titan of business, but it is nonetheless appropriate to apply to him, in his mountainous will to believe, Sinclair Lewis's reference to his subject as "the ruler of America. . . . Our conqueror, dictator over our commerce, education, labor, art, politics, morals, and lack of conversation."

Seventy-five years later, as the free-market faith stands on the verge of becoming a national cult, as superstar entrepreneurs and The Power of Positive Thinking become objects of both journalistic reverence and cinematic homage, *Babbitt* appears more and more like a manifesto of American satire, a model for the sound thrashing so richly deserved by all our contemporary priests of boosterism. Even today, Lewis's characters are still easily recognizable as contemporary types: the authoritative economist, the charlatan business-school professor, the lyricist of the American salesman who writes advertising on the side. Lewis's description of the sometimes-bizarre minutiae of middle-class life is similarly enduring: the story of the man who lords his low license-plate number over his colleagues at the Elks Club; the realtors singing Zenith's official city song on their way to the convention; the characters marveling over the comical slang of the newspaper advertisements. Each could have happened yesterday.

But *Babbitt* is also a strangely limited satire—easy, even for those who inhabit the same social and regional place as George F. Babbitt, to regard as a document strictly of its time, a painstaking description of life in a particular social stratum in the American Midwest in 1922. Despite some surface similarities, the midwestern cities that Zenith has grown into don't really suffocate people in the blunt and obtuse way Sinclair Lewis described. One can even read *Babbitt* as a sort of cultural analog of Upton Sinclair's *The Jungle*, a critique that served its purpose at the time but that progress has superseded. Oddly enough, this was at least partially attributable to Lewis's popularity and his powers of literary demolition: At its best, his writing was capable of obsoleting entire bodies of slang, style, and belief; his inventions became overnight buzzwords and epithets.

Which brings us to the curious relationship between *Babbitt* and the Babbittry—what we might call the Babbitt Equation. Suburban, middle-class Americans loved *Babbitt*. They bought the book in huge numbers; the newspapers of several midwestern cities insisted that their burg was his model for Zenith; and legions of individuals claimed to be the model for George F. Babbitt himself. The book does not include a chapter in which Babbitt sails into a Zenith bookshop and picks up a novel savaging his fellow boosters, but it might well have done so. The real lesson of *Babbitt*, it turned out, was that smug self-satisfaction thrives in a strange symbiosis with self-loathing in the soul of the American businessman, the two driving him to acts that look simultaneously like bold self-overcoming and a dog chasing its tail. What *Babbitt* revealed was that the American business class enjoys few things more than a witty dressing-down of just this type, the author's sympathy for the regular guys showing clearly through his good-natured mockery.

Consider the specific criticism of business civilization that the book makes. George F. Babbitt may be successful but he is a boor, a man who has turned his back on true feeling and filled his life with emotion-substitutes, with empty talk of zest and zip. The guy even sells suburban homes for a living! The commercial imperatives that dominate his world are fake, hollow, and tasteless.

Again and again, Lewis has Babbitt and his fellow Zip Citians encounter bits of the real high-culture stuff (Dante, Virgil, a "marble seat warm from five hundred summers of Amalfi") and follows each meeting invariably and automatically with some crass remark or act of degradation. The reader's response was no doubt meant to be equally invariable and automatic: We cluck disapprovingly, shake our head over the illiteracy of these boobs, and realize that the great tragedy of middle-class life is its distance from the sacred stuff of culture. When Lewis gives us passages like the hilariously banal newspaper poetry of Chum Frink (which celebrates conformity and cultural standardization) or records Babbitt's proud declaration that "in America the successful writer or picture-painter is indistinguishable from any other decent business man," he is setting up one of the criticisms of American life that he would later make explicit in his famous 1930 Nobel Prize acceptance speech. While we Americans had proven our ability to amass capital proper, we were sadly deficient in acquiring cultural capital, the real stuff of social class.

This familiar criticism makes up one side of the Babbitt Equation: The businessman is a boob. This was, in fact, *so* familiar that it quickly became a standard element of business life, just one more item on the long list of self-improvements that we resolve to make as part of *Philistine No Longer!* or the Ten Days to Wit and Culture system.

. . .

THE URGENT CULTURAL STRUGGLE of 1922 was the overthrow of the "genteel tradition" in American letters, the destruction of what H. L. Mencken called "puritanism as a literary force." The enthusiastic public reception of *Babbitt* marked both the victory of the scoffers and the beginning of a great shift in the cultural battleground. What is remembered less clearly is how Lewis's attack on the boorish tastes and unfulfilling life of the bourgeoisie fit the old puritan agenda, especially its tendency toward introspection and self-condemnation. Lewis didn't renounce middle-class life so much as call for a slight alteration of its goals. In Babbitt we can glimpse the first flashes of a new but still unmistakably middle-class style, what we might call bourgeois self-loathing as a literary force. For the left politics in which Lewis ached to participate, *Babbitt* substituted a politics of authenticity, an aestheticized struggle still fought today through TV commercials and in the lyrics of an army of lavishly alienated tattoo boys.

This is the other side of the Babbitt Equation, becoming more ubiquitous with every passing year as Babbitt_2 screams to the world that he's not a "Standardized American Citizen." Babbitt_2 frequents edgy restaurants where he lifts his voice to marvel at his fellow midwesterners' full and total ignorance of radicchio; Babbitt_2 reads *The New Yorker*, where mildly daring slaps at middle-class propriety bracket fawning accounts of the captains of industry; Babbitt_2 reveres not bland Rotarians but the extreme executives whose mad flava is detailed month after month in the business press. But for a truly candid picture of the two Babbitts locked in sham battle with each other, just move your tuner from WYPA to an NPR affiliate for a few hours. One day, NPR presented a lengthy free-trade jeremiad given by a leading CEO and followed it, immediately and quite unproblematically, with an inside look at the Tejano poetry scene, a gorgeously untouched backcountry bohemia where people are still in contact with the natural order, authenticity can be found at every backyard barbecue, nobody has been corrupted by the ways of the big city.

Of course, what makes *Babbitt* a truly great satire is the fact that Lewis seemed to know that he was setting up a largely bogus opposition. Consider, for example, the episode four-fifths of the way through the book in which George F. Babbitt suddenly declares himself "in rebellion" and takes up with a crowd of Zenith bohemians. A number of critics have taken exception to this plot turn, finding a fatal inconsistency in Babbitt's overnight conversion from normalcy into nonconformity. But how different are the two Babbitts really? Contemporary readers find nothing odd about a realtor getting a little jiggy on occasion—if anything, it's part of the job, a mandatory prerequisite for anyone looking to speculate in the next hot neighborhood. For us it's obvious that Babbitt as a consorter with tippling aesthetes is still Babbitt-the-real-estate-manipulator; that bohemia is just as much a boob's game as is selling prefab houses in Floral Heights.

One can only guess at the devastation a satirist like Lewis could wreak in this age of overwrought free-market proclamations, of corporate millennialism and Wall Street astrology. Almost exactly seventy-five years to the day after the publication of *Babbitt*, the *International Herald Tribune* offered as its lead European headline a joyous "New Credo for [the] World." The story's first sentence, penned by Barbara Crossette of the *New York Times*, rivals—even mimics—the gushing phrases of advertising in its transcendent optimism: "Has there ever been a moment quite like this?" Back in America, Crossette announces with the smug confidence of a Rotary Club luncheon speaker, the class problem has been largely solved, as "high-yield retirement accounts are making near-millionaires of thousands of salaried workers and hourly wage earners." Elsewhere in the world, she asserts, ancient conflicts are also disappearing under the benevolent pressure of sound business practices. Crossette is merely trying her hand at the big journalistic idea of the late Nineties, of course, and her effort is distinguished only by the fact that she dispenses with caution and humility more recklessly than last week's entry in *The Financial Times* or *Wall Street Journal.*

Crossette is but a lesser pom-pom on the American free-market cheerleading squad whose big stars are guys such as Robert Samuelson, Thomas Friedman, and Charles Krauthammer. And while their writing may consist largely of twentieth-generation repetitions of the stuff that makes up Babbitt's speech to the Zenith Boosters' Club, lately their ambitions have been anything but provincial. These days American pundits are seeing the old boundaries of taste, humility, and nation-states give way before them, and with an almost supernatural force it has dawned on them that the American booster's way of life can be—*must be!*—extended to the rest of the planet.

AT THE DOWNTOWN CAMPUS of the University of Chicago Graduate School of Business, the contrast between neighborhood residents and students is not quite as remarkable as it is on the main South Side campus. But still the kids are something to see as they come rolling up to the shiny new North Loop complex in taxis and company-provided limos: The designated captains of whatever industry will still be left twenty years from now, the most promising junior executives in the world, hailing from all corners of the globe but still admirably uniform in thought, expression, clothing, and bearing; a homogeneous transnational business class, in straight teeth and standard-issue Burberry, stationed here in Babbitt country for a few years to soak up the timeless principles of Vision, Ideals, Inspiration, and, well, Pep. Tonight the tag-team scholars in charge, postmodern thinkers who celebrate what they call "nonlinear thinking" and the transdisciplinary principles of Flow, have arranged for this golden throng a lecture by a marketplace thaumaturge of the one-thousand-percent variety, a bona fide artist whose talk leads the prodigies of the future directly into their first assignment: comparing the creativity and transgressiveness of Jasper Johns and Warren Buffett.

Then it's on to part two, in which the students are asked to invent personifications of two corporate organizations, one effervescently entrepreneurial, the other supported by (ugh!) state subsidies. To a man, the students have opted to cast the upstart firm as an outsider artist of some kind, the daughter of a Jamaican mother and an Italian father, a painter, a singer, an aficionado of extreme sports and e-communication and exotic travel. The decrepit old company, meanwhile, is said to be a corpulent, tired, middle-aged, and distinctly white male beneficiary of some kind of nepotism—it's George F. Babbitt.

Commencing the evening's sermon, one of the tag-team profs tells the protoexecutives about the weighty yet glorious burden of "vision," about how it sometimes puts one at odds with the little people, the mundanely details-oriented. He reads to them from *Leadership Without Easy Answers*. He informs them that vision is a "spiritual" quality, while "mission" is more of a "left-brain" function. He lists the "Three Enabling Forces." He tells them about "Personal Meaning." And after a taped speech by the late Leo Burnett on the nature of creativity, he dismisses the students back into the night, to the taxis and company-provided limos, off to ponder, with the glamorous sense of responsibility peculiar to those born to power, the pleasantly arduous future stretching out ahead; all the boardroom battles with all the right-brained Babbitts of the older generation that lie before them, and that they are certain to win. What they have heard for the previous three hours is only marginally more useful than what they could have learned from a day's close attention to "Personal Achievement Radio" or a volume by Napoleon Hill. But that's not the point: Corporate bohemianism may be intellectually vacuous, but it works for them like the Great Chain of Being worked for medieval kings, a sound and convincing lesson in class entitlement, in the rightness and justness of the world, and in their own place in it.

Of course, to understand these golden avatars of creative corporate practice as largely identical to the boorish, slow-moving executives they believe to be their forebears is to commit what they would no doubt regard as an act of inexcusable intellectual insensitivity. And as the republic of business extends its benevolent shade over the globe, the minor differences between the Elks Club variant of Babbitt and his China Club cousin—like the distance between radicchio and iceberg or between Bill Clinton and Bob Dole—will expand with it, until that fine day when the Babbitt Equation, the imaginary war of boob and boho, ingenue and ironist, philistine and connoisseur, will be the only public choice we have left.

—BAFFLER 10, 1997

14
Zoned Bohemian

MIKE NEWIRTH

BEHIND THESE PRETTY, pricey streets of West Town lingers a Chicago neighborhood of dim ghosts: the grimy filigree of the Milwaukee Avenue firetraps, the cornices dated to the nineteenth century, the snaking alleys of oxblood cobbles, and the smooth-worn, narrow railway tracks that disappear into brick walls. A neighborhood that for fifty years was serene in its limitations, insulated from the wealth and the speeds of the city. There was plant and factory work, cheap food in lunchrooms and bodegas, cheap rents in the helter-skelter whitewashed warrens, the dozens of large old apartment buildings that were grandly built and now wear thick skins of grime and listing fire escapes. The kids were cutups, playing ball, kicking ass, running with the Latin Kings. Every corner had its tavern that stayed open late. They had empty streets where on lazy summer nights they fixed their own cars, parts strewn on oily sheets. They had their own streets.

It was not so long ago, the late Eighties, that the central intersection of Milwaukee-North-and-Damen was untraveled and desolate at night, a drab part of Chicago just off the Blue Line el where a few worn-out cars sat on the streets, and only the cops, oldsters, and stout Polish regulars moving slowly in the windows of the Busy Bee testified to any neighborhood life. But by 1993 circumstances were beginning to weave a desired destination out of the old neglected neighborhood. The streets packed dense with old homes and six-flats were suddenly valuable to the local landlords and the local media hungry to catch an edge, and soon enough the hipsters and homeowners were trickling in, filling up the smoky bars: the Rainbo Club—which had always been there, and thus could claim the rarefied air and snooty staff of an established spot—and the upstart rooms like Sweet Alice and Uncle Wally's. That was the year *Billboard* anointed the neighborhood as the nexus of cutting-edge Chicago, even printed a *map* of West Town to assist the A&R sharks in searching out the next big thing, which turned out *not* to be Urge Overkill or Loud Lucy. Within a few years a consortium of scene-profiteers had moved into the celebrated intersection, transforming a perfectly adequate shit-kicker bar into a noxious concert hall known as the Double Door. And the youthful explorers, the Art Institute kids and earnest disheveled recent grads, kept on coming, tentatively at first, like tourists with their laminated maps and personal security alarms, then as proud renters, until so many had arrived that the streets were no longer lazy or empty but a rising sea of congested boho cool.

A lot of people saw that big intersection—anchored by the opposing prows of the forebodingly deco Coyote Building and the sleek, white-tiled Flatiron—and decided that this grimy, haphazard neighborhood was *it*, the place for them, the destination they'd been promised. Or else a place for easy speculative profit. Until finally, like an organic change, West Town was transformed into

Wicker Park: Now the cars stack up for blocks to pass under the el, through the same intersection, lined by the somber gray faces of galleries and restaurants. You can't just *park* here anymore; on Milwaukee the valets line up impassively in their orange vests to take your keys and money.

When West Town—a neighborhood dormant for years, torn and frayed, run into the ground—was reanimated in the public eye, its landscape of neglected real estate turned volatile. The space of buildings—houses and taverns and commercial boxes and two-flats—mutated into a liquid, as flexible as capital itself. Even now that the area is so well established in its trendy hipness that it's even become a bit stodgy, there are still enormous profits to be wrung out by the brave. A developer buys a rat-trap house of brick, an old carriage house on the west edge, facing Humboldt Park, hands off an incredible windfall, tens of thousands, to the old Poles or weary Latinos who hold it, spends ten more to renovate, adds a whirlpool tub and Euro-kitchen, and then sells this *deluxe West Village on the Park condominium* for $240,000 or so. And every piece of cheap housing that the developers gussy up is gone for good, whisked upward into the moneyed sphere, as if it were the bourgeois promise itself that the developers were constructing in the air above its foundation, out of ceiling fans and granite countertops.

THE DEVELOPER is an easy figure to hate, but it can be said in his defense that he is a man of the moment, a gelatinous creature who seeks only to expand, to fill the air. All the petulant carpings that make up the do-gooder exposés and complaints—the notion of "community" as anything other than a buyable thing, the concept of persons displaced, the residue of history, the gone jobs of these ghost factories—this entire dusty web of ideas is simply invisible to the developer. So if we're to stoop to the comforting hypocrisy of blame, let's keep things simple and blame the yups, the buyers of the mini-lofts and pale new blockhouse condos. They're the eager participants who should know better, and it's their lust for the correctly purchased life in the city's most *now* quadrant that speeds the teardown of organic neighborhoods, and they really do deserve their portion of blame for that.

But for one who lives in Wicker Park, gentrification seems unstoppable; it seems impossible that the neighborhood's carefully fanned heat and the accompanying rain of greed could have produced anything but this frantic division and degradation of the spoils. The last carousel is finally spinning in Nelson Algren's old neighborhood, as the hard occupations that raised this city sashay back toward the static imaginary past, down the cool lights of the expressways, out toward the endless deathland of industrial parks beyond the city's farthest edge. In the future maybe we'll all be options clerks, or run UNIX networks, piss in a cup, and wear the gleaming suits of movie assassins, and away from our ten-hour office days we'll sleep, orgy, and thrive in our own crisp white boxy condos, all the luxury minilofts fabricated out of the ghost-space of a city gone to history.

The paradox of the Wicker Park scene is that what disappears when all this happens is the very thing of authenticity that all the new arrivals are seeking. It becomes something they can only seek to emulate, both as individuals and as consumers within a larger commercial enterprise. And in that emulation is a growth as invisible as cancer, the hearty hollow boom time that's already left its cement skeleton along the main drags of a thousand suburbs, all the sad Levittowns and Winnetkas. Now each new hello-kitty swinger's retreat or daringly themed post-ethnic restaurant only hastens the collective demise; each new arrival dims by degrees the shine, the buzz, ensures that the cutting-edge Wicker Park scene can only be ephemeral, counts down toward the final disappearance of credibility. From the travails of the landscape here it appears that money, like water, seeks its own aesthetic level: So it is that the favored gritty neighborhood becomes the shunned suburbs, freakish in its whiteness and jut-jawed macho conformity.

In the meantime the new occupants of Wicker Park have little choice but to continue emulating what's gone, what they've come here to find. What remains—what we're left with—exudes the fakey, tacked-up disappointment of a high school talent show. Hence the rise of a new caste of cliquish passivity, the professional bohemians who slouch among the coffee-shop tables, trying out their scowls, buying the lattes, the frappes, the wholesomely ethnicized flesh-free food, obsessing within the secret notebooks, arguing, expounding spittily upon their complicated lives, hatching the diatribes that fill the grotty fanzines—all their needs attended to by the pinch-faced students pulling the teat of the espresso machine, over and over, a sticky eight-hour shift, cash in the register, the tip jar clinking. There is a perfume of insiderdom in the stale air of these coffee shops, a scene built on streams of gossip, news, projects, the ambition to cause some sort of stir that will embed an individual into the public mosaic, the little footnotes and momentary ripples to which urban "edge" culture has been reduced.

Traces of what's been replaced float like ghosts through the streets of the neighborhood. Near Division and Damen was the Czar Bar, a dark, scuzzy rec-room establishment run by middle-aged Poles, where for a few good years touring bands like Unrest and Beat Happening and uneasy local stuff like Homocore found a roost, to the point where the Poles got some money and rehabbed the bar into a light, airy rec room. But now it's shuttered. A few doors away, though, the Smoke Daddy is crowded with white people seated in tight groupings, eating tasty low-country barbecue in quiet reverence beneath the carefully framed and displayed tropes of a po'-folks juke joint: sepia labels of blues 78s, quaint tinted illustrations of the Maxwell Street Market, tin signs from the ol' filling station. Near the big intersection on Damen, one can dine and carouse at the Silver Cloud, one of the many places striving for the dim cultural memory of the swanky cocktail lounge, this one serving funny meatloaf platters, displaying a temptingly fragile pyramid of martini glasses, offering up a booze list dense with the precious goods, the single malts and uncommon microbrews. The Silver Cloud is a handsome space, with that lucrative aura of authenticity lent by a fine old, intricate, dark-wood-and-chrome backbar; this is due to the fact that it was until recently—and for no small time—a Mexican dancing bar, a dark unretouched alcove where the buoyant Tejano music issued into the then-empty street. On Milwaukee, Club Dreamerz, an evil, grafittied concrete shell—which might have been the first place in West Town to have booked arcane rock in the Eighties—exists only in mist. The shell has been awarded a new skin of wood paneling and classy chairs; now it's Nick's, where a clubby benevolence greets the visitor from Lincoln Park, Evanston, the 'burbs, the ones who will be most pleased by this urban-themed suburban tavern, the transplanted smoke and boisterous fellowship of home.

Because the neighborhood is so old—because the dark 1880s Lodge Hall now contains the snotty-mouthed coffee kiosk and the kool krazy shoe store where the discerning employees will be happy to take $40 for a Wisconsin Dells ashtray they dug up at the Salvation Army—an overlay effect can disorient anyone who has lived or traveled here before, say, the past three halcyon years. On Milwaukee Avenue one can track the gentrifying tendrils to where they peter out farther south, where there are still the remaindered husks of the street's former life: El Chino Tacos, the multilingual travel agent, wholesale sneaker stores, and musty Western-wear emporiums. A few blocks more and the storefronts are boarded up, soaped over, closed up early. The street here appears jettisoned, tossed out according to some scheme of benign neglect, a cabal of city pols and landlords ensuring the developers' pickings for years to come. In the early evening there is a creepy silence along this southern section of Milwaukee Avenue—the sound of absence, of still-forming things. In the go-go Chicago Nineties, wealth can take the form of land speculation on the backs of urban strugglers, and the city's longevity withers in the bright fisting gaze of the market.

The celebrated intersection, meanwhile, has become a place of public theater, as tourist-friendly as "Tony & Tina's Wedding." Each weekend day the silvery el cars disgorge streams of visitors, ID'd by the spiffiness of their clothes, the correctness of posture that comes from visiting a heard-about place, the race to judge it against expectations. The voyeurism is in effect at night as well, when the intersection becomes the nexus of Wicker Theme Park, a land of hearty, grinning celebrants with fine clothes and monodimensional faces, hungry to believe the gilded promise of good times and chosen neighborhoods, and stumbling from bar to bar, hissing through their teeth at passing women, tonguing the black poles of primo cigars, pissing on walls and windows as they sullenly search for the car to take them home—all Hondas bearing Northwestern decals looking alike. The ongoing hedon's cotillion is good for business in Wicker, from the Rama Mart with its provisions of ritualized decadence—Miller Lite, E-Z Wides, inhalers, dice, ciggies, Gatorade, Trojans, Advil, Visine, Tums—to the Soul Kitchen, where the well-outfitted swingers of the moment prime themselves for a sexalicious evening by eating the funky food, raw oysters and froufrou'd jambalaya. The money hums like vibrators in all the tight rayon pockets, but it brings with it both the trash of trash—condoms, snack wrappers, the glitter of smashed pints—and human trash, the scam artists, bar bullies, and maybe-rapers, leering around at last call.

For residents of Wicker it is different from the tourist's mode only by degrees. The stakes are personally raised. You are now a part of the scene, one of the fluid links of acquaintance and decadence, and you must act appropriately: purchase coffee-table smut and ephemeral indie mumble; spend bubbly Saturday night hopping from Mad Bar to the Note, wowing a coterie of visiting friends (getting them to pick up the tabs), then slouch hungover all the next day at the Friar's Grill. Or it may also happen that what you feel is a sort of indictment: the uncomfortable knowledge that something has gone wrong, that behind all the hard-priced, slickly bohemian cheer that's been tattooed up and down these old streets is a history—and even a people, a living population—that is ignored, spat on, and forsaken.

The aloof yuppie hipsterism that defines Wicker Park can trace its origins to the decisions of artists and other disreputable sorts to move here around 1983, when Huey Lewis was the King of Rock 'n' Roll, and All The Young Dudes lived in Wrigleyville and Lincoln Park and partied on the Division Street meat-market strip. Today the artist archetype is West Town's equivalent of Joe Camel, a promotional image wafted over the city to help sell condominiums. The dubious contrast between old and new—between a "real" bohemia and the frat party that replaced it—may read like cheap sentiment. Yet the difference here is so sharp and evident as to be undeniable. Today Wicker Park hipsterism exhorts from us only an enthusiastic apathy in return for all the bought objects, the insubstantial retro gear, the puckish publications offering guides to the moment's favored cultural ironies, the focaccia, the electronica. Meantime, any notion of action or protest—to say nothing of resistance—dissolves in favor of shallow self-articulation. The stations of this theme park are manned by the in-crowd, the hipsterists, whose contempt for those they attend and serve oozes out as they giggle and confer over their after-parties and connections and secret schemes.

The hipsterists share a lot with the capitalists—in particular the notion of getting in early, being the first on board a cultural referent like a good growth stock. Raw ambition animates much of the local culture in its race toward the ever-vanishing "edge," a culture whose products—pop-cult–worshipping zines, arcanely abrasive rock, Day-Glo T&A artwork, poetry slams at the sandwich shop—are almost impossible to regard as anything more than grease in the mechanism of self-promotion. When the dust settles in two years or so, a lucky handful of the hipsterists will have extruded careers, signifiers, lucre from the coopted chaos of their Wicker efforts;

others will retreat to the cushioned disappointment of boozy recall within a duller life, grousing over how close they came. Only the landscape will remain constant as it accommodates this discourse, the frantic assertion of competitive difference, underwritten and supported by legions of followers who are as set in their ways as any North Shore Republican.

The cops and bankers who desultorily cruise the intersection can sleep restfully, knowing 1968 will never return to Chicago. For all the irksome young bohemians so urgent in their visibility, it's unlikely that this place will ever see many stabs at actual resistance—no grimy Loisaida squatters at work in Wicker, no one left to terrorize the landlords—nor are there even many echoes of the disgruntled punk-rock scene that flourished in Chicago in the Eighties, the lacerating sounds of Bloodsport, Naked Raygun, Effigies, Big Black, along with the stirring community fostered by the half-populated clubs Batteries and Dreamerz—something almost unknown to the Wickerites, who were then in their Rob-Lowe-on-Div-Street incarnation.

So the scrabbling bohemians set the tone and provide the diverting amusements in the glittering galleries and shops, but it is the handsome, self-assured, well-employed earners who literally own this place. The last laugh of gentrification is—surprise!—enjoyed by its natural constituency, the tidy white strivers who've done so well since the 1991 recession and who have tried so hard to create a permanence for themselves by buying into the sanctioned, praised urban space of a city they never before knew. You can no longer see the frantic pace of land speculation here, only sense it in the absurd muggings of the costs, the public talk of money, of sums that you and I—certainly the people who lived here for thirty or so years—cannot really conceive of pulling together.

Most of the new constructions in Wicker are naked blockhouses of brick and cement, with one significant ornamental feature: an enormous central window, revealing the living room. The big window allows the occupying yuppie to display not just his skinned-looking house but every last thing he's purchased to complete the urban experiment, the brave way he's set out to live.

This sort of ostentation is also routine at Con Fusion, one of the late-Nineties' most chic Chicago restaurants, where the well-dressed and supercilious line up to contemplate an abstruse, variegated cuisine—a beef in port sauce here, some star anise there, edible flowers atop the peppercorn ice cream. The real draw of Con Fusion lies in a certain triumph of design: The restaurant is a large space where nearly every component is the palest white, with furniture of transparent hard plastic, so that the inevitable floor-to-roof windows facing Damen create for those on the street an aquarium of the baroque spending rituals of trendy dining. The management is known to stock the window tables with whichever celebrities drop by, or failing that, to sift out the glossiest among the arriving guests—the tallest, slimmest women, the bejeweled men—just as the red-vested attendants have been ordered to stack up the finest rides—the sterile Mercedeses, the occasional Ferrari—on the narrow slice of street outside. It is impressive to walk past Con Fusion late at night and view this bright scene, the display of the well-heeled and their personal assets, faces frozen above the small helpings of fussily arranged food. The sad austerity of the Con Fusion scene sets it apart from the garden-variety vulgarity of Wicker Park consumption: Watching the patrons squint in vain at the procession of designer novelty, always waiting for satisfaction, is like looking into a specimen case of the future and seeing how vulnerable life is, even in the bright, protected enclosures of the rich.

And there's also that possible future that nobody here wants to talk about, the notion of the pendulum swinging back, that what we've done here will in the end get done to us. A collapse in the housing market, a Midwest recession, a stock market crash, or urban unrest when the thousands of disenfranchised West Siders come around at last to demand their due—each could shred the safe, happy bubble we now inhabit in so many of the colonized neighborhoods of this city. Or, if this notion of urban meltdown seems uncomfortably fantastic here in the autumn of surging productivity, consider instead the ending that is already rushing to meet us, the expiration date, the self-destruct. Already the seams are showing in Wicker Park, as each weekend the streets clog with the loud, well-dressed celebrants in their gleaming new cars and noisy posses, crowding the streets, woozy with drink, uncertain where to go next, coming unhappily upon the inescapable conclusion that the bars and lounges and supper spots in the end are pretty much the same, that there's no place left to go here that will startle or shake them. It seems only a matter of time before Wicker is mostly known for its smog-belching hordes of SUVs, its black-hole real estate loss-leaders, its stogie-huffing sports-bar boozers, and uptight white restaurant patrons. "Wicker Park? That's, like, so 1995!" It is a tantalizing dream: West Town reduced again to its old place, the lofts burnt out, fire-sale real estate signs glutting streets suddenly free of Range Rovers, once again quiet, ignored.

AT THE END of the twentieth century, a certain notion of "artistic community" has become one of our most hallowed social institutions. Maybe it's an ideal that once made some sort of obvious and clearly defined sense, in those sepia garrets where Alice B. prepared the naughty brownies; and maybe somewhere it does still, like among the polite and enthusiastic chosen who appear each summer at Breadloaf, or the sullen polyester-sheathed chosen who grind away in the crowded Art Institute workshops. But the degree to which this cherished ideal has become a public hallucination is the real story of the siege of Wicker Park. After all, it took fifty years for the Greenwich Village of John Reed, Max Eastman, and John Sloan to become the "scene" of Warhol, heroin, *The Basketball Diaries*, and the tourist-squeeze routine of shitty meals, head shops, and bad clubs it is today. The strange and frightening fact about Wicker is that the district's lamination took only five years or so—five years for the bohemian simulacrum to reproduce itself on the rubble of what was real. And the thread has a way to play out still, into the sad finale in which everyone will see past the bright lights and new flashy signs of the Milwaukee Avenue pleasure strip, and the great sheepish exodus that will follow: the big ugly hangover that awaits.

Youth these days consists of the accumulation of money and memory, an effort to make every last frantic experience count toward some ultimate accumulation, some reminiscence to treasure far out in the suburbs when the city at last is left behind. This is why in all the neighborhoods like Wicker Park these days, the young employeds hurry home off the evening el, clutching their Coach bags and cell phones, the tight toes of their shoes tap-tapping. And in the safety of their apartments they shed their constrictive disguises and reappear, no longer drones but dashing and sly, in their tight, gaudy, ill-fitting, carefully coordinated, and expensive designer swinger suits of polyester, stretch, and pleather, hurrying back toward the intersection, past the crackhead panhandlers who soon enough will be gone, toward the bright spangly nightclubs and bars. This is the time of celebration, of the solemn ironic party, and they walk down the dark sidewalks with great haste—the white-collar rebels with their carefully trimmed Van Dykes, the career gals in their important nostalgic shoes—pausing to raise their Zippos to their European smokes, yearning for the walls of their nightclubs, the carefully resurrected cocktail lounges crammed with martinis and cigars, tropes of youth and money ferried to them in the invisible hands of servers, camaraderie and good fellowship trailing gin vapors off the triangular heads of the frosted glasses. This is *their* time. On these evening streets they may brush past occasional former inhabitants of their neighborhood, the old codgers who still live in set-aside low-income housing on Damen, solid grandmas with grocery carts and walkers, crooked-eyed geezers who also wear too-tight synthetics, who might actually dimly recall gambling against Nelson Algren, who knew this city when it was really potent, cruising in their very slow way up the sidewalk, back to their small rooms, hurrying to get out of the way.

—BAFFLER 10, 1997

Afterword

An article in the June 1, 2002, issue of the *New York Times* hails a hot new theory of "creative capital" generated by Carnegie-Mellon professor Richard Florida: "Towns that have lots of gays and bohemians (by which he means authors, painters, musicians and other 'artistically creative people') are likely to thrive." Artist-led gentrification of the Wicker Park variety thus has a theory to go with it. Since authenticity-starved white-collar workers admire the edgy 'n' creative lifestyles enjoyed by artists, artists (if not their art) are now officially great for commerce. Zoning an area for pseudosubversive bohemians is no longer a joke; it's a serious policy consideration.

This fantasy of commodified deviance may sound laughable in theory—just try to imagine edgy performance artists saving Detroit, or modern dance troupes rescuing postindustrial cities like Hartford and Baltimore—but it has produced catastrophic results in Wicker Park. When this piece first appeared, certain parties were outraged by the suggestion that glamour-based real estate trends might somehow be detrimental to existing urban social structures. Five years later, the unchecked development of gated condominiums and franchise entertainment outlets has decimated Wicker Park's minority-owned businesses, as well as the neighborhood's venues for independent cultural consumption. Artists and musicians may have got the ball rolling here, but many of the art galleries and performance spaces are history, and the "creative people" themselves have long since departed for less mechanically boho neighborhoods. Wicker Park 2003 is an arid and pretentious place. By day, boutiques peddle pallid, pricey women's wear, while by night, middle-aged gourmands pose inside daringly themed restaurants. The neighborhood is then given over to a sleazy bacchanalia as collegiates and reckless twenty-somethings pack the bars and drink in the streets, providing in turn targets for the scammers and take-off artists who flock there each weekend.

15
McSploitation

JIM ARNDORFER

HUDDLED IN CHICAGO's neon-scarred River North tourist district, Fadò Irish Pub strains to pass for one of those quaint public houses common on postcards from the Old Sod. Its brightly painted façade, Celtic-lettered signage, and gimcrack-cluttered windows practically creak from the effort to project authenticity. The doorman who checks IDs typically has a brogue. All for naught, alas. None of these cosmetic touches can hide the fact Fadò stands three stories tall, a height completely unbecoming a humble Irish pub. Such bulk is more in the league of Fadò's neighbors—the Hard Rock Cafe, Planet Hollywood, and Rainforest Cafe.

Fadò—Gaelic for "long ago" and pronounced "F'doe"—is the history of Ireland as Disney would "imagineer" it: the past as a preindustrial idyll full of familiar, entertaining, and edifying scenery, with anything that might offend or trouble painstakingly excised. There are no paintings of Cromwell's butchery at Drogheda or reenactments of the Great Potato Famine here; indeed, nothing in Fadò explicitly indicates that for eight centuries Éire was occupied and often brutally exploited by the hated Saxon. None of that bummer blarney!

The prime mover behind the bar is Guinness Brewing—which is in fact a British company, part of the London-based conglomerate Diageo, which also owns Burger King, Pillsbury, and United Distillers & Vintners—so it probably sees little advantage in exhuming such unpleasant facts. Fadò would rather plunder the breadth of Irish history, from the Stone Age through the early twentieth century, to fabricate a pastiche past in which lighthearted bogtrotters worked hard, prayed hard, drank hard, sang songs, and bought quaint things with nary a grumble about their lot.

The past-as-playground rendition of Irish history unfolds as soon as you step inside. At the entrance a fake dolmen—a tablelike megalith prehistoric Irelanders would raise for the honored dead—towers over you. From there the ground level is split into three rooms supposedly representative of different eras in Irish history. First up is the Gaelic pub. Here you're to sip your pint, meditate on the murals decorating the light wood walls, and reach spiritual communion with the fun-loving Goidelic Celts who conquered Ireland around 500 B.C. and sang beautiful ballads when they weren't seizing slaves. A row of semisecluded wooden tables, calculatedly rough-hewn, clings to the east wall.

Moving on, customers enter the stone-walled Cottage Industries pub, which absurdly celebrates the subsistence economy of nineteenth-century rural Ireland. To commemorate that era of famine and want, Fadò has decorated the room with the now-quaint workaday implements of an economy that broke backs and drove hundreds of thousands to board ships for the perilous passage to Amerikay. A loom hangs from the ceiling; elsewhere can be found a spinning wheel, a butter churn, a washstand, farm tools, seed bags, and a collection of buckets and bottles.

The north end of the third story is devoted to the "Dublin Victorian Pub"—which celebrates the queen whose reign saw the Great Famine, two crushed insurrections, and the "dynamite campaign" in England—with luxurious dark woods, velvet curtains, and beveled glass. The area is dominated by a hundred-year-old, forty-piece bar shipped over from Ireland. Off to the sides are "snugs," the intimate booths favored by Irish characters and conspirators alike. A formidable collection of antique barrel taps hangs on the east wall.

Mixed with a few pints, these surroundings are intended to create what the Irish—and especially the marketers of Irishness—call *craic* (pronounced "crack"), a Gaelic word for a convivial atmosphere. Unfortunately, conversation is usually impossible because the sound system is unbearably loud, recycling the same tired hitlist of every pop sensation with even the faintest ties to Erin. Gaelicity assaults from all sides, making cogitation of any sort a futile endeavor. But the politicos, traveling businessmen, and young executives who jam the place don't seem to mind; they simply jostle and holler as if they were in a sports bar.

People choose to visit Fadò for the same reason they go to its theme-restaurant neighbors: They want to be immersed in an entertaining fantasy. The Rock and the Planet provide an escape into the world of celebrity; the Rainforest indulges a fashionable consumerist ecopolitics; Fadò offers a portal into white exoticism. It's the kind of fantasy Chicago has always done well. Consider the blues bar, long a fixture on Chicago's must-do tourist circuit and a virtual emporium of the exotic, even though you're more likely to share your table with a howling fratboy or glassy-eyed management consultant than a hard-bitten migrant from the Delta. A place like Fadò, on the other hand, affords the white American thrill-seeker an opportunity to wallow in maudlin sentimentality and exult in the illicit passions of a subaltern minority without embarrassing reminders of his own place in history—that is to say, without thinking about race. Ireland and Irishness fit such a need perfectly—not only for the more than forty million Americans who claim at least a wee bit of Irish blood, but for Celtophiles who see the Emerald Isle and its people as embodiments of old-fashioned clannishness and underdog pluck.

Irishness certainly is a desirable commodity. Once content to be Irish only on St. Patrick's Day, with all its antics, speechifying, and moronic uses of the color green, Americans—white ones, anyway—now demand more high-minded representations of the Gael. The culture industry has obliged. Michael Flatley has danced, live and on video with prerecorded taps, into the hearts of millions in the bombastic "Lord of the Dance." The New Age Celtic strains of the various *Titanic* soundtracks have served as background music for dinner parties coast to coast. Audiences have adored Edward Burns as the sexy bohemian with a heart of family values in *The Brothers McMullen*, and cried along with Matt Damon's sexy, two-fisted supergenius in *Good Will Hunting*. Frank McCourt's memoir of hunger in New York and Ireland, *Angela's Ashes*, won a Pulitzer Prize.

Marie Antoinette and her attendants played at being peasants; bored nineteenth-century English gentlemen idealized the sensuousness of Italy; Irishness sells to Americans because it represents authenticity and tradition in an often depressingly transient and hollow culture. Religion and faith are untroubled parts of "Irish" lives. Family bonds are strong. Neighbors know and help each other. Work is valued but so is play. Song and dance are in their blood—you saw how those Paddies got down in the *Titanic*'s steerage! Good conversation and a sly, authority-tweaking humor spring naturally from their lips. This perception is nothing new, of course: It was part of the vision of nineteenth-century Irish romantic nationalism and has been propagated ever since by the entertainment industry and the Irish Tourist Board. Only nowadays, deep-pocketed marketers have the latest in demographic marketing tools and segmentation strategies to cram this vision down our throats.

The accepted narrative of the Irish experience in America also bolsters the ideological foundation of the increasingly conservative body politic. In the New World, the Irish contended with bigotry and slaved at menial jobs, but by dint of hard work overcame all obstacles and assimilated into the respectable life of the suburbs and office cubicles. This myth of Irish advancement omits such important factors as political cronyism, the munificence of the New Deal, and the expansion of government, but it does promote self-satisfaction among white folks. If they could make it, the thinking goes, so can anyone. Unspoken but always understood is the contrast of the Irish narrative with that of the other major, if more threatening, exotic group in the United States: African-Americans. The historic travails of the two groups are often compared, and audiences everywhere nodded when a character in the 1991 film *The Commitments*, which told the story of an aspiring Dublin soul band, announced that the Irish were "the blacks of Europe." Of course, at some point the Irish in America "became white," in the words of Noel Ignatiev, but that doesn't figure in the story that *craic* peddlers want to tell.

2.

Beneath its folksy Hibernian veneer, Fadò is a cog in a global marketing strategy engineered by Guinness Brewing. Looking to boost sales of its renowned stout, the brewer has orchestrated an alliance of designers, developers, investors, and marketers in the mass production of a supposedly quintessential Irish institution: the pub.

In the late Eighties, Guinness noticed that Irish investors were making a killing with home-style pubs in France and Germany. Hungry to build its international market share, the brewer decided to get a piece of the Irish pub's new international vogue and create just the right atmosphere to coax skeptical foreign customers, Italian and Estonian alike, to ramp up their consumption of the strange black liquid. Guinness gave a name to its globe-spanning sales strategy: the Irish Pub Concept.

Guinness then started rounding up accomplices. It tapped chefs to design menus, hired recruiters to find appropriately accented bar staff, and commissioned the Irish Pub Company—a newly created subsidiary of Dublin-based McNally Design Group, an international planner and builder of restaurants, hotels, bowling alleys, and discos—to create cookie-cutter pub patterns. Irish Pub architects and researchers spent months visiting hundreds of pubs in Ireland, analyzing and cataloguing such minutiae as joinery details and floor finishes, all to quantify the essence of an Irish pub.

Before long pubs started springing up in Europe, the Middle East, and Asia, in cities from Dublin to Hong Kong. Guinness and its partners waited until 1995 before casting a cold eye across the western ocean to the world's largest beer market, the United States. Putting out feelers, Irish Pub initially encountered skepticism, partly because Irish bars had a bad rap in the States, where they're often seen either as cheesy fratboy hangouts or nondescript dives that draw illegal immigrants and IRA supporters. In fact, Irish Pub had to put up money for a showcase pub before it finally struck a deal with a group of Irish and American investors called Fadò Irish Pub Company. The first bar—named Fadò—opened in Atlanta in January 1996 and before long became one of the country's leading sales outlets for draft Guinness stout and Harp lager.

The designer chose Atlanta as its first site to demonstrate that a city doesn't need a large Irish population to support its establishments. Irish culture had a strong appeal among young professionals, tourists, and conventioneers of all backgrounds, and the Atlanta bar proved it. Fadò Irish Pub Company itself has gone on to open eponymous establishments in Austin, Texas; Washington, D.C.; Seattle; and Cleveland. The Chicago bar opened its doors in

November 1997. Guinness claims it has opened more than fourteen hundred Irish Pub Concept bars around the world.

As novel as the Irish Pub Concept may seem, it follows in the footsteps of a recent and rather unfortunate cultural phenomenon: the theme restaurant, two or three of which seem to occupy every block in River North, thanks to the tireless "vision" of Chicago entrepreneur Rich Melman. Melman got his start in the early Seventies, one of a few savvy restaurateurs who recognized that, in a culture saturated by the entertainment industry and electronic media, there was money to be made by injecting elements of theater and carnival into "the dining experience." He opened his first establishment, R. J. Grunt's, in 1971. Grunt's offered an offbeat, casual vibe with its hanging plants, modern art, and that definitive gustatory innovation of the decade: the salad bar. Catering to the groovy young singles then gentrifying the Lincoln Park neighborhood, the place was a hit.

In the Seventies, restaurants typically needed only to be clean and serve decent food to make a buck. Now it's difficult to find a restaurant not animated by an entertainment concept. When people step into a restaurant these days, they expect to enter a different world. Sometimes, of course, that world is one better left in the dustbin of history, as in the case of the popular Le Colonial chain, which sumptuously evokes the languid, sensuous milieu of French Indochina in the Twenties, with bamboo fittings, lazy ceiling fans, and sepia-tinted photographs of peasants carrying water, harvesting rice, and hefting a sweating, porcine worthy in a sedan chair. The pictures, one gathers, are the next best thing to staffing the joint with real peons. The self-impressed patrons of Le Colonial would hardly be likely to endorse the viciousness of the French regime in Indochina, yet the nostalgia for an era of entitlement, deference, and abject servitude dovetails nicely with the leitmotifs of our own time: the polarization of rich and poor, the no-excess-is-too-absurd imperative to please that is imposed on service-industry employees.

At Fadò, the staff plays along gamely in the bar's exaggerated effort to convince its customers that they are experiencing something other than a denatured spectacle called into being by transnational investors. They proudly boast that the chairs you sit on, the bar you lean on, and the floors you tread upon all were made in Ireland. No one really seems to mind, or even acknowledge, the irony that this "quaint Irish pub" is a very modern creation brought into being by the sorts of large conglomerates that are destroying local institutions ranging from the drugstore to the butcher shop. Everyone's too enthralled with the "authenticity" of the Made in Ireland surroundings and the fun of playing at Irishness; on every visit to Fadò I have either heard someone ape a brogue or seen someone break into a half-assed jig.

Where's the harm in that? Hasn't Ireland been inundated for decades by millions upon millions of Americans searching for their roots, for the Blarney Stone, for the Book of Kells, for 7 Eccles Street? Millions of long-lost and annoying cousins, boring you with stories about their granny from Kerry and trying out their Hollywood brogues and donning their Aran sweaters and tweed flatcaps. And spending billions of dollars. Moreover, isn't the "Celtic Tiger," Ireland's vaunted high-tech and service-economy boom, the tourist trade writ digital?

Ironically, one gets a sense of the real Ireland's predicament in Fadò's re-creation of a post office/grocery/bar supposedly typical of rural Ireland. A telephone switchboard is set in a corner, and stacked on the shelves are boxes of Jacobs cream crackers and Oxo cubes, bags of Mosse's brown bread mix and jars of Fruitfield marmalade. Adverts for Players cigarettes, Marsh Co.'s biscuits, and Wills's Cut Gold Bar tobacco hang on the walls. The whole room effectively subdivides Ireland into brand names. It's the way America understands the world these days.

I once saw, behind the majestic Victorian mahogany bar, two bartenders arguing—Arguing! How wonderfully Irish!—over which artifacts in the pub were authentic antiques and which ones were newly minted and artificially aged impostors. The debate lasted for some time with neither side yielding—another indubitably Irish characteristic. But the disagreement raised a new question: Is Ireland the country doomed forever to live in the shadow of Ireland the brand?

—BAFFLER 12, 1999

16

Rockerdämmerung

Mike O'Flaherty

EDITOR'S NOTE: The slow decline of rock music was one of the most significant cultural shifts of the Nineties. In 1988, according to the Recording Industry Association of America, rock music accounted for a robust 42.6 percent of recordings sold in the United States. And that was a bad year. By the year 2000, rock's market share had dwindled to a feeble 24.8 percent. Ironically, rock collapsed even after the recording industry, in some desperation, had opened its doors to punk and indie rock, genres that had long been excluded from the commercial mainstream. In the following story, Mike O'Flaherty linked the two events—the rise of "alternative" and the fall of rock—by focusing on the content of the indie-rock subculture as it developed over the years. By the early Nineties, when the industry was ready to make its assault on this last frontier of avant-garde experimentation, that avant-garde—for reasons of its own—was ready to surrender. The result has been terminal, irreversible aesthetic stagnation.

WHILE "LATE" CAPITALISM has failed to deal the long-promised deathblows to "ideology" and "history," it did manage a trick that likely took even Francis Fukuyama by surprise: It has killed rock 'n' roll. There was an eerie parallel between the fate of rock's avant-garde and that of the former Soviet Union in the Nineties. The moment of truth came in 1991, when the Soviet Union dissolved itself and loud rock band Nirvana's major-label debut, *Nevermind*, hit Number One on the charts. The "indie rock" scene and the Soviet Union had both defined themselves by their opposition to monopoly capital.[1] Now their vast and hitherto-untapped resources were available for exploitation—or, in the more reciprocal language favored by both IMF officials and recording-industry A&R men, "development." In both cases the corporate overlords were full of hope that their new friends would provide the growth necessary to stave off crisis and stagnation. But in both cases the lucrative new properties were squandered and laid to waste.

At the dawn of the Nineties the Big Six[2] corporations that dominate the recording industry faced the prospect of a protracted sales slump on the order of the 1979–82 postdisco debacle. The industry had managed to recover from that slump by cramming the Top 40 with appropriated black and British styles, but by the end of the Eighties these, too, were bland and codified and yielded diminishing returns. The handful of media-saturated superstars who had so recently served as public symbols of the industry's recovery were (with the exception of Madonna) proving unable to retain audiences as stable and profitable as those of their "classic rock" predecessors.

The fate of the recovery's third element, heavy metal, was more complicated. During the Eighties, the metal audience had bifurcated into rock ("thrash") and pop ("glam") factions. Thrash's purist extremism of form and content deliberately lim-

[1] The term "indie rock" will here denote music derived from punk rock (though often by a few degrees of separation); released on a record label not owned outright by the Big Six record companies; and rooted to some extent in rock forms while investing them with an eccentricity or abrasiveness alien to the mainstream, major-label rock of the moment.

[2] The Big Six, at the time, were Warner-Electra-Atlantic (WEA), Sony (formerly CBS), BMG (formerly RCA), Polygram, Universal (formerly MCA), and Thorn-EMI. Polygram and BMG merged in 1998; then there were five.

ited its sales reach. But that purist extremism also did terrible damage to glam's street cred: It made glam look "fake" by comparison. Something more commercially palatable than thrash would have to be found to take advantage of glam's yawning authenticity gap.

Punk rock did not seem a likely candidate to save the recording industry in the Nineties. In fact, punk's complete commercial failure, along with that of nearly all the early "postpunk" and "new wave" acts, played a considerable role in precipitating the 1979–82 industry bust. Like thrash metal, punk functioned entirely as a negative genre, returning nothing financially but inflicting grievous credibility wounds on such proven bottom-line performers as disco and album-oriented rock (or "AOR," the once-vanguard format that had ossified almost instantly into "classic rock"). But while thrash had carved out a small but profitable subculture niche within the labyrinth of the Big Six, punk and its immediate successors went nowhere commercially. True, a group of vaguely postpunk acts tailored for major-label success ("new wave") had once generated some income for the Big Six, but each succeeding wave of signings from the postpunk underground met the same disastrous commercial fate as that of the punk founders, usually losing their original audience to boot.

Then, in the guise of Nirvana and a few "Alternative"[3] satellites, punk rock finally paid its debt to society. It made its peace with the market. The original punks (and their truest successors) had declared war on all other music subcultures, and those audiences had responded in kind. Alternative promised precisely the reverse: The new sound seemed to offer something for everybody.

3 "Alternative" as a musical genre has been most narrowly defined as a slick commercial version of the late-Eighties "Seattle sound" associated with the indie label Sub Pop—a sound that grafted dissonant, plodding postpunk guitar grind onto song structures derived from early-Seventies hard rock. Though this was indeed the dominant strain, Alternative actually comprised various slick commercial versions of nearly the full gamut of late-Eighties indie rock.

To hard-rock devotees, it combined the street cred, heaviness, and speed of thrash with glam's pop feel and Seventies trad-rock familiarity; in other words, it promised a return to what metal had been before the great glam/thrash schism. To new-wave trendy types—the people who were "alternative" before alternative was Alternative—it offered the frisson of apparent avant-gardism and a new and insurgent wardrobe to match. To hippies of all ages still high on the myth of rock as youth movement, it offered the prospect of an antiestablishment white youth music with genuine mass appeal for perhaps the first time since Altamont. And to the Big Six, it offered more than just a way out of a slump: This was nothing less than the new paradigm, a *renewal.* A new constellation of stars was called for, both big and small, along with fresh styles of publicity and a cornucopia of lifestyle tie-ins. Along with hip-hop, which was finally breaking commercially around this time, and the CD's replacement of vinyl LPs, Alternative solved several problems at once.

INDEPENDENT AMERICAN PUNK ROCK had begun the Eighties dedicated to the destruction of the corporate music industry and the political and aesthetic values for which it stood. Ten years later, now calling itself "Alternative," it was playing a crucial role in saving the Big Six from economic collapse. What happened?

From its very inception, British punk rock had aimed to free itself from the production and distribution networks of the Big Six. The early British independent labels—such as Raw, Beggars Banquet, Step Forward, and dozens of others too tiny and ephemeral to be remembered—formed as a matter of grass-roots pragmatism, essentially to accommodate the punks' fleeting and careless enthusiasms; you didn't have to wait to be "discovered." Oddly enough, most of these labels fell victim to punk's very success. The genre's supernova—the salad days of 1977 when it seemed that punk was going to destroy or absorb the Big Six on its own terms—appeared to vitiate the need to maintain and nurture independent labels for their own sake.

The Sex Pistols' spectacular auto-destruction,[4] however, gave independence a new significance and a new political charge. A crucial portion of the British punk movement concluded that the celebrity framework into which the Pistols had been fitted trivialized their politics of confrontation into a circus of self-destructive outrage. These "postpunks" now regarded indie labels as permanent counterinstitutions in explicit opposition to the Big Six. Though American record collectors may not know it, the postpunk labels (particularly the greatest of them, London's Rough Trade) were thus part of the tide of political radicalism that swept Britain in 1978–79 and culminated in a massive strike wave that shut the country down. Rough Trade people were active in the SWP, a powerful Trotskyist caucus in the Labor Party. Political radicalism was built into the postpunk model, and its implications would reverberate through American indie in the big sleep of the Reagan years like a half-remembered promise.

American indie labels more or less followed in the footsteps of their British peers. American punk bands courted by fashion-conscious A&R men in 1977 were abruptly abandoned the following year, and no further offers were forthcoming. As with early British punk, the first wave of American punk went the indie route simply because nobody else was willing to release their work. Before long, though, the most prominent and emblematic American indie labels (Homestead and SST, among others) embraced the postpunk model of secession and opposition to the majors.

[4] Disgusted by manager Malcolm McLaren's increasing use of cheap publicity stunts, as well as his attempts to screw the band members financially, singer Johnny Rotten abruptly quit the Sex Pistols in January 1978, immediately after the last show of their chaotic American tour. (His parting remark to the audience: "Ever have the feeling you've been cheated?") In one fell swoop Rotten deprived the record industry of one of the leading icons on which the marketing of punk would have depended.

Southern California was far and away America's most prolific and inventive punk scene during the crucial few years following 1978. In response to what seemed a permanent quarantine by the Big Six, Southern Californians developed American punk's first durable institutions and elaborated the affectingly quixotic worldview punk would bequeath to indie rock: a tenacious adherence to unrealizable utopian aspirations, and a principled commitment to "action," no matter how ineffectual or absurd. The early LA scene took comfort, even reveled, in its own absurdity. It had to; while poverty and political upheaval were palpable to their British counterparts, American punks repined in sunny, suffocating prosperity and near-universal political apathy. There, at the heart of the American empire, the mass-cultural contradictions of Seventies America reached a point of hysterical exaggeration: A cult of "niceness" and bland self-indulgence strained to hold back the numbing fear that the economic and military walls protecting the prosperity and security of the great American middle were crumbling. The early LA punks cheered on the collapse, hoping for a new world of danger and surprise, of extreme sensations and emotions. They didn't make many friends around town.

LA punk turned social isolation itself into a virtue. The thrill of secrecy, something utterly alien to the British style, was a recurring theme (consider X's "The Unheard Music" and the Germs' "What We Do Is Secret"). This, too, became a crucial element of what American indie was all about. In the rosy-fingered dawn of hip capitalism, anything you could think of was now a marketable commodity, and overexposure domesticated even the most shocking features of contemporary life: the neutron bomb, Three Mile Island, brutal pornography, and the Sex Pistols. If you wanted to find LA punk (and indie rock after it), you had to discover it. Secrecy restored mystery and adventure to a numbingly familiar world: What looked like an abandoned porn theater was actually the venue where the police- and club-banned Germs were playing tonight under a pseudonym.

But secrecy did not mean secession. The punks were looking out at the world from their hiding places, and the LA punk world was itself a kind of looking-glass version of the "real" world: Familiar social and cultural styles were grotesquely mimicked and put to perverse and idiosyncratic uses. The greatest inversion of all—and the one that survived longest as punk turned to indie and gradually accommodated itself to the outside world—was to find such inventive and audacious work being done in a format as seemingly banal and familiar as rock. It was this feeling of having stumbled into looking-glass land that gave the discovery of punk (and later indie, when it was good) its thrill, whether one found out about it through a friend, a record store, an all-ages show, a fanzine, a radio station, whatever. Punk showed you what the "real" world really looked like.

This impact was made possible by a restless formal adventurousness that in three years took LA punk far beyond its initial British models. The new formal language came to be called "hardcore." Above all it meant playing fast, but the new demands posed by speed forced the musicians to take previously unthinkable liberties with song structure. Melody and comprehensible lyrics were discarded when they got in the way. Songs sped up and slowed down suddenly, ended in the middle of a verse, inverted their chord progressions halfway through. Where previously most punk (to say nothing of the rest of rock) had tried to express original ideas via an inherited, unexamined formal language, now those forms could be adjusted to fit the ideas. If you had a ten-second idea, you could write a ten-second song.

Hardcore expressed a newly comfortable and honest sense of place and identity, no matter how "uncool" such subjects were. This enabled the music to rapidly break out of the bohemian ghetto, where most American punk had previously been confined, and travel to D.C., Boston, and the Midwest. The first full-fledged LA hardcore records appeared in 1980; a mere two years later, dozens of bands, such as D.C.'s Void, Michigan's Negative Approach, and

Boston's SS Decontrol, were releasing records that surpassed most of the LA originators in stylistic daring and sonic extremism. Hardcore gave a potentially huge group of suburban kids a language to engage directly with their specific social context, rather than some faux-universal music-industry fantasy that had nothing to do with anybody's ordinary life. The genre's exclusion by the Big Six created a space for both local scenes and the American punk independent labels, such as LA's SST, Michigan's Touch and Go, and D.C.'s Dischord. And hardcore framed its mutual hostility with the Big Six in the context of its larger hostility to the emerging social world of Reaganite America, a world the hardcore kids knew with the intimacy of a personal grudge: Transnational corporations sold narcotizing pop music to their mall-mad peers and transferred the profits to their missile-development subsidiaries.

Hardcore's radicalism, though, soon began to sound as prefabricated as corporate rock itself, and it quickly degenerated into predictable formula. But hardcore's free-ranging hostility and ruthless self-consciousness also inspired its smartest adherents to go still further in challenging the audience and themselves. Think of Minor Threat's obsessive *jihad* against that most intimate and hallowed of rock rituals, getting fucked-up before the show; or Flipper playing as slow as they could for audiences who'd come to expect high-speed background noise suitable for the mosh pit. Indie rock had arrived.

Unlike hardcore, "indie rock" did not have a single distinctive sound; in fact, it emerged largely as a reaction to hardcore's increasing stylistic rigidity. The common thread uniting the archetypal LPs that the Minutemen, Hüsker Dü, and the Replacements made in indie's watershed year, 1984, is an almost manic eclecticism, ranging from eerie drumless interludes to ragged noise-gush. Indie's aesthetic ideals—musical originality and expression of a personal but compelling worldview—were so banal that scenesters were often embarrassed to state them explicitly, but for once the music itself more than vindicated them.

At the same time, though, the move from hardcore to indie saw the first glimmerings of aesthetic deradicalization that would later explode with Alternative. Reasoning that bad music reflected a dysfunctional society and culture, punk and hardcore bands had built impressive solidarity around an explicit rejection of commercial rock and its trappings—especially rock's Sixties-era mystique of individual genius. Indie rock smuggled a sort of star system back into the underground. Where the leading indie labels, such as SST and Homestead, once had documented the constantly shifting cast of characters of a local scene, they now focused, naturally enough, on the long-term development of a handful of outstanding artists with no relationship other than their label affiliation. And where hardcore had constituted itself as a self-contained counterworld—the Big Six's absolute negative mirror-image—indie's rock fusionists discovered that they could create music that resembled familiar rock styles but was "better" (an impression reinforced by rave reviews from mainstream rock critics who had ignored or despised punk and hardcore). The Big Six noticed the shift, and by the mid-Eighties they began to express interest.

Two of the best and most prominent early indie bands, Minneapolis's Hüsker Dü and the Replacements, made major-label deals in 1985, and the indie scene observed their unfolding fate with no small interest. Hüsker Dü's music was becoming gradually more timid and circumspect even before they were signed by Warner Bros. The band's lyrics moved away from engagement with the social world and toward more "personal" concerns; in mainstream rock culture this move is traditionally associated with increased "maturity," and so it was hailed by the mainstream rock press. At the same time, though, the band's increasing lyrical introversion was accompanied by growing formal complacency and diminished passion in performance. The Replacements' stylistic shift was even more dramatic—so much so that many fans suspected they'd been coerced by Sire into changing their sound: By their second major-label release the once-chaotic band was playing "tight," Stonesy bar-band rock. The band itself seemed deeply confused about what it wanted. The video for their first Sire single, "Bastards of Young," consisted entirely of a static shot of a record player; but this visual middle finger to the Big Six (and MTV) was cover for what seemed a blatant attempt on singer Paul Westerberg's part to write a catchy youth anthem.

A humiliated indie-rock audience responded by vehemently rejecting everything those bands were imagined to stand for. The use of traditional rock forms quickly became deeply suspect, and the genre's leadership passed to a handful of more experimental bands like Sonic Youth, Big Black, and the Butthole Surfers. At the most basic level, audiences turned against nothing less than the Minneapolis bands' heart-on-my-sleeve sincerity, which now seemed more than ever to dovetail with familiar classic-rock banalities (think Bob Seger). Savvier musicians abandoned emotion for sensation—the purer and more wrenching the better—and the confessional for an ambiguity that left tantalizingly open the degree of the artist's identification with his or her (often unsavory) subject.

In many ways this change improved indie rock immeasurably. The new music restored an element of confrontation with the audience. The musicians seemed to have a homing instinct for the most brutally physical aspects of every previous punk and post-punk genre; they fused them into a sound of unprecedented force and visceral pleasure. In terms of sheer stylistic sophistication and formal command, punk and indie reached their pinnacle during the second half of the Eighties. But there were problems as well, complications that eventually would prove fatal. The best bands (think of Pussy Galore) seemed to be those who were most obsessive and extreme in developing some aspect of indie rock's formal language to its logical end point.

The indie scene's disengagement from the social world continued, even accelerated; increasingly, the main subject and interest of indie rock was indie rock. Even politics soon seemed just another variety of the hated "sincerity." About the only credible attitude left for the knowing yet aspiring rocker was irony: embracing illicit social identities, banal musical styles, and so forth, then leaving it up to the audience to decide how seriously to take it. It was a delicate balancing act, and some were undone by their own posturing. Perhaps the most dramatic such instance was the fate of the Dwarves, a band that fastidiously cultivated a reputation for violence in both music and behavior. In 1993 the band announced to the world that its guitarist had been stabbed to death. It soon emerged that he had merely left the group; the remaining Dwarves apparently had decided to use his departure to enhance their menacing legend. Enraged, Sub Pop dropped them in the very year the label's famous alums Nirvana were completing their conquest of mainstream rock. The two events form an eerily appropriate capstone to the indie-rock era.

Indie rock's ironic style was useful, initially, as a kind of game of intellectual "chicken": The threat of being informed that the latest hip thing they'd fervently embraced was actually a joke at their expense might (in theory) lead people to think harder about what they really liked and why. However, in its increasing insularity and disengagement, the indie scene was less inclined to use irony as a critical weapon than to make it a snotty parlor trick. As it was, indie-rock irony rapidly took the path of least resistance: You could sidestep composer's block—or the absence of talent, as the case may be—by retreating to banal forms comfortably familiar to you and your audience and claiming that it was actually a wry comment on rock's formal impasse. Punk and hardcore had used sarcasm, but almost naively, as a way of expressing strongly held opinions. Indie-rock irony, by contrast, belied a fear above all of embarrassment, of being passionate or holding any convictions—of not being cool.

Perhaps the saddest example of this phenomenon was the career of Urge Overkill. On their earlier records, such as 1989's *Jesus Urge Superstar*, Urge deployed the mildewed, time-ridiculed sounds of Seventies "classic" rock to conjure up a world of the forlorn and forgotten and vanished. Slowly but surely, however, Urge shifted from using Seventies rock trappings (and funny Seventies clothes and funny Seventies tastes) as an expression of an idiosyncratic worldview to using those trappings because they afforded cheap, lazy "fun" to performers and audience alike. It was a horrible thing to witness, like watching a suit absorb its wearer. There was still the occasional great song, but the prospect of actual rock-stardom eroded the protective irony that had precariously elevated Urge over the cesspool of their cheesy source material. In 1993, Urge released a major-label debut that, but for its glossy Nineties production and a few witty lyrics, was indistinguishable from the most banal Seventies hard rock. The band had outsmarted itself: It was now too palpably fake and corny to click fully with the authenticity-obsessed alternakids.

Nevertheless, all indie-rock ironies seemed to lead back to the Seventies. Traveling by quite a different road than Urge Overkill, Seattle bands Green River and Soundgarden (both of whom issued records on the Sub Pop label) made their own discovery of Seventies-style hard rock and metal. Within a year the style was epidemic, at least in the Pacific Northwest. Sub Pop quickly became a household word in indieland. It was a return to the womb, with all the comfortable insularity and effortless self-gratification that implied.

Irony ultimately made the crucial difference in indie rock's long-awaited commercial breakthrough as Alternative. Audiences had already been acclimated, of course, to traditional rock styles, and they appreciated the punk and indie seasoning the new bands provided to make them seem so fresh. But more than that: Irony killed the scene's obsessive suspicion of betrayal that had been so evident during the Hüsker Dü/Replacements debacle and substituted a confident sense that the artist was eternally distanced from his or her actions, or their consequences. In the most generic descriptive terms, these bands were making commercially accessible rock music for the Big Six. But the ironic sensibility could explain this as a mocking commentary on same—or (if you were really smart) a bold critique of the hypocrisy of those who claimed to be above such things. Even Nirvana, whose appeal arose from their apparent sincerity, were suffused in irony. True, when contrasted with the prepackaged shit-rock of the late Eighties, their authenticity was obvious. But for those rooted in the indie-rock world—like Nirvana themselves—their success was hardly a clear-cut victory for those who would keep it real: How could Nirvana claim to be sincere when they were now laboring for the very industry that had manufactured the fakes they were now replacing? The band dealt with this problem by drawing on classic indie ironic distancing, appearing in public in "Corporate Rock Whores" T-shirts and so on. Their sound, meanwhile, landed somewhere between mid-Eighties Minneapolis and late-Eighties Seattle. While this tension arguably contributed to the quality of the music, the tragic consequences of Kurt Cobain's balancing act are a matter of public record.

Urge's experience—the sudden raising of commercial hopes to levels unthinkable in the indie Eighties, followed by the rapid obliteration of those hopes along with the bands themselves—epitomized the trajectory of Alternative in the first half of the Nineties. Nirvana's major-label debut *Nevermind*, released in the fall of 1991 to little media fanfare, had topped the *Billboard* charts by Christmas. At the time the breakthrough seemed like a fluke, or a miracle. America's cultural punditocracy was baffled. It was quickly agreed that this had something to do with "disaffected youth" (one had seen this sort of thing before), that these kids resented their hippie/yuppie parents, that they adored flannel and opiates. But as the media catalogue of alleged Alternative paraphernalia expanded, it became less and less clear what (if anything) it added up to—one could make a case that virtually anything was part of such an amorphous entity.

Certainly the Big Six felt themselves on unfamiliar ground; rather than be caught napping by the next unpredictable development of this new popular taste, it was better to be on the safe side and sign everybody. By 1993, acts whose terminal idiosyncrasy and blatant listener-unfriendliness had long been running jokes even within the indie scene now found themselves uneasily ensconced in some Big Six sinecure. I remember well my own shock and amusement in the summer of 1994 when I discovered, at Tower Records in New York City, that Daniel Johnston—an artist then best known for violently erratic public behavior, frequent hospitalization for mental "issues," fervent claims of divine inspiration, and wonderful home recordings that tended to evoke a PCP-addled ten-year-old warbling into a handheld tape recorder over his dad's polka records—now dwelt in the hallowed stables of Atlantic Records, an organization known for such pillars of music-industry tradition as Otis Redding, Led Zeppelin, and Bobby Darin.

By 1994, Alternative had swept up a large portion of the indie scene into its temporarily triumphant crusade for total dominance of the youth market. Optimists saw the triumph of Alternative as a triumph for the punk-rock ethos, which had given birth to indie and, through it, to Alternative; as if the seed of the Sex Pistols, kept alive through the years by indie rock, was now flowering under the sun of mass success. Prominent critics such as Eric Weisbard and Gina Arnold argued that Nirvana's success had grafted indie-rock values onto the corporate record industry and even had progressive political ramifications in the world beyond music. In reality Alternative worked a complete inversion of punk-rock values. Stylistic adventurousness faded as each Alternative success magnetically drew other bands to tailor their sound to the proven formula. Regional distinctions dissolved as bands competed in a homogeneous national market and local scenes were signed up en masse before they'd even had a chance to develop a coherent collective identity. And Alternative's lack of engagement with the outside world was so complete that the very distinction between private angst and social criticism was blurred. On those rare occasions when Alternative figures addressed concrete social or political issues, their pronouncements were indistinguishable from the smug liberal platitudes traditionally associated with the aging Sixties mafia who still set the cultural tone of the record industry. Contempt for the past gradually stripped indie rock of the punk-derived core values that made it worth caring about in the first place. And it was no accident that what replaced them—Alternative—was so compatible with the values of the entertainment industry. Planned obsolescence, the promise of the new and improved, the sneer of willful cultural amnesia—these are the values of the marketplace, radical only in their destructiveness.

INDIE ROCK still exists, sort of. A large minority within the indie scene was not able or willing to get signed; unfortunately, it almost seems as if they decided to fend off cooptation by making their music as repellently self-indulgent as possible. But the inventive formal sense that once redeemed those tendencies has vanished. Indie rock still draws on other musics, but it now does so with the listless dilettantism of a yuppie browsing through the ethnic-foods section at Treasure Island. Punk and its truest indie descendants wanted to destroy and replace the rest of rock music because it was part of a world against which they had declared war. Indie rock now seems driven by a quest to find a safe hiding place away from rock music and the outside world itself.

Still, you can hardly blame indie for wanting to have nothing to do with rock music. What punk failed to do despite years of conscious effort—destroy mainstream rock music—Alternative did inadvertently. Post-hippie rock acts had kept their audiences happy by keeping their expectations low. They promised to provide the hedonistic familiarity of Zep/Stones–derived rock music, and that's what they delivered. Alternative promised a full-blown cultural revolution, and it delivered . . . the hedonistic familiarity of Zep/Stones-derived rock music. By 1996 Alternative suffered from a "credibility gap" of rock-historical magnitude. Having abandoned indie's formal ingenuity, the already stultifyingly formulaic Alternative scene degenerated rapidly into pathetic self-parody. Lionized in the media as the voice of a new generation, Alternative believed its own hype, abandoning the wit and realism of punks whose genuine engagement with the world around them made them self-conscious of the absurd aspects of their project. By the time the solipsism and deliberate vagueness of its putative youth radicalism became impossible to hide, Alternative's political pretensions had been so inflated that it proved impossible to retract them with any grace. This only added to the utter public humiliation its various artists suffered on the way to oblivion.

Alternative's sales curve was plunging by 1996, and it has not recovered. Nor has any other rock subgenre taken its place commercially. And for the first time in rock history, long-term recovery seems uncertain: The mass white youth market that sustained the various rock subgenres for a quarter of a century has largely abandoned rock altogether for hip-hop or R&B.

IF INDIE ROCK has a future, it lies in the cultivation of a sense of its own past. The bands grouped around the Olympia, Washington, indie label Kill Rock Stars, for example, embody everything that's still good about indie rock. The KRS bands could easily have signed on with the Big Six during the "riot grrl" moment a few years ago, yet not one of them has ever defected to the majors: The bands see themselves as part of a specific, ongoing radical political subculture (feminism filtered through punk autonomism) and regional music scene, of which the KRS label is an integral part. When the Kill Rock Stars scene started, there were perhaps fewer women involved in punk or indie rock than ever before, but punk's ancient history offered the examples of Poly Styrene, Penelope Houston, and others, and the KRS bands built on what they'd begun. The problem they faced is one that confronts all radicals today: the dead vacancy of the present culture, which consigns the past to the "dustbin of history," the better to lay infinite claim to the future. All around the world, people are losing their ability to imagine anything outside the eternal present of a transnational corporate capitalism the depth and breadth of which now seems virtually limitless. And they are beginning to forget that anyone ever imagined something beyond it.

In the late Seventies, the punks demanded far more than we even dare to imagine now, and behind them lay more than a century of politics and art built on the idea that people can think and build far beyond the limits of the present. That expansive social imagination may be moribund now; we laugh at the conceit that a mass-market rock subculture can become the functional equivalent of a social or political movement. If a few million people care mildly about an art that advocates some conveniently vague "rebelliousness," it means nothing; their lives are barely touched by it. But if a few thousand people care deeply about an art that challenges them to question everything about the world around them and shows them that they have the power to make something different and better out of it, they may be inspired to transport that imaginative power from art to a project of real political and social change. At the very least they will see and feel more of the world they live in; the depth and creativity of their engagement with it will be immeasurably enhanced. And that's also a beginning.

—BAFFLER 12, 1999

Afterword

Ironically, the death of the rock avant-garde undeniably has improved mainstream pop. Bands such as the White Stripes and the Hives play guitar sounds more off-kilter and abrasive than any heard on major-label releases since the late Seventies. But the impulse behind this stuff is a kind of revivalism, and the music feels too familiar, too calculated to constitute a real breakthrough.

Still, accusations of "sell-out" from indie rockers ring hollow in this case, because the music of these bands is no different, no better or worse, and certainly no more or less original than the majority of contemporary indie rock. Not much has changed there since the end of the Nineties: The leaders of the various indie subgenres continue to do the same thing with an unadventurous professionalism that differs little from the practices of major-label bands. The only difference is that it is now aimed at grad students rather than undergrads. As President Dwight D. Eisenhower once said, "Things are more like they are now than they ever have been before."

17

The Brand Called Shmoo

Li'l Abner from Left to Right

Dan Raeburn

Al Capp was the most celebrated cartoonist of the American twentieth century. Once upon a time he was even the toast of the liberal intellectual world, whose inhabitants saw Capp's daily comic strip, *Li'l Abner*, as rich populist satire. For them Capp was a witty warrior whose pen stabbed the bloated plutocrats lording it over the downtrodden. Years of this kind of populism made Capp a wealthy man. But by the time Capp's career ended in the early Seventies, he had switched sides, becoming the comic Lancelot of the Right. Pundits still praised him as a defender of the average man, but now Capp was going after a different elite: the loony, high-horse student left, those comfy Ivy Leaguers who rode roughshod over us humble commoners of the "Silent Majority." Al Capp began his career as the FDR of the funny pages and ended it as their George Wallace.

Or so the story goes. Capp's left-to-right, head-to-tail flip is the standard narrative one encounters in the various biographies of the cartoonist, and the big question raised by Capp's conversion to the right in the Sixties—namely, why did it happen?—is the toss-up put to the reader by Alexander Theroux in *The Enigma of Al Capp* (Fantagraphics, 1999). Unfortunately, Theroux never decides exactly why Capp changed sides. He comes closest to a convincing explanation when he focuses, as do all Capp's biographers, on Capp's wooden leg as the man's lifelong curse and a symbol for all the insecurity and resentment his impoverished youth bred in him. Using what we might call the wooden-leg-as-Rosebud theory, and running through a list of Capp's other personal disappointments, Theroux retells the usual Capp narrative—that of the eventually curdled sourpuss whose acidic comics were once upon a time sweetened with a little more of the milk of human kindness. According to Theroux, the left lost something great, something almost revolutionary, when it lost Al Capp. "Underneath [*Li'l Abner*'s satire] is social seriousness if not solemnity, and, if it's not an oxymoron, almost Marxist humor," Theroux notes. "It's my belief that the comic strip *Li'l Abner* is one long fable about greed."

To use a word of Capp's own invention, this is hogwash. While it's true that *Li'l Abner* can be read as one long fable about greed, the greed in question was Al Capp's own. As is so often the case, the seemingly irreconcilable left and right sides of Al Capp's politics were really flip sides of our only coin: money.

Like almost everyone else who has written about Capp, Theroux assumes that his subject changed in some fundamental way, and that this change is what explains his political shift. But Capp himself maintained until the end that he had always been the same man; that society, not he, had changed. The truth is, Al Capp did not turn into a bitter, greedy asshole in the Sixties—he was *always* a bitter, greedy asshole. Any fairly critical look at Capp's life and a trudge through Capp's funnies forces upon one the obvious truth that, in the earliest of the culture wars, Al Capp was not a knight but a mercenary. Capp himself put it best when a student asked him what had inspired him to draw a comic strip about hillbillies: "Money," Capp barked.

Viewed from a sociopolitical perspective, Capp's story was that of the middle class's endless fascination with the authentic, unwashed culture of the common man; that of the inflated prices intellectuals will pay for cultural populism of almost any kind. From a personal perspective, Capp's story is a tellingly hollow example of the all-American rags-to-riches fable. Capp's biographers tell the story of Al Capp's victory over poverty, but they often ignore the less-obvious story of poverty's victory over Al Capp.

ALFRED GERALD CAPLIN was born in the first years of the twentieth century, a poor Jewish boy on the ghetto side of New Haven. Class resentment seems to have dogged him from the beginning. Although his family moved constantly, Alfred grew up always in the metaphorical shadow of Yale, the upper-class fortress that haunted his entire life. When he was nine years old a streetcar ran over him and severed one of his legs. Because Alfred loathed walking on his wooden leg, his brother and friends tugged him in a wagon when they made their self-described "Robin Hood raids" on the local Woolworth's—stealing pocket knives, cheap jewelry, and kewpie dolls. In adolescence Alfred would play the part of a Yalie alter ego he had invented, the scruffy-genteel Alfred Von Schuyler, in various ill-fated attempts to seduce powdered and pampered girls from the upper crust. After dropping out of several art schools Alfred began a career as a cartoonist assisting Ham Fisher, creator of *Joe Palooka*. It was during this period of plodding poverty, at the very pit of the Great Depression, that Caplin hit on the idea of making fun of poor people. After he saw a hillbilly revue in a New York vaudeville house, Caplin changed his name to Al Capp and began drawing hillbillies—lazy white people who were poor as dirt, dumb as dirt, and who, like their equally imaginary black counterparts, said "Shonuff." Sure enough, the idea caught on. Al Capp struck gold in them thar hills.

The popularity not just of *Li'l Abner* but of all cartoons in those years is almost inconceivable today. The comics were postwar America's most popular art—as Capp himself noted in an essay he wrote for a supplement to the 1946 *Encyclopædia Britannica*—and by Capp's peak in the early Fifties, *Li'l Abner* was the most popular strip of them all. More than ninety million Americans read *Li'l Abner* every single day of their lives; in quantitative terms this made Al Capp the most important artist in America. Only the arrival of the Beatles a decade later can compare to the chorus of oohs and aahs that rose and fell with the vacillating fortunes of Capp's cornpone heroes, the Yokum family.

Today, only twenty-five years after his retirement, Capp is largely forgotten and for good reason. The only thing about *Li'l Abner* that is funny now is the fact that so many people once gave a hoot about it. After plowing through all forty-three years of Capp's daily comics—comics consisting almost entirely of burlesques, boilerplate dialogue, and contrived situation comedy—one is bored beyond all emotions save irritation. Capp's ham-handed use of ethnic stereotypes is particularly annoying. Whether it was the Polecat tribe, injuns drunk on Kickapoo Joy Juice (a nonalcoholic version of which Capp marketed, and which is still sold today in parts of the Third World); the "Unteachables" (a mob of greaseball, pinstriped Sicilians); or the snoring meggsican hombres and impossibly oversexed, red hot gorls of El Apassionato, racial caricatures were Capp's forte. In a perhaps intentional show of bogus integrity, Capp even drew his own tribe as a bunch of hook-nosed shysters.

Capp's main character was Li'l Abner hisself, the proto-Gump and first mass-media imbecile to serve as an emblem of all the lunkheads that the two coasts imagine to inhabit America's middle. This Brobdingnagian lummox was "the man with the lowest I.Q. in America." As Capp once crowed, "When Li'l Abner speaks, he speaks for millions of morons." The mate Capp fashioned for

Abner was the buxom, brainless Daisy Mae, a naive, chaste, barely clothed shotgun-shack tart who fully, and I do mean fully, embodied the Madonna/whore complex. When not chasing Abner on her fleet bare feet every Sadie Hawkins Day, Daisy Mae was heaven-bent on capturing him for marriage. Capp's idjit Adam and Eve hailed from the mountain hamlet of Dogpatch, U.S.A., a yokel's Yoknapatawpha, a hillbilly Eden where all stayed poor by virtue of their inanity.

As the strip's plot unfolded, Abner clodhopped his way across the landscape of American life, exposing folly and avarice wherever he loped—admirers of Capp, from Theroux to John Updike, refer to Abner as a sort of aw-shucks Candide—and won out in the end by virtue of his stupidity, naiveté, and deep faith in the red, white, and blue. Virtually all of Capp's central cast of characters fit the same profile: lazy, illiterate, barefoot sharecroppers in tattered clothes—charming innocents untouched by sivvylyzashun, mouthing in their every encounter with city folk and all forms of authority a dumb profundity, one all the more compelling for its being untouched by subject-verb agreement.

There's something about this formula of average-dope-confronts-power that has always appealed to middle-class Americans, perhaps because, as with the denizens of Dogpatch, these simpleton protagonists are always portrayed as happy children. No matter what their age, Abner and his lumpen cousins were constantly sleeping, drinking, hoodwinking, and screwing—that last act being of course only suggested, especially on Sadie Hawkins Day. Natcherly, the Dogpatch crowd were good chilluns, prefacing their address of rich folk with "yassuh," "nossuh," and other markers of old-fashioned deference. What Capp invented was a new kind of minstrelsy, one that did without the basic element previously thought necessary for a minstrel show—namely, black people. For all his nasty stereotyping, Capp's great accomplishment was his bleaching of this all-American art.

The overeager intellectuals of the day were convinced that

Capp was the mythical common man in the flesh, a veritable fount of the vox populi. The dialect of Dogpatch was a particular favorite of these ancestors of today's cult studs. For Capp's 1953 book, *The World of Li'l Abner*, John Steinbeck—of all people!—contributed an introduction in which he proclaimed: "I think Capp may very possibly be the best writer in the world today." Steinbeck then recommended that Capp be given the Nobel Prize for literature because, he reasoned, literature is what the people actually read—and everybody read Al Capp. "He has not only invented a language but has planted it in us so deeply that we can talk it ourselves," Steinbeck wrote, apparently forgetting that Sambo dialect had already been around for well over a hundred years. As an example of Capp's "high-faluting, shimmering, gorgeous prose," Steinbeck trotted out this typical Capp passage: "After ah dances a jig wif a pig, Ah yanks out two o' mah teeth, an' presents 'em to th' bridegroom—as mementos o' the occasion!!—then—Ah really gits goin!!" In a 1970 study of *Li'l Abner*, communications scholar Arthur Asa Berger declared: "Capp's use of an American vernacular is, in itself, an 'affront' to the social order, and has strong egalitarian implications." Only an intelligentsia desperate to prove that they were down with the people could claim that mouthing yowza did a democrat make.

Capp's admirers on the left warmed most of all to his savage portrayals of the big fat bad guy. In the Thirties, Forties, and Fifties, Capp reveled in drawing porcine, bejeweled tycoons and big bidnessmen with names like J. Colossal McGenius, Rockwell P. Squeezeblood, and J. P. Gorganfeller. Such caricatures, in and of themselves, were populism enough for most, and the critics duly painted Capp as a dyspeptic, chain-smoking, wooden-legged champeen of the common man. Yet I cannot find one instance of a Capp-champion actually doing the dirty work of looking deeply into the forty-three years' worth of Dogpatch storyline in order to extract evidence of the cartoonist's alleged populism. Maybe the fact that *Li'l Abner* was a comic strip, and hence popular, was sufficient.

The nearest most critics came to a close reading was during Abner's famous 1948 encounter with the blobby, amorphous Shmoo. The Shmoo storyline, more than any other, cemented Capp's reputation as a spokesman for the common man and sent his scholarly admirers riffling through their thesauruses. Shmoos were soft little white penises, cuddly creatures with a perpetual smile and a moozikal song of "Shmoo" on their lips. They reproduced spontaneously and provided everything man needed to survive, laying an endless supply of milk, aigs, and butter. When a Shmoo saw a human look at him with hunger in his eyes, the Shmoo died of happiness on the spot. The hongry Dogpatcher then cut them up and ate them broiled, so they tasted like steak, or boiled, so they tasted like chicken. Sawed lengthwise and dried, they made wood; cut in slabs, they made leather; sliced thinly, they made the fahnest cloth. Abner plucked out the dead Shmoo's eyeballs to fashion buttons for his suspenders and picked their meat from his grin with toothpicks he'd made from their whiskers. If ever there was a metaphor for American abundance, the Shmoo was it. Natcherly such a utopia could not stand. The swine-king of the pork industry, J. Roaringham Fatback, grew pop-eyed and indignant over the Shmoos and, in an apoplectic fit, ordered his double-breasted henchmen to eliminate the Shmoos. Exactly why Fatback killed the Shmoos, nobody bothered to examine—but we will come to that later.

Almost overnight, the myth of Capp as friend of the common man was born. Capp printed the newspaper Shmoo strips as a book in 1948. *The Life and Times of the Shmoo* sold seven hundred thousand copies, and on November 6, 1950, Capp, Abner, Daisy Mae, and the Shmoos made the cover of *Time* magazine. It was official: Comics were now Culture. Steinbeck's recommendation followed soon thereafter, making comics not just pitchers but actual Writing as well. In his 1963 book, *The Politics of Hope*, Arthur Schlesinger Jr. called Capp "the most brilliant and daring of our comic strip cartoonists." Then came the ultimate compliment. In a 1965 article Capp wrote for *Life*, entitled "My Life as an Immortal Myth: How

Li'l Abner Became the Intellectual's Delight," Capp recounted with his characteristically false humility how one morning Alain Resnais, the French film director, had stood humbly on Capp's doorstep and proclaimed *Li'l Abner* to be "America's one immortal myth, and the dominating artistic influence of my life." Rather than regarding this endorsement as a product of that curious Gallic tendency to see buffoons like Jerry Lewis and Mickey Rourke as avatars of a noble American savagery, Theroux presents it as proof of Capp's arteestishness. Capp himself ate up these accolades, dining and wisecracking with the likes of Charles Chaplin, Orson Welles, and the patron saint of lifestyle liberation and bodacious ta-tas, Hugh Hefner himself. Capp even campaigned for Adlai Stevenson and John F. Kennedy. He was a celebrity, and if the liberals embraced him, then a liberal he was.

On the surface, at least. When he wasn't flying to his favorite spot in the world, London's Savoy Hotel, to have his suits tailored on Savile Row, the newly minted populist resided in his home in Cambridge—trading the yin of Yale for the yang of Harvard—and rode to work in one of his chauffeur-driven Cadillac convertibles with the name "Al Capp" painted on the door. All shows of vanity aside, Al Capp the man was in a very real sense not at all who he pretended to be. At his studio the nouveau Brahmin used a number of assistants to help him crank out the products of his imagination in a more efficient fashion. After a morning brainstorming session Capp would rough in the action he and his helpers had concocted. Capp inked in the heads and bodies of the main characters—"getting the look of the strip," as Theroux puts it—and left the rest of the penciling, inking, shading, lettering, and coloring to his assistants. As is always the case in any such relationship, the people who actually did the work knew how to do it better than the bossman. Today Capp collectors pay far, far more for the Abner strips known to be assisted by Frank Frazetta, the unsung genius behind the cheesiest of Capp's oft-ogled cheesecake. (Frazetta eventually huffed out of Capp's studio and went on to great fame as the world's foremost painter of barbarians, Molly Hatchet album covers, and big-hipped maidens in chain-mail bikinis.) The crowning touch of phoniness was this: Capp paid his assistant Harvey Curtis to sign each and every *Li'l Abner* strip with the trademark Al Capp signature. Al Capp was not even "Al Capp."

In the late Sixties Capp seemed to lose interest in baiting industrialists and PR people. He had a new target now, the hippies and the student left, whom he treated with the same contempt he had always held for everyone else. Once again, Al Capp was warping and mocking a kind of white Negro—but this time it was white middle-class kids who consciously tried to be culturally black. First and foremost came that all-important bugaboo of the backlash, the welfare mother. Capp condensed his previous emblems of impoverished fertility, Dogpatch's Misser and Missus J. P. McFruitful and their forty-odd kids, and turned them into the decidedly more urban Miss Ann Yewly Fruitful, the national chairman of Militant Unwed Mothers (MUMs). Capp's caricature of rotund, limousine-riding businessmen (like himself) slimmed into the svelte Joanie Phonie, a thinly veiled lampoon of Joan Baez, who rode to and from her pinko charity benefits in a caviar-laden limousine. Capp tied a polky-dot tie on Abner and replaced the raggedy Dogpatchers with the equally raggedy group of barefoot student protesters he called Students Wildly Indignant about Nearly Everything (SWINE). These new underdogs made a fuss—unlike their yassuh forebears—and for that reason Capp drew them with extra venom and without the sentimentality that some had found so endearing in the good old days.

Once again, Capp's mockery of the underdog made him a rich man. Once again, the middle class leapt at the chance to embrace Capp's attack on the idle rich, but this time it was the Daughters of the American Revolution and the Elks who backed Capp. He became the prophet of the Silent Majority, fulminating against the hordes of longhaired rich kids wearing tea shades, waving placards, and hurling firebombs with their soft, pink hands. Again he made populism into something of an industry: Capp stumped about college campuses on a $5,000-per-appearance lecture tour, where he wagged a nicotined finger at students and growled jowly, spittle-flecked denunciations of their hair, their "hate America" music, their privilege, their youth, and their goddamned laziness. Ever the showman, Capp even crashed John and Yoko's bed-in for peace, barging in and unleashing an incoherent torrent of abuse and invective. Capp prospered from the bitter culture wars, and he took to taking black coffee with Spiro Agnew and Richard Nixon, dining and grousing with Ross Perot and William F. Buckley Jr., and publicly threatening to run for the Senate against Ted Kennedy. Once again, Capp was a celebrity, and if the right embraced him, then a righty he was.

But by the time Capp published *The Hardhat's Bedtime Story Book* in 1972, the jig was up. The book was a set of dystopian essays featuring half-real, half-imagined stereotypes such as Jerry Rubin, whom Capp imagined as president of Harvbaked University in 1984—a Harvard with a Richard Speck School of Ethics and a campus Gestapo run by Abbie Hoffman. It seemed like perfect stuff for the newly populist right—which was learning to portray itself as the ally of the average worker in his fight against a new Establishment—but this time Capp couldn't get anybody to write an introduction. "John Steinbeck wrote the preface to my last book," Capp wrote in his own, self-described "lonely" introduction, "and in it, he nominated me for the Nobel Prize. When they gave it to him instead, it broke his heart and I vowed that never again would I cause a great man pain. And so I have not asked quite a few great men to write this preface for me."

The truth is that the right was through with Capp, and that nobody, liberal or conservative, wanted to touch Capp's book with a ten-foot pole—mainly because Capp had been trying to touch young women with his pole. In 1971 the *Boston Phoenix* reported that Capp had "exposed himself" and made "forceful advances" toward four different girls in the course of one visit to the University of Alabama, after which the cops ran Capp out of town. In 1972 at the University of Wisconsin, Capp waved his cock at a married coed and attempted to sodomize her. She was a "left-wing" girl, Capp protested, a "do-gooder determined to remake me." The coed pressed charges. Capp claimed innocence but pleaded guilty to "attempted adultery" and shortly thereafter retired from comics in disgrace. Five years later he was dead from emphysema.

Where were those true colors during Capp's lefty years? Take a close look at the most celebrated episode from his liberal period—the story of the Shmoo—and you will notice that the Shmoo was much more a metaphor for laissez-faire capitalism than it was for any leftist vision of utopian plenty. J. Roaringham Fatback did indeed exterminate the cute li'l creature and all humanity's hopes for easy prosperity, but not for the reason Capp's liberal-populist admirers imagined. In fact, Fatback ordered his genocide over the protests of his fellow bizmen—savvy capitalists who saw immediately a million new Shmoo markets that would arise for them to penetrate and exploit. "New developments don't ruin American business, Fatback!!" the Suits enthused. "They just open new fields for us!!" "Sure!" piped up another tycoon. "Everybody's got Shmoos—plain Shmoos!! But who's got chocolate-covered Shmoos? There's a tremendous field, right there!!" Their ingenious list went on: salted Shmoos, canned Shmoos, candied Shmoos, Shmoo knives, Shmoo shoop—I mean soup—and so forth, as the barons of business danced in an endless circle of product differentiation and brand extension. Meanwhile, the fat villain Fatback harrumphed, "I hate anything new!! . . . If those things aren't exterminated, I'll have to change my way of life—and I hate change!!" And so Fatback wiped out the Shmoos, subverting the true visionaries of Capp's Shmoo episode: the suit-clad seers of market-based prosperity. Fatback was a villain only because he was a lousy businessman, unable to comprehend or appreciate the eternally provident market—America's actual immortal myth.

The marketplace was always Al Capp's guiding light. In 1949 Capp told *The New Republic*, "All I know about modern capitalism I learned from the Shmoo." Given Capp's cynicism, he probably knew how dead-on his metaphor was. Capp was already selling Shmoo dolls, Shmoo rings, Shmoo clocks, Shmoo soap, Shmoo banks, Shmoo salt shakers, Shmoo records, Shmoo cookie jars, Shmoo pencils, Shmoo stationery, Shmoo soda pop, Shmoo balloons, and Shmoo shampoo. The year prior, during the Berlin airlift, Capp had worked with the 17th Military Air Transport Squadron to supply the besieged city with life-size, inflatable Shmoos. A *Life* magazine article about the Shmoolift rhapsodized about the "CAPPitalistic lessons" the captive Teutonic commies would learn from being penetrated by giant, cuddly, white penises, filled with air, descending from heaven.

—BAFFLER 13, 1999

18

I'd Like to Force the World to Sing

The Making of a Yes Generation

JOSHUA GLENN

EDITOR'S NOTE: How was one to explain the sudden prominence of a cohort of young conservatives in the last few years of the Nineties? One could examine their writings and organizations and congressional testimony and try to unravel their tangled ideas, but that was clearly not enough. When we asked Josh Glenn to come up with some narrative that could make sense of it, he spun the kind of tongue-in-cheek explanation that crazy spectacles like this one deserve.

THE THEORY STARTS like this: Plunged into despondency by the 1992 election, William Kristol, then chief of staff for Dan Quayle, fretted that the pot-smoking, draft-dodging Sixties were once again poised to disrupt the pleasant ersatz Fifties that he and his fellow reactionaries had cultivated so carefully over the Reagan–Bush years. Despairing that his generation of squares would never again see the inside of the White House—which, as Joe Eszterhas confirmed, would shortly be transformed by Clinton and Co. into a satellite office of *Rolling Stone*—Kristol turned his attention to

America's youth, the demographic cohort that makes miracles possible. Unfortunately, as the theory goes, Kristol found little in the so-called Generation X to encourage him. As *Time* magazine had reported, these sullen young men and women were far too prickly and cynical even to vote, let alone vote Republican. Yet somehow Kristol had to convince these kids, schooled in the scorn of the Reagan–Bush era, to rebel against rebellion itself.

Or so, anyway, goes one of the more inventive conspiracy theories now making the rounds. The funny thing is how plausible it all seems once you start looking into it. In 1993 Kristol outlined in *Commentary* magazine a program for selling conservatism as rebellion, declaring absurdly: "Now it is liberalism that constitutes the old order." At the time this seemed quite mad. Today it seems prescient. We all have heard about the clear-eyed youngsters of "Generation Y," with their faith in Wall Street and their uncanny entrepreneurial skills. Well, it's all William Kristol's doing. He has managed to persuade an entire generation with his weird logic. But how?

Two words, according to the theory: OK Soda.

OK WAS "DEVELOPED," as they say in the business, by Coca-Cola marketing chief Sergio Zyman, the same man who'd developed the "brainwater" Fruitopia, at around the time that Kristol was making his appeal to youthful iconoclasm in the pages of *Commentary*. In 1994, OK was introduced into nine strategically selected hotbeds of youth ferment, including Boston, Denver, Minneapolis/St. Paul, and of course Austin and Seattle; it was yanked from the market only a few months later. But wait, back up: *brainwater?* If you've always wondered about the inexplicable popularity of "smart drinks" in the early Nineties, wonder no longer. Remember: It was the CIA that, by experimenting on college students in an effort to develop mind-control drugs, inadvertently introduced LSD into the counterculture. In the Nineties, Kristol and his allies in the CIA simply found a way to perform the trick in reverse. In their impossible quest to conjure up a cadre of conservative youth who would rebel against a Sixties they'd never known, Kristol and Co., the theory maintains, *conspired to dose Generation X with the concentrated essence of what they called "OK-ness."*

Hold on! you object. If OK was a plot funded by the conservative establishment, and carried out with the support of the CIA and Coca-Cola, then why did the thirst-quencher fail? *But did OK really fail?* The transcript of a 1994 National Public Radio interview with Tom Pirko, the president of a food and beverage consulting firm who'd worked on OK, appears significant in light of what has since transpired. Pirko told host Noah Adams that OK tastes "a little bit like going to a fountain and mixing a little bit of Coke with a little root beer and Dr. Pepper and maybe throwing in some orange." When Adams expressed puzzlement that so vile a concoction was supposed to compete with such fruity stalwarts as Mountain Dew, Pirko boasted: "Even though taste is always promoted as the key quality, the key ingredient of any brand, it really isn't. It falls way down in the hierarchy. The most important thing is advertising." ("The most important thing is advertising?" Adams asked incredulously. "No question," confirmed Pirko.) The marketing consultant, laboring perhaps under the weight of guilt for his part in Kristol's conspiracy, was making a confession here: *OK was never intended to succeed as a soda.* The whole point of the project was to inject a hip conservative worldview, as expressed by the soda's advertising, into Xers who'd been rendered deeply impressionable by whatever it was Kristol et al. had put into the beverage. Once the message had been delivered, OK could vanish from the 7-Eleven as mysteriously as it had appeared in the first place.

Of what did that message consist? Recall for a moment the gloomy cloud that hung over Generation X in those days. Even the happiest organs of the mass media were admitting that Xers were right to feel an oppressive sense of reduced opportunity, thanks to (take your pick) globalization and wage stagnation, an unchecked growth in corporate profit-taking, a glut of low-wage service jobs, pervasive undereducation, and the skyrocketing cost of college and home ownership. The young people were, as one *New Yorker* writer put it, "millenarian, depressed, cynical, frustrated, apathetic, hedonistic, and nihilistic."

Coca-Cola knew this litany well. According to a 1994 article in *Time*, the company had been studying the behavior and attitudes of teenagers for two years before it introduced OK—note the timing, again—through something they called the "Global Teenager Program," which employed graduate students from that hotbed of CIA recruitment, the Massachusetts Institute of Technology. Evidently concluding that global teenagers could best be programmed via deliberately downbeat marketing, the company proceeded to decorate OK cans with depressing art, most memorably a set of drawings of a blank-looking young man staring dolefully ahead, walking dejectedly down an empty street, and sitting outside an idle factory with his face in his hands. In the Thirties, such images might have had revolutionary connotations; in the hands of the Kristol/Coke cabal, they meant something very different. This is why the *Time* article, having just described the unhappy plight of Coca-Cola's target market, continued with this telling remark: "At the same time, the OK theme attempts to play into *the sense of optimism* that this generation retains" (my emphasis). Dead industry and optimism? The inscrutable connection was made by Brian Lanahan, manager of—note the ominous department title—Special Projects for Coke's marketing division, who told *Time*: "What we're trying to show with those symbols is someone who is just being, and just being OK." Translation: They were trying to produce young fogies ready to affirm—*to okay*—the existing order, to look up at those silent factories and say, "Whatever."

Enter the wily ad agency Wieden & Kennedy (Nike, Calvin Klein). Charged with the task of transmitting the message of OK-ness to a target audience that had been chemically prepped by the foul-tasting beverage, Wieden & Kennedy developed a marketing campaign that seemed to pander to people's worst fears about mass society; it featured references to indoctrination via television, tongue-in-cheek personality tests, and, centrally, an "OK Soda Manifesto." Copies of the manifesto are hard to come by today; I happen to have one because an article I clipped from a June 1994 issue of the Minneapolis/St. Paul *City Pages* has the ad printed on the other side. I reproduce it here in full:

1 What's the point of OK? Well, what's the point of anything?
2 OK Soda emphatically rejects anything that is not OK, and fully supports anything that is.
3 The better you understand something, the more OK it turns out to be.
4 OK Soda says, "Don't be fooled into thinking there has to be a reason for everything."
5 OK Soda reveals the surprising truth about people and situations.
6 OK Soda does not subscribe to any religion, or endorse any political party, or do anything other than feel OK.
7 There is no real secret to feeling OK.
8 OK Soda may be the preferred drink of other people such as yourself.
9 Never overestimate the remarkable abilities of "OK" brand soda.
10 Please wake up every morning knowing that things are going to be OK.

In every particular, the "OK Soda Manifesto" exhibited those criteria that the psychologist Robert Jay Lifton identified in 1961 with the practice of "thought reform," or mind control. As in all mind-control cults, for example, the manifesto forbade OK drinkers from associating with outsiders and restricted their vocabulary to what Lifton calls "thought-terminating clichés." They were told how to think and warned that the individual's own experiences could not be understood except via the group. The Reverend Jim Jones's Kool-Aid had nothing on this stuff. As a 1995 OK promotional sticker that came bound into an issue of *Might* magazine put it, "OK-ness is that small thing that holds everything else together."

Reading the "Manifesto" now one can see it as an obvious attempt to transform the then-legendary Gen-X disaffection into the watery contentment we associate with "Generation Y." OK-ness, as the manifesto described it, is a doctrine designed for those who grew up in the Seventies and Eighties wondering, "What's the point of anything?" Furthermore, the OK-ness of everything was something one could only "understand" when one stopped looking for "a reason for everything"; learned to distrust the "people and situations" to which one had formerly looked for guidance; and, presumably, learned to trust the market. Sound too counterintuitive? Not to worry, the "Manifesto" assured its readers, "there is no real secret" to figuring all this out, so don't bother trying. Then the purposely vague formula for daily living: OK-ness was a movement, made up of "other people such as yourself," and joining that movement would bring "remarkable" results. All one had to do was to "wake up every morning knowing that things are going to be OK."

This may have seemed insipid, lame, just plain bad advertising, but it worked. Within months the media had spotted a "Generation Y" splitting off from the unhappy X cohort, a cheerful "yes" generation for a cheerful new age. "I'm not really into that rebel thing," proclaimed one zestful participant in a 1994 *New York* magazine profile of American youth. In report after report since then, journalists and analysts alike have agreed that Yers are much better adjusted (read: much better employees and consumers) than gloomy Xers ever were. "Doesn't Smell Like Teen Spirit," gloated the title of an article that appeared in *The Weekly Standard*, a magazine that William Kristol edits. "After a decade of Gen Xers being despondent about their prospects for fulfillment," the story reported, "survey after survey shows teens exuberantly optimistic about their futures." In what can only be a giddy inside joke, it then proceeded to propose, as the anthem of this young, GOP-friendly cohort, Jewel's hit song "Hands," which begins with the line—listen to it yourself—"If I could tell the world just one thing/it would be/we're all OK."

It may sound fantastic, but think about it. Kristol wanted the Nineties to be an inverted Sixties, in which young men would wear their hair short, young women would wear push-up bras, they'd all scorn the Sixties and love swing dancing—and in which passionate young people would add the imprimatur of their youth to the conservative campaign to discredit those concepts, and dismantle those institutions, that obstruct the progress of the free market. All of which has come to pass.

BESIDES, WHAT OTHER than mental scrambling induced by adulterated soda pop can explain the brainless gang of generational "leaders" we evidently are now fated to serve under? Behold the fruits of concentrated OK-ness: twenty-seven-year-old ideologue Mark Gerson, author of *The Neoconservative Vision: From the Cold War to the Culture Wars* (1995) and editor of *The Essential Neoconservative Reader* (1996); twenty-six-year-old economics writer Meredith Bagby, author of *Rational Exuberance: The Influence of Generation X on the New American Economy* (1998) and *We've Got Issues: The Get Real, No B.S., Guilt-Free Guide to What Really Matters* (2000); and twenty-five-year-old "sexual counterrevolutionary" Wendy Shalit, author of *A Return to Modesty: Discovering the Lost Virtue* (1999). When OK was unleashed on young America, Shalit was nineteen, Bagby was twenty, and Gerson twenty-one. Each of them shows clear signs of repeated, heavy dosing.

As in the "OK Soda Manifesto," Bagby's *Rational Exuberance* begins by drawing an unexplained connection between the disaffection of Xers and the doctrine of OK-ness: "Enter Generation X. With caution—and on little cat feet—wary, worn before wear, fearful, and suspicious. Still, and in seeming contradiction, we came wrapped in the passions of newness and with the relentless energy that birth always spawns." Bagby may earn a tearful pat on the head for that maudlin "worn before wear" stuff, but she never does resolve the "seeming contradiction" of people being both fearful and optimistic at the same time. Instead, she rushed forward to define Xers as good junior citizens, their little cat feet dutifully carrying them up the ladder. They are "above all self-reliant and self-defining. We start our own businesses at a staggering rate. We take enormous business risks." For Bagby the proof of her generation's essential OK-ness is not "other-directed" goals such as peace or social justice—although she does demand Social Security "reform," by which she means privatization—but its desire to become millionaires. Her book describes a string of successful young professionals whose rise to the top is supposed to be evidence for Bagby's bizarre assertion that "the 'X' in Generation X is the symbol for multiplication. For us the symbol strikes a chord because the most successful entrepreneurs don't win by adding dollars—they win by multiplying dollars."

Again and again Bagby's work betrays the telltale mental short-circuiting that is OK Soda's gift to American thought. Liking money, business, the market means you are a Republican, right? Nope. Bagby blithely insists that she and her fellow brave new countercounterculturalists are not only nonpartisan ("Neither Elephant Nor Donkey," as the title of a chapter in her book puts it) but actually postpartisan. "In 1991, when I was a college freshman," she gloats in *Rational Exuberance*, "the Evil Empire whimpered its last breath. The world changed. Our ideological battle [was] won." Everything would now be OK forever and ever. All questions had been settled, she insisted, in one shoe-pounding soundbite after another: "We want a government that W-O-R-K-S—that delivers the mail on time, protects the environment, fosters business, secures our future by deficit control, makes our streets safe, and stays out of our way as much as possible while doing it."

Bagby's 2000 book, *We've Got Issues*, offers an even more sweeping declaration of these nonprinciples: "Our generation is making it where it counts," she tells the world, "not in creed or controversy, but in shares and silicon—venture cap, options, start-ups, hedge funds, broadband, plug-ins, digital, IRAs, 401(k)s—those are our buzzwords." And a fine set of buzzwords they were indeed—especially for William Kristol's pals on Wall Street during that recent bout of national madness known as the Internet bubble. But beyond controversy? The cat does make one effort at leaping from the bag on its cute little feet when Bagby wonders at the book's conclusion "whether or not I stealthily interjected some of my own prejudices (oh, of course I did) or whether I remained nonpartisan and aboveboard throughout." Otherwise, though, Bagby is fairly consistent, insisting that free-market capitalism somehow transcends politics, that she and her entire generation have been liberated from "ideology." A more accurate description of what has befallen her and countless other tidy young strivers, according to the theory, would be a kind of political hydrolysis, a chemical conversion to a politics that otherwise made no sense.

Another victim is Mark Gerson, author of the 1996 book *In the Classroom: Dispatches from an Inner-City School That Works*. Gerson, too, insists on his nonpartisanship—he just wants things to work! But while his book ostensibly recounts a year Gerson spent as a teacher in a Catholic school in Jersey City, the plot is just there to give Gerson an opportunity to mock bilingualism, diversity training, and the idea that standardized exams may be culturally biased. Gerson's most important contribution to the literature of young conservatism is an extended meditation on the central OK activity of sucking up to authority. He expresses shock at his inner-city students' marked failure to suck up to him. Tongue nowhere near his cheek, he recounts that he and his suburban schoolmates were accomplished bootlickers; that sucking up was the most valuable skill he learned in school. Indeed, Gerson even gives readers a taste of his ability, heaping on the praise for neoconservative mentors and heroes such as Gertrude Himmelfarb ("one of the world's great social historians"); Norman Podhoretz ("a literary phenomenon"); Michael Novak ("one of the great economic philosophers of our era"); Daniel Patrick Moynihan ("perhaps the most gifted thinker to serve in public office in this century"); and Irving Kristol ("a brilliant writer of remarkable insight and great wit"). He describes a book by James Q. Wilson as "one of the best works of nonfiction in recent memory," and his Williams College professor and mentor Jeff Weintraub as "something of a cross between an oracle and an encyclopedia." As for William Kristol, the man who drugged and brainwashed him, Gerson describes him as "a key figure—some would say the key figure—in the transformation of the modern Republican Party [into] the party of intellectual imagination and ideological excitement." When it comes to your conservative elders, apparently, "The better you understand something, the more OK it turns out to be."

Wendy Shalit, who went to Williams College with Gerson, is the younger sister of Ruth Shalit, the *New Republic* writer whose plagiarism helped discredit that magazine. Wendy became a conservative mascot in 1995 after launching a courageous journalistic crusade against coed bathrooms. "A Ladies' Room of One's Own," her call to arms in *Commentary*, was duly reprinted by that bastion of nonideological OK-ness, *Reader's Digest*. She's even dated John Podhoretz, the straightforwardly conservative son of the professional ex-leftist Norman Podhoretz. Shalit's *Return to Modesty*—which proposes that anorexia, date rape, and all the other "woes besetting the modern young woman," are the natural "expressions of a society which has lost its respect for female modesty"—also identifies liberal feminists as the real enemies of womankind. "It is no accident that harassment, stalking, and rape all increased when we decided to let everything hang out," she writes.

Shalit, who's been known to defend the Promise Keepers and religious modesty laws for women, has declared: "The patriarchy, in the form of a stable structure of traditional values, and the protective authority to enforce it, is precisely what women are missing, and desperately want restored."

Not only is it hip to be square nowadays, Shalit would have us understand, it's hip to be brainwashed. Describing her youthful conviction that feminists "exaggerate the difficulties of being a woman," Shalit begs the reader not to "ask me how I was so sure of this, or what this had to do with any other part of my ideology. As anyone who has ever had an ideology knows, you do not ask; you just look for confirmation for a set of beliefs. That's what it means to have an ideology." In other words, "Don't be fooled into thinking there has to be a reason for everything."

What's So Bad About Feeling Good? asked the title of a 1968 musical comedy that tantalized Bill Kristol's generation with a plot in which nihilistic beatniks were straightened out by a happiness virus. It might well have been the blueprint for what has actually happened to our generation. Thanks to OK Soda, the frustrated idealism of Generation X has been converted into a passionate complacency. The patriarchy is neat-o, Shalit insists; Gerson gives the nod to the social and economic hierarchy; and Bagby puts the seal of youthful approval on free-market capitalism. It's, like, get with the program already . . . OK?

—Baffler 14, 2001

Afterword

In the aftermath of the recent stock-market collapse, two of the fresh-faced ideologues I had profiled in my conspiracy theory quietly stepped down from their soapboxes. In 1999, Wendy Shalit had unbuckled her whalebone corset long enough to write a blistering op-ed piece about delusional union spokespersons outraged by the vast discrepancy between the pay scales of CEOs and workers. But now that those same CEOs are taking perp walks, she's nowhere to be found. Mark Gerson, whose butt-kissing technique had paid off a few years back, when George Gilder and others invested in his start-up market-research firm, seems to lack any further motivation to write valentines to older market triumphalists. Although they didn't recant, at least Shalit and Gerson no longer insist that everything's OK.

Meredith Bagby, on the other hand, still hasn't kicked the habit. The Bagby Group, a consulting company "for businesses seeking to attract the Generation X market," never took off—so she's become a professional yea-sayer. A few weeks after the events of September 11, Bagby helped represent "young Americans" at a hearing of George W. Bush's infamous Commission to Strengthen Social Security. Abasing herself before the assembled appointees, each of whom favored the privatization of Social Security, Gen X's Most Respected Economic Writer asked that her generation be permitted to throw itself upon the actuarial grenade. "You must ask us to accept a plan that could raise our eligibility age and index it to average lifespans, lower our future benefits by altering the way they are calculated, and tax our future benefits at a higher rate," she declaimed. "If you do this, we will not oppose you." I can only repeat, in conclusion: "Never overestimate the remarkable abilities of 'OK' brand soda."

19

Dreams Incorporated

Living the Delayed Life with Amway

Matt Roth

What is your dream? demanded a booming voice. The ballroom went dark and the audience settled in for a fifteen-minute video catalogue of the stuff dreams are made of: a blur of luxury cars, sprawling mansions, frolicking children, pristine beaches, hotdogging Jetskiers, private helipads, and zooming jets—all set to caffeinated, John-Teshy instrumental music. The voice returned: "It's about *family!*" (A shot of kids collapsing on an oceanic lawn, love-tackled by Dad.) "It's about *security!*" (A shot of a palatial house.) "It's about *you!*" (A close-up of toes, gently lapped by the incoming tide, wriggling in white sand.)

This was Dream Night, and it was about Amway.

There are some one and a quarter million Amway members in the United States, roughly one for every two hundred of the rest of us—all of them eager to spread the gospel of salvation-through-selling-Amway-products. Considering Amwayers' penchant for compiling long lists of names, accosting strangers, and generally striving to collapse the degrees of separation between them and other humans, the chances of an American being asked to an Amway meeting are quite good—somewhere between having a condom break during sex and being dealt a straight in a hand of poker. For a certain segment of the struggling middle class, where there's a magic mixture of disposable income and status insecurity, the odds are nearer those of catching a cold. And for someone like me, a postcollegiate preprofessional with a solid future in temping, Amway is more or less a mandatory rite of passage.

Dream Night was not the first Amway event I had attended, but it was the most hallucinatory. It began with the triumphal entrance of the Amway Diamond couples, half-jogging through a gauntlet of high-fives to the theme from *Rocky*, as the audience whooped and hollered and twirled their napkins over their heads. When the standing ovation finally tapered off, the emcee offered a prayer thanking God for (a) the fact that we lived in a free-enterprise system, where there were no government agents kicking down the doors of meetings like Dream Night, and (b) His Blessed Son. As dinner wound down, the video screens displayed a picture of what the guy next to me was quick to identify as a $20,000 Rolex watch.

As its hands reached "midnight," the Rolex dissolved into a series of video montages depicting the consumer Shangri-la that our own forthcoming Amway success would open for us. A day in the life of a typical jobholder—all alarm clocks, traffic jams, and dingy cubicles—was contrasted with that of an Amway distributor, who slept in and lounged the day away with his family. Real-life Amway millionaires strutted about sprawling estates (proudly referred to as "family compounds") and explained that such opulence was ours for the asking. There were chortles as a highway patrolman stopped an expensive sports car for speeding—only to ride away a moment later with an Amway sample kit strapped to his motorcycle. The laughter became a roar of delight as the camera zoomed in on the sports car's bumper sticker: JOBLESS . . . AND RICH!

The Amwayers who had taken me to Dream Night were flying high on the drive home, whooping occasionally just to vent their exhilaration. I felt as though I had just sat through a year's worth of infomercials, with some high school pep rallies and a few Tony Robbins lectures thrown in. But to see all this as an exercise in mass hypnosis, according to Amway's literature, would be to "misunderstand" what is, simply, "the best business opportunity in the world"—an assessment, strangely enough, with which the rest of world is starting to agree.

The Best Business Opportunity in the World

The Amway Corporation was founded in 1959, ostensibly as a small-scale manufacturer of "biodegradable" detergents (beginning with Liquid Organic Cleaner, the patent for which Amway acquired from a struggling Detroit scientist). It has since grown into a $6 billion-a-year consumer-products behemoth selling everything from groceries to lingerie to water-filtration systems. These products aren't available in stores, though. The key to Amway's success is its curious distribution system: Instead of using retail outlets and mass-media advertising, Amway licenses individual "distributors" to sell its goods from their homes. The distributors are independent franchisees; they buy products from Amway at wholesale and resell them at the "suggested retail" price, pocketing the difference as profit. Distributors are also paid a percentage of their sales (from 3 percent to 25 percent) by Amway itself. But the detail that distinguishes Amway's "multi-level marketing" scheme is that it rewards distributors for bringing new recruits into the sales force. Distributors get a cut not only of their own sales revenues but also of sales made by their recruits, their recruits' recruits, and their recruits' recruits' recruits, a branching pyramid of lineally descended Amwayers known as a distributor's "downline."

The Amway approach supposedly avoids impersonal door-to-door sales, as each distributor need only sell directly to a small customer base of friends and family. Business "growth"—and an ascent to the flashier "bonus levels" (Ruby, Emerald, Diamond, Executive Diamond, Double Diamond, Crown Ambassador)—comes mostly through expanding one's downline. In theory, this odd marketing system ensures that benefits accrue not to Madison Avenue slicksters but to ordinary folk capitalizing on their close-knit community ties—a scheme that seemingly reflects the small-town, Protestant populism of Amway's cofounders, Rich DeVos and Jay VanAndel.

Its pandering to heartland values notwithstanding, the company has also had its share of critics. In the Seventies a succession of defectors charged that The Business (as the faithful call it) was a pyramid scheme, a fraudulent enterprise that made money by recruiting new members and channeling their fees to higher-ups in the organization. A 1979 Federal Trade Commission investigation concluded that Amway was not in fact a pyramid scheme because most of its revenue came from sales of actual products.[1] But that

[1] The FTC's ruling that Amway is not a pyramid scheme is based partly on the "70-10 Rule": To qualify for Performance Bonuses based on downlines' sales, an Amway distributor is required to sell, according to Amway's *Business Reference Manual*, "at wholesale and/or retail at least 70 percent of the total amount of products he bought during a given month"—this is supposed to prevent "inventory loading," the forced purchase of unsellable merchandise. Amwayers are also required, for the Performance Bonus, to sell to at least ten retail customers in a given month, which ensures that real business is being conducted.

Both parts of the 70-10 Rule have major loopholes. According to the *Business Reference Manual*, "for purposes of [the 70 Percent Rule], products used for personal or family consumption or given out as samples are also considered as part of sales volume." Thus, overbuying for "personal use" is not ruled out. As for the Ten-Customer Rule, the *Manual* states that the "distributor should not disclose the prices at which he or she made the ten retail sales." This makes possible a practice alluded to by a World Wide speaker:

didn't end the company's troubles. During the Reagan years, Amway was the butt of jokes and the target of exposés. Senior distributors set up private "distributor groups"—organizations dealing in motivational materials and notorious mass rallies.[2] Dexter Yager, founder of the Yager Group, was known to leap around stages brandishing a giant gold crucifix.

Amway blamed its seamy image on a few "bad apples," impossible to avoid in a business that is open to all. Since the Eighties, the corporation has dealt with the issue by encouraging distributor groups to train Amwayers in "professionality" and by promulgating an official code of ethics.

---

giving away Amway products to ten people and calling them "retail sales." He added that the income from the Performance Bonus made the giveaways well worth it.

The FTC also cites Amway's "Buyback Rule" as a feature distinguishing The Business from a pyramid scheme. Distributors can return any "products, literature, or sales aids" for "whatever refund is agreed upon between the departing distributor and his or her sponsor." The *Manual* adds this note: "To return Amway literature for credit or refund, the literature must be sent back in its original wrapping, unopened and unused."

[2] Nowadays, nearly all Amwayers identify with a "distributor group." Dream Night, in fact, was arranged not by Amway but by World Wide Dreambuilders LLC, consisting of the downlines of Crown Ambassador Bill Britt. These groups, which do the heavy lifting of building and inspiring downlines, have no legal connection to Amway (as indicated by the disclaimers on the back of tickets for Dream Night and every other World Wide function I attended: "This event is produced and offered independently of Amway Corporation and has not been reviewed or endorsed by Amway"). The corporation uses the legal independence of distributor groups to its advantage. In a class-action lawsuit brought by former Amwayers charging Amway Corporation, World Wide head Bill Britt, and Dexter Yager with fraud and price-fixing, Amway claimed that it was itself, in effect, a victim of Britt and Yager's tactics—and thus not liable. (The case has since been settled out of court.) Having repudiated Britt and Yager, Amway promptly welcomed them back into the fold: Both recently made the cover of Amway's in-house magazine, *Amagram*, and Yager received the Founders Distinguished Service Award.

The reform efforts seem to have paid off. Today Amway is portrayed as a model business. Articles in newspapers around the country have crowned "multilevel distribution" as the Third Wave of marketing: If it looks like Amway, we're now told, then it's *not* a scam. Trade magazines laud Amway as a high-quality manufacturer; the United Nations has given it a rare Environmental Award; Jay VanAndel, the recipient of a score of business awards, served a term as president of the U.S. Chamber of Commerce; Ted Koppel has cited Rich DeVos as one of America's premier philanthropists; Larry King blurbed DeVos's book, *Compassionate Capitalism*, as "a credo for all people everywhere." Even the *Wall Street Journal*, which delights in mild ridicule of Amway spectacles, never completely laughs off The Business. The paper is always careful to mention Amway's billions in annual sales, the new class of professionals flocking to it, the FTC decision ruling it legal, and its remarkable global expansion—especially in Eastern Europe.

But Dream Night brought all the questions back to the surface. If Amway isn't a scam, why did it seem so much like one? It may win heaps of praise nowadays, but Amway doesn't seem to have changed much at all. Perhaps what's changed is us. Maybe capitalism has finally reached the stage of self-parody, unblushingly celebrating a house of cards as its highest achievement. And maybe Dream Night, far from being the ritual of a fringe cult, is the vanguard of the future.

First Look

Fittingly, my encounter with Amway began during a long-term temp assignment at Andersen Consulting's ENTERPRISE 2020 (E2020), an ongoing exhibit to which consultants would bring potential clients to scare them about the future. The main attraction was a battery of "industry experts" who would discourse gravely about globalization, accelerating technology, managed chaos, self-organizing supply chains, flex-this, flex-that, and nano-everything, eventually coming to the take-home lesson: The future was not to be faced without an Andersen consultant on retainer.

Sales pitch though it was, E2020 subscribed to an increasingly ubiquitous worldview at once overheatedly Darwinian—the global economy as nature run riot, lush for the dominant, unforgiving for the slow to adapt—and strikingly theological. In the next millennium, a resurgent Market would act as the vengeful (invisible) hand of God, laying waste to the Second Wave's many Towers of Babel—government planning, welfare states, unions, warehouses, consolidated factories, even mega-conglomerates. Wage earners, surviving solely on the basis of their own laboriously amassed "human capital" would repeatedly face having it wiped out by successive "paradigm shifts," at which point they would have to uncomplainingly accumulate more: This was called "being adaptable." Progress required clearing the ground for a new order of pure Nietzschean struggle: E2020 regularly held a seminar entitled, "Dominate or Die."

If the forecast looked pretty grim, I wasn't the only one who felt it. How else to explain the behavior of Sherri, a coworker, who in addition to her sixty-plus hours a week as E2020's "Events Coordinator"—charged with showing corporate swells a good time while they were in Chicago—took MBA classes at night and mentioned that she was starting her own "distribution business"? One day she asked me to attend a meeting at which a "millionaire from the West Coast" was to talk about "business trends of the Nineties." I had my suspicions—about this time, Amway Dish Drops appeared in the E2020 kitchen—but my inner anthro major was curious.

The meeting was hosted by Sherri's friend Josh and his wife Jean,[3] he a commodities broker, she a high school math teacher. Sherri and Josh had attended the same small Christian college. Before that, he had been an Indiana farm boy, and he still had the

[3] The names Sherri, Josh, and Jean are pseudonyms.

look: a beefy, boyish face with a grin that verged on gaping, mussed hair with perpetually sweaty bangs, a brown suit that flared in all the wrong places, and a general air of guilelessness. This cast in high relief his awkward attempts to put on city airs: the firm handshake, the breezy small talk, the man-of-the-world asides.

Scott Coon (the millionaire from Seattle), on the other hand, was the genuine article: *His* breezy small talk projected sincere interest, *his* well-fed face reflected self-assurance. After a mumbled intro from Josh (followed by whoops from the audience), Scott stood beaming at us, rubbing his hands in anticipation.

This was a "First Look"—the initial meeting where Amwayers bring prospects to scare them about the future—and Scott delivered it with gusto and verve: two and a half hours of fast patter without notes, touching upon such diverse topics as the high divorce rate, the quality of McDonald's hamburgers, IBM's strategy of diversification, and the number of cupholders in the minivan he had recently bought *with cash*. I would later realize that this was a typical Amway speech: somewhere between an infomercial and a sermon, a loosely organized string of riffs that bespoke either improvisational genius or, more likely, countless repetitions.

Scott spent the first hour explaining America's economic crisis, rooted in a betrayal stretching back to the late nineteenth century. That's when big corporations, with the help of government-run public education, first convinced Americans to abandon their entrepreneurial instincts and accept jobs. Before that, everyone was either a small-business owner or apprenticing to be one; afterward, it was all about benefits packages. Emasculated by wage slavery, Americans had muddled along fairly well until, as stagflation rent the land in the 1970s, we realized in horror that mere wages were helpless against "exponentially expanding costs."

As he reprised decades' worth of conservative alarmism, invoking inflation and national debt and other flat-earth bugbears, Scott built to a doomsday climax. The Second Wave, like Communism, like all the works of man, was destined to decay and collapse, making way for the coming entrepreneurial kingdom—which, for those who lacked faith or zeal, would bring a day of reckoning. Were we ready? To prove he "wasn't making this crazy stuff up," he littered the floor with copies of *Fortune*, *Money*, and *Forbes*, citing the relevant disaster stories. I felt like I was back at ENTERPRISE 2020.

But unlike E2020, which catered to the upper echelons, Scott offered a berth on the ark to the common worker, the middle-level manager, the petit bourgeois professional. Moreover, what he offered was so entrepreneurial, so Third Wave—so purely capitalist—that it transcended the Darwinian struggle altogether, promising an escape into tranquil early retirement. He held up a copy of *Success* magazine trumpeting the "Young and Rich in America." "It's still possible to make it in this country," he declared. "There's no hammer and sickle over this deal yet!"

He was about to show us the sure bet in the coming high-stakes society.

The Plan

Everyone in the room had long since flipped the cassettes in their handheld recorders by the time Scott revealed the secret behind his own "out of control" income. He worked, he said, in the cutting-edge field of distribution, where the real money was to be made nowadays. Through his business, he could get thousands of quality goods, many of them brand names, at a cut rate. The company that organized this amazing system did $6 billion a year in sales—Scott helped us to understand this awesome figure by describing the height of a billion-dollar stack of hundred-dollar bills—and was, on top of this, debt-free. It might surprise us that this company was Amway![4]

[4] As soon as they mention Amway, First Look speakers always hurry to dispel "myths" about The Business: that it's a rinky-dink soap company, that it

According to its Sales and Marketing Plan, there were two ways to make money in Amway. You could simply buy products cheaply, at wholesale costs reportedly 30 percent below retail, and sell them dear. On top of this, however, you teach others to do the same: The income you garnered through "duplicating" yourself, Scott explained, would add up quickly, as all of your downlines' sales would count toward your bonus awards. We were to imagine recruiting six distributors, each of whom would bring in four more, who in turn would snag an additional two. Our respective downline groups, according to this "6-4-2" formula, would have seventy-eight members. If each of our underlings did $100 a month in sales, we'd make an extra $2,000 a month in bonuses.[5]

And for those of us who had no taste for sales, here was the best part: A group of Amway millionaires had come up with a surefire system for making The Plan work without all the selling—and had formed World Wide Dreambuilders LLC, a corporation independent of Amway, to spread the word. All that was required to ensure an Amwayer's success, Dreambuilders taught, was that each distributor simply bought $100 of Amway products a month for his own "personal use." That meant no high-pressure pitches, no Tupperware parties. You could meet your $100 monthly goal by selling to yourself—at 30 percent off retail to boot! This was such a self-evidently great deal that your downline would practically

---

requires door-to-door sales, that it's a pyramid scheme (if you do an organizational chart of a typical corporation, guess what, that *looks* like a pyramid too!), that you have to be a Christian to join (there's nobody The Business wouldn't accept), that it's a crazy cult (Amway provides an opportunity to everybody, meaning that it inevitably lets in some bad apples who damage its reputation).

5 This wasn't exactly true: The bonus is calculated on the basis of sales of 100 PV a month; PV, or Point Value, is a play currency that converts to American legal tender at a rate of about 1 to 3.5. Each distributor in one's pyramid would have to spend around $350 a month in real money to generate the $2,000 bonus.

build itself. You could quickly 6-4-2 to that extra $2,000, and once our six "legs" did likewise, you'd pull down a cool $50,000 a month; or, if other "factors" were considered, more like $100,000! And that was just the beginning: There were some truly spectacular incomes to be made through The Business—which Scott would have told us about but for FTC regulations barring him from doing so.

Suddenly the future looked bright: We could do all of the twenty-first-century things—work from home, engage in cutting-edge marketing, become part of a decentralized network, and nurture our inner entrepreneur—and not perish from it. All the "human capital" we needed was the ability to shop and be effusive about it, and these were practically American birthrights.

Judging by the herculean efforts made to seduce me into The Business, however, The Plan wasn't quite as effortless as it sounded. Josh and Jean adopted a strategy that consisted mainly of driving me, at untold inconvenience to themselves, to as many meetings as possible in far-flung suburbs. Blocked bodily by Jean from climbing into the back of the car, I would sit captive in the passenger seat while Josh tried out the various small-talk techniques he'd learned from World Wide. Our trips always ended with Josh proffering a Sample Kit, mainly so that he could visit me later to retrieve it. It was a large white box with a Happy-Meal handle filled with detergents and propaganda, including *Promises to Keep*, a slim paperback by the suggestively named Charles Paul Conn, and numerous photocopied articles explaining why Amway was the most "misunderstood company in the world."

Meanwhile, Amway products didn't exactly seem to wing off the shelves. Sherri complained that she couldn't even get her own family to buy from her business: Her mother preferred to go to the local Costco. ("A *communist* store! Gee, *thanks*, Mom!") Of course, you couldn't rely on intimates, she explained; the real way to build The Business was to "make casual acquaintances out of strangers." Techniques for doing this, basically pickup lines, were an important part of Dreambuilder curriculum. Josh spoke admiringly of Diamond Distributor Randy Sears and his many suave "ice-breakers": Randy would pretend to know someone, for instance, and they'd often pretend to know him right back. Or he'd walk right up to somebody and say, "I like your belt!"[6]

In their zeal, Josh and Jean shuttled me to at least one meeting too many. The worst was a Seminar, an afternoon of "professional training" definitely geared to insiders. Here, during a marathon transfusion of spine-stiffening resolve, I got a glimpse of just how demoralizing the travails of Amway could be. The speaker, Conrad Halls, a Hollywood cameraman with over-the-hill golden-boy looks, who had been loose and congenial in a First Look the night before, was much sterner in the Seminar's light of day. He emphasized that Amway was not a get-rich-quick scheme, that the "difference between *trying* and *triumphing* is a little *umph*," and that—and here he pointed to his head—if you didn't already have a positive attitude, you had better "reprogram your computer." He praised a woman in the audience who was missing her daughter's birthday party to attend the Seminar. She lived what Amwayers call a "delayed life." "In a few years, when you're spending all day, every day with your daughter, you'll look back at this investment into your business," he reassured the woman, "and know it was the best birthday gift of all." Those who slacked in their attendance at World Wide functions, he warned, might just as well forget about being successful. After this short homily, Conrad's wife, Lisa, gave us an important pointer for living the delayed life: You were never to let your doubt or discouragement show, because that would scare off prospects. Instead, you had to learn to "fake it till you make it."

6 Once, when we had arrived at the wrong Holiday Inn for a World Wide meeting—right interstate, wrong unincorporated area—Josh wrung some victory out of defeat by coming up with a "great icebreaker" to use on the lone airline pilot in the lobby: "You're with United? You must be *friendly!*"

It was a strange adage for bucking people up. The Seminar, in fact, had a desperate atmosphere of good money being thrown after bad. Amway might not have grown through offering great bargains after all, but rather through a process of recursive "faking it": screwed people trying to get unscrewed by screwing others. I couldn't be sure, of course, until I saw a wholesale price list and could gauge the money to be saved by buying through Amway. As it happened, the price list was the one document that Josh always neglected to have in his briefcase.

One night, after he had taken me out to dinner (we went Dutch), Josh told me that there was a price list in the back of his car—sealed in an Amway Starter Kit. I could have it right away; I just had to give him the $160 fee to officially join Amway. Uncertain about taking the plunge, I claimed my checking account couldn't cover $160 that week. That was all right, he insisted: I could write a postdated check that he would hold until I gave the OK to deposit it. I still resisted, and he got out of the car with me, opening the hatch to show me the sealed white box within. Eventually, he settled for giving me a book called *Being Happy*, which he could later retrieve.

The next week, I made up my mind. I would never learn the truth about Amway until I joined. I left a message on Josh's Amvox voicemail, telling him I had the $160 check ready. A week later, I left another message. By my third attempt, I got Josh himself (who had been intending to return my calls) and finally was able to arrange a time to separate me from my money. It wasn't the last time I felt he and Jean weren't exactly cut out for the rigors of The Business.

Buying Through The Business

Figuring out the arcana of Amway took months. The price list, for instance, is denominated in two artificial Amway currencies called "Point Value" (PV) and "Bonus Volume" (BV), which are listed alongside the U.S. dollar–denominated wholesale and "Suggested

Retail" prices. But for all the rigmarole, the system's core concept was simple.

Imagine that you've struck a deal with a company to give you discounts for buying in bulk: If you buy $100 worth of stuff, they'll send you a 3 percent rebate. The percentage goes up incrementally the more you buy, up to 25 percent back on $7,500 worth of purchases. Now, let's say you personally are unable to spend more than $100 a month, but you manage to get seventy-four other people to go in with you. Together, you spend $7,500 and share equally the 25 percent rebate. The upshot: Everyone saves money. That's the idea behind a consumer coop or wholesale buying club.

Now, let's say you get the 25 percent rebate from the company but tell the other seventy-four participants, "Look, you've each spent only $100, so you'll get only a 3 percent rebate." Not only would you save 25 percent on your own purchases, but you would also make a 22 percent profit on everyone else's. *That's* the idea behind Amway.

If you sit atop the canonical 6-4-2 Amway pyramid as a "Direct Distributor,"[7] you make 25 percent on what your entire group spends, minus the 12 percent you pay out to your six legs, who in turn pay out 6 percent to their legs. If you're one of the forty-eight distributors on the bottom layer, with no downline of your own, you get back 3 percent of what you spent—while, remember, 13 percent of what you spent goes to the guy on top. It would amount to the

[7] A "Direct Distributor" is one whose group does 7,500 PV or more in monthly sales (which is almost $25,000 a month in U.S. currency, a far more daunting figure that the artificial PV currency helps to disguise). Direct Distributors are entitled to order directly from Amway without going through their upline sponsor, as the lower ranks must do. Once you are a Direct Distributor, your group is no longer nested in your sponsor's. From then on, your sponsor gets only a straight 4 percent cut (the "Leadership Bonus") of your group's sales. You accrue more bonuses by lining up DDs under your direct sponsorship: Six DDs make you a Diamond, twelve a Double Diamond, twenty a Crown Ambassador.

same thing if the distributors at the bottom received the full 25 percent rebate—and then gave all but 3 percent of it to their uplines.

Disguising the upward flow of fees within a downward flow of commissions, all calculated and paid out by Amway central, has its advantages. One of the decisive factors in the 1979 FTC decision exonerating Amway from allegations of pyramiding was that most of its revenues came from product sales, not from enrollment fees. The assumption is that those sales are based on rational consumer choices—made on the basis of price and quality—and that the money paid into the bonus system is not an extraneous surcharge but merely the portion other corporations would pour into their marketing budgets. Amway claims, in fact, that it's able to save money even for its small-time distributors by avoiding such things as pricey mass advertising. These savings are the source of the alleged 30 percent Basic Discount that every distributor is supposed to enjoy even before the bonuses kick in.

To test these claims I took my new Amway wholesale price list to the local supermarket for a price comparison. As it turned out, Amway *wholesale* prices were only slightly better than supermarket *retail* prices, although a few Amway products, such as freezer bags, were significantly cheaper. And this was giving The Business the benefit of many doubts: I factored in its claim that its detergents are more "concentrated" than other brands; I compared Amway with high-quality brand-name products, not store brands or generics; and I compared only regular prices, ignoring the fact that the supermarket, unlike Amway, always has items on sale (not to mention coupons).[8] The same results obtained at the local drugstore in comparisons of vitamins and cosmetics. All in all, the 30 percent Basic Discount was nowhere to be found.[9]

[8] To be fair, the *Amagram* occasionally has a "Catalog Sale" section, where a handful of items are offered at discounts.

[9] The Amway *Business Reference Manual* itself gives the lie to the 30 percent figure. It calculates the Basic Discount by subtracting a product's wholesale

To get the full Amway experience, I started buying my groceries through The Business. I found that, despite Amway's growth, its "cutting-edge" distribution system preserved all the pitfalls of a small buying club run out of somebody's apartment. Ironically, my local supermarket actually had started as a buying club run out of someone's apartment way back in the 1930s; as it grew, however, it accreted all the efficiencies of the retail system. Now it was open fourteen hours a day, seven days a week, with professional managers, stockers, and checkers; a visit there was quick and hassle-free. To make my "pickup" at Josh and Jean's apartment, on the other hand, required an hour-long el ride and arrangements with a friend to haul the stuff back home, all scheduled for those brief windows of opportunity when Josh and Jean could be there to meet me.

And these inconveniences paled next to the emotional shock of entering Josh and Jean's apartment. Not big to begin with, its thorough occupation by the Amway Corporation made it positively claustrophobic. The living room was dominated by huge metal cabinets displaying Amway cleaning and food products; shelves along the wall were devoted to toiletries; boxes of cereal lined the top of the couch. Next to the window was an eraser board listing upcoming World Wide Dreambuilders meetings; free wall spaces and the outsides of cabinets were decorated with motivational slogans ("I AM A WINNER!") drawn in crayon.

When I arrived for the first time, Jean had already bagged my order. She apologized for the absence of some items, which were on "backorder." (Among them were the Big Fiber Fudgies, high-fiber brownies that Josh, Jean, and Sherri rated among the tastiest

---

distributor cost from the suggested retail price (both denominated in dollars) and then dividing them by the BV price, which is set by Amway for each product but which is usually lower than the U.S. dollar price. If the calculation is done *solely* in dollars, the Basic Discount shrinks to about 17 percent. And when I did a real price comparison, that 17 percent came down to about 4 percent.

delectations on earth. Jean urged me to be brave about the Fudgie delay.)

The supply chain rigidly followed the line of recruitment. Some of the items I ordered had to be sent by mail all the way from Seattle, since that was where Scott and Shelley Coon, our upline Direct Distributors, happened to live. Others could be shipped from a regional warehouse in Michigan—one of Amway's attempts to make the system more workable—but still had to be ordered through the Coons. Some items—unavailable from the warehouse—could be sent directly to me via UPS, but my building didn't have a doorman. Jean suggested I have them sent to her apartment to be picked up with the rest of my order.

While Jean explained all of this, Josh, by way of chatting up my friend who was driving me home, offered him some Glister Anti-Plaque Gum. This was a companion to Glister Anti-Plaque Toothpaste, something so caustic-sounding that I never dared put it in my mouth. "It's actually illegal in Canada," Josh declared incorrectly, adding, "I guess they just don't worry about plaque up there." My friend excused himself to go to the bathroom, from which he emerged with an odd look on his face. Once safely in the car, he described the bathroom as something not to be missed.

I did pickups for several depressing weeks. Apart from Sherri, I never saw any sign of another customer. It was like one of those dusty, deathly still mom-and-pops frequented only by regulars who come mainly to chat—and I was oppressed with a similar sense that the proprietors needed my money more than I needed their merchandise. It was actually a relief when, one week, Josh and Jean had left town without warning me.

What with backorders and unexpected disappearances, it took me a few weeks to gather enough items for my next experiment: a blind taste-test pitting Amway food against brands from "communist" supermarkets. Unfortunately, a bias crept into the data when my subjects learned to identify what they called the Telltale Amway Aftertaste. Even correcting for this, Amway food rated low: Only the Critics' Choice Cherry Flavored Toaster Pastries (a Pop-Tart analog) managed to eke into second-to-last place. The Goglonian Bagels were universally declared the worst ever experienced. And the Big Fiber Fudgies? Let's just say that they were pretty much all Telltale Aftertaste.

Despite the mediocrity of Amway products, I couldn't help being impressed by their sheer number and variety. Other multilevels offer one or two miracle products, such as nutritional supplements—blue-green algae or "minerals in colloidal suspension," for instance, about which wild claims can be made with impunity. Such products defy conventional sales methods, usually because they require either elaborate instruction or some sort of conversion experience on the part of the customer. Amway, with its Liquid Organic Cleaner, began this way but eventually came to insist that *all* products were better sold through multileveling: couches, VCRs, cookies, socks, toilet paper, you name it. Amway didn't push one exceptional product so much as offer a complete alternative universe of consumption, giving Amwayers the maximum number of opportunities to switch their buying to dues-paying mode.[10]

Dreambuilding

From time to time the paradoxes of The Business would surface in Josh's conversation. In one of his many unguarded moments, he voiced a preference for Amway Scrub Rite because it ran out more quickly than the "superconcentrated" Amway cleaners, enabling him to buy it more often. Catching himself, he quickly added, "Of course, it still lasts a *long time*." This puzzled me. Why was Josh so eager to shovel money at Amway? The rational thing would be to minimize his own purchases while strong-arming his downlines

[10] Not that there aren't limits. The food in Amway leans heavily toward the pricey, overpackaged "meal kit" and portable "nutrition bar." Woe to those who try to buy a bag of rice through The Business—not to mention fresh produce or meat, though you can have frozen steaks airmailed to you.

into buying as much as possible. But, of course, if everyone did that, the whole business would evaporate. This was Amway's central dilemma.

There were some rational explanations for Josh's behavior. To recruit others, he needed the propaganda talents of his upline World Widers, who made it clear to their underlings that they had to be "fanatical about personal use," holding this up as an index of a distributor's positive attitude. Another rationale was provided by the well-worn anecdote, often retold in the first person, about the distributor who missed a new Performance Bracket by a few dollars when *a little bit more* personal use could have taken them over the edge. The story always ended, "Well, you better believe I never made *that* mistake again!"

But as I came to know Josh better, I realized he was acting not so much out of a calculated strategy as out of a deep faith in "duplication." Josh believed that whatever he did, his downlines would imitate: If he set the example of filling his house with only "positive" (i.e., Amway) products, so would they. Rich DeVos, more philosophically, calls this the Law of Compensation: "In the long haul, every gift of time, money, or energy that you give will return to benefit you."

Josh felt that duplication worked in the other direction as well. If he emulated the multi-multi-millionaires ("multi-multis" for short) above him—and did exactly what they said they had done—he would succeed as they had. In his mind, his interests were already merged with theirs. He would boast of *their* accomplishments, tell me that *their* bonuses just kept "getting better and better all the time!" For him, of course, bigger bonuses for uplines simply meant a more powerful upward suction on his income. But that kind of self-defeating "stinking thinking" missed the point, as far as Josh was concerned. By "visualizing" great wealth and by imitating the consuming habits of the great and wealthy, he would somehow obtain great wealth.

I only learned the extent to which he and Jean had convinced themselves of this when I worked up the courage to visit their bathroom. It was a strange spectacle indeed. The wall opposite the toilet was decorated with Post-its, each with a biblical proverb or chestnuts like, "A drowning man doesn't complain about the size of the life preserver," and "If you don't stand for something, you'll fall for anything!" I was startled when a reggae song about "winners" suddenly filled the air (I located the speakers in the medicine cabinet). Most impressive, however, was a wish list taped above the toilet. Scrawled in pencil, it was presumably lengthened whenever Josh or Jean had a flash of covetousness in the shower. It included, among other items,

- A bathroom as big as our apartment and someone to clean it every other day (but not Sunday)
- A whirlpool as big as our bathroom
- Seven pairs of tennis shoes and seven courts
- A black helicopter seating 12
- Horses, 21
- A chateau, with seven gardens and seven fountains and a chauffeur

With Amway, extravagant desire was obviously *the* motive force: To desire what your upline had—even those things that nobody could realistically hope for—was what kept the scheme in motion.[11] Josh and Jean's wish list, as well as the many other

[11] At the top, the multi-multis seem to attain a Zen of conspicuous consumption. Brad Duncan, brother of the great Double Diamond Greg Duncan, described seeing a dusty Rolls-Royce among the many cars in the garage of his upline mentor, Ron Puryear; when he asked what he paid for it, Ron answered, "I don't know. Whatever the sticker price was." Brad took him to task for this, until Ron lectured: "That dealership is somebody's livelihood—somebody with a family. I'm not so hard up that I need to haggle the food out of a child's mouth." Brad was chastened, realizing that only small minds pay attention to sticker prices.

"visualization" exercises involved in dreambuilding, was simply part of their training to ever more expansively *want*.

But, like my friend who had first eyeballed that bathroom, I was particularly struck by the numerology that invested even tennis shoes with a mythic charge. If Josh and Jean were greedy, it was a fairy-tale greed: a fantasy of escape into a land where the rules of everyday life no longer applied. Amway promised to transcend the downsides of American capitalism—the increasingly long hours, the job insecurity—by indulging its excesses. With realistic, collective solutions off the docket, people turn to miracles. In this way, Amway is not so different from other mutations of the American Dream: the notion that grass-roots entrepreneurs would save the urban poor, that the stock market would save Social Security, that casinos would fund our schools. All of these salvation schemes preserve a core myth of capitalism: that the instruments for distributing wealth also somehow create it. Or as Double Diamond Distributor (and Überparasite) Greg Duncan put it at Dream Night while discussing Washington bureaucrats divvying up the economic pie: "I *make* pies!"

It's a myth hard to resist—insofar as the exchange floor and the casino offer dramatic visible spectacles of people getting rich while real wealth-creation is the arcane stuff of productivity figures and efficiency studies—but it has tragic consequences for people like Josh and Jean. Perfectly capable of leading enjoyable lives, they nonetheless surrounded themselves with Amway propaganda, subsisted on Amway food, immersed themselves in Amway culture, talked and thought in Amway jargon, and siphoned their income to Greg Duncan in the hopes of learning the "secret" of his wealth.

Saturation

As much as Josh ignored the contradictions of his faith, he could always be relied on to express them. A typical Joshism (uttered while describing the photos of new Directs that appear in the

Amagram each month): "People are amazed that there are that many new Directs each month—at first, they think it's per year, but no!" The point apparently being the great odds of success. Then, in the very next breath: "I look through them every month to make sure there aren't too many from Illinois. I'm worried that Chicago will get saturated. Last month, though, there were only two." Now he was selling the *poor* odds.

All Amwayers are haunted by the specter of saturation, the success that spells disaster. The 6-4-2 scenario tells it all: To keep one promise of $2,000-a-month requires that seventy-eight more be made. The problem is that growth doesn't improve this ratio: Were Amway to conquer the known universe, fewer than 2 percent of its distributors would be (or mathematically *could be*) Directs or higher. Of the rest, about 90 percent would actively lose money, and without a pool of prospects to give them hopes for the future, they would surely quit. Amway would collapse from the bottom up.

The prospect is alarming enough that Charles Paul Conn, in *Promises to Keep*, works hard to prove it'll never happen. "The reality," he tells us, "is entirely different from what might be predicted by a statistician with a slide rule." He points to the millions of untapped prospects—youths, retirees, downsized professionals, foreigners—although he fails to acknowledge that recruiting them would only make The Business hungrier. More plausibly, he adds that Amway will always remain a small part of the population. The Business's high dropout rate, he explains, though "often cited as a negative factor, actually serves to keep the pool of potential distributors large." In other words, Amway's salvation is its high rate of failure.

This hard truth belies Amway's populism, its promise that success simply requires getting in on the ground floor—and that *every floor is the ground floor.* Deep down, Josh may have realized that an Amway easy enough even for him to master would soon self-destruct. This buried consciousness surfaced, for example, in the way he consoled himself with weird probability statistics. He knew how many levels deep he had to extend his downline (something like six) before he was certain to recruit someone with a knack for huckstering, someone on whose tide he could rise. It was unlikely, of course, that a guy like Josh could spawn a six-level downline without the help of such a person, but that fact simply masked a deeper improbability: that there were enough of these theoretical master salesmen to prop up every schlub who couldn't succeed otherwise.

He ultimately dealt with this Catch-22 through simple fantasies of escape. He was adamant that someday he'd be a millionaire, his current predicament no more than a bad memory. His hand would trace a hyperbola as he explained that The Business was hard at first, but if you'd just stick in there, you'd soon enjoy *exponential* success. This would happen so soon that he wouldn't have to prospect long enough even to get particularly good at it. "The point is not to get good," he insisted, "It's to get done!"

It was unlikely Josh would ever be one of the few to "get done." Amway actually didn't thrive through exponential growth, but rather through the fanatical consumption of a relatively small number of people who believe that everyone can be a "winner."[12]

[12] Amway gives some idea of real chances for success in its *Amway Business Review* pamphlet, which the FTC requires it provide to all prospects. The *Business Review* is an ingenious mixture of mandated honesty and obfuscatory spin: The average monthly gross income for "active" distributors, for instance, is revealed to be a meager $65 a month; but the *Review* leaves out the *median* income and the *net* profit, both of which probably would be negative. Likewise, it states that "2 percent of all 'active' distributors who sponsor others and approximately 1 percent of all 'active' distributors met Direct Distributor qualification requirements during the survey period." From this, it derives the optimistic conclusion that, "once again, the survey demonstrates a substantial increase in achievement for those who share the business with others." *Increase* implies that there are some nonsharing distributors who succeed; an alternate reading of the statistics would be that all distributors *try* to share, none succeed *without* sharing, but only half are *able to share*. It's also a

Josh was in denial—and it was in Amway/World Wide's interest to keep him that way.

The Power of Association

After a year in The Business, Josh and Jean were scarcely able to devote eight hours a week to distributing goods and showing The Plan, activities that required a good supply of prospects, customers, and downlines. They were desperate for new leads and regularly alarmed me with proposals that we all go to some public place and *mingle*. Of course, that would have required overcoming shyness and other gag responses, impediments that Josh, Jean, and Sherri never really overcame (most of their leads seemed either to be family or, like me, coworkers). They would, on the other hand, devote entire weekends to "recharging their batteries" at First and Second Looks, Seminars, Rallies, and Major Functions (Dream Night, Leadership Weekend, Family Reunion, Free Enterprise Day). These meetings required only insecurity and neediness, which all three had in spades.

These functions, all sponsored by World Wide Dreambuilders, were rhetoric-fests where Amway's self-help message was pushed to its logical addiction-recovery extreme—although with the roles curiously reversed. "J-O-B people," meaning those who were *not* Amway-style entrepreneurs, were portrayed as the helpless addicts, hooked on the "immediate gratification" of a weekly paycheck. It was *they* who were in denial, telling themselves that they didn't have a problem, that they were happy working all day for practically nothing. In contrast, the "delayed life" was a healthy process of withdrawal, of gradually replacing the "negatives" in your life (including non-Amway products) with "positives." Most important, you learned to "dream" again, reconnecting with the

---

measure of Amway's PR savvy that every article I've seen (even the critical ones) that mentions the number of Directs uses the 2 percent, rather than the more accurate 1 percent, figure.

inner child who, before the nine-to-five beat it down, had fantasized about big houses and fast cars.[13]

Whereas The Plan is supposed to provide a simple means to a desirable end, for Josh, Jean, and Sherri, the process of recovery had become an end in itself. Josh and Jean would constantly tell me how World Wide's books and advice had enriched their marriage and helped them to communicate with each other. (The bolstering of marriage and family was a major theme in Amway.) The Amway lore is also full of distributors, perhaps abused as children, who "couldn't even look people in the eye" when they joined, but who now were confidently showing The Plan to all and sundry.

Dreambuilders' impact on Sherri's life was far less salutary. Its most tangible financial effect was the used car that Josh advised her to buy, which came complete with a weird smell and a glove compartment that didn't close. But Sherri felt that she had undergone a profound psychic transformation. "Before Amway," she would say, "I just wasn't *thinking*!" Her new clarity made her scornful of mass pursuits: When the E2020 staff went to a Cubs game, she could hardly believe that people would waste their time that way. (Josh counseled her just to sit next to strangers and *mingle*.) Her "j-o-b," even with a promotion to Internet Expert, certainly didn't interest her any more: She wanted to spend the whole day talking

[13] The recovery slant also solves a troubling logical conundrum for Amwayers. On the one hand, Amwayers are utterly dependent on jobholders—not only to manufacture and transport their products but also to provide them with clerical assistance when they're Diamonds (Greg Duncan boasted of the size of his staff, which does his actual distribution work) and, above all, to make their millions worth something in the outside economy. On the other hand, Amway is supposed to offer a surefire alternative to wage labor. What will keep all of the essential workers from becoming distributors? The answer lies in weakness of the flesh: Just as there always will be alcoholics, junkies, and overeaters, so there always will be many people without the resolve or courage to join Amway.

about The Business.[14] And she now regarded unambitious coworkers, family, and friends as, in Scott Coon's words, "slugs."

As her world shrank, she immersed herself in World Wide culture. For entertainment, she listened to the motivational tapes, laughing and crying at the tales of hardship and triumph. She read the WWDB recommended books, memorizing snippets of Norman Vincent Peale and *Psychocybernetics*. She urged me, likewise, to move to the "next level": to hook into Amvox voicemail (where I could listen to messages from my distant upline Greg Duncan courtside at Bulls–Magic games);[15] make plane and hotel reservations for the upcoming family reunion; and get on "standing order" to automatically receive six World Wide cassettes a month at six bucks a pop—which Josh claimed simply covered costs—presumably of meetings recorded onto very cheap tapes. ("I'd gladly pay more for them," Josh insisted, "because they're helping me to become financially liberated!") Sherri told me, in hushed tones: "Greg Duncan judges you more on the number of standing orders in your downline than on your PV!" I didn't doubt it. The upper ranks of World Wide and other groups rake in enormous profits from their speaking engagements and the sale of motivational materials. Dexter Yager, head of the Yager Group, reput-

[14] I got the impression that she was becoming a laughingstock at work, an experience common enough to have spawned a whole genre of revenge fantasies in the Amway lore. Speakers always describe the retirement party you'll be able to throw for yourself, complete with fireworks, to stick it to the naysayers who once laughed at you. They also describe the houses and vacations you'll give to your parents, who'll finally realize how wrong they were about The Business. The yearning to save face—especially with people you urged to join Amway—seems to be a major factor keeping people in.

[15] Rich DeVos owns the Orlando Magic basketball team, and Amway uses the nickname of former Magic center Shaquille O'Neal for its "Shaq Bars," treats that taste like chaff stuck together with heavy-duty, honey-flavored adhesive. When I reluctantly ate one at a meeting, a passing World Wider commented, "I *love* those. You need to eat them with a *lot* of water, though."

edly made more from his propaganda syndicate than from his actual Amway business.

While the whirlwind of meetings and events was great for cultivating denial, it seemed to do little to help distributors develop "strong and profitable businesses." Nor was it much good for attracting new blood into The Business. With the exception of First Looks, the extreme cultishness was distinctly off-putting to newcomers. Still, Josh, Jean, and Sherri continued to make the mistake of indiscriminately taking prospects to whatever meeting was being held. Even a Second Look (described ominously as more "motivational" and less informational than a First Look) was inadvisable for outsiders, as Sherri discovered when she took her friend Elizabeth to one.

The car ride to the meeting went swimmingly. When Sherri mentioned job insecurity and the need to "diversify," Elizabeth couldn't have agreed more. When Sherri mentioned the time–money trap, Elizabeth knew just what she was talking about. A First Look might have had a real impact.

Elizabeth was clearly expecting some sort of business seminar. (Sherri hadn't mentioned Amway and also cautioned me against doing so. "I've found that when I say 'Amway,' people get all . . ." she said, miming "running-away-screaming.") What she got, however, was closer to a Pentecostal revival meeting. The featured speaker, Executive Diamond Brad Duncan (Greg's younger brother), was more Billy Sunday than financial analyst; he yelled, joked, screamed, and sermonized past the audience at "sinners" who pretended they didn't want to be rich and who dumped on anyone with ambition. He exhorted us to stop listening to our "broke" friends and relatives and to allow ourselves to be influenced by successful millionaires: "I believe in the *power of association!*"

Brad spoke in parables: There was Brad's father-in-law, who, upon being given a brand-new souped-up truck, sat down and wept. After a few years, the "newness wore off," so Brad again bought him the latest model. And again his father-in-law sat down and wept. (Brad's own fluid dynamics were more spectacular: When he first saw the jazzed-up truck, "urine streamed down" his pant legs.)

I was sitting next to Elizabeth and couldn't imagine what she was thinking. (True to form, Brad didn't mention Amway for more than an hour.) At first, she laughed and clapped with the rest of the audience; as the evening wore on, however, there was a lag. Her responses became more tentative as the crowd of hundreds became more wildly, foot-stompingly enthusiastic. Afterward, she was dazed and hollow-eyed. In the parking lot, Josh, Jean, and Sherri encircled her, urging her to meet with them the next day to learn more about The Business. Cornered, she agreed. After a few minutes in the car with Sherri, however, she regained enough strength to put off the meeting to the indefinite future. (Months later, she was still on Josh's "hopeful" list.)

Disappointments like this got Sherri down, and keeping her outlook positive was beginning to strain even World Wide Dreambuilders LLC. At one First Look, Dave Duncan (Greg and Brad's father, a straight-talkin' Montanan who had given up a successful construction business to build dreams with Amway) reassured Sherri with a timeline he drew on the eraser-board showing that you could make millions within ten years. Afterward, however, during the mingling—while Dave warned a young couple that, sure, some brain surgeons did well, but only the ones at the top—Sherri started eyeing the evening's hosts with despair. They were "crosslines," her Amway cousins from a different downline, in this case a brother-sister team who had broken 7,500 PV with an all-out one-summer campaign. Sherri, almost beside herself, insisted that Josh, Jean, and I have a meeting to "figure out what we're going to do. Because we've got to do *something*!"

Josh also showed signs of breakdown. After the presentation, he took his customary position near the speaker, a handheld recorder jutting provocatively from his hip; but because he wasn't in Dave's downline, he wouldn't be able to accompany him to dinner. Josh claimed that it was at such dinners that speakers, unfettered by FTC restrictions, could reveal "the good stuff." He proposed tailing Dave to the restaurant: "They couldn't stop us, could they?" When Jean talked him out of this, he became desperate simply to "go somewhere and meet people." Jean reminded him it was a school night for her. "Well, maybe we should talk to the hotel staff," he suggested.

My uplines' despair made me reluctant to add to their failure. But I had stayed in too long already. Having run out of other things to buy, I had resorted to subjecting my cat to Amway pet food. And I began to sense that when Josh and Sherri looked at me, they—in their last-ditch hopes—saw Diamonds. Before I disappeared from their lives, however, I accompanied them to one last Rally.

Rallies always began with a ritual called "crossing the stage," in which distributors who had attained a new bonus level would go up to receive their commemorative pin and shake hands with a Diamond. From the crowd of about 500, two couples "crossed" at the 1,000 PV level (the lowest warranting a pin) and received a standing ovation from the audience. From the stage, the host then called out all the levels from 1,500 PV to 7,500 PV. Nobody emerged from the audience—which, nonetheless, remained on its feet applauding. The host kept cajoling, "C'mon, there's plenty of room up here," as if it were shyness that was keeping people away. It was the archetypal Amway moment: a crowd giving a standing ovation to nobody.

The centerpiece of any Rally is the life story told by the guest of honor, emphasizing the depths of his pre-Amway rut and his resurrection through The Business. That evening's featured guest, Executive Diamond Bill Hawkins, however, was too arrogant even to feign the requisite humility in his testimonial. He had been great all his life: a talented musician in one of Minneapolis's best bands, a brilliant schoolteacher, a voracious reader, a charming companion with hundreds of loyal friends, and an unbelievably prodigious drinker of beer (about which he was now "ashamed"). When he saw The Plan and realized that he was much smarter than the guy showing it, he knew that his ship had finally come in: Here, at last, was something that would adequately reward his greatness.[16]

Bill was one of the two types you find in Amway: the smarmy predator who knew a good hunting ground when he saw one. Confident in his superiority, he didn't need to think that Amway would work for everybody, but he didn't shy away from pretending that it would. Josh, Jean, and Sherri, of course, represented the other type: the dupes.

Bill signaled his disdain for the dupes by launching into a monologue that would have caused a scandal before a more critical audience. He told us, matter of factly, that World Wide had $8 million in assets, in which only those at the Diamond level had any equity; that the twenty World Widers who sat on its board frequently had food fights that splattered the HQ's silk wallpaper; and that World Wide tapes were so bad that Bill himself regularly threw them out his car window. In short, he was tossing us rope to hang him with, baldly acknowledging that World Wide was nothing but a support system for a bunch of fast-talkers who lived high on the hog by charging their bamboozled underlings outrageous prices for spurious advice. This was the most damning critique of Amway I had ever heard. Yet none of it mattered to the crowd; they seemed only to be dreaming of the fancy wallpaper that they might one day be able to soil.

[16] His tedious auto-encomium was enlivened only by occasional chilling anecdotes of violence: Hawkins told the audience how his mother hit him as a child until, old and strong enough, he could credibly threaten to hit her back; how his frat brothers, drunken and rambunctious, tried to shave his head one night, whereupon he barricaded himself in his room, audibly cocked a shotgun, and threatened to kill them; and how his family needled him about Amway until, one Thanksgiving, he jumped up and shouted, "I don't dump on what you do, and if you keep dumping on what I do, I'll take you outside and knock your block off; and if you're a woman, I don't know what I'll do!"

He ended by riffing on *The Wizard of Oz* as a way to remind us to stay positive and focused: "You have to stick to that yellow brick road. Just like Dorothy. She followed it all the way to the Emerald City—and picked up three legs along the way! You know what? *The Wizard of Oz* is really an Amway movie!" The crowd erupted in laughter and cheers. In the midst of their long applause, they seemed to have forgotten what the Wizard turned out to be.

—BAFFLER 10, 1997

Afterword

Grappling with its most troublesome asset, Amway Corporation has devoted a lot of energy in recent years to coming up with new names for itself. The chosen style has been sci-fi corporate, where each name sounds like a contraction of something too nefarious to be uttered at full length. Amway itself is now wholly owned by "Alticor," whose other subsidiaries include "Access," "Pyxis," and "Quixtar." Its official publications proclaim that "Alticor" now does $4 billion or $5 billion in sales each year, down from the $6 billion Amway sources were trumpeting just a few years ago. Clearly, Amway thrives best in those magical periods, such as that of the preceding article, when rising prosperity coincides with persistent feelings of insecurity. Take away either the anxiety or the extra pocket change, and Amway is hit hard. How the company will fare in the years to come, with our new alertness to business scams and irrational exuberance, is anyone's guess. But one shouldn't underestimate the ability of Amway to adjust to new realities. After all, as any Double Diamond might tell you, gambling on the stock market has always been a fool's game, and when the bubble bursts, it's the little guy who suffers. No, what you need to do is build your own business from the ground up, a business that will provide you with a secure residual income that will just keep expanding and expanding. . . .

A Bull Market in Bullshit

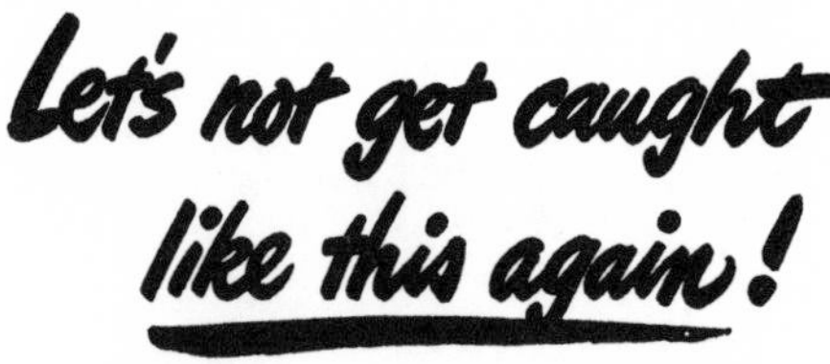
Let's not get caught
like this again!

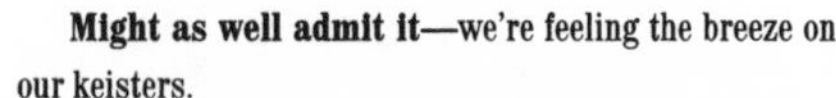

Might as well admit it—we're feeling the breeze on our keisters.

Sure, for the better part of three decades we've had the other team by the short ones. And maybe, as a class, we thought we had it in the bag. But it wasn't enough to sit back and pile up the dough. Oh, no. We had to install leadership teams to blubber about core values.

Not only that—we had to be cool. Now, I don't care if some dot-com punk wants to make a commercial taking a dump on guys like me. Jackass wants to burn his money, let him. But I'm a rich white dude with all the burdens that rich white dudes have grimly borne for over a century. And I want these New Economy jockeys to know that they didn't invent libertarianism. Or union-busting. Or positive thinking.

It took a half-century of hard work to get us where we are today. Lowest corporate taxes since the Big One. Social Security on the ropes. Our guys running the White House, all of Congress, and the courts.

And then the kids screw the pooch with this goddamn Nasdaq boondoggle.

Now our asses are in a sling. But I'm one guy they're not going to fool again. I'm signing up my own boys with subscriptions to The Baffler Magazine—the one irregularly published periodical that didn't fall for all that dot-com malarkey. One boy's in college, and the other's at Wharton. They're at an age when somebody's got to tell them what assholes they are, and unfortunately it just doesn't mean the same thing coming from Dear Old Dad.

Subscribe to THE BAFFLER.
P. O. Box 378293, Chicago, Ill. 60637
www.thebaffler.com

20

Three Scenes from a Bull Market

J. W. Mason

Editors' Note: Like everyone else, writers like to eat, go to the doctor, and pay their rent. So it would be unkind to belabor any young dude simply for drawing a paycheck from the business press. Indeed, we may recall how many important social critics—Dwight MacDonald, Jane Jacobs, and Daniel Bell, to name a few—made their livings and published important work in the pages of magazines such as *Fortune*.

Still, that was during the high tide of liberalism. In the Nineties, as the Nasdaq floated into hyperspace, the business press had a hard time distinguishing itself from the free market. What was the market, after all, but "information"? Business journalists became bad reporters and worse arbiters of history. Their millenial bull market is now an irretrievable dream, but their most important work has yet to be undone: The campaign to privatize Social Security marches on, sub rosa.

Extraordinary Popular Delusions

Every Friday evening, a rumpled thirtyish young man in a badly fitting suit jacket dispenses stock picks on CNNfn. He's a columnist for *Worth* magazine and publisher of a successful financial-advice newsletter. No surprises there—except to veterans of the

Chicago rock scene, who may rub their eyes when they see the name "Ken Kurson" flashing at the bottom of the screen. Hey, didn't he used to be front man for the Lilacs? Sure was—and before that, bassist for Green, a moderately successful Eighties pop band, from which he's taken the name for his magazine. At first glance, it looks like the Repo Man scenario: punk rocker, with serious misgivings, gone to work for The Man. It is, minus the misgivings—and with some strange complications.

Green, according to the manifesto included in every issue, is a financial magazine "for the rest of us—those who know that 'the man' really couldn't care less if we young 'uns approve of his larceny. . . . for those who don't care how cool it is to admit that they care about their lives and their futures." As it turns out, *Green*'s operational definition of caring about your life and future is: *Buy mutual funds*. *Green* operates under the odd conceit that promoting mutual funds is, as the passage just quoted suggests, a daring and transgressive act—or, in Kurson's words, "*Green* is based on the premise that moneytalk is the last taboo."

Of course, The Man does care if we approve of his larceny; for proof, look no further than Kurson, whose vocal and enthusiastic approval has been rewarded with that columnist's gig at *Worth* and that spot on CNNfn. What's his secret? It's sure not the advice. An ad for *Green* suggests that you'll find it useful "if you don't know exactly what a mutual fund is." This is correct. If you *are* familiar with the concept of mutual funds, though, it's far from clear what you'll learn from reading *Green*. Typical nuggets include answers to questions like "What's a bond?" or "What's a stock split?" One issue devotes three pages to demonstrating that if you owe money on several credit cards, you should pay off the one with the highest interest rate first.

What sets *Green* apart are its treatises on the hipness and even the morality of investing: Mutual funds are what separates the men from the boys, the sole alternative to a lifetime of humiliating dependence on one's parents.

> *Green* was conceived because its editor is frequently asked about finance by friends, coworkers and relatives, a diverse gaggle who share only one thing in common: None would ever be caught dead trying to master something as uncool as money. It's not punk rock, it's not rebellious, it's something of which my parents might approve, whatever. So they wallow in financial purgatory, ringing up astronomical debts on credit cards and student loans, many of which are taken to finance education in vanity disciplines that will never pay enough to make good on the loans. That's not rebellion and it's not freedom. It is the modus operandi of privileged and spoiled kids who know their parents will bail them out when things get too rough.

Getting the relation between youth culture and stock ownership right has been a vexing problem for the authors of the vast literature on Gen X, torn as they are between the fantasy that twenty-somethings are a uniquely frugal generation who will save the stock market and the fear that they've been spoiled by Social Security and commercial TV. Kurson himself is of two minds on this subject: On the one hand, it's the frugal Gen Xers who are supposed to be his readers, but on the other, he regularly berates his peers as pampered and indolent. In his TV and radio appearances, where he invariably is treated by interviewers as envoy and interpreter for the mysterious tribe of Youth, Kurson prefers to talk about how much his generation loves to save: "I think people in Generation X . . . feel that the Social Security system is by no means guaranteed to be around by the time they retire, that self-directed retirement plans, 401(k)s and IRAs, are really mandatory now." But in the privacy of his own pages, he's more liable to vent his rage against the popular kids who mocked him for his forbidden love of Mammon. "I had to be very secretive about my interest in money," he recalls, looking back at those painful years. "I've been at parties where people are discussing every kind of perversion and admiring the host's Gacy paintings, but just try to bring up compound interest and watch the room clear."

The kids are wise; the kids are fools. What is it about *Green*'s self-contradicting mass of resentment and braggadocio that has so caught the ear of Wall Street's image masters? And when else but during the most superstitious of bull markets could a writer with few qualifications to offer investment advice make up for it with nothing but stylish (Kurson has style in spades) expressions of ingenuous wonder at the institutions and public mores of capitalism? *Green* is continually agog at the fact that under capitalism you don't necessarily have to work for money, you can compel money to work for you. Each of the first few issues of the magazine even featured a panegyric on interest, with titles like "The Magic and Beauty of Compound Interest" and "The Glory and Magic of Compound Interest, Redux." There's also plenty of talk about self-reliance, but it seems self-reliance is something you do with your stocks. Indeed, to read this stuff you'd think the world contained no one but bedridden invalids pampered round-the-clock by private nurses, and brawny loners forging their way with naught but two strong arms and a well-balanced portfolio.

But all that stuff about stocks and interest is for people who don't know the game of ideology. The real way to make money in a bull market isn't mutual funds, it's working up a highly visible enthusiasm for mutual funds, letting yourself be seen reinventing the wheel of capitalist ideology in the language and garb of Generation X.

The most important element of that ideology, of course, is the political. Criticizing an article in *Harper's* expressing skepticism at the idea that stock investing can replace our current system of public provision for retirement, *Green* says, "It's difficult to see why he's wringing his hands. Sure, it'd be wonderful if some benevolent government or corporation were genuinely looking out for us," but it just ain't so. "Better to know the score while there's still time to stuff your mattress." That's our choice: benevolence from on high, or mattress-stuffing down below. If we can't count on our leaders to care for us, then it's every man for himself and devil take the hindmost. Notice what's excluded here: the possibility of any kind of collective political action. But that—not government "benevolence"—is what brought about Social Security and employer-provided pensions and the rest of it, in the first place, and that's the only kind of action most people can take to ensure their well-being forty years down the road.

Tulipomania

With an unbending moral code balanced by a promise of plenty in the hereafter, the speculation craze—whipped into a frenzy by the many investment-advice publications that have sprouted during Wall Street's long sunny season—has all the makings of a vernacular American religion. True to form, the ebullient promoters have dark alter egos following in their wake, a platoon of Jeremiahs whose abiding fear is that even the gravity-defying market of the Nineties has not drawn in *enough* money. With the feverish intensity of street-corner preachers, they collar any passerby foolish enough to make eye contact, pressing the literature into their hands with an impassioned plea: Jesus saves, and so should you.

The high priest of this cult is undoubtedly Pete Peterson, millionaire investor and advisor to a half-dozen presidents, whose brief is for probity, parsimony, and self-abnegation. "People may think this will be painless," he likes to say. "It won't." His obsession, as he let the world know in his 1996 book, *Will America Grow Up Before It Grows Old?*, is aging. The argument goes like this: The country is getting older, people are living longer and having fewer children. This "age wave" will mean many more unproductive retirees with expensive health-care and nursing-home habits, and fewer workers to pay for them. It also will mean a much bigger bill for government programs for the elderly, like Social Security and Medicare.

As it turns out, the "age wave" is a remarkably easy fear to debunk. While it's true that there are more old people than ever, the number of children and housewives (the rest of the dependent population) is decreasing; in fact, the ratio of nonworkers to workers has dropped steadily over the past century and is now at its lowest point. Honest fiscal conservatives should take as their slogan, "No more housewives!" But these facts don't interest Pete Peterson. For him, the demographic story is just a hook on which to hang his view of the world: a vast struggle between the forces of good and evil, where to be good is to save and to be evil, to spend. "When I was a child," he lectures the impecunious boys and girls of today, "I witnessed firsthand what can be accomplished by parents who dedicate themselves to posterity. For decades on end, my father, in Kearney, Nebraska, kept his small restaurant open 24 hours a day, 365 days a year. Every penny that didn't cover necessities or get plowed back into the business he set aside for his children's future. To him, being called a 'big spender' was the ultimate insult."

Like most of his ilk, Peterson emplots his narrative (as the historians say) into a tale of psychocultural decline. Naturally, the self-indulgent Sixties play no small role in his story, but he also goes back further: to the end of World War II, when an America besotted with its own strength abandoned the thrift his father practiced in the Thirties and Forties. Did Peterson expect birthday presents when he was boy? Not a chance! Just "a small metal barrel with a slot in the top—a 'gift' from a local S&L—in which my brother and I were expected to save our pennies, nickels, and dimes. My parents assumed we would make regular trips to this local S&L and deposit these savings for our future." Peterson's obsession draws him into some strange alliances. Unlike other conservatives, he's pro–public television, at least for children, because it offers an alternative to "endless commercials, all telling them to 'buy now.'" Victory in World War II was also a problem, since it encouraged Americans to grow proud and lazy and insist on working shorter hours for higher wages, which they then spent rather than saved at the trusty neighborhood S&L.

But soon, Peterson insists, as the country overflows with geezers, we will be in for our comeuppance. No more entitlements—not for the poor, and not for the middle class either. No more assuming you deserve a decent job, a home, an education. And certainly no more assuming you deserve to retire. Peterson points admiringly at the Japanese, who, "unlike Americans . . . are unencumbered by the idea that people are entitled to live the last third of their adult lives in subsidized leisure." Never mind that Peterson nearly doubles what is in fact the average length of retirement; the sight of anyone lazing around in a retirement home fills him with fury. Those people should be out flipping hamburgers!

But it's not just retirees who will have to bear the burden—we'll all have to tighten our belts and save like madmen. Only by saving and investing, Peterson assures us, will we be able to fill the insatiable maws of "a nation of Floridas." Some people may think "this will be painless," he cackles. "It won't. . . . There are no free lunches! To save more, we must consume less."

But does productive investment really depend on increased savings? The short answer is no (for the long answer, check out Doug Henwood's book *Wall Street*). According to John Maynard Keynes—and to the best evidence available today—investment is constrained not by a lack of savings but by a lack of sufficiently profitable investment opportunities. The typical big corporation is swimming in capital but demands a 10, 11, or 12 percent return before investing in plant or equipment on a significant scale. Such returns, understandably, are hard to achieve. Saving more and consuming less will merely make them rarer still—and leave us poorer, not richer, when the Baby Boomers retire.

Bad economics though they may be, calls for increased saving have an undeniable emotional resonance for some. Certainly this is the cathexis that all the young Social Security alarmists are tapping into. Viewed more dispassionately, though, there's something just a little odd about the idea of people in their twenties obsessing over retirement. I have no idea what I'll be doing in four years, let alone in forty; it's as likely as not that life as we know it will by then have been brought to a halt by global war or ecological collapse (or, if you believe the techno-futurists, have been transformed into one continuous virtual orgasm). It's a safe bet that what's really on the mind of the readers of personal financial magazines is not the size of their bank account in 2040 but its size today, and for all the usual reasons, punk rock or not. But for the moment, let's address the alarmists' arguments as though they were in earnest: Is it true that how much you save and invest when you're young is the main determinant of your standard of living when you're old?

The answer is no. For the vast majority of people who are currently in retirement, private savings do not contribute significantly to their income. From all the millions of words devoted each year to urging saving for retirement, you'd never guess what a small proportion of most people's retirement income such saving actually represents: Barely 10 percent of the income of the typical elderly household consists of income from assets—and an unknown but significant portion of this represents payments from defined-contribution pension plans rather than private savings per se. If you measure the average income from the four major sources—earnings, Social Security, income from assets, and pensions—for elderly households with each type of income, income from assets ranks dead last, at about $1,700 per year.

In other words, our grandparents' best investments by far were a job with a decent employer who provided a pension, and membership in a society civilized enough to take care of people's essential needs. According to the young bull-market thinkers, though, all that is going to evaporate one of these days, but, hey, banks and bull markets are forever!

The Madness of Crowds

I read somewhere that the attribution of the line "Let them eat cake" to Marie Antoinette is unfair; the French word she used really referred to a cheaper kind of flour (a better translation might be, "Let them eat Wonder Bread"). Those who say, in the words of a one *New Republic* headline, "Let them eat stock," have no such excuse: They mean exactly what they say. James Cramer, who wrote the *New Republic* piece, seriously suggested that the solution to layoffs is to give the fired workers stock options: "No government intervention is needed; it would be voluntary, but, once a handful of companies adopt these packages, all will follow." Naturally, existing shareholders, those kindly souls, would never object to having their stock diluted for the benefit of laid-off workers.

Cramer's is only one of the more imaginative (i.e., stupid) schemes floated in recent years to dramatically broaden stock ownership. Stock ownership is still limited almost entirely to the wealthiest 10 or 20 percent of the population, but within this group it's lately become much more evenly distributed. Just as in the 1920s, people who never before owned stocks have been lured into the market by the prospect of 10 percent returns year after year, and their purchases have driven prices still higher, drawing in even more investors behind them.

Of course, it takes an enormous promotional apparatus to keep the money flowing and the prices ever-rising. *Green* is just one very small, though strategic, cog in this machinery. Even on its home turf, it's overshadowed by much bigger players: Fidelity, whose TV ads hype its appeal to twenty-somethings; Morningstar, which packs its cubicles with goateed, nose-ringed mutual-fund analysts and newly graduated (but skill-less and experience-less) "consultants"; and brokerages and pension companies such as State Street Boston, which lubricate their plots for Social Security privatization with appeals to an imaginary generational conflict in which they, naturally, are on the side of the young. "Excluding senior citizens, there's probably no age group more obsessed with Social Security than post-boomers," write State Street execs Marshall Carter and William Shipman in their 1996 book, *Promises to Keep: Saving Social Security's Dream*. Obsessed in a good way, of course. Brad—a character the authors have made up, but, we're assured, is as typical a Gen Xer as can be—muses, "Why can't I relieve Social Security—and my fellow taxpayers—of the burden of caring for me in my old age and let me care for myself by letting me save for my own retirement? After all, this is America, isn't it?" To Shipman and Carter—and to *Forbes* magazine, which waxed euphoric over what it called "the most entrepreneurial generation in American history"—Gen Xers seem like a dream come true: They hate Social Security (and their parents and grandparents, who receive it), they love to invest, they're ambitious and hardworking, but "they're not expecting gold watches after spending twenty or more years with one company as Dad or Grandpa did. Besides, who'd want to?"

All this pales in significance alongside the greatest scheme of them all, the privatization of Social Security. Writers such as Peterson, Carter, and Shipman want to junk the program in favor of a system of private accounts. Their arguments are motivated by the phenomenal returns on stocks over the past few years. The unmentionable flip side of the last decade's boom, though, is that stocks are now wildly overvalued. A model developed by Robert Shiller of Yale relates the stock market's average price-earnings ratio over the last ten years to the expected return over the next ten. Price-earnings ratios are now well over 25; plugging those numbers into Shiller's formula yields an expected return for the next decade of negative 68 percent. In other words, if historical experience is any guide, the average company's stock is priced at triple what the underlying profits can sustain. For a while, as with any bubble, there are enough suckers to buy overvalued assets at an even higher price to seemingly justify the valuation; but sooner or later, you run out of suckers and the bubble bursts.

Dumping the nation's collective retirement account into one of the most overvalued markets since the days of Dutch tulips, though, would neatly bail out the speculators who bought when all the signals said sell. It would also be the scam to end all scams.

No wonder the rich are selling their stocks; they'll soon be buying them back at bargain prices from bankrupt yokels who thought that money would work for just anyone. As they say on the Street, it's during bear markets that money returns to its rightful owners. Dumping Social Security into the stock market will add drama (the numbers will be higher while the fun lasts, and the headache will be much worse afterward), but it won't change the story in any fundamental way. In the long run, stock prices can grow faster than the economy as a whole only if profits rise at the expense of wages. And economic growth shows no signs of exceeding 2.5 or 3 percent a year, while wages can fall only so far. According to calculations by Dean Baker of the Economic Policy Institute, for 10 percent returns on stocks to continue for the next forty years, wages would have to fall by a third. Two decades of flat wages have produced Timothy McVeigh and the first major urban riots since the Sixties. Does anyone want to chance what four decades of falling wages would produce? Does anyone want to *advocate* it?

Soon, in all likelihood, we will be entering an extended bear market. The privatization of Social Security will be deservedly abandoned. *Green* will be forgotten, as will, we hope, Pete Peterson. The lambs will have been slaughtered and the money brought back where it belongs. People will find other uses for their spare time and spare cash than playing with stocks, and, most likely, the apologists for capitalism will become a little more circumspect in their praise for unregulated free markets. But only for a while.

In his epic *Feudal Society*, the French historian Marc Bloch describes how in the sixteenth century, at the very end of the feudal period, when the mounted knight and his personal followers were already long an anachronism, young noblemen could still be found reinventing, apparently from scratch, oaths of allegiance indistinguishable from those used by Charlemagne's vassals 800 years earlier. Just so, under capitalism, until That Day comes, we shall always have with us the Ken Kursons and the Pete Petersons, naively rediscovering the virtues of laissez-faire.

—BAFFLER 9, 1997

21
Ursus Wallstreetus

Doug Henwood

In January 1996, I got a call from Jim Grant, editor of *Grant's Interest Rate Observer*, a Wall Street newsletter focusing on the credit markets. Jim was a bit nervous that the dockers' strike in Liverpool had attracted sympathy strikes, demonstrations, and other actions around the world—a solidarity campaign organized in part through the Internet. The rise of labor is always bad for the bond market, and Jim was afraid that in all the hype about fiber optics, it had been forgotten that rebellious proles can get wired, too. Was the historical tide of the last twenty years reversing itself, and labor beginning to rise again?

It was my duty to tell Jim that labor's attempts at international solidarity, as inspiring as they are, have typically burned out quickly. Maybe someday a global labor movement could sustain itself, and if it did, it'd certainly be wired, but it'd also use phones and letters.

Ursus Wallstreetus is a strange species. Almost without exception, bears adore capitalism as the most wonderful institution that humans have ever devised, the goal of all social evolution. But the true bear—not the temporary cyclical bear, but the temperamental permabear—always expects all kinds of disasters to befall his beloved capitalism: inflation, deflation, boom, collapse, in turn or in various strange combinations. Whatever seems a plausible reason for a sharp and sustained drop in security prices will do. Aside from a few catastrophist Trotskyite sects, Wall Street bears are virtually the only people in America who have faith in an imminent labor uprising.

Though stockbrokers can often be giddily optimistic, a sizable portion of Wall Street, especially those around the bond market, are staunch partisans of gloom, if not outright doom. Gloom is as much a part of the bondbroker's sales effort as optimism is of the stockbroker's. Bond investors love sluggish economies and servile workers; anything that threatens these two factors, such as strong growth and tight labor markets, is regarded with alarm. So it's not surprising that the overall culture of rentiers and traders is often gloomy, even sadistic. Daily newspapers have so absorbed this worldview that drops in unemployment are described as "alarming" (*New York Times*), and a low rate of unemployment something against which experts "warn" (*Washington Post*).

Since stocks rarely do well if the bond market isn't also prospering, mainstream Wall Street wants a happy bond market. So if selling securities is your business, then you don't want to have economists forecasting strong economic growth. This made for trouble between 1993 and 1997, when the U.S. economy often showed far stronger growth than Wall Street predicted or wanted. One economist who was rightly forecasting growth above the Wall Street consensus in 1993 and 1994 was called in by his boss and told to mark down his numbers. Meanwhile, Ed Hyman, Wall Street's favorite economist (according to the *Institutional Investor* poll, which he won for about a dozen straight years), predicted all sorts of slowdowns that never materialized. By coincidence, in addition to sending out his own commentaries and forecasts, Hyman also sells bonds and manages a large bond portfolio.

Most of the time, these gentlemen are rarely called to account for their bad forecasts. A rare and delicious moment, however, came in late 1994. Every January, the *Wall Street Journal* does a roundup of predictions for the coming year. One of the most prominent gloomsters on the Street, Phil Braverman, had predicted that 1994 would be a year of a torpid economy, meaning lower interest rates and an indulgent Federal Reserve. Instead, the economy proved strong and the Fed tightened rates six times during the year. Asked to explain what went wrong, Braverman replied that he hadn't made the mistake, the Fed had.

The most intriguing form of bear is the one gunning for a generalized financial collapse. Many permabears hew to some brand of right-wing political economy and blame the always-imminent disaster on various statist perversions of the Free Market. (Their notion of a pure, stateless Ur-market, of course, is complete fantasy; it's always taken powerful states to create markets and keep them from spinning out of control.) Some are "Austrians"—followers of Hayek and von Mises, who hold, among other things, that the ceaseless extension of credit, supported by indulgent central banks, leads to vertiginous booms and punishing busts. Central banks, of course, are institutions of the hated state, which prevents the body economic from undergoing a ritual depressive purge every ten or twenty years. Sure, such a purge would bankrupt millions and drive up the unemployment rate toward 20 percent, but if you don't let the purifying ritual of depression do its work now and then, the consequences will be even worse—the inevitable crash that never seems to arrive.

Probably the most entertaining bears are the ones who inhabit the edges of respectability. One of the most amusing such outposts is the newsletter *Strategic Investment*, edited by James Dale Davidson and Lord William Rees-Mogg. Davidson, who also runs a loopy antitax foundation, is constantly scouring the globe for a retreat in case of global meltdown; right now, his favorite potential retreat is one in the "delightful green hills" of New Zealand. Meanwhile, virtually every issue includes a dispatch from house stock-market pundit Michael Belkin declaring the great bull market of the 1980s and 1990s to be already over. Every additional 1000 points tacked onto the Dow simply serves as further confirmation of the crash's imminence. In his more fevered moments, Belkin circulates tales of the Fed's "safe houses," from which Alan Greenspan's agents buy stock-index futures to boost the market whenever it sags.

Wall Street is supposed to be a place of great sophistication. In one sense, this reputation is deserved; it takes a certain degree of imagination and technical skill to devise instruments like inverse floaters, poison put bonds, and remarketed reset notes. But when it comes to political and economic analysis, denizens of the Street are as crude as any barroom philosopher. All of which might be overlooked if Wall Street's bears came up with better investing advice or pleaded allegiance to higher truths. Unfortunately, they live in a world that knows no higher truth than statements of profit and loss.

—BAFFLER 9, 1997

22
Boom Crash Opera

Shadowboxing in the Culture Bubble

Chris Lehmann

"From every corner of the earth where the unfettered industrial system was grinding out the raw materials for wealth, crushing men's bones, parching their blood, following them in a perpetual orgy of chicane and debauchery, came the onrushing flood of pennies pilfered from the poor, from the ignorant and from the savages, from indentured slaves who treaded the death mill to beat a rhythm to the saturnalia of America's unbridled profits."

Thus did Kansas Republican and onetime Hoover man William Allen White recall the great bull market that lifted off in 1927 and crashed two years later. True, White had always kept a certain moral and political loyalty to the Progressive era, but it's nonetheless striking to ponder how peremptorily the business boosterism of the 1920s curdled into rhetoric that might have made Marx himself blush. White delivered his thunderous judgment, by the way, not in some street-corner anarchist tract but rather in a sympathetic 1938 biography of President Calvin Coolidge, the stiff New Englander who silently fidgeted while the economic order burned.

Now, of course, we have pretty much banished the thought of White's death mill and its tenders. Indeed, the whole industrial system has, in the popular mind, been magically effaced and the historical table reset with the goblets and aliments of Information Age capitalism. Wealth is now created in suburban office parks, pleasantly minded by the Dockers-clad geeks and engineers who preside over the end of history. Who, after all, could picture aw-shucks Microsoft supremo Bill Gates in an orgy of "chicane and debauchery"?

However, the unquiet shade of the Twenties is not staying put. Its shimmering surface—that high old time of flappers, speakeasies, hopheads, and jazz fanciers—exerts a continuing fascination among our keepers of the zeitgeist. Nostalgic cable channels schedule "1920s weeks," and ads for Beefeater gin taunt: "There was a decade called the Roaring Twenties. What will yours be called?"

Happy Days Are Where, Again?

But it's in the field of economic prognostication that the Twenties have their most persistent cachet. In a cover story on "The New Rich," *Newsweek* christened our own purblind time of greed and info-idolatry "the Roaring Nineties" and confidently declared that the bull market is "making instant billionaires—and changing America." Of course, *Newsweek*'s frantic bandwagon-hopping raises certain suspicions about its own grasp of history: It was only in 1996, after all, that the magazine ran a downsizing cover with the headline, "Corporate Killers"—and it would obviously be too much for the zeitgeist-happy *Newsweek* brain trust to pause and reflect that the new ranks of "Microsoft millionaires" have seen their investor returns skyrocket thanks to the killing sprees of downsizing CEOs.

Newsweek, in any event, only brings up the rear of the sanguine permaboom parade. In fact, the financial press has been boosting the tableau of perpetual prosperity since the bull market took off in 1995. And of course, the most blinding reveries of pelf ascendant come from that tireless exponent of Information Age capitalism, *Wired* magazine. *Wired*'s massive July 1997 cover story plumbed "The Long Boom," a conceit hatched by *Wired* features editor Peter Leyden and Peter Schwartz, doyen of the Global Business Network—a visionary think tank of the digiterati that boasts among its members such cyberseers as Stewart Brand, William Gibson, Laurie Anderson, and Brian Eno.

The countless cracked details of the Schwartz and Leyden scenario don't bear repeating. Mainly, "The Long Boom" is a wish list for an info-imperium, a society in which all sectors of life cop the same techno-buzz and spontaneously do things like devise "a new information-age standard of measuring economic growth" and "begin to shift from hierarchical processes to networked ones." Imagine *Newsweek*'s own feel-good economic columnist Robert Samuelson drooling over his fortieth bong hit, and you begin to get the picture.

Here, in fact, the notion of a resurgent Twenties culture starts to get rather interesting. The Twenties were, in fact, obsessed with parallel questions of communication and civilization, even as they were steeped in equally foolish prophecies of a permanent prosperity.

Where do such preoccupations come from? One likely source is a striking, and feverishly repressed, instability in the distribution of the largesse kicked up in the wake of great speculative booms. In economic terms, no recent era in American history bears a greater resemblance to our own than the Twenties, mixing runaway growth in the paper economy with ever-steepening social inequality underneath.

The Culture Sublimation

Yet then, as now, few Americans were greatly exercised over, or even aware of, the downward ratcheting of the citizenry's comparative economic advantage. Instead, they clamored—then, as now—about crises of cultural self-definition. The "great fear" of the Twenties, historian Warren Susman writes, was "whether any great industrial and democratic mass society can maintain a significant level of civilization, and whether mass education and mass communication will allow any civilization to survive." Strewn atop the squalor of the era's inequality, in other words, was the elastic scrim of culture, beneath which the unaddressed issues of the day got rearranged into various grand questions of civilization's destiny.

Indeed, as Susman argues, the era developed a certain Hegelian mania for fusing the talismans of civilization atop the sprawling infrastructures of communications. Hence the mad rush to catalogue and popularize most fields of knowledge, chiefly through imposing tomes such as H. G. Wells's *Outline of History;* the reverent Art Deco palaces erected as monuments to the mass-disseminated miracles of the motion picture and the automobile; the fevered excitement of intellectuals over the modernist dispensation captured, for example, in Vachel Lindsay's celebration of America's new "hieroglyphic civilization."

But such questions of cultural-cum-civilizational meaning permeated far beyond the keepers of higher culture and practitioners of high modernism who people Susman's argument. The Twenties were in fact every bit as much a decade of runaway popular *Kulturkampf* as they were an era of thinly distributed prosperity. Indeed, we can say that the decade inaugurated an arresting leitmotif in modern American history. Call it the Culture Bubble: the inflation of the terms of cultural debate while conditions of social inequality teeter on the brink of intolerability.

Cultural conflict is at least as old as the American republic, as any cursory look at Puritan election-day sermons will confirm. Yet in their modern-to-postmodern incarnation, the Culture Wars—the paint-by-numbers ritual in which the warring parties trade accusations of depravity, repression, and historical obsolescence, with the state usually conscripted as referee—made their bones in the Twenties. Fundamentalists railed against evolution; eugenicists, Klansmen, and patrician pseudoscientists inveighed against runaway immigration and racial mongrelizing; apostles of uplift conspired with religious crusaders to produce Prohibition; less genteel reactionaries weighed in with still cruder measures of sociopolitical control, such as the Palmer raids against foreign-born radicals and campaigns against union organizing; the New Woman and the Lost Generation marked the first appearance of the twentieth century's Great Amoral Youth Question; jazz, radio, and the popular cinema all furnished incontrovertible evidence to scores of bush-league Spenglers that the long slide into barbarism was under way; the growth of the automobile, modern advertising, and a commercialized mass culture erased the incorrigible regionalism and parochialism of America's rural village life, prompting intellectuals such as Sinclair Lewis and Robert and Helen Lynd into fervid denunciations of small-town homogeneity and lodge-brother groupthink.

One could go through this litany and glibly substitute latter-day civilizing themes and culture crusades into the templates the Twenties left behind: the war on drugs for Prohibition; the V-chip for the Hays Code; *The Bell Curve* for Madison Grant's *Perils of the Great Race*; Generation X for the Lost Generation; *Fargo* for *Main Street*; Buchananite immigration hysteria for Klan-led immigration hysteria; and fundamentalism for, well, fundamentalism. Yet such one-to-one correspondences only elide the broader point regarding the Culture Bubble: These elaborate contretemps over the culture's robustness and behavior-policing efficacy are rarely about the country's real troubles or much of anything at all. Indeed, they furnish the compass by which the embarrassing, discomfiting matters of social class can be endlessly skirted.

This point can be nailed down, with reference to both that distant Roaring time and our own present one, with a few bracing statistics. Surveying the economic changes wrought during the Twenties, historian Robert McElvaine notes that as the decade ended, the richest 0.1 percent of the population—some 24,000 families—enjoyed an aggregate income equivalent to that of the poorest 42 percent of the American population—or 11.2 million families. From 1920 to 1929, total aggregate American disposable income rose by 9 percent, while among the top 1 percent of the population, it rose by 75 percent—from 12 percent of the nation's total in 1920 to 19 percent in 1929. The distribution of wealth—stocks, equity, and savings—was even more upwardly skewed. By 1929, the top 0.5 percent of the population controlled 32.4 percent of individual net wealth in America—the highest such concentration in American history.

Until now, anyway. Even though all the returns aren't in from the Nineties bull market—which will only accelerate current trends—all the indications suggest, as *Business Week* economists William Wolman and Anne Colamosca argue, that the Nineties have "witnessed a concentration of wealth that is without historical precedent in the United States," making the upward consolidation of wealth in the Twenties "only a pallid prelude." Between 1983 and 1992, the top 1 percent of Americans increased their net wealth by a whopping 28.3 percent; in the same period median wealth declined by 8.1 percent, and the bottom 40 percent of the population lost 49.7 percent of its net wealth.

The landscape of American enterprise in the Nineties remains, despite its many new info-bells and whistles, a playground of unprosecuted leviathans and trusts. Just as Andrew Mellon (who played both sides of the street as an aluminum baron and the Harding–Coolidge Secretary of the Treasury) has his Nineties analog in Goldman Sachs don/Treasury boss Robert Rubin, so does Henry Ford, who lorded over the dominant growth industry of his day, beg comparisons with Bill Gates. Likewise, entire industries—from Gates's software empire to the merger-happy military, aerospace, media, and entertainment complexes—are effectively controlled by a handful of cartelized players, much as utilities, banking, and oil were seventy-odd years ago.

Cartelization proves in all ages to be unquestionably good for business—or, rather, for the charmed circle of business owners. From 1923 to 1929, the income of workers inched up by 11 percent. That may look positively socialistic next to today's labor-soaking economic order—but only until one notes that over the same period, corporate profits rose by a staggering 62 percent, and dividends shot up 65 percent. And while the book has yet to be closed on our own decade, this parallel, too, is unmistakable: The Economic Policy Institute notes that corporate profit rates took off in 1986 and have been rising steadily ever since. Nineteen ninety-six saw the greatest boost in the rate of both before- and after-tax corporate profits (11.39 percent and 7.57 percent, respectively) since recordkeeping began in 1959.

Pretty Vacant

It's not hard to see why, in a social order as individualistic as America's, these rather straightforward matters of distributive injustice get sublimated, as it were, into inherently insoluble matters of cultural identity. This isn't to say that all culture is reducible to material inequality, as the yeoman Marxist oversimplifications blithely assume. But it is arresting to ponder the ways in which submerged grievances of class send American discourses of culture and morality into a curiously weightless kind of hyperspace.

In part, of course, social inequality makes only the most muffled peep amid the tumult of America's great cultural barbecue for quite obvious reasons. The myth of classlessness is the most reverently enshrined article of our social faith. There are no savagely truncated life opportunities or bitterly marginalized outcasts in American social mythology—only entrepreneurs waiting to happen. Thus, popular discussions of poverty in America almost never engage the core questions of blighted, rapidly resegregating urban schools and industrial employers that gleefully decamp from urban neighborhoods for cut-rate labor markets in the developing world. Instead, they chase the ever-receding tails of the "culture of poverty" and "underclass" debates, which open obligingly onto the great question of how best to police the black family.

But critical distinctions between class and culture stubbornly elude us, since the logic of the Culture Bubble is, in many ways, the story of the past American century: Time and again, steepening class polarization sends American public discourse a-dithering into queries over What It Means to Be an American. We seek to shore up the edifice of unfair life outcomes with the crumbling mortar of behavioral reform.

To help maintain this airtight state of denial, moreover, the news media willfully veer from any material touching on the public weal. Frederick Lewis Allen, one of the Twenties' ablest chroniclers, writes that the era of Coolidge prosperity stands out in historical memory for "the unparalleled rapidity and unanimity with which millions of men and women turned their attention, their talk, and their emotional interest upon a series of tremendous trifles—a heavyweight boxing match, a murder trial, a new automobile model, a transatlantic flight." These interests were stirred, as it happens, by a media industry that, like its latter-day counterpart, was consolidating its institutional ranks as it multiplied its audience: The number of newspapers dropped from 2,580 in 1914 to 2,001 in 1926, as their readership shot up from 28 to 36 million. By 1927, fifty-five newspaper chains controlled 230 papers with a combined circulation of 13 million.

Today, as the income gap widens to an unprecedented scale, we have again watched the money culture modulate into so much celebrity planespotting. Global financial markets may shudder and once-secure unionized workforces may spiral into temp and part-time limbo, but we worry that surly White Sox slugger Albert Belle may not be worth $55 million, that maybe Jim Carrey isn't hilarious enough to merit $20 million a picture, or that Elaine, Kramer, and company—our *Seinfeld* buddies—might be overpaid at $400,000 an episode. These celebrity glyphs allow us to formulate nonthreatening judgments on individual character—that Julia

Louis-Dreyfus always seemed a little too stuck up, and didn't Jim Carrey ditch his first wife?—in lieu of asking whether it's patently delusional to imagine that eight-figure incomes can be "deserved" in the first place. Or, for that matter, asking just what the culture of celebritism is doing in the forefront of national consciousness.

Celebritism, indeed, provides a key reading of the Culture Bubble's progress. The degree to which questions of personality subsume substantive political debate roughly corresponds to our impatience with the more ponderous matters of social equity. In the early Twenties, the American farm economy was plunged into a decade-plus depression by the postwar boom in European credit and the deflation of commodity prices, but Washington stolidly hewed to the laissez-faire line in deference to the stock market's keepers. The farm-relief measures that managed to pass through Congress were dutifully vetoed by President Coolidge as intemperate meddling with the market. The consequences? Rural America's plight was magically distilled into H. L. Mencken's and Sinclair Lewis's hectoring of the booboisie or into Klan/lodge-brother mobilizations of bigotry. The great symbolic clash between rural and urban civilization climaxed in 1925 with a stage-managed drama in Dayton, Tennessee, where William Jennings Bryan debated evolution on a courthouse lawn with big-city agnostic Clarence Darrow.

Now consider, in our own day, the many efficacious uses of the culture wars and of celebritism for short-circuiting political debate. Why should we demand crackdowns on the new global sweatshop's subcontractors, as long as Kathy Lee did enough damage control for her clothing line to start feeling perky again? Few people today remember that 1992's great "Murphy Brown" flap was not merely a symbolic controversy over single motherhood, but also Dan Quayle's official pronouncement on the causes of the LA riots. That the federal government's most sustained response to the second-greatest civil disturbance in American history could be a fight picked with a television character speaks volumes about the suction power of the Culture Bubble. Candidate Bill Clinton made his own statement on race that same long, daft summer by picking a fight with a rap artist.

Five besotted years later, we don't find it at all unusual that our discussions of race are principally shaped by perceptions of a celebrity murder trial, that Hillary Clinton should chide a motion-picture character for smoking on screen, that the scale of Bill Gates's estate commands more attention than the collapse of federal inner-city housing, or that a princess who was evidently not versed in the operations of a seatbelt becomes a postmodern saint.

Enterprises such as *George* magazine are, of course, premised on the notion that celebrity culture and political discourse are identical—a claim it sought to demonstrate by publishing photos of its avatar, JFK Jr., in the virtual buff. Meanwhile, in an entirely apt grace note to the forward march of celebritism, the only recent successful defense of liberalism in the marketplace of ideas was a book called *Rush Limbaugh Is a Big Fat Idiot*—penned, of course, by a TV personality.

The Right-to-Lifestyle Movement

But another coefficient of the Culture Bubble is a general exhaustion of political ideas. Every history of the decade notes that the charming, gregarious nitwit Warren Harding inadvertently christened the Twenties a time of "normalcy," misreading the word "normality" in his inauguration speech. What is less widely noted is that the substance of the speech itself called for the burial of Progressivism, widely discredited as the liberal dogma of social experimentation that led to the catastrophe of the Great War. Rededicating the Republic to its historic "concern for preserved civilization," Harding warned that "our most dangerous tendency is to expect too much of government" and pronounced the mandate to keep wages and prices within their "normal balances." This meant trusting the "unmistakable" momentum of "the forward course of the business cycle" and, naturally, "the omission of unnecessary interference of Government with business." Harding's laconic successor, Calvin Coolidge, stopped all the flowery talk of civilization and cut to the chase, pronouncing redundantly that "the business of America is business."

In our age, of course, liberalism, rather than Progressivism, has become the great untouchable political doctrine, a bacillus to be vigilantly quarantined in the gleaming laboratory of global business civilization. Clinton's declaration in his 1995 State of the Union address that "the era of big government is over" was his valentine to Wall Street—and confession of intellectual bankruptcy—that Coolidge's tautologies and Harding's paeans to civilized normalcy were in their day.

Clintonism made good on the rhetoric of Government Lite, and not only through such blunt and unlovely means as the Personal Responsibility Act of 1996 (another nice touch, this—defenestrating federal entitlements to millions of impoverished mothers and children with disciplinary culturespeak about individual "responsibility"). Indeed, the Clinton era will likely be remembered as the time when government wandered around like a bored child on a rainy Saturday, dreaming up busywork to make itself feel like it was up to something important. Entire sectors of public life have been dumbed down into miniature culture crusades in flailing efforts to bulk up and define a postideological presidency. Education, in many ways the mother of all contemporary American inequalities, is given the digital civilization treatment—glib national-standards rhetoric and millennial talk of VDTs on every desktop—as school infrastructure crumbles and urban districts hemorrhage away their tax bases. Racism is to be assuaged with official apologies and a national "conversation." Teen anomie is to be micromanaged with feel-good measures such as drivers'-license drug tests and the V-chip. In short, citizens in need have become the moral equivalent of trick-or-treaters—dismissed at the door with paternal good wishes (or perhaps a lecture and an apology) and a fistful of morsels that will, likely as not, rot their teeth.

The forces of dissent, meanwhile, nicely fit the sobriquet that reformer Walter Weyl used in 1921 to describe the spent Progressives of his age: "tired radicals." Indeed, they have become the great tenders of the Nineties' culture wars, devoting more attention to the symbolic defense of the National Endowment for the Arts than they have to the defense of the shrinking welfare state. Curricular requirements at elite universities, and the tediously rehashed legacies of the Sixties campus revolt, invite more sustained comment among the left intelligentsia than wage inequality, strikes, or the explosion of the global sweatshop. As often as not, in fact, the global market's rhetoric of shopping-as-liberation is indistinguishable from our atrophied left's allegiance to Lifestylismus—which is how an enterprise such as *Wired* can simultaneously shill for global capitalism and brandish an alternative, even revolutionary, edge.

Indeed, much of altcult politics nowadays has fallen, like the aesthetic and literary revolts of the Twenties, into a facile, reflexive market libertarianism, which revolves around the classic libertarian aim of securing the optimal conditions of faux-daring self-expression. Today's cyber-rebels trumpet their heroic exploits against the Helmses and Bennetts of our age, much as the bohemians of the Twenties fancied themselves a fearless insurgency, scandalizing a nation of Comstocks and Protestant bluenoses with their ethos of literary realism and sexual liberation.

Even more unfortunately, *Wired* again provides the paradigmatic example of revolutionary cyber-praxis, via the labors of its in-house prophet of political culture, Jon Katz. A former CBS news producer and NYU Journalism School professor, Katz plies a vision of the republic eerily well-suited to the Twenties campaign of self-styled literary radicals against a largely mythical Puritan culture. "Culture is politics" to today's young cyber-insurgents, Katz announces in his Digital Age manifesto, *Virtuous Reality*, which bears the fearless, incendiary subtitle, "How America Surrendered Discussion of Moral Values to Opportunists, Nitwits and Blockheads like William Bennett."

Katz's estimation of the Digital Age's numberless virtues is every bit as nuanced and complicated as his reading of the culture wars. Tirelessly apostrophizing the "revolutionary," "free," and "democratic" virtues of the Digital Age, Katz detects *samizdat* rebellion bursting out of every e-mail account—he even, with embarrassing attention to detail, succumbs to a prolonged reverie of Revolutionary pamphleteer Tom Paine as a Web surfer. But since all the great Web controversies seem to take place within the terms of the Culture Bubble, the exercise of telling rude and liberating truths to power seems to concern matters a tad less world-historic than the questions that preoccupied Tom Paine. "The young have a moral right of access to the machinery and content of media and culture," Katz thunders, as though the central target demographic of the entire culture industry had been banished overnight by William Bennett into internment camps littered with books and broken radios. "Kids should not have to battle for the right to watch MTV," Katz goes on to declare. Only in the giddy precincts of the Culture Bubble could the most banal of consumer choices—the freedom to watch frenetically edited advertisements—be worked up into a constitutive political "right."

Whether it's Katz's hectoring, or the Ayn Rand–ish literary stylings of Silicon Valley novelist Po Bronson, or the countless cinematic, sitcom, and indie rock productions that baptize gadget-happy entrepreneurs as latter-day Dantons, the Culture Bubble has quietly spread its casement around every conceivable outpost of would-be rebellion. In point of fact, of course, the matrix of prosperity in our own speculative times is nearly identical to the brutish global repression that William Allen White denounced with, to our ears, quaint moral outrage: Capital treads nimbly across more and more of the globe, romancing and discarding ever-cheaper labor markets and in the process consigning even the once-comfortable middle class to downward wage pressure and chronic job insecurity. It took a global economic cataclysm for reformers like White to regain their voices in the wake of the Twenties Culture

Bubble; every one of the great questions that had recently exercised public opinion, from the revolt against literary gentility to the Prohibition crusade suddenly became embarrassingly puerile.

—BAFFLER 10, 1997

Afterword

Ah, the permaboom prophecies of the late 1990s. Someday, one imagines, there will be a brisk market on eBay for the works of Peter Schwartz and Peter Leyden, Jon Katz, Kevin Kelly, et al., that will outstrip collectors' clamor for a Calvin Coolidge grapefruit squeezer or a Charles Lindbergh handkerchief. If the Nineties were a Twenties redux, the Oughts are right on schedule to rival the economic profile of the Thirties—with the important caveat that the Depression years ushered in a revived Democratic liberalism and a historic party realignment of the American electorate. After November 2002's off-year elections, Republicans controlled both branches of representative government—together, of course, with the U. S. Supreme Court, which was thoughtful enough to start the ball rolling by awarding the presidency to a new scion of an old GOP dynasty. Culture and ideology, which back in the benighted "Red Decade" were waved off as mere superstructures wobbling on the hard core of economic life, now supply the basis of a libertarian economic age. It matters little that the New Economy is rapidly obsolescing by all its most important measures; it's acquired the grand, impermeable potency that Murray Kempton (writing again of the Thirties) described as "social mythology." Or, as a Soho model coos over the ambient street noise of a Kenneth Cole TV spot, "I'm *so* over politics."

Interns Built the Pyramids

THE FUTURE HOLDS GREAT PROMISE

THE PRICELESS ASSET

It takes many things, all put together, to give you a good literary magazine at low cost.

There are writers and editors and publishers; there are desks and chairs and waxers and blue pencils and carpets. There are all the review copies of books and records that people send in. There are the lamps and the stamps and the photocopiers.

These are important. But they could not possibly do the job without the vital human spirit that brings life to all this equipment and makes it work smoothly and efficiently for dozens of readers.

Yes, nothing would go without abrasiveness. It's the quality that inclines us to accentuate the negative and cast the shining future in such gray, depressing tones. It's the characteristic that makes this magazine so irritating to so many.

We happen to think that abrasiveness is a quality worth hanging around for. And we hope you stay with us over the remaining years of the American Century.

Subscriptions to The Baffler are $20 for four issues, $36 for eight. Please specify which issue you'd like to start with.

Subscribe to THE BAFFLER.
P. O. Box 378293, Chicago, Ill. 60637
www.thebaffler.com

23
When Class Disappears

THOMAS FRANK

Let Them Eat Pizza

It's a Thursday afternoon in May 1996, nearly ten months into the Detroit newspaper strike. The city's downtown, where the offices of the *Detroit News* and *Free Press* are located, is a dead zone of boarded-up skyscrapers, vacant lots, and empty, litter-strewn streets. Down in the shadows in front of the *Detroit News* building, underneath the wall on which an inscription proclaims the paper an "Unrelenting foe of privilege and corruption," members of the six unions on strike against the newspapers are joined by union workers from across the city, assorted city councilmen, and a smattering of religious figures to sing "Solidarity Forever" and watch as this week's volunteers block the entrance to the *News*'s internal parking lot, undergo ritual removal by a squad of Detroit police, and get hauled off to jail. In the bright sunshine on the roof of the *News* building thirty feet above, professional strikebreakers from the Vance International security company look on. Were it not for their black uniforms, the thick-necked, sunglassed, and short-haired Vance guards could be actors from a beer commercial. They're certainly jolly enough: For them, the union doings appear to be rich comic spectacle. They smirk and joke. They chew gum in uncanny synchronization, their powerful jaws moving up and down in unison. And although one of them occasionally lifts a video camera to capture the moment for company lawyers, it seems as though they're here mainly to provide a living tableau of public indifference.

It's not a coincidence that the most important labor struggle of the mid-Nineties is taking place in the information industry, and specifically within the smiling newspaper empires of Knight-Ridder, publisher of the *Free Press*, and Gannett, producer of both the *News* and *USA Today*. Labor is becoming invisible here, and the strikers know it. Most of them are Detroit lifers; many are second- and third-generation newspaper workers, with strong feelings about the traditional blue-collar status of journalists. Talking with them below the photos of newspapermen past in the Anchor bar or in the offices of their pugnacious strike paper, the *Detroit Sunday Journal*, one begins to suspect that they might be the last of the hardened, rooted, class-conscious species of journalists that defined American literature for most of the twentieth century; that the strike has, among its many other effects, served rather efficiently to weed out people of exactly this type from the workforce. Within a week after the strike began, Gannett and Knight-Ridder management had replaced them with an army of footloose gannettoids, interchangeable information workers who can be flown into any city on a moment's notice. While the scabs' metropolitan reporting (and, naturally, labor reporting) leaves a bit to be desired, they have had few problems cranking out the lifestyle features that draw the gaze of suburban readers. In the glazed world that the info-conglomerates are building for their readers, the old newspaper workers serve about as much purpose as the buildings that once stood in the vacant lots across the street from the *News* offices. Class is disappearing from both the journalistic workplace and the public culture of this most class-conscious city.

In February 1997, the strikers make an offer to return to work unconditionally and newspapers around the country quickly decide that the time is finally right to cover the Detroit newspaper strike. When it is printed, though, their reporting is wrapped in a mythological package so uniform and so smugly confident of the direction in which civilization is heading that it reminds me of the black-clad Vance guards on the roof of the *News* building, filming and chewing. Hear the new breed of journalists confront the big questions: What is labor? Why, labor is a relic of the deluded Thirties. What are strikes? Why, strikes are sad.

The *Chicago Tribune*'s version, page one on February 24, 1997, is positively at war with the idea of causality. It introduces its readers to the subject not by discussing the issues at stake but by delivering a soft-focus enumeration of "the often-overlooked wounds when labor and management can't agree." There is a certain "complexity of emotions" brewing in Detroit, the *Tribune* reported, including "bitterness," "anguish," and an occasional bright patch of understanding (of strikers for scabs). The Strikes Are Sad theme permits the *Tribune* writer all sorts of personal-relationship metaphors. "Friendships have been broken," he notes. He likens the struggle to "a troubled marriage, where both spouses have said too many damaging things to simply forgive." He quotes a striker who says, "People have become like enemies." The article concludes with these statements of random cosmic misfortune: "It's a real tragedy," and "Why did it have to happen here?"

Since the whole mess was just a bit of bad luck for both sides, neither the means by which management forced its employees to the wall nor the immediate issues that precipitated the walkout in the summer of 1995 are important enough to merit more than one sentence in the *Tribune*'s account. Other facts have to go unremarked altogether: for instance, that Gannett is a notoriously antiunion employer regardless of what city it's in; that newspaper management has often boasted about what the strike has allowed it to accomplish; that Detroit civic leaders, including the mayor and the archbishop, have been outspoken on the side of labor in this dispute; and that the whole thing was only made possible by one of those legislative gifts that the federal government has been showering on media conglomerates for the last ten years (in this case, the Newspaper Preservation Act, which was interpreted in 1989 in such a manner as to permit a joint operating agreement, or federally sanctioned monopoly, between the two competing papers).

The *Tribune*'s apparent desire to deny the larger significance of the Detroit battle is almost palpable—and it's an especially interesting maneuver given its own union-busting past. But the *Chicago Tribune* hardly invented this kind of journalism. Check out the *Reader's Digest* rendering of the Detroit story, a nasty bit of moralizing that concentrates almost exclusively on the damage that strikers did to cars and windows in the happy Detroit suburb where the newspapers are printed. Even though it's openly hostile to the strikers, the *Dige* concludes its coverage by summoning up sentiments identical to those in the *Tribune* article (although here they come from the mouth of a manager, not a striker): "anguish," broken friendships, and regret over the strikers' mulish refusal to stop "living in the past." To describe labor conflicts as personal and unhappy but fundamentally without causes that outsiders can understand simply seems to be the way we think about the subject these days. "Unions are obsolete/Strikes are sad" is the industry standard, like "Eternal China" and the curious notion that the Balkan peoples have been at war basically forever.

Some find the strike-as-heartbreak narrative so poignant that it has already become a narrative framework in advertising, the great showplace of consensus. "Strike Break" (no kidding, that was really its title), a Pizza Hut commercial from a few years ago, presents the now-orthodox vision of organized labor so concisely and realistically that, were it not for its more-conspicuous-than-usual product placement, the ad could easily be substituted for TV news strike coverage. The scene: Anyconflict, USA. Outside the plant, striking blue-collar exotics wave signs and hubbub noisily. Up in their offices, beleaguered managers, like the concerned parents of a runaway teenager, wait for the workers to come to their senses. "I thought we were friends," one executive moans. Not to worry, sir! By having a Pizza Hut delivery truck intervene with a cache of hot pies for his disgruntled employees out on the picket line, he is able to salvage the situation. Everyone knows how going on strike can build up a real hunger, right? And sure enough, the workers drop their flimsy "On Strike" signs in a rush for the pizzas, then look up gratefully to the benevolent corporate provider in the window. Who needs negotiations, contracts, or unions themselves when friendship, the glue that really holds industry together, can be reaffirmed at the cost of a few pizzas?

The labor movement may be waking up from its Cold War coma, but in terms of the nation's official myths, it might just as well have gone on sleeping forever. In the millennial dreaming of the businessman's republic, labor's critique, with all its intimations about social class and workplace democracy, no longer makes sense. For contemporary American media-makers, complacent with an unprecedented self-assurance, the market is the only appropriate matrix for understanding human affairs. Business is life; management is government; markets are democracy; entrepreneurs are artists. And the more directly these principles are stated, the better. Using a style only slightly less heavy-handed than the official art of Stalinist Russia, serious journalists join with TV commercials to lead us in worship of the great executives. It is speculators and mutual-fund managers, we are told, who create wealth, and the business pages teem with tales of wise blue-collar investors who have accepted the market for the universal-prosperity machine that it is and have transferred their faith from union to broker. *Fast Company*, a magazine that has successfully merged rock 'n' roll hip with managerial efficiency, offers up a manifesto baldly equating office work with society and announces that "corporations have become the dominant institution of our times, occupying the position of the church of the Middle Ages and the nation-state of the past two centuries." The movie *Jerry Maguire* understands human relationships as questions of more or less honest salesmanship; French advertising executive Jean-Marie Dru writes that "people perceive countries as they do brands." Is this a great time or what?

As market-worship becomes the monotheme of official economic commentary, class disappears. The objective facts can be recited easily enough. Most daily newspapers once had writers or editors who worked the labor beat; almost none do now. As late as the 1960s, newspapers could assume that the issues and specialized language that were part of labor coverage were familiar to readers; that people knew why unions existed and what they did; that unions were a normal part of working life; and that readers had some personal interest in the fate of workers elsewhere. Now, writers routinely address whatever labor questions they think it appropriate to raise in the specialized language of investment authorities (How will this affect the company's dividends? Its share prices?), or by avoiding them altogether with the condescending usual: Unions are obsolete, strikes are sad.

Labor unions continue to exist, of course. When one considers the millions of workers whom unions represent, the millions more who would like to be represented by them, and the vast millions in whose interests they act, it's easy to conclude simply that contemporary journalists are doing their jobs poorly. In fact, according to the great archetypes of our time, they're doing them correctly. Business has captured the high ground of normalcy; unions only make sense as a troublemaking special interest. The troubles and battles of working people only sound through to us as meaningless pulses from a distant universe, as personal grudge-matches between those too stupid or too stubborn to board the incredibly liberating and fulfilling pleasure-train of information capitalism.

Let Them Eat Lifestyle

It's not that Americans deny the existence of social conflict. In fact, we've got our hands full these days, and with a most exciting battle: a full-on "culture war," a pitched struggle for lifestyle liberation from the dark forces of dance-floor prohibition and church-herding authoritarianism. We've got commentators who are ready to paint the entire history of the twentieth century in terms of our glorious progress toward full enjoyment of lifestyle, with only a few brief interruptions in the unhappy Thirties and Cold War Fifties. We've got an entire academic pedagogy devoted to the notion that symbolic dissent—imagining, say, that the secret police don't want us to go to the disco, but that we're doing it anyway—is as real and as meaningful as, or, better yet, more real and more meaningful than the humdrum business of organizing and movement-building. But most important, an enormous segment of corporate America has declared its "radicalism" and is busily inventing all sorts of colorful new products that will free us from mass society.

The trade-off between lifestyle and labor has been so direct that it's hard to imagine that these two features of contemporary American life—one triumphant, one in total eclipse—aren't connected in some cosmic fashion. It's as though the revolutionary legacy of the Sixties somehow effaced the revolutionary legacy of the Thirties; as though workers had to be put back in their place so that rebel lifestylers could take their pleasure properly; as though urban deindustrialization had to happen so the rest of us could enjoy our authentic-proletarian conversion lofts in peace.

The culture wars have also helped to make plausible the otherwise-bizarre fantasy common in contemporary management theory: that Information Age capitalism has made moot the once-divisive issues of social class. Ad-man Dru suggests that by means of "disruption"—his dramatic term for strategic attacks on social convention—lifestyle marketers have permanently replaced the extra-corporate left altogether. For Dru, audacity is more than just the quality we admire in such figures as Martin Luther King, George Bernard Shaw, and Robert Kennedy—it's the secret to brand success. Dru blithely presents a catalogue of successfully disruptive brands that says more about the decline of the labor left than a dozen PBS specials about Rush Limbaugh: "The great brands of this end of the century are those that have succeeded in conveying their vision by questioning certain conventions, whether it's Apple's humanist vision, which reverses the relationship between people and machines; Benetton's libertarian vision, which overthrows communication conventions; Microsoft's progressive vision, which topples bureaucratic barriers; or Virgin's anticonformist vision, which rebels against the powers that be." The Body Shop owns compassion, Nike spirituality, Pepsi and MTV youthful rebellion. We used to have movements for change; now we have products.

Before the practice was outlawed in 1935, manufacturers commonly set up in-house pseudounions that made great displays of addressing workers' concerns while allowing management to avoid the costly concessions that a real union would demand. While the Republicans' best efforts have proved insufficient to revive the company union (the "Team Act," which would have done so, was vetoed by President Clinton in 1996), the principle has been successfully extended to society as a whole: We're all in the company union now, our needs for social justice served without having to go outside the system. Lifestyle capitalism comes complete with its own social justice and its own "revolution."

In the Thirties, the steel industry advanced what it called "the Mohawk Valley Formula" to discredit and suppress organizing efforts. A PR campaign of the old school, the scheme combined a barrage of antiunion propaganda (emphasizing words like "agitators" and "law and order") with fantasies of "Citizens Committees" and loyal, prosperity-minded workers, and an overwhelming display of private police power. Today's equivalent might be called, in honor of Nike, the Beaverton Formula: First, move your tennis-shoe manufacturing operation to the union-free and largely invisible Third World, where you can enjoy maximum "flexibility" and pay your compliant menials starvation wages courtesy of the most barbaric of all possible regimes. Second, hire the hippest of all possible advertising agencies to fetishize your products as tools of "empowerment" and "revolution" and thus make them appealing to exactly those Americans whose world has been shattered by the departure of operations like yours to the union-free South and Third World. Third (optional), build minimuseums to your seamless, self-feeding marketing vision, equating your company with human civilization generally; enjoy the plaudits of that greatest culture warrior of them all, *Advertising Age*, which recognizes you as Marketer of the Year, the brand that no longer needs to speak its name.

Let Them Eat Pepper Gas

How different is all this from the days when the *Chicago Tribune* covered labor by screaming for the execution of the Haymarket defendants? We suspect it's still true, as John L. Lewis said at the start of the great organizing drive of the 1930s, that shooting people down in the streets is no longer a permissible response to union efforts. But lesser gradations of coercion are certainly still acceptable, and while calling for blood might not allow the makers of national opinion to feel as noble as they'd like, the implications of their kinder, gentler understanding of work are substantially the same as they were a century ago: Unions fly in the face of everything that is modern; strikes are inexplicable and tragic. The global-market ideology may gleam with new technology, but its smugness about the direction of history is familiar stuff indeed.

What has changed quite dramatically is the way we think about the potential power of workers. Classic labor writing clings almost obsessively to the possibility of transformation, the feeling that the conditions that determine people's lives are things we can control. This is the feature that made the genre so powerful, and also the feature most noticeably absent from contemporary reporting on the subject. Although the ideology of the culture trust insists that these are the most democratic times of all (since there's entertainment available now for every conceivable demographic), we seem to have lost altogether the sense of democratic possibility that animates unionism. Even those who are sympathetic to the victims of downsizing (and, hey, who isn't?) understand workers as victims, not as historical actors capable of reversing the whole thing. We have the power to demand, say, toothpaste that both whitens our teeth and bemints our breath, but things that happen in the economy as a whole are simply inevitable. Wages are stagnating even while the economy grows? Well . . . the market works in mysterious ways. Economics is something we complain about; the power to change our lives is a role we reserve exclusively for business. Louis Adamic entitled his 1931 history of class conflict in the United States *Dynamite;* a contemporary treatment of the subject would be called *Tears*.

It's a Saturday afternoon in October 1994. The workers at A. E. Staley, a corn-processing plant in Decatur, Illinois, have been locked out of their jobs for more than a year by their employer, a teamwork-touting multinational conglomerate. In the course of the year, they've been joined on the picket lines by strikers from Caterpillar and Bridgestone/Firestone, the town's two other major industrial employers. The global economy has dropped the bomb on this once-complacent blue-collar city. But still I had been surprised when I was told all this by a friend in Springfield; I had seen nothing about it in the Chicago papers besides the standard tragedy tales. Yet the issues in Decatur are as compelling as they can possibly be: Workers at all three plants are in danger of losing the eight-hour day, the reform upon which the American labor movement was founded, and with it any hope of leading a normal life outside of work. The situation is also maddening: The rank-and-file Staley workers have mounted a campaign marked by innovation, careful planning, and even genius, but their international union has made no secret about its reluctance to support them. Nor has Secretary of Labor Robert Reich raised a finger to help them win their fight. Wanting to save only their jobs, they have taken on two powerful enemies at once. Staley has locked them out and sends pepper-gas-spraying goons after them when they protest in front of the plant; union hierarchs, threatened by the specter of rank-and-file activism, want no more to do with them than their employer. Two years later, their struggle having ended in defeat, many of the Staley workers will accuse their international of undermining their campaign and engineering their capitulation.

But in late 1994, the battle for visibility is at its height, with billboards near the interstate highway proclaiming Decatur a "war zone" and locked-out Staley workers touring the country as "road warriors" to spread the word about their experiences. On this Saturday afternoon, 15,000 union workers from around the country have arrived for a march through Decatur in the hopes that by sheer numbers they can reclaim this city, give this struggle a prominence that is impossible to ignore.

Before heading back to Chicago, we stop for dinner at a Decatur Denny's, whose only other clientele is a gaggle of drunken Decatur high schoolers wearing whimsical hats. When the Denny's manager, an efficient fiftyish fellow with clip-on tie and name tag, hustles out to clean our table or to tell us why Denny's can't cook a hamburger rare, he is the object of some hilarity at the kids' table. They pelt his back with fries as he hurries here and there.

This is sordid, depressing stuff. But there are important qualitative differences between his predicament and that of the Staley workers. He inhabits a clean orange world free of labor struggles, union halls, and pepper-gassing by cops. But it's also a world free of history and meaning, free of the kind of energy and friendship we had seen in the streets of Decatur that day, and, most important, free of the sense that the city was something you had made, that the future was a question you were answering. Do we want to be a postindustrial country? Do we want to entrust our lives to the whims of the market? Once, these were things we would have decided for ourselves; now, sitting alone at Denny's reading *USA Today*, I realize they are none of our business.

—Baffler 9, 1997

24

The Intern Economy and the Culture Trust

JIM FREDERICK

FOR A BRIEF PERIOD not too long ago, I was the "chief of research" at a glossy yet rugged men's lifestyle magazine. An industry darling, this "practical guide to the sensory thrills and psychological rewards of an active physical life" (as its 1995 National Magazine Award write-up swooned) was one of the most celebrated and award-laden start-ups in recent memory. As they say in the industry, *Men's Journal* was "a very hot book."

Not coincidentally, it was also an advertiser's dream—a place where we took press releases at their word, where we reshot photos for "personal grooming" stories because the toothbrushes didn't look "exciting" enough, and where being a "complete guide for high-performance living" (we used this phrase seriously) meant giving lavish coverage to every sexy consumer product we could get our comp-crazy hands on. In the pages of this morally bankrupt advertorial, this himbo of a magazine, you could, any given month, learn that speed-skiing was not only fun but fulfilling ("Courage wasn't what would propel me down Willamette. Innocence. I would become innocent."); read about the religious significance of mountain-biking equipment ("There's a Zen-like mystery about Giro's new Helios helmet."); be the first to know that this particular style of Nikes was much better than the one we said was the best ever a month ago (this one uses aircraft tubing!); and discover all the reasons why Howie Long is a really good actor.

But do not be impressed by the lofty title I held there. "Research chief" was pure euphemism for "the-fact-checker-whose-head-will-roll-if-anything-goes-wrong." In charge of the "legal invulnerability and factual accuracy" of the magazine, I occupied the bulk of my days by determining whether octopi have pancreases (they don't), what the hell "aircraft tubing" actually is (nobody knows), and whether ex-Oakland Raider wide receiver Warren Wells would sue us for calling him "compulsively felonious" (playing it safe, we cut the "compulsively" and never heard from him).

I was also partly in charge of finding interns to send our faxes, answer our phones, and, among other sundry responsibilities, go shopping for the products in photo shoots that we couldn't get gratis. Compared to fact-checking, hiring interns was difficult stuff. Not because no one was willing, mind you. On the contrary, I was spoiled for choice. The applicants would walk in, these college kids, recent graduates, and grad students, always punctual and always white, sheepish but confident, polite, and well fragranced. They would hand me clips from their school newspapers while I looked over their résumés, which always went something like this:

Interview magazine
May '95 to Sept '95
Summer Intern

CBS News
Oct '94 to May '95
Fall Intern

The Village Voice
May '94 to August '94
Summer Intern

"Very impressive," I would say. By my quick calculations, they had each contributed, conservatively, five or six thousand dollars' worth of uncompensated work to various media conglomerates. I would tell them that they surely already had all the "experience" they would ever get by following this strategy, and that while I had positions open (who doesn't have unpaid positions open?), I was reluctant to fill them with people who were already competent cub writers, reporters, editors, and fact-checkers. They should have been demanding real jobs a long time ago. They would try not to look too crestfallen at this news. They would explain to me that they were indeed the perfect persons to work for me for free. Hell, they sometimes said, they had been doing it so long that they were good at it by now.

Internships have never been more popular. According to the *New York Times*, the number of interns toiling for free has increased 30 percent in just three years, and internship guides, growing fatter every year, list anywhere between 50,000 and 100,000 positions. As tales of layoffs, "downsizing," and "right-sizing" continue to flood the general-business and mass-market publications, internships invariably are presented as refreshing bright spots of "opportunity" for the younger generation.

Don't worry that "cost controls and job cuts in the 1990s pushed many companies to shrink their training and recruiting departments," counsels an article in the December 4, 1996, *New York Times*. Big business is still looking out for you, and "the surge in internships has created new opportunities for people like Jim

Morabito," a guy who, it turns out, held four internships before he even hit his senior year in college. While the vagaries of the Information Age visit hardship and ruination on families, towns, and entire regions, the intern economy is humming along unhindered, ballooning constantly, becoming an increasingly significant yet largely invisible segment of the American workforce. A study by Northwestern University determined that 26 percent of college graduates hired in 1993 had done some type of internship, compared to only 9 percent in 1992. And, according to the author of the *Student's Guide to Volunteering*, volunteering alone comprises a $176 billion industry. Training may have been the paid beginning of your father's first job, but today you're supposed to get it on your own, often on your own tab.

With all the books, magazine articles, and pundits barraging us with an alarmingly unified rhetoric of, "Internships give you the edge in a competitive job market"; "It's a win-win situation for both employer and intern"; and "It's not a job, it's an education," it's easy to forget that internships are free money for big business.

Somewhere over the past two or three decades, a secret and shrewdly undeclared war has been fought between the titans of the glamour industries and a small undefended segment of the labor pool, and labor has lost. By deft public-relations maneuvering, innovation in the face of decreasing cash flow, and the merciless leveraging of an ever-younger, starry-eyed, and unwary segment of the population, the media mandarins have cemented the institution of the internship—working for free—as not merely an acceptable route up the corporate ladder, but the expected one. Tomorrow's Mike Ovitzes, David Geffens, and Barry Dillers won't have started in the mailroom at William Morris, they will have been interns there.

IT'S SAFE TO SAY that when thirty-five black sugar workers were shot dead while striking for a dollar a day in 1887, or when 500,000

Southern textile workers walked off the job in 1934, no one was thinking ahead to the summer of 1996, when Jessica from Swarthmore would be sweating over the green glow of the Xerox machine, logging hundreds of unpaid hours as an MTV intern, assuring herself that this doesn't suck because now her CV will have "résumé radiance," as the authors of *America's Top Internships* like to put it. And granted, the intern class does not make a particularly sympathetic symbol of exploitation. It's hard to care about the plight of privileged college students when they themselves have volunteered for—demanded, even—this demeaning servitude. But the willingness of the rich, white, naive, and stupid to work for nothing affects us all.

There are almost as many definitions of "internship" these days as there are "internship programs" (more than 100,000 by the Princeton Review's count). "Apprenticeships," as free-labor pundits such as Bob Weinstein, author of the formidably shameless *"I'll Work for Free!"* call them, are as old as the Code of Hammurabi itself, suggesting a long and noble tradition of uncompensated tutelage in the workplace. (I often wonder if anyone will go the extra mile and assert that "interns" also built the pyramids, but they never do.) The Fair Labor Standards Act (FLSA) of 1938—a typically meddlesome piece of federal legislation, in true Second Wave fashion—prohibited child labor, established a minimum wage for any kind of work within a for-profit institution, and stipulated that no one may work more than forty hours a week without extra pay. The law was a major setback for employers of every stripe. For more than half a century, it forced the captains of industry (barring significant exceptions, of course) to cooperate with the newly established and accepted labor unions. A thoroughly blue-collar piece of legislation, the FLSA targeted only the most abusive employers of the time: factories, farms, and other heavy industries. It provided exemptions for charities, churches, and other perpetually cash-strapped nonprofit organizations that had always (and still do) filled their ranks with young volunteers.

There is, however, another exemption in the FLSA. Vaguely worded, it concerns "trainees," or the oddly redundant "student learners." It allows for-profit institutions to pay short-term employees less than the minimum wage if they are there in an educational capacity. The Department of Labor requires that six criteria be met before it considers someone not an "employee" but a "trainee" exempt from the FLSA: The training is similar to that one would get in school; the training is for the benefit of the trainees, not the employer; the trainees do not displace regular workers; the employer derives no immediate advantage from the activities of the trainees, and may even incur some loss; the trainees understand that they are not entitled to a job at the conclusion of the training; and the trainees understand that they are not entitled to wages for the time spent in training.

Even though the Department of Labor doesn't use or even recognize the word "intern," this clearly legitimate educational arrangement is what certain branches of industry—banks, law firms, tech companies, engineering companies, and many federal agencies—refer to when they use the term. College students follow a highly structured path of seminars, lectures, on-the-job training, personal "mentors," and company-assigned moot projects. And, despite the exemption, many of these interns are still quite well paid.

The real abusers of the intern economy are the glamour industries. Fashion, architecture, and virtually every media outlet (except for newspapers and some magazines, with their fussbudgety unions) piggyback on the credibility of the more legitimate programs by hiring college kids as little more than clerical temps, paying them not a dime, and disguising the whole operation as a "learning experience." It is not a coincidence that the industries offering youngsters an unending parade of subversive cartoons, daring advertising, and rebellious photo spreads are also the ones most likely to strip their earning power from them. It's almost their duty, as the institutions that have taught us to value style over substance, to take advantage of our resulting faith that working someplace cool is better than getting a paycheck.

But why should the rest of us care if Chip from Brown, who fetches coffee for the green-room guests, is an "intern," not a "temp"? Or if the entire student bodies of Mount Holyoke, Amherst, Columbia, and Vassar are stupid enough to sign away their summers to Wenner and Eisner, Geffen and Redstone?

First, a bit of basic employment-market economics. The glamour industries enjoy a tremendous surplus of labor. There are more people who want media jobs than can be employed. Therefore, labor is cheap, as demonstrated by the industry's already low salaries ($18,000 a year for an editorial assistant is not uncommon, which is about $9 an hour, assuming the most optimistic work schedule possible).[1] Left to its own devices, a rational market with surplus labor will bid wages down almost to the point where no one will accept a job. If it can, a market will bid the wages all the way down to zero—as long as someone, anyone, will do the work, for whatever real or imagined benefit. Which brings us back to Jessica and Chip. For them and their classmates, the imagined benefits of an internship are so great that real benefits—you know, wages—have been bid out of existence. Businesses have a real, bottom-line incentive to encourage the trend toward labor that is not only free but also without any type of obligation whatsoever. In other words, interns are restructuring the labor market. Thanks to those who can afford to win the labor auction with the lowest possible price—*I'll work for free!*—those without outside (read: parental) support are forced to take tremendous real-dollar losses to stay competitive. Or they are simply priced entirely out of com-

[1] Entry-level wages in the glamour industries improved substantially in the late Nineties, and many first-job salaries now range from the mid-20s to the mid-30s. If such wage levels turn out to be sustainable, then some good might have come of the great Internet/stock market/labor market bubble after all. But that's a big *if*.

petition. This ensures that the glamour industries remain the land of the rich and privileged, for they are the only people who can absorb a short-term loss to get an imagined long-term gain.

But why stop there? Left unchecked, a labor market knows no boundaries when it comes to exploitation. Although the intern price floor can't go any lower dollar-wise, it can go lower by the amount of time served, or by the size of the labor segment drawn into the swindle. As more people do internships, the supply of intern-alums increases, driving down the value of that "experience" even further—a phenomenon you could call "intern inflation." So college kids feel pressure to do more of them, or for a longer stretch of time. And those previously thought of as obvious employee potential, such as college graduates, grad students, and career-changers, are increasingly told, "Have you thought of doing an internship?"

Without some sort of check, this admirably efficient market will just continue on its merry way. Not long from now, we will begin hearing: "Summer internships don't really give you that much experience because they are only twelve weeks long. You need at least a semester or even a year to get a real grounding." It is not outlandish to imagine a day when a year's internship is explicitly required before you get hired for a new job, or when employers start charging interns for, let's say, "training costs." Before we laugh at Jessica and Chip for exploiting themselves, we should consider that years of Jessicas and Chips have already made unpaid internships an unspoken requirement for certain jobs, and the longer the intern economy hums along unhindered, the more this labor inflation will increase. By giving away work, interns reduce the value of everybody's labor.

How much have they cheapened our lives? Since statistics concerning interns aren't counted by the Department of Labor, it's nearly impossible to estimate. But the figures for individual intern-exploiters are readily available. Take MTV, which alone uses between 150 and 200 interns at any given time and requires from each at least two days a week of work. There are three seasons—summer, fall, and spring. A twelve-week summer intern is forfeiting $989 if he works the minimum two days a week; $2,472 if full time. A twenty-week spring and fall intern gives up $1,648 if he works two-day weeks; $4,120 for full time. How does MTV make out in all this? Very well, thanks. Granting MTV the minimums for all variables of its program (150 interns working only two days a week), MTV saves $642,270 a year in unpaid wages. To extend these calculations nationwide, assume there are 40,000 internships every year (the low end of the internship guides' estimates), and they all work only two days a week for only twelve weeks (again, all low-end estimates). What do you get? Every year, kids forfeit and businesses gain more than $39,522,000.

And that's not all internships do. Take a trip to any design studio, advertising agency, or editorial office (even the most responsible left-wing publications) and you'll see one of the glamour industries' dirtiest secrets: There's not a black face in the joint. If you can't get a job unless you've had an internship, and you can't take an internship unless you can be supported by daddy for at least a couple of months, then the system guarantees an applicant pool that is decidedly privileged. But you needn't let a little arithmetic and your innate sense of decency bother you. Do what the free-labor advocates have been doing for years now: Simply holler, "Internships are not racist and elitist!" as loud as you can; repeat as necessary until you believe it.

All Internships Lead to MTV

It should hardly surprise us, given the amount they stand to gain from the unfettered operating of the intern economy, that the hippest publications are among the most regular and most sanguine chroniclers of the intern's happy lot. *Rolling Stone*, a notorious intern abuser, runs gooey features on the glories of unpaid internships in its annual college issue. One year, it profiled the lucky guy who drove the Oscar Mayer Wienermobile; the even luckier guy who got to fetch lunch for Howard Stern; and, luckiest of all, the New York Knicks towel guy. But *Rolling Stone* doesn't want Chip and Jessica getting swollen heads just because they get to sweat for the stars, so on occasion it will tincture the standard categories of the intern story with a certain wholesome contempt for the young people who so put themselves out for the glamour business. "You would be surprised how many intelligent people cannot take a cohesive phone message or Xerox more than one copy of a document," it quoted Victoria Rowan, a woman who had risen from internhood to be a powerful and glamorous assistant editor at *Mirabella*, as saying back in 1993. "It's not a game of shit on the peon. Coffee has to be ordered." Indeed it does, gentle Victoria. But if you're not paying the peon minimum, you are, in fact, shitting on her. Even girl-empowering *Sassy* gets in on the act, following in 1995 the heroic exploits of an intern at—surprise—MTV: "Biggest perk: We got to go to Madonna's Bedtime Story Pajama Party at Webster Hall (a huge club in New York City). Worst part of the job: We have to go up to the 50th floor a lot, and the elevator makes me nauseous."

But to read the most addle-eyed intern-economy glorification of all, you have to turn to *The New Yorker*, which in October 1994 ran "Rocking in Shangri-la," a story by John Seabrook about interns at—you guessed it—MTV. The story actually attempts to convince readers that "the real power brokers" at MTV are not President Shirley McGrath, Chair Tom Freston, or even Viacom Chair Sumner Redstone, but rather its "employees under the age of twenty-five." "When you are in your early twenties and you are working for MTV," Seabrook writes, in one of the most appallingly misguided tributes to the Culture Trust to appear to date, "you carry in your brain, muscles, and gonads a kind of mystical authority that your bosses don't possess." After fourteen long pages, it turns out that the "authority" possessed by the low-paid production assistants and the unpaid interns boils down to this: They are walking, talking demographic surveys who tell executives what is cool and what sucks. In exchange, they get free MTV stuff! And they're allowed to listen to music as loud as they want! Often, observes the venerable *New Yorker,* interns will "rock out together for a moment before continuing along the hall," because, we are told, "employees who think that a particular song 'rules' are encouraged to crank it."

IT IS NEARLY IMPOSSIBLE to raise a battle cry for a war that already has been lost. Knowing too well that old notions like government protection for the exploited, fair wages, and—not to sound quaint—common decency probably will never catch up with the go-go Information Age, the Culture Trust has won this battle even before the other combatants had realized it started. The tide of indentured college servitude is unstoppable, and the market for free labor can only get worse in the near future.

Don't bother looking to government. The people who passed the FLSA have long since been supplanted by the likes of Ohio Republican Representative Joe Knollenberg, who fights courageously to liberate employers from the tyranny of paying a fair day's wage for a fair day's work. Knollenberg introduced an amendment to the FLSA, entitled the Job Skills Development Act of 1997, which aims to revoke the basic provision that labor contributing to the wealth of someone else must be compensated. When he had introduced a virtually identical bill in 1995, Knollenberg told the House Subcommittee on Workforce Protections that the FLSA "places an unnecessary burden on individuals seeking employment in a competitive profession. . . . Frankly, the FLSA restrictions on volunteer services illustrate why the American people believe their federal government is too intrusive." What Knollenberg doesn't mention is that without that "intrusiveness," any sweatshop proprietor or factory foreman could legally claim that the work their underlings are doing is "volunteer work" aimed at "furthering their career goals." After all, they're only trainees at the drill bit, learning skills that will help them get ahead in a competitive job market.

Curiously enough, there have been some hopeful developments in fields where the would-be exploiters of interns are bound by a professional code of ethics. The American Institute of Architects (AIA) instituted a program a few years ago to combat unfair labor practices by its members. Every architect who receives an award from the AIA or makes a speech at its meetings must sign a document affirming that his or her company upholds all tenets of the FLSA and the association's agreed-upon labor practices. But this is an anomaly permitted by the unique position of the AIA within its industry. Any hope that the National Association of Broadcasters, the Council of Fashion Designers of America, and the Academy of Motion Pictures Arts and Sciences would follow suit is almost laughable.

As for the interns themselves, it would be a little naive to imagine that the children of the white-collar class could make some stand of solidarity and resist working for free. The era is simply too selfish, EMI Records too alluring, MTV too sexy, *Spin* too hip, and CBS too powerful. The glamour titans will have all the free labor they will ever need. And in a world where we are forced to mortgage pieces of our soul every day, we are increasingly going to have to give it away for free.

—BAFFLER 9, 1997

Afterword

After the brief job-market insanity of the late Nineties (signing bonuses for entry-level jobs, stock options that were actually valuable for a while, etc.), the ruthless efficiency and downward pressures of an unchecked labor auction have returned. Wipe that smile off your face and forget about bringing your pet to work, because the newspapers are again filled with scary stories about how few jobs are out there. And it has been shocking, but not surprising, to learn that many of this essay's most outrageous, just-for-a-gag predictions have in fact come true. Some students are now, indeed, paying thousands of dollars for summer internships, and some middle-aged career changers are competing in ever-greater numbers for the opportunity to answer phones and open the mail for free. Corporate America, of course, couldn't be more thrilled that the great intern scam thunders on unhindered, while the underlying ethics and legality of the whole institution go completely unquestioned. As the *Wall Street Journal,* that proud chronicler of the Intern Economy, delightedly reminded its readers not long ago, "It's a way of getting better help for less, and without the long term commitment." Right on!

25

Chapters of Eleven

Kim Phillips-Fein

An hour before closing time, the Chicago Mercantile Exchange hardly seems like a dignified institution at the center of American finance: It's more like a sports bar. Throngs of grown-up frat-boy traders stare at numbers flashing on a gigantic screen. Moments of calm alternate with paroxysms of activity, as the *Animal House* lookalikes pump their fists into the air and gesticulate to the clerks ringing the pit. Pieces of paper fly through the air, deftly handled by college-age runners wearing the baggy gold jackets of Team Merc. Abstract pork bellies and livestock—and the abstractions of abstractions, stock indexes and interest rates—are furiously tossed back and forth in a never-ending game that seems always to be in the ninth inning.

Does bankruptcy ever enter the minds of the wild-eyed millionaires who bounce like cheerleaders in the panicked atmosphere of the pit? If so, they can forcibly expel the thought with a few trades. But come October 1998, the wizards at the Merc—alchemically spinning loss into gold—won't be able to take their minds off going bust. That's when the Merc begins trading a brand-new future index based on the quarterly number of bankruptcies. Though the Quarterly Bankruptcy Index may sound bizarre, it's supposed to function like insurance: The credit-card companies stand to lose a small amount if bankruptcies fall, but they'll offset potentially great losses if bankruptcies rise. Peach farmers and hog merchants can buy futures to lower risk; why shouldn't banks, credit-card companies, and department stores be able to use the derivatives market to offset their mounting losses to bankruptcy?

The notion of people getting rich betting on the spiraling number of bankruptcies may seem a little odd to the uninitiated. But personal bankruptcies hit an all-time high in 1997, with more than 1.3 million people filing, and even more are expected to file in 1998; bank-card companies claim to have lost between $10 and $12 billion as a result. Not that anyone should feel sorry for the credit industry, which borrows money at standard rates and lends it out at exorbitant ones. But they are simply on the lookout for some new financial tool to help insure themselves against loss—that is, when they aren't busy pressuring Congress to stiffen the penalties for bankruptcy. What makes the "deadbeat index" unusual is its casual nonchalance toward bankruptcy. While moralists vent public outrage over the spiraling number of bankruptcies, the master financial minds of the Merc have admitted the truth: Bankruptcy is normal today, an aspect of economic life to be insured against as though it were a fact of nature like drought or flood.

This routinization of bankruptcy is the polar opposite of the old Weberian version of economic behavior. The farmers and artisans of centuries ago felt a strict identity between self and pocketbook. Financial dealings were thought to reveal the most intimate truths about one's character. In the old precapitalist world, bankruptcy received the stiffest of punishments; the debtor relinquished freedom, property, and sometimes life itself. In England, bankruptcy was punishable by death through the eighteenth century; imprisonment for debt remained the norm until the days of Dickens. But advanced capitalist states have long since given up pushing business moralism to such extremes and have ceased to equate financial death with the real thing. Nineteenth-century reformers were horrified by the cruelty of debtor's prisons, but they were also disturbed by the fact that their own bourgeois peers could be thrown willy-nilly into the bin simply for making a bad deal or two right before a recession. As our contemporary economists might say, an economy built on rewarding risk can't afford to mete out too-harsh punishment for daredevil entrepreneurs whose stunts occasionally leave them lying bruised on the ground.

During the last fifty years, though, bankruptcy has been democratized. Today it's a condition that might be faced by anyone, not just entrepreneurs. And while the spending binges that land most of us in bankruptcy are hardly deeds of heroic capitalist risk-taking, they are far more important in reality to our larger economic well-being.

Nonetheless, this latest phase in the development of bankruptcy has brought loud public calls for a revival of the old precapitalist horror toward debt. Credit-industry hacks and their minions on Capitol Hill have taken up the mantle of personal responsibility and have sought to transform the Nanny State into the Daddy State, a stern federal superego that will scold debtors along with pregnant teens, divorcees, and other bearers of bad values. "Bankruptcy has become like a carwash. People go in, spend a little time inside, and come out spotless," laments Mallory Duncan of the National Retail Federation, apparently longing for the days of public stocks and debtor's prison. "Bankruptcy is becoming a financial strategy for too many Americans," moans Donald Ogilvie, executive vice president of the American Bankers Association, in a letter to the *Wall Street Journal*. "There are a whole lot of child-like adults with adult-like credit lines," keens Ronald Utt, senior fellow at the Heritage Foundation. But the ain't-it-awful crowd, harking back to yesteryear's business moralism, blithely ignores what the Merc cannily admits. Bankruptcy is a crucial safety valve for an economy that depends on mass consumption and low wages.

IF THE REAL CAUSE of the rising number of bankruptcies was some sudden erosion of moral fiber, it would be testimony to the malleability of the human spirit. In fact, we really don't need to juice up our econometric model with a virtue variable to see what has caused the increase. As it turns out, the change has fairly mundane origins: Bankruptcy is closely correlated with the ratio of debt to income, which has been rising rapidly ever since real wages stopped rising in the early Seventies. In other words, as people began to borrow to make up for stagnant wages, bankruptcies started to rise.

It's commonplace to blame the rise in bankruptcies on the new bankruptcy code, which, starting in late 1979, made it easier to discharge credit-card debt. But bankruptcies had actually been climbing throughout the Seventies, from 173,000 personal and business bankruptcies in 1973 to 254,000 in 1975, before falling slightly to 226,000 in 1979. During those years, bankruptcy law didn't change, but consumer indebtedness did: Between 1973 and 1979, the ratio of total household debt to total household income rose from 58.6 percent to 64 percent. After the new law took effect, it's true, personal bankruptcies rose by 100,000, but the law was more a response to the bankruptcy trend than a cause.

The debt-income ratio rose steadily through the Eighties and Nineties, reaching 83.4 percent of household income in 1994; by 1997, debt-service payments reached a shocking 16 percent of total household income. Credit-card use climbed especially sharply during the Eighties and the Nineties. Between 1984 and the present, revolving credit (short-term debt, mainly credit cards) has more than tripled. And with rising debt, bankruptcies have rocketed, climbing from about 300,000 a year in the early Eighties to more than one million in 1996.

This mountain of new debt may seem a sure sign of a country headed for the poorhouse. But in fact, the seemingly exorbitant amount of consumer debt is in large part responsible for the prosperity we've enjoyed these past few years. The Nineties expansion, in contrast to the Keynesian expansion of the Sixties, is fueled by consumption; consumption has averaged 67.8 percent of GDP in the Nineties, a higher proportion than during any other expansion since World War II. Debt explains the otherwise-mysterious appearance of a consumption-driven boom at a time when real wages have been falling or stagnant. The fact that the debt-to-income ratio has been climbing since 1973—the postwar peak for real wages—suggests that families have taken on debt in order to compensate for slow wage increases. Today, credit-driven spending is at historic levels, accounting for about 29 percent of the growth in consumption in the expansion that commenced in 1991. Today's credit explosion makes *The Bonfire of the Vanities* look sober; during the Eighties, credit accounted for just 23 percent of growth in consumption. From the standpoint of economic growth, there's no doubt the handy income supplement made possible by debt has been a lifesaver. But the corollary is a much larger number of bankruptcies, since stagnant wages and rising debt together mean that at some point people—well, lots of people—inevitably are going to default.[1]

Debt also has ideological benefits. By putting purchasing power into the hands of the vast majority without increased wages, it creates a fiction of social equality and sustains mass purchasing power even as income inequality widens. A million-odd bankrupt-

1 GDP figures are from Doug Henwood's Bureau of Economic Analysis database; figures on the proportion of growth in consumption financed by credit are calculated using his flow-of-funds database.

cies is a small price to pay for such a handy illusion. Without the cushion of widely available credit, we'd risk a broad economic contraction, not to mention a whole lot of demands for higher wages. Rising profits, meager wage growth, and manic consumption are what drives the Nineties boom. Someone's gotta pay—and for the time being, the bill's going to Visa.

But who are the debtors? Are they the bearers of a new strain of shortsighted selfishness? Actually, they are more or less a cross section of the middle class. In occupational makeup, they mirror the country as a whole, but their incomes are far lower, and their debts far higher, than the general population. Median family income for bankruptcy petitioners in 1991 was $18,000—half the national average—and almost 30 percent of debtors had incomes below the poverty line. Many owed one-and-a-half times their yearly income in short-term debt.

What these numbers suggest is that bankruptcy is now a routine part of middle-class American life. People borrow heavily, especially during expansions, when they expect—perhaps irrationally—that they'll be able to pay back all their debt. But should a single crisis befall a heavily indebted household, it's easy for it to fall hopelessly behind. Much of the rise in bankruptcies has occurred during economic upswings, which puzzles pundits, though it may not be so complex: In good times, banks are willing to lend, credit-card companies hawk their wares, and people are lulled into a false sense of economic security. But when disaster hits, they topple right away: More than half of 1991 bankrupts reported interrupted employment in the two years before they filed. Forty percent of older bankrupts faltered under heavy medical debt. Many are single parents. Their commonalities are not immorality but a brush with a single financial disaster—divorce, layoff, catastrophic heart attack—which is all it takes to collapse a debt-ridden family's finances. So an extremely high bankruptcy rate is pretty much to be expected in a society with scant social-welfare provisions, stagnant wages, easy credit, and a high cultural premium on status-through-consumption. You may have lost your middle-class salary; you may not have the job security of a degree or a union. But your debt is as good as anyone else's.[2]

But for other debtors, the rude disruption of their middle-class lifestyles hasn't been the result of sudden disaster; it's been mere pretense from the start. These are spenders who aren't weighed down by a rare big-ticket item but who bankrupt themselves with spending sprees totally out of keeping with their incomes. Poor people are the credit industry's growth sector; between 1977 and 1989, the proportion of households earning between $10,000 and $20,000 who have at least one credit card rose from 33 percent in 1983 to 44 percent in 1995, according to Federal Reserve economist Peter Yoo. Even among households with incomes under $10,000, 32 percent owned credit cards in 1995. Lower-income households also use their cards more heavily than they used to. (Although wealthy households still account for the majority of credit-card debt, average credit-card debt for households in the lower half of the income-distribution scale increased at a 14 percent annual rate between 1992 and 1995, compared with an 8 percent annual rate for households in the top half of the income-distribution chart.)

For poorer families, debt is an irresistible supplement to low incomes. I went to Chicago's federal bankruptcy court and looked through some of the petitioners' files. Among them I found Mary B., a middle-aged woman, married with no children. She's worked at the National School Towel Service for sixteen years; her annual salary is $12,000. She probably will never buy a home or get a degree. Nonetheless, she declared bankruptcy in April 1998, after running up credit-card bills of $9,200. According to court docu-

[2] Financial profiles of petitioners from "Consumer Debtors Ten Years Later: A Financial Comparison of Consumer Bankrupts, 1981–1991," by Theresa Sullivan, Elizabeth Warren, and Jay Westbrook, *American Bankruptcy Journal*, Spring 1994. Also see "Consumer Bankruptcy: Issues Summary," by Elizabeth Warren of Harvard Law School.

ments, she charged $5,300 of "ordinary household goods and supplies" to her Discover Card, and $3,200 more to her First Chicago card. Let's reflect on what these expenses might be: a trip to Sears for a new washer dryer? A jaunt to Marshall Field's, perhaps for a cute pair of earrings and a chi-chi black dress? Marie Anne T.'s files tell a similarly ordinary story. A nurse technician for five years, earning a salary of $18,000, this single mother with two young-adult children managed to ring up bills of $13,700 on her credit cards in 1997, increasing her disposable income by 76 percent and making stops at Sears (for a new lawn mower and stereo, according to court files) and at Montgomery Ward (new tires for the car?). She also owed $46,000 in secured debt, mostly for no fewer than three automobiles, shared with her children. Neither Mary nor Marie Anne realistically could have hoped to pay the exorbitant bills, no matter how bountiful the economy seemed. Instead, each one simply "passed" as middle class for a year, flaunting her new clothes and household goods.

There's an odd poetic justice in the bankruptcies of Mary and Marie Anne. Banks and credit companies are, strictly speaking, the direct source of their illusory "income." But, considered more abstractly, it is their bosses who are lending them money. Most households are net debtors, while only the very richest are net creditors. In an overall sense, in other words, the working classes are forever borrowing from their employers. Lending replaces decent wages, masking income disparities even while aggravating them through staggering interest rates. If Mary's wages were higher, she might not have needed those credit cards—and, of course, her boss wouldn't have quite so much money lying around to lend. Credit and bankruptcy can sometimes even seem like class warfare by other means: Mary and Marie Anne are simply treating themselves to a long-delayed raise.

But there is also something tragic about quick bankruptcy and easy credit, about the buying frenzies of folks like Mary and Marie Anne or their wealthier counterparts who are laid low by exclusive summer camps, music lessons, and private schools. Bankruptcy may provide short-term relief for consumers locked into endless debt servicing, but it can't deliver on the promise of sunny days and blue skies held out by the lawyers shilling on late-night TV. Upper-class moralists may gnash their teeth, but bankruptcy serves their interests fairly well: By obscuring collective problems, credit provides easy individual escapes into a world where everything can be yours. Frustration with empty, boring work, a stagnant salary, and the tedium of making ends meet can be expressed as the craving for a waffle iron, a piece of lingerie, a bright plastic toy for the kid. Bankruptcy transforms the nasty crunch confronting the middle class—"downsizing," rising housing prices, slow real-income growth, attacks on unions—into an individual morality play of desire, gluttony, confession, and finally redemption, as the forgiven debtor goes out to borrow once again.

—BAFFLER 11, 1998

Afterword

The credit industry is still lobbying to get the government to crack down and help it collect its debts, even while it floods responsible borrowers—for example, college students—with credit-card solicitations. A bankruptcy reform bill was narrowly held up in the Senate in 2002, but the bill—which makes it more difficult to enter Chapter 11, forcing people instead into state-supervised debt-repayment plans—will likely be law before long. This looks like another case of short-term financial interests interfering with the long-term needs of business. Since credit and bankruptcy have kept the economy pumping through the recession, it's anyone's guess what will happen if this embarrassing excuse for a social safety net is removed.

26
Dilbert and Me

TOM VANDERBILT

IF WE MAY BELIEVE the authors of *Chicken Soup for the Soul at Work*, a "tremendous malaise" grips the workplace today, and with "all the downsizing, the work going offshore . . . people need to feel inspired." Luckily, it's not a problem too big to be fixed with some Norman Vincent Peale homilies. Thus we read, in a lesson titled, "Santa Comes to Joan":

> Every office has a Joan, or should have. She's the one everyone looks to when the workload gets too heavy. She's the one with the good story and the ready laugh. For our Christmas party, she's the one who transforms our sterile corporate conference room, Christmas after Christmas, with tiny white lights, real teacups, teapots and plates she had brought from home.

There was a "Joan" at the media conglomerate I used to work for, and one day during the company's year of near-20-percent profits, I went to work to find she was being let go, the result of some silent machinations from above (wherever that was). And even as the company "aggressively expanded its position" by purchasing other media entities, we would occasionally feel the brush of distant rumor telling us that our days, too, were numbered. So what was the talk around the watercooler? Plans to organize? Formal protests over the company's shoddy personnel practices? No, no, and no.

We talked about *Dilbert*. Hardly a day passed in which we made no reference to that great subverter of corporate hierarchy, in which I didn't see Dilbert's winsome visage flickering on a neighboring screen saver or peering out from a mug in the employee kitchen. In the face of real threats from a ruthless and all-too-knowing management, we turned to a fantasy office world in which managers were obvious incompetents, in which new motivational schemes were self-evidently ridiculous, and in which anonymous cubicled office drones held the real power. Even downsizing seemed innocuous in *Dilbert*, a practical joke that was always happening to someone else.

What seems remarkable about all this now is the curious relationship between *Dilbert* and all the absurd management fads and mission statements that it mocks. Its refusal to do anything more than gripe helped more to naturalize the managerial culture than to subvert it. As corporate America tears up the social contract, it should come as no surprise that *Dilbert* books have become a popular gift from managers to employees, or that executives have begun to ask the comic's author to lecture at their conferences, or that *Dilbert* books have become a "business bestseller" (an entirely new category indicative of the proliferation of corporate-culture commodities), or even that Hallmark should issue *Dilbert* mugs for "Boss Day" (the holiday invented in 1954 by a Kansas woman who says she wanted to honor her father). Symbolic acts of everyday resistance, it turns out, are healthy. They are exactly what the boss wants to see on your cubicle wall.

Dilbert helps to humanize and insulate us from what is actually happening in corporate America. The two fill the same cultural need as the TV commercials that show family farmers using geosynchronous technology to plow their tracts, even though the ad's sponsor is an agribusiness concern that has made family farmers virtually extinct. Or as all the writing about homespun investment groups such as the Beardstown Ladies, whose folksy tips and "recipes" make believable the ridiculous conceit that Information Age speculating is as familiar and safe as stowing bags of money under the bed, and that the global market, which uproots whole cultures and seeks to render locality obsolete, is somehow A-OK with the small-town values and personalities they symbolize.

Meanwhile, sales of less savvy and less cynical corporate ideoproducts are suffering from a devastating backlash. *The New Republic* reports that the Conference Board, the folks who bring you the Consumer Confidence Index and other accoutrements of the Kinko's economy, has announced a scalding assessment of the motivational industry. As it turns out, posters of mountain climbers and rowing crews don't spur the unmotivated, and the already motivated don't need them. Even Successories, the nation's leading purveyor of corporate incentiana, has been forced to sack its management team and replace workers after a few quarters of lackluster performance.

Other dealers in positive thinking and management chicanery have been able to stay ahead of the curve. Hallmark Cards, for example, a leader in the "social expressions" category, has already supplemented its "business expressions" line with one called "Out of the Blue," a series of small, inexpensive cards bearing some quickly digestible fragment of workplace uplift. A Hallmark spokesperson informed me that the line was part of a nationwide trend toward what *Harper's Bazaar* reported as a "nicening of the workplace." The "Out of the Blue" cards, I was told, were designed to fit in employee mailboxes, or to be left discreetly on desks, somehow providing salve to the increasing tension over layoffs, outsourcing, mergers, and the rest.

Even more noxious is the "corporate soul" movement, which argues that downsizing organizations need to inject "values" into the company or bring "healing" into the workplace in forms ranging from mass bouts of therapy to flowers left on desks (as if downsizing were some affair of the heart gone awry). It was, of course, only a matter of time before the hucksters of wellness, those ubiquitous checkout-counter gurus such as Deepak Chopra and James (*Celestine Prophecy*) Renfield, began tailoring their soulcraft to fit the hulking frame of corporate culture. Renfield now explains how spirituality and capitalism are compatible, observing that "the greatest fulfillment comes when we make the world a better place, and this connects with our deepest traditional need in capitalism—find a need and fill it." Given the increasing taste for euphemism, I suspect it may only be a short while until Fortune 500 companies follow the lead of the New Agey firms, replacing their CEOs with "Keepers of Dreams and Beliefs."

The spirituality kick reaches an illogical extreme in *Jesus CEO*, a book that finds Christ's teachings applicable to today's business world. "Jesus knew his mission statement," the author observes, "and he did not deviate from it." Or, taking a metaphor from the ever-relevant world of sports (a longtime corporate-inspirational favorite), "As quarterback, Jesus knew his game plan could not be to take truth up the middle." The book essentially updates Bruce Barton's *The Man Nobody Knows*, which argued Jesus was, before anything else, a salesman. Barton's book appeared in 1925, at the tail end of several decades of effort to bring "that old-time religion" into line with the new mass consumer economy, a process that spun off such marvels as Mind Cure and spirituality-tinged bestsellers like 1907's *The Efficient Life*.

"It's like a religion," one office worker told *The New Republic* about Successories. And the comparison is entirely apt: Just as

Protestant ideas of salvation in the next world were once retooled into visions of abundance in this world, so is the new impetus toward spirituality in the workplace and Scripture-like motivational tales offering assurance to those caught amid the convulsive shifts of the reengineering corporation, the corrosion of loyalty and security, and the terrifying ruptures of the globalizing economy. Religion, too, drifts toward market logic, in everything from mainstream megachurches to the most outlandish cults. Note in particular the Heaven's Gate group, whose mass suicide was so much in the news. Rather than the traditional bunch of sandal-sporting mystics, they were a forward-looking, entrepreneurial organization (willing to demonstrate "teamwork" and confront "risk"), flourishing in a sci-tech haven by the sea. Indeed, in the weeks after the group's "departure," I stumbled across this suggestive passage in *God Wants You to Be Rich*, a book about the "theology of economics" by libertarian economist Paul Zane Pilzer: "To survive today, the corporation must look frequently at every task as if it were about to embark on a journey to a new kind of planet on a new kind of spaceship."

In South Korea, in Russia, and in Europe (where, a Smith Barney analyst observed, "there have been decades of coddling the job holders"), the big changes of recent years have bred massive protests in the street by those whose lives are scheduled to be destroyed. Here we line the barricades with greeting cards and Fortune 500 faith healers.

—BAFFLER 9, 1997

27

Us Against Them in the Me Decade

CHRISTIAN PARENTI

> Rising unemployment was a very desirable way of reducing the strength of the working classes. . . . What was engineered—in Marxist terms—was a crisis in capitalism which re-created a reserve army of labor, and has allowed the capitalists to make high profits ever since.
>
> —*Alan Budd, chief economic adviser to Margaret Thatcher, 1992*

THE LATE SIXTIES AND EARLY SEVENTIES were tough times for the owners of American industry. The postwar recovery had peaked. Europe and Japan had rebuilt their industries and transformed themselves from hungry markets for American goods and capital into aggressive economic rivals. Newly industrializing countries, too, were joining the game. After more than two decades of virtually uninterrupted growth, there was just too much stuff circulating the planet. Too many cars, too many shoes, too many refrigerators, and not enough people with money to absorb the abundance. It was a classic formula: Too much success glutted markets and shrank profits.

To complicate matters, mass rebellion—particularly of the socialist and Third World nationalist sort—was breaking out around the globe. As the United States continued to lose badly in

Vietnam (and not for lack of lethal effort), the American political establishment—liberals and conservatives alike—lost credibility. The civil rights movement and peaceful antiwar rallies on campuses had given way to massive urban riots and homegrown "terrorism." As the war dragged on, even American GIs were a liability, on occasion casting their antiwar vote with hand grenades. In 1970 alone, the military, which preferred to suppress news of dissent, reported that 363 officers were "fragged," or assassinated in the field by subordinates.

And where was labor in this political maelstrom? Where was the mainstream American working class, that supposed host of somnambulant Archie Bunkers? They sent their boys to die in 'Nam, grieved quietly by themselves, and, as the official image informs us, donned their hardhats for the occasional prowar, flag-waving Nixon rally, right? Actually, the real saga of labor during those troubled years is one of disobedience, chaos, "counterplanning," malingering, and huge, militant wildcat strikes. It was in response to this crisis—a crisis of excess democracy and excess working-class power—and the vicissitudes of overproduction, that the great right-wing backlash of the last three decades was born. To understand what happened next, it is crucial to understand that for the first time since the Great Depression, the American business class felt its back pressed against the wall.

The Sleeping Giant Stirs

Labor's "new mood" first made headlines in 1968, the year political revolt broke out around the world. The United Farm Workers were gaining national attention and winning contracts. Walter Reuther, president of the behemoth United Auto Workers (UAW), was taking an increasingly progressive stance against racism, the war in Vietnam, and the AFL-CIO's pampered, pussyfooting leaders. In May 1968, AFL-CIO President George Meany suspended the UAW from the federation. A little more than a month later, Reuther formed the Alliance for Labor Action with the Teamsters, the country's largest union. All the while, the UAW was bringing home the bacon, having just beaten Ford in a two-month strike.

Around the same time, public-sector workers—who by and large did not have the right to strike—began to agitate. In February 1968, New York sanitation workers, ignoring the law and threats of jail, walked out and left the city's refuse to mount in frozen, rat-infested heaps for nine days. Mayor John V. Lindsay called the strike "blackmail" and refused to give in to workers' demands, until the more sober Governor Nelson Rockefeller overruled him and boosted wages for the garbagemen. But their strike had become a spectacle of national proportions. A fretful *U.S. News & World Report* noted "a new, aggressive mood among public employees." Soon came word of the American Federation of Teachers' drive to collect a million-dollar "militancy fund" as teachers staged small but widespread illegal strikes in Maryland, Florida, and New Mexico.

Strikes hobbled American industry in the first four months of 1968 to an extent they hadn't since 1950, and labor emerged victorious in most of the disputes. By late June, federal mediators were involved in 353 strikes, which had idled 219,000 workers in trades ranging from construction to journalism. In Detroit, for example, workers shut down both of the city's papers for seven and a half months, while the building trades brought the construction industry to its knees for most of the summer. And labor was only beginning to feel its strength.

Nineteen sixty-nine brought the first of several truly titanic showdowns. In October, General Electric faced off against a coalition of twelve unions. Since the Forties, GE had been known as one of the most antiunion corporations in America. Its take-it-or-leave-it approach to contract negotiation and its ruthless cost-cutting went by the moniker "Boulwarism," in honor of the company's notorious personnel manager, Lemuel Boulware. The company's heavy hand was of no avail in the strike of 1969–70, when workers shut hundreds of GE plants from Burlington, Vermont, to Oakland, California. With 133,000 strikers coast-to-coast walking picket lines, production at the nation's fourth-largest employer ground to a halt.

The stakes were high for both sides. "If we're beaten like we were in 1960," said one shop steward with the International Brotherhood of Electrical Workers, "that's the end of the union at GE." Across the trenches, corporate officers saw their worst nightmare coming to life: Not only did the twelve-union alliance opposing GE bring together some of the most formidable personalities and organizations in labor's camp, it united once-bickering factions of the labor movement. The UAW even kicked in more than a million dollars and a few veteran strategists and negotiators to aid the smaller electrical unions on their sectors of the front. Among the rank and file, another frightening unity was forming: Along with the white, crew-cut, old-school workers were legions of long-haired, pot-smoking youths, men and women, black and white, who unlike their elders did not recall the depression and didn't fear the threats of GE's labor experts. The youth brought with them all the fury and iconoclasm of their generation—they were militant, pro-union, and ready to fight.

As Christmas 1969 came and went, the strike's economic impact reverberated through other industries. Eleven weeks of impasse at GE left Learjet holding a half-dozen executive jets in Wichita, Kansas, with empty nacelles awaiting GE engines. Tecumseh's compressor-fabricating operations had no electric motors, forcing the company to lay off three hundred workers. Meanwhile, retailers began to feel the pinch as a boycott of GE consumer electronics and appliances gained momentum. Direct losses to GE were tallied at $100 million in missed profits.

On the picket lines, the mood remained strangely calm. Even in the company's northeastern strongholds, the press reported that strikers were settling in for the long haul, with little of the anxiety seen during big strikes of years past. Why? To the horror of businessmen, the answer soon arrived with all the sting of a shiv from Brutus. Not only were strikers receiving union funds, but tens of thousands of them also were drawing welfare checks. The government was subsidizing labor's side of the battle! "It's a mind-boggling situation," declared Thomas Litwiler, a GE executive in Pittsfield, Massachusetts. "The strikers are living reasonably well on welfare, and nobody knows what to do or what it really means any more." By the end of the victorious 122-day action, GE strikers had collected an estimated $25 million in welfare. To their employers, this was a disaster.

Welfare-subsidized class war, troubling enough in itself for the honchos at GE, also pointed to larger problems. Working-class power was being institutionalized within the state, and the state in turn was being transformed. Collectivism, the hoary bugbear of the right, was nigh.

Consider the fact that between 1964 and 1979, the federal government enacted sixty-two health-and-safety laws meant to protect workers and consumers, and thirty-two other laws to protect the environment and to regulate energy use. Many of these interventions, it should be noted, were endorsed by Richard Nixon, who presided over the creation of the Environmental Protection Agency, the Occupational Safety and Health Administration, the Consumer Safety Administration, and the Mine Enforcement and Safety Administration. The Brookings Institution estimated that by 1983, pollution controls alone had cost American business between $13 billion and $38 billion, and that measures to protect health and human safety cost between $7 billion and $17 billion.

Showdown 1970: Labor's Tet Offensive

Labor's victory over General Electric presaged turbulent times. According to government statistics, contracts covering some five million workers would come up for negotiation in 1970, and unions were preparing to make significant wage demands. Employers braced for combat, and by the end of the year, more than sixty-six million days of labor time would be lost to job actions, the highest toll due to strikes since the great postwar labor offensive of 1946.

As the storms of 1970 approached, the National Association of Manufacturers and the U.S. Chamber of Commerce entreated Nixon to help impose labor discipline. But before long, the federal government faced a labor-relations shitstorm of its own: On March 18, more than a thousand angry letter carriers in New York City dropped their bags and grabbed placards. Twenty-five thousand drivers and clerks honored the pickets, and postal operations in New York City ground to a halt within hours.

The action was illegal. Just for walking out, each striker faced a possible felony charge carrying a minimum prison sentence of a year and a day, along with a $1,000 fine. A federal court immediately ordered postal employees to return to work, while James Rademacher, head of the national postal union, issued bellicose back-to-work orders of his own.

It didn't matter. Within two days, the New York wildcat strike had spread across the country. Along with banners, the strikers now carried effigies of "Rat-macher." In all, more than 200,000 of the nation's 740,000 postal workers were out in more than two hundred towns and cities. Hundreds of thousands of drivers and clerks halted before even the flimsiest of the letter carriers' picket lines. By March 21, the U.S. mails had completely stalled. "We're very close to paralysis," a postal official complained. "What is still functioning is hardly worthy of calling a postal system."

As local after local joined the strike, panic set in among opinionmakers and business leaders, and the press predicted a national "disaster." Nixon went on TV to plead with the nation that nothing less was at stake than "the survival of a government based upon law." To restore order and move the mails, he called out the armed forces. But even these scabs in olive drab displayed a voguish lack of discipline: Of the twenty-six thousand National Guard, Army, and Air Force reservists ordered to report for duty, only sixteen thousand showed up—and, according to *Newsweek*, many of those "got mixed reviews as postal workers," preferring to grab empty mailbags and "disappear for the day." Others fraternized openly with the strikers.

The worst-case scenario was unfolding. In a perceptive assessment of the situation, *Time* magazine warned that "the government's authority was placed in question and the well-being of business, institutions, and individuals in jeopardy." The price of order, it seemed, would be surrender to wildcat postmen who were demanding amnesty and a 40 percent pay raise.

After a week without mail, negotiations had begun and the strikers returned to work, but they remained defiant. "It's got to be good and it's got to be quick," one letter carrier said of the talks in Washington, D.C. "Otherwise, we'll stay out till we get the money." In material terms, the postal strike was a modest success: All government workers won an immediate 6 percent pay raise, and postal workers carried off an additional 8 percent. Politically, though, the impact of the strike was enormous, increasing the momentum that resulted from the ass-whipping administered to GE months earlier. "We've learned from the postal workers that if practically everybody strikes, then nobody is going to get hurt," one government worker told the *Washington Star*. "They can't fire everyone."

Almost immediately, state and municipal workers started striking for better wages and more control on the job. Teachers, garbagemen, gravediggers, hospital workers, cops, and city office workers walked off their jobs in huge illegal strikes. Even the skies grew calm: Air-traffic controllers, recently organized into the two-year-old Professional Air Traffic Controllers Organization (PATCO), called a rolling sick-out and threatened an illegal strike. Just as the postal strike was winding down, PATCO's chief, attorney F. Lee Bailey, announced that his union's issue was safety, and that unless their demands were met, the controllers would "shut down the air traffic system." PATCO won its pay increase and other concessions without having to go that far.

Due to strikes in the construction trades, many cities suffered industry-wide work halts for weeks at a time. In Kansas City, commercial construction projects were halted for more than three months. "Settlements are coming in . . . higher than last year, which was an extraordinary year," commented a perturbed Secretary of Labor George Shultz. "This is a formula for disaster."

In what would become a trademark phrase of the era, William W. Winpisinger, Machinists president and chief negotiator for the angry railroad unions, described his rank and file as "running right on the edge of being out of control." Far from making threats, he was pleading with employers to help him maintain power. It was a common theme. Everywhere one looked, workers were spoiling for a fight. By the early Seventies labor leaders had to learn to fight on two fronts: After squeezing concessions from employers, it was not uncommon for even generous contracts to be rejected by the pugnacious rank and file. By 1971, it was estimated that 15 percent of all contracts were being rejected, up from around 8 percent in 1964. At the UAW, Reuther even took to staging small strikes just to placate his action-hungry and increasingly youthful rank and file.

But one contract rejected by angry Teamsters trumped all others. The trouble began on April Fools' Day 1970, after what was described as "the most orderly" series of contract negotiations in Teamsters history. The independent union's new president, Frank Fitzsimmons, had won his truckers a $1.10-per-hour wage increase, but the rank and file wanted sick pay and wouldn't take the contract. Immediately, drivers walked in sixteen cities, including many key hubs. In the Midwest, the strategic chokepoint of the strike, renegade locals set up mobile pickets and blockades. Trucks moving eastward found most key crossing points on the Mississippi River occupied by huge squads of wildcat Teamsters. Only trucks carrying food, medicine, and beer were allowed to move. Trucks that tried to smuggle other products underneath loads of soup or behind racks of beef wound up with smashed windshields, slashed tires, and sabotaged engines. As freight movement ground to a halt across the country, layoffs in other industries began to mount. Within a week, an estimated half-million workers were directly or indirectly idled by the Teamsters' wildcat. Greyhound buses, the airlines, and inland river barges all increased their freight volume exponentially, but it did little to fill the breach. As stranded merchandise piled up in poorly guarded heaps, manufacturers and wholesalers reported expensive waves of theft.

Fitzsimmons, the employers, and the courts closed rank against the outlaw strikers. In state after state, injunctions rained down from hostile courts; employers swore no compromise; and union leaders did all they could to force the drivers back on the road. The governor of Ohio called out the 145th Infantry—the same National Guard unit that had just gunned down students at Kent State and put down several urban riots—to escort small convoys of scab-driven trucks. None of it worked. After twelve weeks, trucking firms in Chicago capitulated to the wildcats' demands. With that, the employer unity crumbled, and the Teamsters won their right to sick pay.

Meanwhile, in coal country, wildcat strikes were becoming epidemic. As *Fortune* magazine put it, management faced "a work force that is no longer under union discipline." Among the miners' grievances were the industry's abysmal health-and-safety standards. In 1969, miners in West Virginia had begun what was called the Black Lung Wildcat. Within days, nearly all of the state's forty-four-thousand miners had dropped their tools. After twenty-three days in which no coal came up from the shafts, the West Virginia legislature passed a law compensating three thousand victims of coal-dust pneumoconiosis. But it wasn't enough. For the next two years, wildcat strikes continued in the mines. Nineteen thousand Pennsylvania miners walked in 1970, protesting lack of enforcement of new safety rules; fifteen thousand miners staged another wildcat in West Virginia to demand hospital benefits for disabled miners and their widows. Under union bylaws, the rank and file had long been denied the right to vote on their own contracts. By 1972, after years of internecine strife and bloodshed, insurgent miners had overthrown union despot Tony Boyle and democratized the United Mine Workers. They also won significant wage increases from the mine owners.

The Scales of Class Power, Tipped

There are many ways to measure working-class power. One is what economist Juliet Schor calls "the cost of job loss"—that is, the amount of income, measured in terms of potentially missed wages, that the average worker loses between jobs. When the cost of job loss is high (e.g., when unemployment benefits are reduced, or when welfare benefits are slashed or restricted), workers will be less likely to risk being fired for militant labor activity—so their power is reduced. Another indicator is the ratio of quits to layoffs and quits to job openings. When more employees quit than are laid off or fired, one can conclude that employers have lost a degree of control over the workforce. That is exactly what happened during the late Sixties and early Seventies: The ratio of quits to layoffs reached two to one, almost twice what it was in the late Fifties. The share of the workforce involved in some strike activity between 1967 and 1973 reached 40 percent—even though in the same period the unemployment rate crept up from 4 to 8 percent.

What terrified businessmen in the early Seventies was not just that the price of labor was going up, but that it was going up regardless of unemployment rates. As the American economy cooled and slid into recession in 1973, the unemployment rate pitched upward, yet wages and prices did not fall in response. This combination of stagnant growth and rising inflation became known as "stagflation."

The inverse relationship between wage levels and unemployment is known among economists as the "Phillips Curve." For the first time in American history the two components of this economic "law" were out of whack. This led in part to a precipitous decline in the general rate of profit. In *The Great U-Turn*, Bennett Harrison and Barry Bluestone explain: "From a peak of nearly 10 percent in 1965, the average net after-tax profit rate of domestic non-financial corporations plunged to less than 6 percent during the second half of the Seventies—a decline of more than a third." The nadir was 1974, when the general rate of profit reached a low of around 4.5 percent. Throughout the rest of the Seventies, inflation and unemployment persisted, labor unrest continued, and profits stagnated. Workers were claiming an unprecedented share of the wealth they produced. It was an unmitigated disaster for those who owned, and they would soon take terrible revenge.

The counterattack began in 1979, when President Jimmy Carter appointed Paul Volcker as chairman of the Federal Reserve Board. Now it was capital's turn to "shut it down." Within months of taking office Volcker dramatically boosted interest rates—they hit 16.4 percent in 1981—thus cutting borrowing and buying power and chilling economic activity in general. As a direct result, the United States plunged into its most severe recession since the Thirties. The plan was simple: Punish uppity American workers with a "cold-bath" recession and they would learn to work harder for less. "The standard of living of the average American has to decline," Volcker told the *New York Times* in 1979. "I don't think you can escape that."

The war on labor—along with Ronald Reagan's proposals to cut taxes for the rich, to gut welfare, and to deregulate health, safety, and environmental standards—was intended to boost corporate profits back to comfortable levels. But getting to yes took time. Not until 1982, when Continental Illinois Bank began to collapse under the weight of its bad loans, did Volcker relent and open the Fed's spigots. By then the deep recession had worked its magic: Ten million people were unemployed, and the press was running stories on the "new poor." Wage reductions became the norm in contract negotiations. Weekly take-home pay fell more than 8 percent between 1979 and 1982 and failed to recover for the next five years. But the most amazing measure of the recession's political success was this simple fact: Before the 1980–82 recession, wage freezes and pay cuts in unionized industries had been almost nonexistent. In 1980 not a single union contract negotiation had ended in a pay freeze or cut. By 1982, however, 44 percent of new contracts conceded wage freezes or outright cuts. Wages had been rising more or less consistently since the end of World War II, but now the tide had turned.

But macroeconomic medicine went only so far. Reagan began stacking the National Labor Relations Board, the federal body that arbitrates labor disputes, with antiunion activists. The courts, too, were salted with union-hating judges. To put labor firmly back in its place, the Reagan administration chose a direct confrontation. When PATCO struck in 1981, Reagan instantly fired all eleven thousand striking controllers, even though they had endorsed him during his election campaign. This massacre sent a clear signal: The war was on and the government would back business to the hilt.

The Reagan administration also sanctioned the use of contingent labor; it even set an example in 1985 by allowing the government to hire temp workers at below union wages. Then in 1986 the Reagan administration legalized home work, a practice many trade unions argued would lead to exploitation and child labor and would undermine established minimum levels of health and safety. And that is exactly what happened. According to Harley Shaiken, the doyen of labor studies, the U.S. Labor Department reported twenty thousand child-labor-law violations in 1988, up from thirteen thousand in 1986. There was a 500 percent increase in the number of New York City sweatshops employing children. The number of minors illegally employed in sweatshops increased 128 percent nationwide in the second half of the Eighties.

So it is today. It is easy for us mortals to forget this aspect of the Sixties' legacy, but others never will. For capital those years brought a glimpse, however abstract, of its own mortality. It was the nightmare that has spurred the right-wing backlash ever since, as the fear of falling rides the collective psyche of the business class like some tenacious and leering incubus. To keep the horror at bay, the leaders of the rich deploy their policy amulets and political mojos: ruthless austerity for those who toil; constant racist demagoguery; paranoid and irrelevant moralizing; and always more cops, more laws, more prison, and more discipline for working people.

—BAFFLER 13, 1999

Vox Populoid

28
Birchismo

Dan Kelly

> We'll teach you how to spot 'em
> In the cities or the sticks,
> For even Jasper Junction is just full of Bolsheviks
> The CIA's subversive, and so's the FCC
> There's no one left but we and thee
> And we're not sure of thee.
>
> —*"The John Birch Society," by The Chad Mitchell Trio*

Somewhere in the green blankness of southern Michigan, just off Highway 94, stands a lonely little sign declaring, "Get US Out of the UN!" If you're paying attention to the road you'll miss it, but trust me, it's there. I first noticed the sign on the way from Grand Haven to Chicago a few summers ago, and as a rubbernecking spectator of fringe political thought, I assumed it was the work of a local militia or perhaps even a cell of cantankerous Constitutionalists, afeared the New World Order was encroaching on the sovereignty of New Buffalo, Michigan. Filing it away in my memory jar, I planned to uncover the sign's mysterious origins at another time.

Two years passed, and while visiting a gun show in Grayslake, Illinois, my question was answered. There as much to collect kook literature as to peruse Glocks and SKS rifles, I came across a gentleman in red flannel selling books, videos, and pamphlets, each pushing various fringe-dweller hot buttons. Topics ran from the dreaded New World Order to Her Satanic Majesty President Hillary to, hello, the United Nations, which we had to get US out of, pronto. I was mildly surprised to discover the source of this particular enthusiasm, the same one I had noticed in Michigan's black-stripe wilderness: the John Birch Society. I had discovered a dinosaur bone in my own backyard—the bone, though, was still connected to a reasonably lively dinosaur.

If your first reaction to the phrase "The John Birch Society" is a bewildered "Whoozat?" it's a telling sign of your youth. The John Birch Society was, is, and ever shall be the world's most stringently anticommunist organization, dedicated to finding, exposing, and squashing out every aspect of the global communist conspiracy. The group was founded in 1958 by retired candymaker Robert H. W. Welch, who, rather than playing checkers or wandering the beach with a metal detector, chose to spend his golden years assembling a cabal of industrialists and declaring holy war on Marxism. Welch had grand plans for his little society. Star-chamber visions filling his head, Welch imagined a titanic secret organization that would checkmate the even more secretive communists' every move.

The John Birch Society's heyday came during the early Sixties. While many recall that decade as an age of butt-naked radicalism with a Jefferson Airplane soundtrack, the Sixties were also the salad days of the far right. Culture-shocked average folk desperately sought a way out of the oncoming sybaritic morass, and Welch was only too happy to give directions: Take an extreme right and drive on forever.

As for John Birch, we'll never know what he would have thought of his eponymous society. Unlike Horst Wessel or Nathan Hale, he never joined the club that would have him as a martyr. A young Bible-banging missionary from backwoods Georgia, Birch relocated to China in the Forties to evangelize the heathen Chinee. When the United States entered World War II, Birch rearranged his career plans, enlisted in the Army, and quickly rose to the rank of captain. After several years of pushing Jesus, performing OSS intelligence work, and earning a chestful of medals, the twenty-seven-year-old Birch was nabbed by the Red Chinese and executed a scant nine days after the end of the war. In all probability, Cap'n Birch might have slipped between history's cracks had Welch not learned of his plight in the files of the Senate Internal Security Subcommittee.

According to contemporary accounts, John Birch was a decent enough fellow, albeit one whose sphincter never knew the meaning of the words "at ease." But in Robert H. W. Welch's approximation, Birch was much more. To hear Welch tell it, Birch was an amalgam of Jimmy Stewart and John Wayne, with a jigger of James Bond to boot. As a martyr he was ideal—a clean-cut, God-fearing, good-looking kid cut down in his prime by pinko scum. Indeed, for Welch he was nothing less than the first casualty of the nascent Cold War.

As for Welch, he was born to do battle on the home front. As Birch literature proudly recounts, the candyman was something of a child prodigy. Born in 1899 and home-schooled, he entered the University of North Carolina at the age of twelve. In 1917 he moved on to the U.S. Naval Academy, and the following year to Harvard Law School where, according to society literature, "his stubborn mind vexed his liberal professors." Their vexations soon ceased, though, as Welch dropped out in 1920—strangely, at the top of his class. Welch then entered the family business, applying his "stubborn mind" to vice-presidential duties at the Welch Candy Company and inventing Sugar Babies along the way. (Welch was outdone, however, by his brother James, who was both company president and creator of the more popular Junior Mints.) Not coincidentally, JBS charter members were men very like Welch—cronies from his big-business days, retired from years of overseeing production and managing underlings, now eager to apply their knowledge to this great land of ours.

Welch was, naturally, an avid reader of Spengler's *Decline of the West*, from which he deduced the idea that the Old World was sliding into the dotage of collectivism, and if America wanted to avoid the same fate, it had to reactivate George Washington's isolationist policies. The literata who gave the Birch Society its paranoiac frisson, however, was Nesta Webster, a high-born British lady who wrote several standbys of the conspiracy theorist's library. Webster spent her life exposing the intricate web betwixt the Bavarian Illuminati, Jews, Communists, and all those in between in such tomes as *Secret Societies and Subversive Movements* and *The World Revolution*. Inspired by Mme. Webster, Welch became convinced that the Illuminati—supposedly founded in 1776 to bring "illuminated" individuals together to solve all the world's woes—survived to the present day as ghosts in the global machine, pulling the levers and causing the historical events we of the hoi polloi assume to be accidental. Welch's stroke of genius was to extrapolate that the Illuminati's ultimate goal was to create a one-world socialist government. Communism was their most devastating weapon, its enervating influence sucking the life from a nation and converting its population into a huddled mass of hollow men.

Add to all this conjecture the all-too-real cabals of high-ranking government officials and plutocrats who *do* meet periodically to tug at the world's puppet strings, and who were ecstatically celebrated in historian Carroll Quigley's 1966 book, *Tragedy and Hope*. The Illuminati may have been a projection of Welch's imagination, but the Council on Foreign Relations, founded in 1920, David Rockefeller's Trilateral Commission, founded in the early Seventies, and the ultra-spooky Bilderberg Group are all very real and have corporate presidents, media kings, and financial czars at their helms. Quigley thought all this was just jake, as the industrialists, world leaders, et cetera, were no doubt coming together for the good of humankind.

Welch saw things differently. Such stuff was not only dangerous, it was an outright offense to American sovereignty, the Constitution, apple pie, proper flag-folding technique, and all else Welch held dear. Outrageous though it seemed, the Birch Society's obsession with conspiracy ran deep in the American grain, arising directly from the widespread nineteenth-century belief that secret societies were antithetical to democracy. Welch saw the shadow government's imprint everywhere, and in keeping with his own era's notions of the Republic's enemies, he simply recast communists as the villains, rather than the traditional Masons, Jesuits, or Jews. His small-government politics were equally unremarkable. The society's motto could easily have been the credo of some state Republican Party: "Less government, more responsibility, and—with God's help—a better world."

Despite their admirably homegrown paranoia, the Birchers were nevertheless considered a trifle dotty. Every reformer has his critics, but Robert Welch kept providing his with devastating ammunition. Welch's first book, *May God Forgive Us* (1952), started the wrecking ball swinging with its revelation that rather than fighting Communism, as they were supposed to do, our government had actually been aiding and abetting the Red Menace. Joe McCarthy, predictably canonized by the Birchers, had been right all along. The "loss" of half of Europe and all of China was the work of high-level pinkos in the U.S. government—with a special commendation awarded to Truman administration secretary of state/evil genius Dean Acheson.

What really tattooed Welch and the society with oddball status forevermore, though, was his declaration that President Dwight D. Eisenhower was a card-carrying Leninist. In the early years of his crusade Welch penned a long letter to selected friends outlining Eisenhower's alleged side-job as a puppet of his Soviet masters. Welch closely examined Ike's military career, describing his every move as yet another tactic to gain precious postwar ground for the occupying Reds. In 1963 the letter became a book, *The Politician*, and it established Welch's reputation in the public's mind as a cast-iron kook.

Today the thought of dubbing Ike a pinko seems merely strange, but back then it had an air of treason about it. While America was not exactly ready to roll in the hay with the Soviets, people were equally reluctant to wallow once again in the McCarthyist mud. Welch had no such scruples. In *The Politician*, FDR, Truman, both Dulles brothers, and favorite Birch Society punching bag Chief Justice Earl Warren were all said to be witting agents of The Conspiracy, ready to roger Lady Liberty at the snap of Moscow's fingers.

And the list rolled on. Birch targets included the Social Security system, the Federal Reserve, income tax, welfare, foreign aid of any sort, urban renewal, the American Medical Association, compulsory integration, the civil rights movement, and the brain-bending practice of water fluoridation (cf. General Jack D. Ripper in *Dr. Strangelove*). Even defense spending was in doubt since Birchers believed that the real communist threat arose from within. If that wasn't terrifying enough, almost all America's universities, corporations, foundations, more than seven thousand of its clergymen, and a guesstimated 60 percent-and-rising segment of the mass media were rife with hardcore communists, fellow travelers, and "Comsymps" (a word coined by Welch for those he could not directly accuse of being communists). Our once-great nation now glowed pinker than Pepto-Bismol. Welch admonished his troops in no uncertain terms: "Get to work, or learn to talk Russian."

Many contemporary conservatives, such as McCarthy revisionist Richard Gid Powers, try to pass off the Birch Society as something of a liberal invention, a particularly lunatic bit of fringe on which the media focused in order to discredit the worthy cause of anticommunism. But the Birchers were far more than that. For all its Chicken Little paranoia, the JBS popularized the strategy that the right would employ so ably for the next three decades: unremitting war on the snobbish, effete intellectual elite—a gang the neoconservatives soon learned to call by their correct name, "the new class," rather than the more inflammatory "communists."

Not surprisingly, before Welch turned on his weird-idea faucet, the right was happy to welcome the JBS on board. The Birch Society not only brought together the usual GOP constituents—"wealthy businessmen, retired military officers, and little old ladies in tennis shoes," in the words of one contemporary observer—but also attracted a fair number of young people, who appear in photos of Bircher meetings dressed in sensible suits and flower-print dresses.

What was most frightening/inspiring about the Birch Society was that, despite its flaky reputation, it worked. It was an ideological juggernaut, structured like a corporation and filled with dues-paying members who were that rarity in Sixties American politics: right-wing activists. One contributor to the 1964 anthology *The Radical Right* estimated that, at its peak, the JBS had more than four thousand chapters and a hundred thousand dues-paying members. (Exact figures are unattainable, as JBS membership lists have always been classified.)

Mass-mediated memories of the Sixties always give prominence to the SDS, the Yippies, and other left-wing organizers and protesters, but the Birchers were out there too, banging on doors, organizing protests, and writing to their congressmen. And that wasn't all they did. As it turned out, the Birchers weren't playing by Dale Carnegie's rules.

Welch once said, "It is one of our sorrows that, in fighting the evil forces which now threaten our civilization, for us to be too civilized is unquestionably to be defeated." The answer, then, when fighting Communism, was to use Communism's tactics. Like an underground army of Hugh Beaumonts, the Birchers collectively heard and obeyed. Through his monthly *Bulletins*, Welch taught his local chapters the finer points of fifth-column activity. In order to better oversee the proper dispensation of education to

America's youth, members were advised to seize control of their local PTA. Members were also to infiltrate groups suspected of having socialist leanings and to attend and disrupt "pro-communist" gatherings—which could mean anything from heckling a professor at a nearby university to protesting a Russian art exhibit. Also, as the JBS's popularity began to wane, the head Bircher set up front groups and ad hoc committees to lure those who wouldn't be caught dead at a Birch Society cell meeting. Such fronts included the well-known Committee to Impeach Earl Warren, the innocuous-sounding Freedom Club, the Realtors for American Freedom, and the double-dutch mouthfuls of the Committee Against Educating Traitors at Government Expense and the Committee to Warn of the Arrival of Communist Merchandise on the Local Business Scene. It was often possible for an everyday citizen to attend a Birch meeting without realizing it.

Birchers also took it upon themselves to flood newspapers, radio and TV stations, and local, state, and national government offices with barrages of letters and phone calls, whenever one or the other dared to act in opposition to Birch philosophy. Other psychological blitzkriegs brought the war home to the Birchers' perceived enemies. Repeated anonymous late-night phone calls; false fire alarms; embarrassing and annoying classified ads featuring the mark's home address—these and other "I didn't order these pizzas"–level pranks filled the Birchers' black bags.

Despite all this fiercely patriotic activity, the JBS's days were numbered. Whether it was by an ingenious Masonic plot, or simply enough decent folks growing tired of the Birchers' bullshit, the inevitable karmic backlash occurred.

Owing to their unequivocal views and quasifascist structure, the Birchers were often, at times lazily, lumped in with the likes of the Klan, the neo-Nazis, and the more reactionary militias. No surprises there: As a superpatriotic organization, the JBS was a freak magnet. As fast as Welch and a handful of conscientious chapter leaders kicked out the bigots filling their ranks, more joined up—

promoting their poison behind Welch's back, and often right under his nose. The bigot label left its mark. The JBS became viewed as a gateway drug to the harder stuff.

Charges of anti-Semitism kept cropping up. Welch himself wasn't an anti-Semite—even the Anti-Defamation League grudgingly conceded that—and the JBS, while not a model of strength through diversity, was established to discriminate against commies and commies alone. In the lower ranks, on the other hand, those of anti-Semitic inclination cut society literature with racist classics such as William Guy Carr's *Pawns in the Game* and American Nazi Party ephemera. The JBS ideology of "US versus the Insiders" was equally worrisome. Use of such Bircher buzzwords as "Illuminati," "Insiders," and "Internationalists" as euphemisms for "Jews," "Jews," and "Jews," respectively, was not unheard-of. Welch may not have been an anti-Semite, but his apparent naivete about the sources of his theories was hard to swallow. In his book *Birchism Was My Business*, Gerald Schomp, a former chapter leader, recounted that Welch was one day seized by the bright idea of rounding up as many right-wing Jews as possible (no easy trick, according to Schomp) and creating yet another front group: the Jewish Society of Americanists.

The Birchers' pro-cop tack—"Support Your Local Police" is undoubtedly their best-known slogan—also spooked many non-cop Americans. Cops gravitated to Birchism like hippies to hash, enticed by the JBS's pooh-poohing of civilian review boards, whose presence would have had a chilling effect on the thin blue line's God-given right to crack skulls. JBS cells sprang up in police departments from coast to coast. Regional manager Thomas J. Davis proudly trumpeted the presence of one hundred Birchers on the NYPD payroll in 1964. In Santa Ana, California, a cell of twenty or thirty Birchers in blue waged a campaign to oust their chief and replace him with one of their own.

. . .

These days, the lot of the professional paranoid grows ever more difficult. The world has lost both Robert Welch (he died in 1985) and the Soviet Union. New times call for new ideas, especially about who "THEY" are, and how best "THEY" can be combated.

Fortunately, Welch discovered a new world of revelations well in time for the end of the Cold War. It dawned on him that he had it backward all along: It was the United Nations that ran the Soviet Union, not vice versa. Forget learning Russian; it's Esperanto that we'll have to study, unless we are willing to disrupt UN preparations to overrun our streets, seize our homes, violate our womenfolk, and use the Constitution as toilet paper. This new apocalypse even has a name, found beneath that freakish "pyramidclops" on the back of every dollar bill: "Novus Ordo Seclorum," the New World Order invoked by Presidents Nixon and Bush.

To give the devil his due, the modern JBS still advocates education over insurrection, even in this age of militias and ATF showdowns. Furthermore, Birchers are not flying-saucer, cattle-mutilation, or hollow-earth theorists—they deal only in the implausible, not the improbable. Surprisingly, they even oppose organized militias, believing that the Second Amendment's reference to a "well-regulated militia" permits firearm ownership but does not give free rein to form private armies.

Allowing cooler heads to prevail hasn't necessarily swelled the JBS's ranks. In comparison with what it once was, the JBS undoubtedly suffers these days from a severe dearth of manpower. Of the alleged hundred thousand members of the Sixties, only eighty thousand or fewer remained in the Seventies, leading to an even more dramatic depopulation during the Reagan years, according to some sources. An e-mail request to the society for a current head count was met with claims of confidentiality—rarely a sign of a boisterously healthy organization.

Ah, but while Birch numbers are small, the hardest of cores remains. Like the red-flanneled gentleman at the gun show, today's Birchers are a passionate lot, driven to expose what their literature now describes as a "satanic Conspiracy." More than six hundred thousand copies of the "Conspiracy" issue of the JBS house organ, *The New American*, were hawked by loyal Birchers in 1997—both independently and through the society's American Opinion bookstores. Passion is definitely a prerequisite for JBS membership. Even with the not-smallish membership fee of $48 a year (lifetime memberships have soared from the $1,000 bargain rate of the early Sixties to $2,000 today), one is entitled to little more than a subscription to the JBS bulletin, regular chapter meetings, and a clean conscience, I suppose.

Thirty-nine dollars arranges for delivery of the thin, four-color *New American*, which emanates from Appleton, Wisconsin, a town significant only as the hometown and current receptacle of Saint Joe McCarthy. To read the magazine is to realize how almost mainstream the Birchers have become—due more to the nation's successive listings to the right since 1968, of course (*The New American*'s Website carries a ringing endorsement from Pat Buchanan), than any behavior modification on the JBS's part.

The New American dedicates itself to providing those "facts and perspectives omitted from other national media," as they put it, including, in recent issues, a detailed nine-thousand-word story on the august nobility of Pinochet and the infamy of that former despot's present persecution by "the global elite"; a complaint about "gynecological probing" in the public schools; reach-for-your-revolver headlines such as "Christian Slaves Freed, UN Objects," and "UN Wants to Tax E-mail"; an essay comparing and contrasting the nefarious Bill Clinton with then-fugitive hippie murderer Ira Einhorn; and, of course, the latest dispatches from the ongoing war over water fluoridation.

Historically, only a few openly acknowledged Birchers have been able to win high public office. Most Birchers with any real political experience joined after leaving office, as in the case of one-term congressman Howard Buffett, father of billionaire investor Warren Buffett. Similarly, those politicians who, unmindful of the effects of political poison, proudly declared their JBS membership—as did California Republican Representatives John H. Rousselot and Edgar Hiestand in 1962—often found themselves promptly ousted by the voters. They didn't have far to fall. Most former Bircher politicos easily "transitioned" to positions within the JBS. The number of closet Birchers who have held legislative power, on the other hand, probably will never be known. In 1961, conservative paladin Barry Goldwater stated that a search for Birchers through the hallowed halls of the Capitol Building "would turn up a lot of embarrassed people." The last noteworthy and open member of the JBS to hold national elected office—the society's chairman, no less—was Representative Larry McDonald of Georgia, back in the early Eighties. McDonald also made the unfortunate decision to board KAL 007, the passenger plane shot down by the Soviets in 1983, undoubtedly sending the Birchers into paroxysms of shivering paranoia.

With the recent flowering of the right, though, one hardly has to be a JBS member to support the society's once-kooky beliefs. Representative Ron Paul, a former Libertarian candidate for president and a major proponent of taxpayers' rights (namely, the right to pay few or none), has proposed measures to withdraw U.S. membership and funding from the United Nations. A particular sweetheart of the Birch fraternity is the notorious Representative Helen Chenoweth of Idaho, who finds time in her busy schedule to write for *The New American*. "Thank goodness for those, such as the John Birch Society," gushes Congressman Chenoweth (as she insists on being addressed), "who are unashamed to advocate love of country, defense of nation, and an abiding commitment to our Constitution."

As for potential future Birchers, today's JBS has had better luck getting in touch with the kids than Bob Welch ever did. One pet project is Robert Welch University, which, the good Lord willing, will soon become a fully functioning, four-year liberal arts college, empowered to issue degrees in God-fearing 100 percent Americanism. One particularly fun aspect of the JBS is the summer camp held under the Bob Welch U. banner. While the program includes the typical activities of volleyball, canoeing, hiking, and singings of "Kumbaya," campers can also take classes designed to remediate the bum education they pick up at Illuminati-run public and private schools: "Our Godly Heritage," "What Is Humanism?" "Global Tyranny—The UN," "The Life of John Birch," and, as an alternative to making wallets and weaving lanyards, "Salesmanship." Other activities include the "Night Patrol," wherein camp counselors brandishing swords and funny hats mount raids on the campers' cabins at random hours, teaching them the hard-learned value of hating secret police. Parents can also be assured that no funny business takes place between campers of opposite, or even the same, sexes. Counselors oversee the campers' activities twenty-four hours a day. What was that about oppressive governmental control?

TODAY'S RESPECTABLE CONSERVATIVES, looking down from their amply funded think-tank posts, find it convenient to cry boo to the John Birch Society, dismissing it as a political curiosity for which they claim neither affinity nor responsibility. Yet, for the past thirty years, these same right-thinkers have fueled their successful reconquest of government with a blaring populism that bears a red-haired milkman's resemblance to the wacky faiths of the JBS. Silent, righteous majorities rising against a hated liberal elite; defiantly normal Americans versus a sneaking, manipulative "new class" of journalists, professors, bureaucrats, and social workers. However contemporary conservative thinkers might protest, this is a strategy for which they owe the John Birch Society a debt of gratitude. Welch and company converted the McCarthyite witch-hunt into something more universal: a culture war between God's patriots and an international, octopod cabal of quivering Great Society Clintonistas.

While it is true that the contemporary right takes great pains to keep talk of The Conspiracy far from its public presentations, and while it is also true that the Birchers hold no truck with the likes of Newt Gingrich or the Bushes (globalists all), their weird theorizing was an important bridge between the Joe McCarthy sideshow and the more successful right-wing populism of Irving Kristol and David Horowitz.

Most crucially, the Birch Society was among the first to crystallize and capitalize on that most compelling of right-wing faiths: the feeling, shared by so many of the nation's privileged and powerful, that they are, in fact, the persecuted ones, the ones whose towers are forever in danger of being toppled. Welch's true accomplishment was calling together into a protest movement a generation of strutting, financially solvent, middle-aged Americans, fresh from bombing the hell out of Dresden and Hiroshima and still intoxicated with their new role as the first superpower; a generation for whom the landmark events of the Sixties were an unpleasant series of pimp-slaps. Welch did more than he could ever know to prove his hero Spengler's theories, beckoning his followers into a uniquely American brand of collectivism.

—BAFFLER 13, 1999

29

Paradise Shot to Hell

The Westbrook Pegler Story

JEFF SHARLET

WHAT KIND OF TIMES do we live in when syndicated radio host G. Gordon Liddy can "neutrally" remind listeners to shoot for the head when targeting federal agents? Times pretty similar to the heyday of Westbrook Pegler, the It Boy of attack journalism, now a tragic and largely forgotten figure. "The angry man of the press," as he was known in his mid-twentieth-century prime, Pegler was one of the most widely read newspaper columnists in the country. From the Great Depression through the Cold War he tilted at suspects familiar to Rush Limbaugh's fans: foreign subversives, swindling politicians, the First Lady, corrupt union bosses, the elite, the effete, and, of course, homosexuals. For guys like Pegler and Liddy, These Days are always understood to be After the Fall: This used to be a damn good country until "they" made a hash of it.

Pegler wielded his well-sharpened prose like a knife in a street fight. He was the kind of writer who could cheer on a lynch mob (as he actually did in 1936; he sincerely believed the victims had it coming) or exhort solid citizens to join strikebreakers "in the praiseworthy pastime of batting the brains out of pickets." In his lighter moods, Pegler refined his homophobic invective on minor targets such as the literary critic Clifton Fadiman—"the bull butterfly of the literary teas"—and then, more encouraged by the wounds such words inflicted than any particular dislike for homosexuality, he turned his antigay guns on bigger game, "outing" Woodrow Wilson and Frank Sinatra. (When Sinatra sought out Pegler to give him a beating, the singer brought Orson Welles as a witness. Pegler made a getaway, but he retaliated in print by praising Welles as a "dear, roguish boy [whose] whole nature seems to chitter and cheep in the language of the elves.")

Light moods were uncharacteristic of Pegler, though; more often he aimed to maim, even to kill. He channeled hatred so pure that more than one colleague blamed the death of Heywood Broun, his liberal contemporary and ex-friend, on a column in which Pegler labeled Broun a liar. And Broun got off easy. In 1965 Pegler wished of Robert Kennedy that "some white patriot of the Southern tier will spatter his spoonful of brains in public premises before the snow flies." By the time he called the hit on RFK, Pegler had declined into unhinged dotage, bitter and banished from respectable journalism by his own cussedness, and quickly alienating even his friends on the far right with his unabashed anti-Semitism.

So what would prompt an old lefty like Murray Kempton to write, upon Pegler's departure from the mainstream press in 1962, that "he goes with honor as he has lived with honor," and that "he was true to us at the end, truer than we are to ourselves"?

Perhaps Kempton was feeling nostalgic for what was even then a dying breed of journalist: the tradesman, the uneducated skeptic, the worker whose product was prose. In his prime Pegler was that and more: He understood his job as a kind of combat, and he recognized his enemies as power and authority. Unlike Limbaugh, a self-styled entertainer who wouldn't dream of biting the hand that feeds him, Pegler not only bayed at the amorphous, alien forces of moral disorder but often enough turned on his masters themselves. That's why Pegler is worth recalling even now—not for the substance of his anger, but for its quality, the rage that drove him to swing again and again at anyone he thought had it in for the common man.

Pegler's common man was the beleaguered man in the middle, getting it from both sides. His columns plied a deluded nostalgia for a golden age of small-*r* republicanism he believed had passed in America, a time when every man made his own way, when "government" meant the military, and pampered rich men were a European disgrace. So Pegler bellowed to throw out the crooked union bosses, and the unions too; throw out the politicians and the tax men and the luxuries their collections paid for; throw out the immigrants; throw out the New Deal and bring back the Old. After all that, the golden age would be ours again. In 1938 Pegler elaborated this notion on the front page of the *New York World-Telegram*, where his column occupied the space usually reserved for breaking news stories. In a rant titled, "Those Were the Days" (curiously presaging the theme song of Norman Lear's *All in the Family*), Pegler demanded: "Next time Mr. Roosevelt or Honest Hal Ickes, the House Dick of the New Deal . . . or any of those honorary proletarians who swing towels in that corner of the ring sound off in disrespect of the Old Deal I would appreciate it if somebody would refresh my memory on just what was wrong with it." In Pegler's world, the years before the Crash had been good not just for the rich, but for regular folks too:

> Wasn't that the time when they were sticking up tall buildings in all the big towns? And building swell new suburbs and kicking out new cars by the millions, including some which retailed for around $6,000 and, what's more, selling them? Wasn't everybody

> working who could or would work? . . . [W]eren't ordinary, forgotten men able to fish up the price of $25 seats [for the fights] a couple of times a year? . . .
>
> Yes, I know, the bankers and speculators and hustlers shoved us a lot of wall-paper stocks and bonds, and everybody was knocked in the creek when the wagon threw a wheel. But you wait and see what happens to Morgenthau's Mavourneens one of these days and then tell me whether, and if so why, it's any more fun to be rooked by a political party and a lot of wabble-wits stuck away in offices in Washington than by a banker. . . .
>
> I just don't know, neighbor. For a long time when I would hear them say Old Deal in that curl-of-the-lip way I went along, too, feeling that, yes, it certainly was terrible, but let me ask you this: How were you doing back in those terrible days, and if this New Deal is going to be so swell when are those boys going to get through that long windup and let us see what they have got on the ball?

That's Westbrook Pegler in top form: sitting in the populist bully pulpit, trumpeting the cause of the corporate elite on behalf of the commoners. Not that *he* thought of it that way. Long before most Americans, rich and poor, began to fancy themselves members of the middle class, Pegler was the real deal; he embodied its contradictions and felt its bruised vanity. Pegler truly believed in his lost republic. Caught in the disorder of the Depression, he lashed out to vindicate the dispossessed man in the middle, the guy who resented the freeloaders and always feared getting played for a chump by his betters.

PEGLER WAS BORN to hate. His father—a liar, a brawler, and a drunk to whom Pegler remained devoted throughout his life—loathed the rich just as Westbrook would, even as both eventually prospered as well-paid laborers for William Randolph Hearst.

Arthur Pegler was credited by some as the originator of the "Hearst style," a populist tongue of blood and cliché, expressive of the sentiments of working people but emptied of any real political content. A British immigrant, the elder Pegler came of age as a member of the Boomers, a hard-drinking, wandering generation of journalists known for their inventive writing and their hatred of their own bosses and managers. In later years, Arthur Pegler turned against even Hearst himself, writing (still in Hearst style) that Hearst papers resembled a "screaming whore running down the street with her throat cut."

Such spectacles appealed to readers unsatisfied with the self-righteous new "objective" style of upper-middle-class papers like the *New York Times*, which, with its claim to depersonalized reality, presented itself as omniscient and unquestionable. Hearst, on the other hand, offered spicy treats, news to consume, stories that offered visceral sensation in place of critical perspective. Both approaches operated like machines built to produce particular political results, but at least yellow journalism served up some sauce along with its propaganda.

Pegler *père* spent much of his career in Chicago, home to one of America's finest political machines, and he worked hard to keep its gears well oiled. Westbrook loved his dad, and from an early age, he dreamed of taking up the same trade. He got his chance at the 1912 Republican convention in Chicago, where his career was born in a burst of disillusionment. That was the place and time, he later remarked, that America "began to go to smash."

The nineteen-year-old Pegler saw the convention as a gallery of the grotesque. Incumbent William Howard Taft's three-hundred-plus pounds symbolized to him the gluttony of a Republican Party gone rotten, and Teddy Roosevelt, whom Pegler had long admired for the way he stood up to Wall Street, revoked his promise not to run again for no other reason Pegler could discern than vanity and a feverish hunger for power.

"We stand at Armageddon, and we battle for the Lord!" TR

roared, and the crowd, exhilarated by TR's "New Nationalism," screamed back in what Pegler deemed blind ecstasy. Meanwhile, Taft's "Regular" faction greased their man's path to victory. In response TR stormed out to stage his own convention just down the street. In the months that followed, TR was shot (he survived and resumed campaigning that very day with the bullet still lodged in his chest); he decided that big business wasn't so bad after all when faced with the loss of financing from J. P. Morgan; and Taft, paralyzed by the Republican split, stayed silent. As a result Democrat Woodrow Wilson claimed the White House on a platform Pegler thought combined the worst elements of both his opponents' business appeasement and popular grandstanding.

To top it all off, the 1912 convention afforded Pegler an introduction to the Hearst empire's ace hack—an episode Pegler never forgot. He was standing around on the convention floor, he later recalled, when

> a big man with a brow like the belly of a medicine ball ripped off a few sheets of copy and, without looking up, handed them to me saying, "Boy, copy." I was a boy, but no longer a copy-boy. I was a leg man, and I tossed it back at him, saying, "Run it down yourself, I am a reporter." The Hearst super nearly died, and said, "Run that copy downstairs, or I will kill you. That is Brisbane."

As in Arthur Brisbane, the jingoistic crook whose one-sentence paragraphs Hearst himself quoted when he wanted to say something he thought was profound. If Arthur Pegler invented the Hearst style, Brisbane was its master exploiter, using his front-page column to promote real-estate schemes—just the kind of greed that Pegler could neither stomach nor ever stay altogether clear of.

If that was the moment that the United States went to smash, you might say Pegler tumbled right after. He was disposed to cheer for TR despite his misgivings, until his father explained to him that politics—and journalism—wasn't about who *should* win, but who *would* win. And when Pegler moved from politics to police court later that year, he remembered the lesson. Surveying the petty thieves, prostitutes, and down-and-outers who made up the court's clientele, Pegler saw people without power who, to his way of thinking, didn't help themselves any by breaking the law. When it came to role models, Pegler looked to "the ham-handed sergeant of the Harrison Street station," a cop who set things right with his fists. As Pegler's biographer Oliver Pilat wrote, 1912 was when Pegler recognized that "there were two layers of people in the world, the weak and the strong; he sympathized with the weak, but he lined up with the strong."

Pegler spent the next several years bouncing from one newspaper job to another, in Des Moines, St. Louis, Dallas, Denver, and New York. He traveled to Europe to cover World War I. But with his lack of social graces, he managed to offend every officer and editor necessary to get him booted out of the press corps. War wasn't really a good topic for him anyway; his nationalism blunted his cynicism, without which he wrote like a blind man. Back in the States, though, he found a natural—and lucrative—journalistic niche at the ballpark and beside the boxing ring.

Pegler had never been an athlete himself, aside from a few clumsy attempts at boxing, so perhaps it was his distance from the experience that allowed him to approach it with his eye on the cash register instead of the ball. He wrote that he wanted to deglamorize sports, "in rebuke to grubby box-office mercenaries." And he began turning out original stories, written for fans who felt they were getting ripped off. Readers looked to his byline as much for his skepticism as for the scores. His editors took notice and put him on a steady schedule of raises. Pegler was getting rich.

As he joined the class he'd spent his youth loathing, Pegler continued to sharpen his knives. By 1929, Pegler was making $25,000 a year. In 1932, Hearst himself came courting, but Pegler was sitting so pretty he could afford to turn down an invitation to

San Simeon to discuss contracts with the Old Man. Instead, he made a bigger move—from the sports section to the front page of the flagship Scripps-Howard paper, the *New York World-Telegram*. For $75,000, Pegler was to share Page One with Heywood Broun, each allowed to comment however he pleased on the passing scene. Broun's "It Seems to Me" was a space for liberal (and soon to be socialist) manifestos. Pegler's "Fair Enough," though, was a mystery. Pegler didn't seem to have any politics; all he had was rage.

In his second column, Pegler declared that "my hates always occupied my mind much more actively than my friendships . . . [and] the wish to favor a friend is not so active as the instinct to annoy some person or institution I detest." Mob bosses were a sort he particularly hated, especially when such men also happened to head up unions. Although Pegler eventually came to see all unions as octopi strangling his common men with dues that went directly into their leaders' bank accounts, he did pause a few times in his decades-long union-bashing rant to expose real corruption. At least two well-deserved jail terms can be attributed to "Fair Enough" columns.

Pegler carried on his campaigns in the name of one particular "little guy" known as George Spelvin, American. "Spelvin" was the stage name an actor used at the time when, in addition to his main role, he doubled in a small part. The Spelvins of the world were servants, butlers, messengers, clerks, men-on-the-street, and passersby. Pegler's Spelvin, though, was an early Archie Bunker. Union men, uppity women, swells, bubbleheads, and eventually foreigners, blacks, and Jews all gave Spelvin a stomachache.

In 1942, Spelvin went looking for a job because "Mrs. R." (Roosevelt) had "said she thought everyone should be ordered what to do by the government," and her orders were to fit into the war effort anywhere you can. Turns out, though, there were no more jobs in America that didn't require a union card, and "Bigod nobody is going to make him join anything whether it is the Elks or the Moose or the Mice or the Muskrats or whatever. It is the principle of the thing with George, and, moreover, being a native American and a veteran of the last war, he has a rather narrow prejudice against being ordered around by guys who talk like they just got off the boat."

Pegler's problem was that it was always the principle of the thing. He adored making stands where it was one man against the mob or the masses, and bigod, he'd go down swinging. And so he did, again and again, picking losing fights at every turn. His audience loved him for it. But Pegler failed to grasp that his readers appreciated his rants because they offered a momentary respite from the trials of their daily lives. They may have liked to hear him rail against Roosevelt's riches, but they never abandoned FDR. Pegler voiced their doubts and, in his inability to grasp the complexities of the world that shifted around him, also dissipated them. "By his own standards, he was incorruptible, honorable, and sincere," commented his biographer Pilat. "But sincerity is only an effort to gauge reality and conform to it, and his tools for that effort were inadequate." Pegler could evoke phantasms and fantasies similar to the ones that captivate countless talk-radio buffs today, but when the stories were over, his readers went back to Roosevelt, unions, taxes, and the modern world—what looked to most like the only deal around.

PEGLER'S HATRED WAS PURE, but it wasn't enough to save him. In the end, the contradictions of what he believed was a classless society buried him even as they made him a wealthy man. Class was Pegler's bogeyman: Even as it determined his world he refused to believe in it or to name it, calling it instead "the bosses," then "the unions," and finally "the Communists" he seemed to see everywhere in his old age.

By then he'd gone over to Hearst and beyond. In 1943, the National Maritime Union had put a thousand pickets around the *World-Telegram* to protest a column he'd written about what he considered the royal wages of union seamen. The paper's publisher, Roy Howard, decided Pegler had to go. Pegler agreed; he'd recently received another offer from Hearst, and despite his longstanding personal affection for Howard, he relished the jump in pay and readers. *Newsweek* estimated that the new job would give him access to ten million loyalists.

But Pegler remained, in Murray Kempton's words, "the man who hated publishers," and in the end he couldn't spare Hearst his scorn. After two decades of selling Citizen Kane's papers with a column that increasingly resembled a blast furnace; after turning against the Newspaper Guild, the one union to which he'd held a little bit of loyalty; after abandoning the religious tolerance of his youth in favor of ever-more-obvious and loathsome anti-Semitism (international bankers and "prophets" came to be staple fare); after staking Joe McCarthy to a run with relentless good press and watching him tire on the rail, Pegler came around at last to the original enemy, the boss.

When Pegler was a younger man, the boss of bosses had been Hearst Senior himself—in Pegler's words at the time, "the leading American fascist." By 1962, almost two decades into the Cold War, Pegler was praising Old Man Hearst as a "great founding genius." The problem now was his son, W. R. Hearst Jr. Before the thirty-five hundred members of the Anti-Communist Christian Crusade in Tulsa, in a speech warning of a new "coercion" that ruled the press, Pegler excoriated the younger Hearst for lacking "character, ability, loyalty, and principle."

No doubt Hearst did. But he shared his father's intolerance of dissent, and the next day Pegler was banished from mainstream journalism forever. By then, he may not have cared, for he had observed throughout the Fifties the degeneration of the newspaper columnist's craft into assembly-line production of "packaged goods" designed by the publisher. Pegler had discovered that newspapers were becoming indistinguishable from other branches of the entertainment industry. His own employer, King Features, was, as he described it to the audience in Tulsa, "a subdivision of the Hearst empire dealing in comic books, comic strip books, sweet powders to make soda pop, toys, and a very ingenious variety of dingbats for the immature."

By the time he was blacklisted, Pegler had already exiled himself, setting up a private retreat in the desert outside Tucson. From there, he cultivated a revolving roster of rich men with far-right views who adopted Pegler for various journalistic endeavors. But not even crackpot rags like the John Birch Society's *American Opinion* could contain Pegler's obsession: Its editor finally ended their relationship, complaining of the "monotony of Pegler's articles" about the twin demons, Eleanor and Earl (Roosevelt and Warren). His next employer, a conservative business monthly called the *Toledo Monitor*, begged him to lay off "1) New Deal & Roosevelts; 2) Kennedys; 3) Jews." Not long after he lost one of his last jobs, his beloved wife died. Although Pegler married twice again, from there on out, he was alone, and his loneliness made him even meaner. He fought his distant desert neighbors over the howling of their dogs. He brawled in the streets of Tucson. Much of what he wrote was no longer publishable, but he sat in his empty, pure, American landscape pounding out more and more of it, trying to get at the monster he couldn't name.

In 1966, when the *New York Herald Tribune*, *World-Telegram*, and *Journal-American* all died, Pegler wrote to Kempton, one of his last friends: "If you have a spare half-hour, please write what happened to our world. Peg."

Three years later Pegler died too, without ever realizing what had happened to the once-dazzling cosmos of journalism in which his uncompromising columns had shone. The masters he willingly served (even as he thought he fought them) had killed it. He had helped.

Pegler went to his death a true believer in his own virtue, broken and uncomprehending. His life epitomized the conservative backlash of the Cold War—a tragedy made possible by real adversity and fear. Pegler's spirit lingers today as a faux-populist puppet show, with the "common people" reduced to one of Limbaugh's props. But with Pegler himself there was always something more. When he raged against fat cats and fascists, and held forth on the unbearable arrogance of power, he hit some nice notes. Those columns still offer something for readers and writers both: the civic virtues of well-tuned fury.

—BAFFLER 13, 1999

30

Modernism as Kitsch

Hilton Kramer's Thirty-Year Culture War

Daniel Lazare

If you are one of those who dismiss the art critic Hilton Kramer as a kind of antiquated aesthete with a deep anger against the modern world and a mad glint in his prose, you should know that it wasn't always that way. Although nowadays his magazine, *The New Criterion*, specializes in Allan Bloom–style laments about leftist barbarians undermining Western culture, there was a time when he was capable of writing about high- and not-so-high-culture figures with humor, insight, and even balance. Here, for example, is how he described a 1978 Whitney Museum show devoted to the enigmatic *New Yorker* cartoonist Saul Steinberg (he of the famous "View of the World from Ninth Avenue"):

> The public that attends a Steinberg exhibition . . . does not resemble the public at other exhibitions. It moves differently and

> behaves differently, for it does not look as much as it reads. It also smiles a lot. Its whole manner of absorption—and there is no question about its being absorbed—is quite different from that of people looking at painting or sculpture. A Steinberg exhibition arches the back and concentrates the mind. It is an intellectual puzzle as well as a visual entertainment. It abounds in ideas. It both embraces the world "out there" and yet obliterates it, turning everything the Steinberg mind touches into—what? A comedy of manners, certainly. But also a comedy about art and its processes of thought. . . .

This was lively and interesting, the sort of observation that makes even those of us who don't particularly care for Steinberg (such as this writer) want to keep on reading. Now consider a typical bit of late-Kramer bombast, circa 1987, in which the writer rages like a sidewalk crazy person at the leading cultural institutions of American society:

> From the lecture halls of the Harvard Law School to the glossy pages of *The New Yorker*, from the boardrooms of innumerable universities, museums, and publishing houses to the classrooms where the arts, the humanities, and the social sciences are being deconstructed and destroyed, it is the policies and doctrines bequeathed to us by the New Left in its alliance with the counterculture that determine the principal agenda and exert the dominant influence.

And if you think that's a remarkable bit of conspiracy theorizing, have a look at Kramer's, er, *unique* take on American cultural history from the vantage point of the fourth year of the Clinton administration:

> About the cultural as well as the political consequences of Stalinism, our historians are only now—thanks, in part, to the opening

> of the Soviet archives—beginning to tell the full story of what amounted to a massive and largely successful campaign of ideological brainwashing, conspiracy, and intimidation. . . . [A] good deal of American cultural life may be said to have been Stalinized, and at certain intervals—in the cultural life of the 1960s, for example, and with the imposition of political correctness and multiculturalism in the 1980s and 1990s—has been repeatedly re-Stalinized ever since.

Despite repeated red scares, purges, and right-wing crusades, it seems that Communism—the official Moscow variety, spelled with a capital *C*—is as powerful as ever. Although less astute observers might take certain developments, e.g., the fall of the Soviet Union in 1991, as evidence that Communism had weakened as an ideological force, Hilton Kramer, art critic, knows better.

In a superficial sense, Hilton Kramer seems like just another member of the old *Partisan Review* circle of intellectuals who started out left and wound up moving farther and farther to the right in response to Sixties radicalism—some would say in response to figuring out where the money came from. The political landscape is full of such converts, ex-Stalinists, ex-Trotskyists, or ex-SDSers such as Peter Collier and David Horowitz. What makes Kramer's case more interesting than most is, first, that he did it all in the name of modernism, a movement that, at least as far as art is concerned, has always had certain vaguely antibourgeois connotations and, second, that he has taken aesthetic modernism much farther to the right than most people would have thought possible. While some might recall the right-wing antics of T. S. Eliot, Ezra Pound, or Louis-Ferdinand Céline, in our own times it is generally assumed that the only aesthetic opinions one is likely to hear in the land of reaction are Tom Wolfe–style snipings at the New York art set with their white wine, black-on-black clothing, funny pictures, and impenetrable theoretical discourse. But Kramer reminds us that it ain't necessarily so: One can defend

Picasso and even write appreciatively about Julian Schnabel and still be a card-carrying member of the loony right. How long he'll be able to keep it up, though, is another question. On one hand, there's no doubt that his presence has provided the random collection of cranks who make up the American right with a certain intellectual credibility they wouldn't otherwise enjoy. On the other hand, a man of refined sensibilities like Kramer can't help but be increasingly uncomfortable among the gun-toting, Darwin-denouncing, militia-forming know-nothings who are the constituency for the only politics Kramer now finds he can stomach. Perhaps this painful situation is what explains his increasingly wild-eyed rhetoric.

But the Hilton Kramer story is best understood as an epilogue to the remarkable 1983 study by Serge Guilbaut, *How New York Stole the Idea of Modern Art* (published, by the way, at just about the same time that *The New Criterion* was getting off the ground). Guilbaut traced the evolution of abstract expressionism from the anticapitalism of the Thirties to a movement so mainstream that the State Department ultimately was able to make use of it in its anti-Soviet *Kulturkampf.* Since one of the few things everyone could agree on about action painters splattering pigment onto oversized canvases was that they had verve, then the society that produced them also had to have verve—a syllogism that, Guilbaut showed, served the early U.S. culture warriors well. But before the State Department could utilize abstract expressionism in this manner, it had to strip it of its depression-era radicalism. Rebellion had to be firmly separated from revolution so that it could be rendered as 100 percent American as blue jeans, bubble gum, and bebop jazz. Radicalism had to be domesticated. As the art critic Clement Greenberg—Kramer's mentor and one of the main players in this affair—put it in 1961, without the least touch of irony: "Someday it will have to be told how anti-Stalinism, which started out more or less as Trotskyism, turned into art for art's sake, and thereby cleared the way, heroically, for what was to come."

What was to come was formalism at its most hermetic, a theory that held that art could succeed as art only if left undisturbed in its own separate realm, sealed off from any and all outside forces.

This process was well under way by the time Kramer happened on the scene in the early Fifties. Born in Massachusetts to a solidly Democratic, working-class family in 1928, Kramer graduated from Syracuse University in 1950, bounced around as an English grad student for a bit, and then, after an unhappy year at Indiana University, got his first big break when Philip Rahv, one of *Partisan Review*'s two founding editors, accepted an article he had submitted on new developments in the American art scene. Such was the magazine's influence that Kramer (whose "dirty little secret" was that he had never taken an art course) became an instant authority. Offers to write poured in from *Art Digest*, *Commentary*, *The Nation*, and elsewhere. Then, in 1965, came the ultimate plum, a job offer from the *New York Times*, where he eventually would serve as cultural-news editor and chief art critic.

Why did Kramer do so well? A look back at some of his early criticism suggests that it was a combination of an infectious, enthusiastic style, an air of authority (even if not totally earned), and political dependability. As Kramer was later to write, modernism by this point was enjoying an unprecedented hegemony over the art field. Its rivals—the regionalists, the social realists, etc.—had all been banished to Siberia, victims of a new orthodoxy that held that anything that was not abstract was not modern, and that anything that was not modern was not genuine art. It was an orthodoxy that Kramer not only supported but also believed in—politically, intellectually, and morally.

Kramer nonetheless spent his first years in and around the *Partisan Review* carefully picking his way through the ideological mine field. While veteran *PR*-istas argued about Trotsky and the Bolshevik Revolution, and Clement Greenberg struggled to hold on to some vestige of Marxism along with his ever-more-severe formalism, Kramer held his tongue. All the while, though, he was moving toward a class analysis of his own, one that rejected any ideological connection between the avant-garde and the left. The real connection, he was coming to think, was between the avant-garde and the bourgeoisie. For years, the two had been mortal enemies. But then a few wealthy collectors eventually broke the ice, purchasing works that previously had been despised, and rapprochement soon led to a full-scale embrace. For most critics this union of Bohemia and Babbittry has been a little embarrassing, to say the least. For Kramer, though, it has carried the sort of millennial promise his colleagues once pinned on "the revolution." "Like partners in a stormy but enduring marriage," Kramer wrote in 1985, "the avant-garde and the bourgeoisie came more and more to depend on each other and even to resemble each other." One side learned how much it could shock and mock its patrons without alienating them completely, while the other learned to suffer along with their new creative-genius friends as they explored new forms of expression. Indeed, not only did the capitalist class embrace modernism, Kramer wrote, it "created special institutions—museums and exhibition societies, schools, publications, foundations, etc.—which functioned, in effect, as agencies of a licensed opposition." The result was something new in the history of Western culture.

Kramer was no radical at this point, but neither was he the merry volcano we know today. In retrospect, the incident that seems to have pushed him over the edge was the 1964 publication of Susan Sontag's "Notes on 'Camp'" in *Partisan Review,* an essay that purported to announce a whole new way of looking at things, a new sensibility. Sontag's essay is best read as a delayed rejoinder to an equally epochal piece, "Avant-Garde and Kitsch," that Clement Greenberg had published in *PR* back in 1939. Greenberg's essay had been an attempt, simultaneously ponderous and naive, to enlist high modernism in the service of socialist revolution. Kitsch, or what later would be called mass culture, was the very antithesis of real art, he argued. It served as an instrument of totalitarian control, lulling the public into complacency by assuring them that they knew what was right without having to think. Modernism, on the other hand, challenged the masses with its very difficulty. The purpose of modern art was not to declare "all power to the Soviets," "down with the imperialist war," or anything else so heavy-handed, but to inspire its audience to think—to think about art, about culture and politics, about the human condition in all its aspects.

To which Sontag replied a quarter of a century later, the hell with it: If kitsch is cheap and anti-intellectual, it can also be fun, and fun is the truly revolutionary quality. "Many examples of Camp are things which, from a 'serious' point of view, are either bad art or kitsch," she declared. But so what? "The whole point of Camp is to dethrone the serious."

The essay seems to have had the same effect on Hilton Kramer that the young Bob Dylan had on Michael Harrington—one of complete shock and dismay. Kramer had *believed* when Greenberg laid down the law about modernism's moral engagement. Art was going to change the world! Yet here was Sontag celebrating kitsch precisely because it was liberated from "moral relevance." Over the years, Sontag would turn into something of an obsession of Kramer's, becoming the epitome of the self-aggrandizing literary politician he most despised. He followed the various twists and turns in her career with morbid glee. Here was Susan Sontag as the enemy of whiteness ("the white race is the cancer of human history . . . "); Susan Sontag as the lifestyle revolutionary ("Rock, grass, better orgasms, freaky clothes, grooving on nature—really grooving on anything—unfits, maladapts a person for the American way of life"); Susan Sontag as the born-again anticommunist (readers of *Reader's Digest* "would have been better informed about the realities of Communism" than readers of *The Nation* or *New Statesman*); Susan Sontag as a latter-day Joan of Arc in war-torn Sarajevo; and, finally, Susan Sontag as laptop bombardier urging NATO to give the Serbs hell. Every time his audience's attention seemed to wander, Kramer would haul out yet another dumb Sontag quote as if to say, "See? This is what we're fighting against!"

After thirty years of official irony it's not hard to sympathize with Kramer's outrage. But Kramer just couldn't walk away from it. When Sontag went left, he went right; when she returned to the center, he went farther right still. Kramer was caught in a dilemma, as he sometimes realized in his more lucid moments. Camp was not just a new style, it was a disease, an aesthetic parasite. It needed modernism—his modernism!—in order to strike its supercilious poses. The problem, though, was that modernism seemed too old to fight it off. It was weak, enervated, "at the end of its tether," as Kramer would later write. To make matters worse, the more Kramer struggled, the more serious he became, the more he seemed to strengthen his postmodern enemies, providing them with exactly the puritanical butt their japes required. But Kramer fought on, and as he did, all his ideas and his insights and his brilliance were reduced to a single point: the absolute moral authority of Art.

This was the passion of Hilton Kramer, the desperate effort to save what could not be saved. The more hopeless it became, the more frenzied his efforts grew. In his hands, Greenbergian notions of modernism as a stringently moral exercise were becoming something dangerously authoritarian. Modernism was becoming a fetish, an icon, as Kramer bowed in prayer five times a day in the direction of the Museum of Modern Art. His position became conservative in the most literal sense—he was struggling to conserve what he could of a tradition he knew to be dying.

Kramer's neocon proclivities were evident by 1970 when he lashed out at painters in New York for calling on museums to shut down temporarily to protest the invasion of Cambodia. By 1982, when he launched *The New Criterion*—"a monthly review edited by Hilton Kramer," as every cover has proclaimed since—with a half-million-dollar grant from the Olin Foundation and other such sources, they were at full boil.

The New Criterion started out cranky and ended up worse. In an opening statement, the editors quoted Sir Walter Scott (a kitsch writer if ever there was one) to the effect that the entire enterprise was motivated by outrage over "the disgusting and deleterious doctrines with which the most popular of our Reviews disgraces its pages." "Not since the 1930s," the editors went on, "have so many orthodox leftist pieties so casually insinuated themselves into both the creation and criticism of literature, and remained so immune to resistance or exposure." Within a few years, the magazine had published a neo-McCarthyite attack on the Princeton historian Lawrence Stone that was so over the top that it earned a rebuke from the neocon doyenne Gertrude Himmelfarb herself. In 1986, it published a wacky piece by Ronald Radosh asserting that a republican victory in the Spanish Civil War would have resulted in less freedom than a fascist one. (While correctly pointing out that the Soviet secret police ran riot behind republican lines, Radosh's article made one wonder why, if Franco was preferable to Stalin in Spain, Hitler would not have been preferable to Stalin in Eastern Europe. After all, Franco saw his and Hitler's struggle as one and sought to repay Hitler for his support during the Civil War by contributing a military unit, the Blue Division, to fight alongside the Nazis on the Eastern Front.)

And it only got worse. Before long Kramer was seeing feminists and deconstructionists under every bed and behind every tree, united in the common project of ransacking his precious modernist canon. By 1988, he was damning an entire generation of academics to perdition because they were conspiring to ensure that art be "categorically removed from the realm of aesthetics and placed firmly in a realm where the only legitimate questions are those that can be asked about the material—which is to say, the political and economic—conditions of its production."

Loopy as this sounds, it made perfect sense in terms of Kramer's alternative universe: If art is holy, its mysteries must be defended against those who would pry too deeply into the circumstances in which it is created. Faith must be secured against reason. By 1989, Kramer was calling on academia to abandon sociological analysis altogether and return to the high ground of connoisseurship, "the clear, comparative study of art objects with a view to determining their relative level of aesthetic quality." The operative word here was "relative"—Kramer was calling, in effect, for a return to the old cultural hierarchy in which artists were arranged in descending order of importance from the godlike to the semidivine, and so on.

By the mid-Nineties, *The New Criterion*'s tone had become so gloomy as to be positively Spenglerian. Thanks to the rock-loving, pizza-chomping, cigar-smoking Bill Clinton—in many ways, a figure even more distasteful to Kramer than Sontag—culture everywhere was going to wrack and ruin. "Culturally, morally the world we inhabit is increasingly a trash world," sang Roger Kimball, Kramer's tory colleague, "addicted to sensation, besieged everywhere by the cacophonous, mind-numbing din of rock music, saturated with pornography, in thrall to the lowest common denominator where questions of taste, manners, or intellectual delicacy are concerned." Kramer meanwhile took to writing a column for that well-known fount of intellectual delicacy, the *New York Post*, devoted to complaining that his former employer, the *Times*, was becoming a PC stronghold. As a member of the Adelphi University board of trustees, he got caught up in the Peter Diamandopoulos scandal when it came out that he and Adelphi's free-spending neocon president had run up a $552 bar tab one evening at university expense.

THERE ARE MANY IRONIES in this saga. The saddest and most compelling is the evolution of modernism from a movement coinciding, as Clement Greenberg once put it, "with the first bold development of scientific revolutionary thought in Europe," into something more and more associated with the authoritarian right.

But another has to do with the evolution of kitsch itself. Greenberg used the term to describe art that discouraged critical inquiry and rewarded political quiescence. But this is exactly what modernism itself has become in the hands of Hilton Kramer. For him modernism is an object of worship, not a tool of experimentation; a weapon to employ against those who would probe, analyze, or otherwise demystify power. The result is not modernism *versus* kitsch, as it had been for Clement Greenberg, but modernism *as* kitsch.

—BAFFLER 13, 1999

31
The Poetry of Commerce

Minou Roufail

> Not a great dealer, perhaps, since she had more of an ear than an eye, and not a classic art dealer, either, since she preferred selling to counting . . . but when the conditions were right, as they had been yesterday, when she could set the poetry of commerce in motion, as she had done, she could fucking sell some art. —*Dave Hickey,* Stardumb

"Who needs God when you've got Capital?" mused art critic Peter Schjeldahl in a 1997 salute to Las Vegas. The saying might well have stood as art criticism's motto of the Nineties. After all, it's clearly the guiding sentiment of Schjeldahl's mentor, Dave Hickey, an art critic whose influential 1997 book, *Air Guitar*, is in its third printing and whose ideas pervade the little world of contemporary art. A self-styled renegade, Hickey has spent years proposing a vision of cultural renewal sparked by the forces of the free market, or, as he likes to call it, "democracy." That vision, in short, is this: The expansion of state-sponsored arts institutions in the Fifties, Sixties, and Seventies ultimately led to the people's disenfranchisement and the rote manufacture of artists by a modern-day Academy. Both artist and art lover, alienated from the local communities that should rightly sustain them, are now hostage to the mandates of big government agencies. The commercial sector, however, promises liberation. Only unfettered entrepreneurs can create a vital art, and only paying customers can escape the predigested dispensations of the liberal state.

Like champions of the market everywhere, Hickey cloaks his hostility to the public sector in the rhetoric of democracy and freedom. But Hickey is no watchdog for Western civilization à la Hilton Kramer or Allan Bloom. He distances himself from both cultural conservatives and the lefty intelligentsia, fancying himself instead a man of the people. A product of the Sixties (he even played guitar for Janis Joplin), he is a perennial hipster, outsider, and establishment-basher. Along the way Hickey made a living as a gallery owner, a music critic, and an editor at *Art in America*, and his criticism is wide-ranging and eclectic.

Air Guitar, a collection of Hickey's writings for *Art issues*, is dedicated to such unpretentious pleasures as basketball, cars, and the Gorgeous Ladies of Wrestling. The back flap tellingly sports a photograph of the youthful Hickey accompanied by the caption, "The author as art dealer, 1967." As it turns out, this youthful dip into the world of buying and selling is the key to Hickey's criticism: At the age of twenty-six, convinced that his professors were too ideologically hidebound to appreciate his ideas, Hickey quit graduate school at the University of Texas for the more honest, more all-American profession of gallery-owning. (His disdain for academia has only intensified since he took a job as, um, an academic at the University of Nevada at Las Vegas.) The story of how he came to reject the scholarly "priests of institutional virtue" to "make one's way in the world through wit and wile" is classic Hickey, one in which our hero defies the shit at the top and the shit at the bottom in favor of the democratic, "Emersonian" way. Hickey is his own ideal American.

It is Hickey's aesthetics, however, that made him famous, and the connection he draws between the experience of beauty and the power of the market that have made him such a characteristic figure of our age. *The Invisible Dragon*, a 1993 Hickey polemic that almost singlehandedly inspired a revival of interest in beauty, fortuitously appeared in the same year that the Whitney Museum mounted its notorious "political" Biennial, a ham-handed effort to showcase identity politics that bombed spectacularly. Enter *The Invisible Dragon*, an attack on the art-world bureaucracy and its "administration of virtue." Although only sixty-four pages long, the book was enthusiastically embraced by an art world weary of pseudoradicalism and self-righteous posturing. Hickey received the Frank Mather Jewett Award for Distinction in Art Criticism for 1994. His ideas on beauty started cropping up in exhibition catalogues, gallery statements, and the effusions of acolytes like Schjeldahl and *Los Angeles Times* art critic Christopher Knight. By the mid-Nineties, Hickey was the latest vogue in an art world he affected to despise. (He returned the favor by publishing, in 1999, a series of vignettes on art-world types called *Stardumb*.)

Viewed in terms of the larger American rage for markets, though, Hickey seems less like an innovative thinker and more like the Fred Barnes of art criticism: In his universe, all things bad come from elite liberal institutions like government and museums; all things good emanate from ordinary people working through their trusted democratic medium, the free market. Hickey simply makes this familiar scheme palatable to the art world by steering clear of right-wing wackos and pretending to derive it instead from sophisticated thinkers such as French philosopher Gilles Deleuze, whose politicized theory of sadomasochism Hickey uses to ground his views on aesthetic experience and, ultimately, liberty. In Hickey's spin on Deleuze, "'the sadist is in need of institutions,'" while the masochist craves "contractual relations." Eventually Hickey manages to conceive of art as a contract between the beholder and the image, with beauty as its "signature." Art both gratifies the beholder aesthetically and instructs her in freedom of contract. Ooh-la-la!

Hickey applies Deleuze's theory to the avant-garde's old whipping boy, the museum, while equating it helpfully with the state. The curatoriate may make overtures to alienated beauty—the "invisible dragon"—but these are farcical, for in Hickey's scheme of things, the true artist and the ideal beholder can't transcend the imperatives of the institution. Addressing a hypothetical aspiring artist, Hickey advises: "When your movement hits the museum, abandon it. Your demure emblem now adorns the smooth state—resides in the domain of normative expression, its status greatly magnified and its rich social contextuality effectively sterilized." Hence the book's cover illustration, Ed Ruscha's rendering of the Los Angeles County Museum of Art on fire. Quirky, demotic organizations like the Liberace Museum in Las Vegas are, by contrast, said to be more authentic representatives of American expression.

For several years Hickey could be found dispensing this free-market philosophy of culture in his column in *Art issues* magazine. Ostensibly "devoted to unfashionable enthusiasms, unlikely objects of desire, and other phenomena held in mysterious esteem by the author and citizens of his acquaintance," the column was even more powerfully devoted to the programmatic identification of Hickey's tastes with all that is righteous and democratic. But Hickey's love affair with the people is ambivalent at best. Indeed, the tuned-in "citizens" with their "unfashionable enthusiasms" are the only ones for whom Hickey has any real sympathy. These people are members of local, intimate communities like the ones in which Hickey grew up, where culture is ordinary, and where "participants" consciously gravitate toward good art—essentially, the place where Norman Rockwell meets Andy Warhol. The rest of us—that is, the majority—are but fodder for the sadism of the institution, and Hickey pretty much can't stand us.

"Romancing the Looky-Loos," an essay dedicated to the *pensées* of Hickey and country-music star Waylon Jennings on the burdens of the true and authentic sensibility, is typical of Hickey's preoccupation with these cultural constituencies. Jennings reminisces about the good old days when he played "for people who come from where you come from," like-minded people who "understand what you're doing, so you feel like you're doing it for them." But things have changed:

> "Right now, hoss," he says, "it's completely out of my hands. I'm looking at those people out there, but I don't know what I'm seeing. And they're watching me, too. But they don't know what they're looking at. My best guess is that they'll keep on loving me till they start hating me, or their Waylon duds wear out. Because they already hate me a little, just because I'm me and they're them. That's why they always go on about how talented you are. Because they hate you. Because if they had this talent, they would be you. The fact that you've worked like a dog, lived like a horse thief, and broke your mama's heart to do whatever you do, that don't mean diddly-squat. To them, it's talent. Supposedly, you got it, and, supposedly, they don't. So eventually you're bound to disappoint them."

"Looky-loos" are, of course, philistines, enviously looking in from the outside. They are fickle, insensitive clods who will never really understand you. Jennings's brooding self-image—"worked like a dog, lived like a horse thief, and broke your mama's heart"—invokes the heroic artist who suffers for his art (and all for the sake of "them"). Indeed, in Hickey's story, he and Jennings are literally going down that lonesome highway, "sitting in the shotgun seats at the front of his bus, slouched down with our heels up on the chrome rail, watching the oncoming highway between the toes of our boots." Either you lived like a horse thief, etc., or you're one of those people, who as Hickey says, "did not live the life—people with no real passion for what was going on."

Hickey's association of "real passion" with freedom-loving capitalists and of philistinism with the liberal state is a staple of his writings. "Pontormo's Rainbow," for instance, recounts an early encounter with an authoritarian sociologist he sourly dubs June Cleaver, who grills him in the school cafeteria for the purposes of a national study on the deleterious effects of cartoons on children. The moral is supposed to be obvious: Invasive, puritanical bleeding-hearts want to deny the TV-watching boy Hickey the glorious pleasures of being "ravished by color." Then there's Professor Walthar Volbach, a refugee from Nazi Germany who taught Hickey that "the government" and "the universities" only sponsor "Aryan muscle-boy" art—that is, "official art"—as opposed to the commercial sector, which was "a Jew thing, a queer thing, and a silly woman thing," a place where truly vital and truly diverse culture can flourish. So Hickey rejects his birthright as an Aryan muscle-boy to become a "soldier of desire doing a little business in the night"—that is, an art dealer. For Hickey, as for many American libertarians, fascism and liberalism are indistinguishable because both promote the power of the state. Advancing from this brilliant insight, Hickey proceeds to liken various art figures to Nazis. In *The Invisible Dragon*, Hickey actually compares the Museum of Modern Art's founding director, Alfred Barr, with Joseph Goebbels.

Hickey's response to the triumph of the "looky-loos" and their big nanny government is not to withhold his genius from the masses, like the best and the brightest in Ayn Rand's *Atlas Shrugged*, but rather to retreat to Las Vegas, a city that he imagines somehow to embody democracy itself. For Hickey, art is "a betting sport," and gambling is a metaphor both for the free market and the free individual. Hence he is able to argue that Las Vegas possesses both the "only indigenous visual culture on the North American continent" (you know, the neon thing) and freedom from class stratification. Since the city's culture is a product of the market's response to "private desire," it is unmediated by the state-sponsored custodians of fine art. In Las Vegas, he writes, "there are only two rules: (1) Post the odds, and (2) Treat everybody the same. Just as one might in a democracy (What a concept!)."

This is, of course, preposterous. From the hard-fought union-organizing drives to the penthouse suites of the high rollers, Vegas is a city of profound and obvious class discrimination. And while Hickey has remarked on the "queasy dread" inspired in him by the state's "diffuse network of proprietary surveillance," he seems to have no problem with the Orwellian surveillance technology used by the big Vegas casinos. Furthermore, as James Surowiecki has pointed out in *Slate*, the city is "a supply-sider's dream: no corporate income tax, no personal income tax, no local earnings tax, no inventory tax, no capital-stock tax, no franchise tax, no admissions tax, no inheritance tax, low property tax, and a right-to-work state. Difficult not to make money when you're the only game in town in a Third World city-state."

But at least Vegas is not Washington, D.C., the capital of "this nasty little Puritan republic," and while relaxing among his beloved neon, Hickey is free to deliver his overheated libertarian attacks on the public sector. In Hickey's version of democracy, it's all quite simple and direct: Works of art are submitted to the public referendum of the free market without recourse to the state's artificial sanction. Meanwhile, the individual, practiced at negotiation and consensus through cultural relations, becomes a free participant in democracy. And Hickey himself cheers us on in our war with the liberal state while his books and articles are published by the Foundation for Advanced Critical Studies and his salary paid by the state of Nevada. It's hard to argue with Hickey's longing for a resurgent counterculture; indeed, genuine discontent with the art world of the Nineties is what paved the way for Hickey's conspicuous success. But rugged individualism is hardly a new alternative. In fact Hickey merely replaces the radical democratic vision of the left that has dominated art discourse since the Sixties with a radical democratic vision from the right. Nothing better describes the bankruptcy of this vision than his chosen city of Las Vegas, a place with no cultural commissars and no taxes, and where the majority of the people are losers.

—Baffler 14, 2001

32

The Earl Butz Farm

Albion, Indiana

MICHAEL MARTONE

EXCEPT FOR THE INTERPRETIVE CENTER in the trailer of a North American moving van, the Earl Butz Farm, the boyhood home of Earl Butz, secretary of agriculture under Richard Nixon, is now part of a larger, privately owned farm. The land itself, four hundred acres in Sycamore Township, is currently owned by an Italian insurance company and is leased to the Big Mac Management Group, a subsidiary of Central Soya Industries of Decatur, Illinois. None of the buildings known to exist during the former secretary's childhood (two houses, summer kitchen, root cellar, storm cellar, mow barn and silo, tool shed, tractor shed, corncrib, coops, pole barns, pumphouse, springhouse, horse barn, grain bins, garages, greenhouses, mill, machine shop, manure tanks, cannery, warehouse, fuel bunker, loafing shed, pigpens, nursery and farrowing houses, child's playhouse, woodshed, and outhouse) survives. Before the land is planted, it is possible, with a bit of imagination, to reconstruct the bare outlines of the domestic structures' footprint by using the small stands of rhubarb and horseradish that somehow germinate each year to outline the buildings' lost foundations. One can easily discern the remains of the former dirt-floored basketball court bordered by foxtail and milkweed. There are the ruined and rusted struts of a windmill tower, the well beneath it being too deep to fill, that serve as a base station for the citizens-band radio employed by the seasonal field hands. There is not a fence or fence post in sight, though the interpretive center has a collection of barbed wire. The fertile family graveyard, however, still yields, after all these years, a rich assortment of artifacts and human remains, which are freshly turned up each spring by state-of-the-art mold board chisel plows. Agronomy experts from Purdue University believe that such material will continue to be produced for, perhaps, several years more as the topsoil is routinely eroded.

—BAFFLER 14, 2001

Contributors' Notes

JIM ARNDORFER is a journalist who lives in Chicago.

MARK DANCEY was one of the co-conspirators behind *Motorbooty* magazine. Presently he paints pictures, prints posters, and provides illustrations for deserving clients. Mr. Dancey lives in Detroit, Michigan.

THOMAS FRANK is author of *One Market Under God* and *The Conquest of Cool.*

JIM FREDERICK is a senior editor for the Asian edition of *Time* magazine. He lives in Hong Kong.

JOSHUA GLENN is the editor of the journal *Hermenaut;* he's also on the editorial staff of the *Boston Globe*'s weekly "Ideas" section.

DOUG HENWOOD is the editor of *Left Business Observer* and the host of a weekly radio show on WBAI, New York. He is the author of *The State of the USA Atlas* (1994), *Wall Street* (1997), and the forthcoming *After the New Economy*. He hasn't owned a share of stock since 1987.

DAN KELLY lives in Chicago with his wife, Michael, and two sons, Travis and Henry. Besides THE BAFFLER, his writings have been published by Feral House, *The Imp*, and the *Ragtime Ephemeralist*. He is a regular contributor to the *Chicago Journal* and Chicago's *New City* newspapers.

GREG LANE is the publisher of THE BAFFLER. He's the mean one who answers the phone.

DANIEL LAZARE is a freelance journalist in New York. He has written for *Harper's Magazine, Playboy, Le Monde diplomatique*, and *New Left Review.* He is also the author of three books: *The Frozen Republic* (Harcourt Brace, 1996), an iconoclastic study of the U.S. Constitution; *America's Undeclared War* (Harcourt, 2001), an examination of American urbanophobia; and *The Velvet Coup* (Verso, 2001), a constitutional analysis of the Bush-Gore election debacle. He lives in Manhattan.

CHRIS LEHMANN is deputy editor of the *Washington Post Book World*, scourge of the subversariate, and a blue state bon vivant.

PAUL MALISZEWSKI's writing has appeared recently in *Harper's Magazine, The Paris Review*, and the Pushcart Prize anthologies.

MICHAEL MARTONE is currently working on his memoir, *Contributor's Notes. The Flatness and Other Landscapes*, published in 2000, won the AWP Award for creative nonfiction.

J. W. MASON is policy coordinator for the Working Families Party in New York. His writing has appeared in *In These Times*, the *Boston Review*, *City Limits*, and *The American Prospect.*

BEN METCALF was born in Illinois and raised in that state and in Virginia. He currently makes his home in New York City, where he is the literary editor of *Harper's Magazine*.

DAVID MULCAHEY, managing editor of THE BAFFLER, is a member of the leisure class (Division II). He occasionally manages, edits, and even writes for money in his twelve-block habitat on the South Side of Chicago.

MIKE NEWIRTH is fiction editor of *Bridge* magazine, and his writing has recently appeared in *In These Times*, the *Chicago Reader*, and *Matte*.

MIKE O'FLAHERTY is a freelance writer who lives in Chicago. Under the nom de plume Luther Bagby, his food criticism can be read in such publications as *Fashionable Male*, *Reptile Fancy*, and *Proletarian Vanguard*.

CHRISTIAN PARENTI is the author of *Lockdown America: Police and Prisons in the Age of Crisis*, a Soros Senior Justice Fellow of the Open Society Institute, and a Visiting Fellow at the CUNY Graduate School's Center for Place, Culture, and Politics. His writing has appeared in *The Nation, The San Diego Union-Tribune,* and the *Washington Post*. His new book, *The Soft Cage: Everyday Surveillance Past and Present*, will be published by Basic Books in fall 2003.

KIM PHILLIPS-FEIN, a writer in New York City, is working on a book about the roots of Reaganism and the free-market right. She is also a graduate student in history at Columbia University.

DAN RAEBURN writes and publishes *The Imp*, an irregular series of booklets about comics. He lives in Chicago.

MATT ROTH lives in New York City, where he is a graduate student at Columbia University and holds down a j-o-b. He has written for *In These Times* and the *Chicago Reader*. He is not currently attending any inspirational meetings.

MINOU ROUFAIL lives in Connecticut with the requisite husband, son, and dog.

JEFF SHARLET is cofounder of the online magazine KillingThe Buddha.com and coauthor of *Killing the Buddha: A Heretic's Bible*.

NELSON SMITH is a Manhattan-based freelance advertising writer and essayist whose work has appeared in the *New York Times Magazine*, *Harper's Magazine*, *In These Times*, and several defunct literary zines. He is currently working on a definitive cultural history of pigeons, from Genesis to Skinner, tentatively entitled "Lessons of an Organic Widget."

CLIVE THOMPSON is a sniveling, envious, po-faced writer in New York, whose work has appeared in *Wired*, the *New York Times Magazine*, and *THIS* magazine.

BRYANT URSTADT is a writer living in Guilford, Connecticut. He has written for *The New Yorker*, the *New York Times*, *Rolling Stone*, *Boston Globe*, *Details*, and *Outside*.

TOM VANDERBILT is author of *Survival City: Adventures Among the Ruins of Atomic America* (Princeton Architectural Press, 2002). He lives in Brooklyn and has written for many publications, including the *New York Times*, the *Wall Street Journal*, *The London Review of Books*, *Atlantic Monthly*, and *Metropolis*. He also writes the "Exploded View" column for *BOOKFORUM*.

EMILY VOGT is the associate publisher of THE BAFFLER. She is finishing a PhD dissertation in anthropology.

PATRICK WELCH is an idiot. A stinking, worthless idiot. He is married and lives in Chicago.

Acknowledgments

A GREAT NUMBER OF PEOPLE AND ORGANIZATIONS have sustained THE BAFFLER over the years—so many that it would be impossible to thank them all within the space of a few pages. Instead we will limit our acknowledgments to those who made a direct contribution to the contents of this book. First, we would like to thank the writers and artists whose names appear in the table of contents. Writing and illustrating for THE BAFFLER has never made anybody rich, but we like to think it has made them happy. Alane Mason, our editor at Norton, tightened and burnished the writing in this volume, making it considerably better. Joe Spieler, our agent, took care of us as he always does, which is to say expertly. Mark Dancy, our cover artist, came through again. We thank Studs Terkel, not only for his kind remarks, but also for being the North Star of humane journalism in this country. Our longtime colleague Matt Weiland helped shape these essays when they first appeared in the magazine, as did our trusted cronies George Hodak and Chris Lehmann. Dan Peterman and Rick MacArthur were key in ways that must remain classified. We are fortunate to be associated with all these people.

Index

Index